# Sketches in the Theory of Culture

# Zygmunt Bauman

# Sketches in the Theory of Culture

Edited by Dariusz Brzeziński

Translated by Katarzyna Bartoszyńska

polity

First published in Polish as *Szkice z teorii kultury* by Wydawnictwo Naukowe Scholar, Warsaw, 2016

Polity Press
65 Bridge Street
Cambridge CB2 1UR, UK

Polity Press
101 Station Landing
Suite 300
Medford, MA 02155, USA

ISBN-13: 978-1-5095-2829-5
ISBN-13: 978-1-5095-2830-1 (pb)

A catalogue record for this book is available from the British Library.

Library of Congress Cataloging-in-Publication Data

Names: Bauman, Zygmunt, 1925-2017, author.
Title: Sketches in the theory of culture / Zygmunt Bauman.
Other titles: Szkice z teorii kultury. English
Description: English edition. | Medford, MA : Polity, 2018. | Includes bibliographical
    references and index.
Identifiers: LCCN 2018006738 (print) | LCCN 2018033005 (ebook) | ISBN
    9781509528332 (Epub) | ISBN 9781509528295 (hardback) | ISBN 9781509528301
    (pbk.)
Subjects: LCSH: Culture. | Semiotics. | Social structure.
Classification: LCC HM621 (ebook) | LCC HM621 .B388 2018 (print) | DDC
    306–dc23
LC record available at https://lccn.loc.gov/2018006738

Typeset in 11 on 13 pt Sabon
by Toppan Best-set Premedia Limited
Printed and bound in Great Britain by CPI Group (UK) Ltd, Croydon

This research was funded by the National Science Centre in Poland on the basis of the grant awarded after obtaining a doctoral degree, based on the decision No DEC-2014/12/S/HS2/00391.

For further information on Polity, visit our website:
politybooks.com

# Contents

*A Message in a Bottle: on the Recovered Work of
Zygmunt Bauman*
Dariusz Brzeziński     vii

From the Author     1

**Part I Sign and Culture**

I    The Origins of the Semiotic Theory of Culture,
or the Crisis of Cultural Anthropology     7

II    Towards a Semiotic Theory of Culture     31

III    Man and Sign     62

IV    The Problem of Universals and the Semiotic Theory
of Culture     94

V    Some Research Problems in the Semiotic Theory
of Culture     119

**Part II Culture and Social Structure**

I    Cultural and Extra-Cultural Organization of Society     155

II    Economics, Culture, and Typologies of Societies     172

III    Cultural Determinants of the Research Process     203

IV   Three Observations About Problems of Contemporary
Education     216

V   Masses, Classes, Elites: Semiotics and the
Re-Imagination of the Sociological Function of Culture    231

*Afterword*     251
Zygmunt Bauman, 2016

*Notes*     256

*Index*     269

# A Message in a Bottle: on the Recovered Work of Zygmunt Bauman

Dariusz Brzeziński

## INTRODUCTION

'The "message in a bottle" allegory implies two presumptions: that there was a message fit to be written down and worthy of the trouble needed to set the bottle afloat; and that once it is found and read (at a time which cannot be defined in advance) the message will be still worthy of the finder's effort to unpack it and study, absorb and adopt it' (Bauman 2005: 142).[1] These words of Zygmunt Bauman's can certainly be applied to *Sketches in the Theory of Culture*, which is finding its way into the hands of readers half a century after it was written. The book was to be published in 1968, but because of the events of March 1968 and the repressive measures that its author was subjected to, it was withheld. The original text was not preserved by the publishers, and the only copy that Bauman had was confiscated when – forced to emigrate – he crossed the Polish border. The book was considered irretrievably lost for many years, both by the author and by researchers studying his work (see Tarkowska 1995b: 320; Bauman Janina 1988: 200, 201). Meanwhile – like a message in a bottle, coursing the ocean – it managed to survive in one, incomplete set of proofs. They were recently found, and, thanks to studies undertaken, it was possible to reconstruct the entire text of the work.

*Sketches in the Theory of Culture* is remarkable both because of its history, and because of the value of the ideas presented within it. In the book were articles devoted to theoretical reflection *sensu stricto*, and to issues such as: the condition of mass culture, the demands of pedagogy, changes in rural regions, etc. In his analysis, the author referred to studies undertaken in various fields, creating an interdisciplinary discourse that comprises the *signum specificum* of his work even today (Tester 2001: 7, 8). On the one hand, this work can be read as an examination of the transformations that were taking place in the social sciences during the 1960s. A lot of space was devoted to the crisis of cultural anthropology and to the potential of structuralism and cybernetics. Bauman penetratingly and critically analysed developing currents, and presented his own, very interesting propositions as part of his studies of culture. On the other hand, the book contained reflections on the birth of a new type of society, characterized, among other things, by a greater dose of individualization, the intensification of a global network of relationships, and incredibly quick, impossible-to-predict transformations. The sociologist wrote about the world of the second half of the last century under the rubric of 'liquidity' and 'amorphousness', thus anticipating his later thoughts on the transformation of modernity by a few decades (Bauman 2000).

The following text is devoted to acquainting readers with the 'message in a bottle' that is the *Sketches in the Theory of Culture*, and also indicating its value for the reader of today. In the first part, I will present the circumstances of finding the work and the steps that were taken to reconstruct it. Next, I will move to the time when the book was written; I will describe some events from the intellectual biography of Bauman that are important to this context, and will sketch out the context of the socio-cultural events in Poland during the year of 1968. The following two portions of the text will be devoted to the contents of *Sketches in the Theory of Culture*. First, I will describe the problematic of particular chapters, and then I will point to the evolution in Bauman's view of culture, which is clearly visible in this text. I will conclude by presenting the messages for the present that can be found in this work, which was written half a century ago, and recently, fortunately, 'washed up on the shore'.

## THE HISTORY OF THE PRESERVED COPY AND THE RECONSTRUCTION OF THE TEXT OF THE BOOK

The particular circumstances of the survival of a large portion of the proofs of *Sketches in the Theory of Culture* will almost certainly remain a secret forever. We can only speculate on the basis of meagre evidence. The copy was found in the premises of the combined libraries of the Department of Philosophy and Sociology of the University of Warsaw, the Institute of Philosophy and Sociology of the Polish Academy of Sciences, and the Polish Philosophical Society, located at Krakowskie Przedmieście 3 in Warsaw. It was hidden, under a layer of other material, in a metal cabinet that no one had had access to for many years. It was found by Janusz Siek, the director of this unit, during a time of general cleaning that was connected to his retirement. The copy came into my hands during research undertaken in the years 2014–17 for a project funded by a grant from the National Science Centre of Poland: 'The work of Zygmunt Bauman in the context of contemporary theories of culture'. To hold in my hands a text that was officially considered lost, one that unveiled heretofore unknown aspects of the intellectual work of the author of *Modernity and the Holocaust*, and that was simultaneously an excellent account of a problematic considered in current studies, was a remarkable experience for me. The discovery of the surviving copy of *Sketches in the Theory of Culture* was a shock – and simultaneously a cause of great joy – to its author, Zygmunt Bauman. I was able to meet with him personally to discuss it when I was an academic visitor at the University of Leeds in February 2016. At the time, he told me about studies he had undertaken in connection with his work on the book, and also about the events connected to its destruction in 1968. I acquired further information on the subject of the preserved copy during the course of an archival inventory undertaken at the Ossolineum Publishing House in March 2016, where the book was first prepared for publication.[2] The documents collected in the editor's files for *Sketches in the Theory of Culture* assisted in the reconstruction of the text, and also shed light on the history of its creation and the attempts to destroy it.

From the official documents, it emerges that the Ossolineum backed out of publishing *Sketches in the Theory of Culture* and dissolved its contract with Zygmunt Bauman on 13 April 1968. They justified this with a statement about 'him being politically compromised, as revealed during the events of March'.[3] It is worth considering this decision in the broader context of the repression which fell from the arms of contemporary leaders onto the academics who were acknowledged to be the political opposition. The latter were deprived of their posts,[4] their published works were censored, and sometimes they were also deprived of the opportunity to conduct academic work (see Krajewski 1982: 106–10). Bauman – as one of the greatest revisionist thinkers – met this fate in full. He was one of five independent academic employees who lost their jobs at the University of Warsaw as a result of the March events.[5] He was removed from all functions in academic assemblies and editorial groups, and his published works were placed under *de facto* censorship. What is more, as Nina Kraśko observes: 'As a result of his ethnicity, his position in Polish academic life, his active role in the Polish United Workers' Party, his identification with Marxism, Bauman became the target of the witch hunt conducted by the mass media and politicians. His name appeared in journalistic publications as a general name, written in lower-case letters and in the plural form' (Kraśko 1995: 33). This situation forced the sociologist to join the so-called 'March emigration' (Bauman 1969). First, he went to Israel, where he worked at a university in Tel Aviv. Then – from 1971 until his retirement – he was the director of the Institute of Sociology at the University of Leeds in Great Britain.

Efforts to preserve the one copy of *Sketches in the Theory of Culture* should be considered in light of the above-mentioned facts. This required, no doubt, both bravery and a conviction of the value of this text. Today, we can only suppose – such a hypothesis was proposed by Janusz Siek in a conversation with me – that an employee of the Ossolineum Publishing House, wanting to save the book, passed on a preserved fragment of the proofs (in the form of so-called 'galleys') to the then-director of the libraries named above, Janusz Krajewski. He had the text bound, and hid it in a place from which he could retrieve it in more welcoming times. But he did not live to see those times.

The preserved copy contains six and a half – of a planned ten – chapters of the book. On the basis of the Introduction and editorial materials preserved in the Ossolineum it was possible to reconstruct the remaining portion of the book, which was supposed to be composed of articles that had appeared earlier in academic journals.[6] Because of the passage of time, it is now difficult to establish to what degree they were to be revised for the book; we can only assume that those changes – if they were indeed to take place – were minor.[7] Adding the portions of the text missing from the proofs was one of the decisions made by the publishers in order to reconstruct the fundamental contents of the book. Wanting to respect fully Zygmunt Bauman's wishes pertaining to the preservation of the historical character of the text, it was decided to refrain from making a majority of the editorial changes that, because of the passage of time since its writing, might be justified. It was decided, for instance, to preserve the author's translations of the works he cited, though many of them have since been translated into Polish.[8] Interventions undertaken during the editorial process were based on making changes to the text that were indicated in the editorial proofs, unifying the citations, and introducing minor typographical changes stemming from the evolution of Polish grammar.

## SKETCHES IN THE THEORY OF CULTURE IN THE CONTEXT OF BAUMAN'S EARLIER WORK

If *Sketches in the Theory of Culture* had been published in 1968, it would have been the fifteenth book that Bauman published – as author or co-author – during his time as an academic in Poland.[9] Along with the work entitled *Culture and Society: Preliminaries* (Bauman 1966c), published two years earlier, this book attested to the meaningful transformations that took place in his academic interests during the 1960s. Earlier, his analyses were concentrated mainly on the sphere of the sociology of politics, in both an international framework and the framework of People's Poland (Wiatr 2010).[10] His doctorate – defended in 1956 – was on British socialism (Bauman 1959), and the subject of the work that led to his habilitation in 1960 was the English labour movement (Bauman 1972). Among the array of Bauman's works pertaining to Polish politics (see, for instance: Bauman and Wiatr 1953; Bauman 1957a: 3–26, 1957b, 1962b, 1962c), it is worthwhile, above all, to direct attention to his reflections on the subject of the fundamental changes that were supposed to take place after the October thaw (Bauman 1957b). The worsening of the situation in Poland during the following years confirmed his belief in the illusory nature of those expectations and placed him in the position of being an ever greater critic of political leaders. This had consequences for both his political views and his academic work.

As for the former, it must be emphasized above all that Bauman abandoned the official doctrine of Marxism and became a revisionist (see Brzeziński 2017: 61–80). The most fundamental role was played in this regard by his being inspired by the thought of Antonio Gramsci (Gramsci 1971; Bauman 1963). He spoke about this in his interview with Keith Tester in the following way: 'I read good tidings in Gramsci's *Prison Notebooks*: there was a way of saving the ethical core, and the analytical potential I saw no reason to discard from the stiff carapace in which it had been enclosed and stifled' (Bauman and Tester 2001: 26). The 'ethical core' referred to in this response was a sensitivity to exploitation, injustice and socially produced suffering. Bauman gradually cast off, however, his conviction in the Party's meaningful role in eliminating these problems. In its place, he began to re-evaluate the merits of grass-roots initiatives (Bauman 1967c). He had very limited opportunities to present these views in publications, however. His first wife – Janina – remembered the difficulties he encountered in the second half of the 1960s, years later, in the following way:

All of his books and articles were strictly censored, his public appearances sharply condemned, every step carefully watched. He awaited the decision about his professorship without any chance of approval from the appropriate powers. He particularly infuriated the Party when, during the famous trials of Kuroń and Modzelewski, he spoke out in defence of a student connected to him. A black cloud hung over his head, and thickened with the passage of time. (J. Bauman 1998: 138)[11]

The above response serves as a good introduction to the changes that took place as part of the second of the aspects described above – that is, in the character of academic work undertaken by Bauman. The impossibility of communicating his own views, and his ever greater disagreement with the politics conducted by those in power, contributed to the metamorphosis in the sociologist's research interests. They lit on the problem of culture (Tarkowska 1995a: 11). This was not a completely new topic for him. His earlier analyses were focused, however, on the belief – characteristic of Marxist–Leninist thinking – in the primacy of the base over the superstructure, and mainly on the question of the range of implementation of socialist and capitalist values (see Bauman and Wiatr 1953; Bauman 1962a; Bauman 1965a). Bauman's studies of culture from approximately the second half of the 1960s onwards took a completely different form. Above all, they were characterized by a strong theoretical drive. From 1964 to 1968, the sociologist wrote a series of articles devoted to reflections on the essence of culture, its relation to social structure, and also the relationship between it and the personality of individuals (see, for instance, Bauman 1964a; 1965a: 58–74; 1965b; 1967d). He also published a book entitled *Culture and Society: Preliminaries* in which he presented his own vision of the transformation of cultural realities, using a method of ideal types. At the time, his interests in culture also had an empirical dimension. This was reflected in his work as the director of the Department of General Sociology in the Division of Philosophy at the University of Warsaw, the Office of Polish People's Anthropology. Although it only functioned for a year, it left a permanent mark on Polish sociology, thanks to the projects and concepts developed by its members (Tarkowska 1995a).

For the purposes of *Sketches in the Theory of Culture*, Bauman wrote completely new texts or adapted a few articles earlier published in academic journals. This book gives a good idea of his research efforts at the time, and makes it possible to track an evolution in his beliefs on the essence and meaning of culture. In his review of the book, Stefan Żółkiewski wrote: 'The book prepared by Z. Bauman is distinguished by a great academic timeliness; it adapts to Polish conditions, in an original way, ideas being developed today, especially in the West and the East, of grasping theoretical questions of culture, popularizing among us this contemporary problematic, while adding at the same time his own solutions and point of view.'[12] The directive to destroy this publication was thus not only yet another blow that was aimed at Bauman in the aftermath of the March events, but also a major loss for Polish research. Thus, the opportunity to be acquainted with it after many years is now all the more valuable.

## THE PROBLEMATIC OF *SKETCHES IN THE THEORY OF CULTURE*

*Sketches in the Theory of Culture* is composed of ten chapters, and divided into two parts. The first of them, entitled 'Sign and culture', contains reflections inspired primarily by structuralism and semiotics, two currents that are combined here with the premises of Marxist thought. The question organizing the author's efforts is an attempt to work out a theory of culture that would be general, rigorous, and intersubjectively verifiable. Bauman was inspired primarily by the work of Claude Lévi-Strauss, whose thought he adapted in a creative way, and frequently also critiqued. The texts contained in the second portion of the book – 'Culture and social structure' – stemmed primarily from the author's fascination with structuralist thought, and were focused on a different problematic. There, the sociologist analysed the relationship between the cultural and structural dimensions of the organization of social life. He did this both as a process of theoretical reflection *sensu stricto*, and also by referring to concrete examples, historical as well as contemporary. The chapters comprising this part of the book are a continuation of the problematic investigated in a different guise in *Culture and Societies: Preliminaries*, which was published two years earlier.

In the chapter opening the first part of the book – entitled 'The origins of the semiotic theory of culture, or the crisis of cultural anthropology' – Bauman reflected on the transformations that were taking place at the time in cultural studies. He proved that the currents dominating the previous decades, based on the collection and scrupulous analysis of information pertaining to the functioning of specific collectives, turned out to be *de facto* dead ends. In this critique, he followed in the steps of the creator of *Structural Anthropology*, whose idea of creating a general theory of culture he saw as very attractive. He did not agree, however, with Claude Lévi-Strauss in the matter of the need to concentrate on the universal laws of the functioning of the human mind. He claimed that it was necessary to

apply the methodological solutions proposed by the French structuralist to the analysis of reality, in which culture played a semiotic function. This question was developed in later chapters that formed the
first part of the book. In the next – 'Towards a semiotic theory of
culture' – he analysed various theories of the sign and indicated their
meaning for research on culture. He claimed that the fundamental
property of culture is the organization and structuring of human
behaviour. The most important tool in realizing this function is, according to him, the 'pattern of behaviour' – or the 'act' – whose relationship to action Bauman compared to the relationship between a phoneme
and spoken sound. The conclusions emerging from this comparison
he saw as the basis of the interpretation of culture as a sign structure.
The topic of the reflections contained in the third chapter – titled
'Man and sign' – is the specifics of the semiotic system proper to
*Homo sapiens*, and also – *pars pro toto* – a reflection on the essence
of the human species. Bauman referred in these reflections to research
conducted in biological and technological studies. He analysed the
function of the sign systems of other living creatures, and also referred
to predictions about the future of machines. In the debate about the
particularity of the human, he emphasized the meaning of technology
and patterns of behaviour, acknowledging these factors as tools for
organizing the world. On the basis of the assumption fuelling the
analysis in the next chapter – 'The problem of universals and the
semiotic function of culture' – 'there exists, common to all people,
comprising the particularity of their species, a schema of thought-
action, imprinting on the structure of their systems of kinship and
judiciary, the structure of medical care, and political systems, and all
the other "items" so diligently dissected and grouped by professional
categorizers' (see pp. 95–6 below). This schema is materialized, in
Bauman's opinion, in the efforts to structuralize and organize the
external environment. The sociologist emphasized, however, that this
process never reaches an end, and the regions that are not encompassed
by it are the source of cultural dynamism. The supplement to the
above analysis, simultaneously opening new perspectives on research,
is the final chapter of the first part: 'Some research problems in the
semiotic theory of culture'. In it, Bauman reflected on the subject of
patterns corresponding to specific cultural fields. He distinguished
societies in which 'position-creating' signs or 'position-derivative' signs
dominate, indicating the consequences of this state of affairs in the
terrain of the dynamic of cultural changes.

The chapter opening the second part of the book – 'Cultural and
extra-cultural organization of society' – begins from this renewed

description of the informational and controlling function of culture. This time, Bauman placed this reflection alongside the problem of structural limitations. He wrote: 'The legal–political arrangement, working in concert with the economic one, serves the same function, generally speaking, as the cultural system: its task is the limitation of the collection of abstract possibilities by maximizing the likelihood of some and eliminating others' (p. 160 below). The sociologist described the conflict between culture and structure in terms of the theory of alienation; in his view, the proper direction of efforts leading to his solution should be the realization of the Marxist idea of activism. An interesting exemplification of the relationship between the cultural and economic systems was presented by Bauman in the following chapter – 'Economics, culture, and the typologies of societies'. In it, Bauman sketched out the transformations that were taking place in rural societies, using the concept of urbanization. The main subject of his reflections was the multi-dimensional – both social and cultural – consequences of the process of including these areas into the sphere of market mechanisms. The sociologist also referred to the changes that took place in Polish villages after the war. The third chapter in this part of the book – bearing the title 'Cultural determinants of the research process' – is devoted to reflection on the process of shaping ways that people perceive the world. In this regard, Bauman emphasized the crucial role of environmental factors – clearly indicating, however, that they do not have a determining character. In his view, they influence, among other things, the delineation of general positions of the individual towards reality, shaping the most important research goals and the subordination and organization of facts. In this context, he emphasized the meaning of so-called 'cultural brokers', a term he used in reference to teachers, writers, priests, monks, etc. A deeper analysis of the role of pedagogues is to be found in the next chapter, 'Three observations about problems of contemporary education'. The context of those reflections was socio-cultural transformation, which in an earlier work Bauman connected to the formation of a 'heterogeneous developing society' (Bauman 1966c: 374–450).[13] In this situation – the sociologist claimed –

> The main pressure, the strongest, must be placed on individual responsibility for their own choice. A young person must be prepared by an enlightened education, and not by the streets, for the fact that their life will be composed of a collection of individual decisions and choices and that no one and nothing, neither divine plan nor historical necessity, will remove from them the burden of responsibility for their own actions. (316–17)

The final chapter of the book – 'Masses, classes, elites: semiotics and the re-imagination of the sociological function of culture' – is devoted to reflections on the structural effects of the growth of means of mass communication. In it, Bauman proved that the constitution of a new type of culture required previous social transformations, based first and foremost on the birth of a universal dependence on the market, organization, and technology. In turn, the achievements of technology contributed to the disappearance of the division of values into higher and lower.

An important commentary on the reflections contained in *Sketches in the Theory of Culture* is the Afterword to the book that Zygmunt Bauman wrote in 2016. In it, the author discussed the transformations that took place in his work in the second half of the 1960s. He wrote, among other things, that 'The biggest shock for me was how much I could rely on my memory, discovering culture as a *process*, rather than as a body of material that was constant, or set up for self-stabilization and permanence' (see p. 252). The change described here in the perception of culture – moving from a vision of 'structure' to the idea of 'structurization' – will be discussed further in the following section of this text. I will also explain how some of the ideas presented by Bauman in the work discussed here anticipate his insights about the theory of culture from the beginning of the twenty-first century.

## THE EVOLUTION OF ZYGMUNT BAUMAN'S THEORY OF CULTURE

In the Introduction to *Culture and Society*, written in 1966, Bauman wrote: 'Culture is a resource of created or borrowed, but always possessed by a given collectivity of people, information, transmitted to each other in turn by individuals through the mediation of symbols with meanings that are fixed for that given group' (Bauman 1966c: 95, 96; my translation – KB). In accordance with this definition, the sociologist placed a particular emphasis, at the time, on questions of the coherence and integratedness of culture, and also on its isomorphism with regard to the social system. He indicated that its role is to create shared meanings, and also the values, positions and motivations associated with it. Thanks to this, culture can participate in an essential way in the process of creating feelings of unity between people of a given group.[14] At the time, Bauman presented the relationship between the individual and culture – both in this book[15] and in the majority of analyses contained in *Sketches in the Theory of Culture*

(p. 29)[16] – in a fairly one-sided way, in terms of a process of internalizing specific contents. This did not mean, however, that he settled on deterministic positions, because he juxtaposed the structuring function of culture with the notion of volition: 'an individual whose behaviour is regulated by goals and by patterns of behaviour can behave in a certain way, but does not have to', wrote Bauman in *Sketches in the Theory of Culture* – 'That is why their behaviour is significantly less stereotypical, and adjusts more readily in response to the environment' (pp. 204–5). Although the sociologist strongly emphasized the modelling role of culture at the time, he also pointed to the fact that it only contributed to the individual's process of decision-making.

In the portion of reflections contained in the book being considered here, the role of the agency of the individual was emphasized to a much greater degree. For example, at the conclusion of the chapter opening the second part of the book, Bauman juxtaposed a positivist and humanist vision of the world. According to the former, the human is a being that reacts to stimuli; their actions, however, are based on a specific socio-cultural arrangement. The latter conception assumes, however, that the human individual is not so much the receiver as the creator of the world – a subject capable of actively participating in its constant transformation. Inclined towards this view, Bauman wrote:

> The presence of a creative act in every human event means that it evades the positivistic perspective – that it can only be partially contained in a schema with a finite number of measurable variables. That which remains beyond the limits of the positivist schema is a fighting and active human, endlessly engaged in choosing, evaluating, organizing the world. Who is not only an endpoint of energy vectors but also a point of departure. (p. 171)

The source of such a vision of the human was at the time for Bauman, among other things, a revisionist reading of Marxist thought (see Bauman 1967c). It had other sources as well, however, among which we should point to cybernetics (pp. 155–71 below) or – subject to very interesting interpretation – the thought of Claude Lévi-Strauss (pp. 251–5). All of these currents played a role in the evolution of the sociologist's theory of culture, based on a transition from a concentration on the act of organizing specific values to a reflection on the active role of these same processes of creating and structuring social reality.

The observations described above coexisted in Bauman's works of the time with ideas stemming from yet another perspective. Its emergence was tied to the sociologist's reflections on the growing process of differentiation of culture. He described his perspective at the time as a consequence of the shaping of the world of technological civilization, the intensification of contacts between different regions of the globe, and the ever more essential role that market mechanisms began to play. In the context of all of these events, he wrote: 'The culture of society, in which various research perspectives and values criss-cross, ceases to be a system. It becomes a loose collection of not-necessarily-coherent models and meanings. It becomes mass culture. A plethora of accidental cultural contacts take place' (Bauman 1966c: 433; my translation – KB). *Eo ipso*, in the sociologist's opinion, heterogeneous developing societies are characterized by the development of individualization; within them cultural norms to an ever greater degree became an object of choice. This simultaneously meant – in accordance with the perspective on culture described before – that the ties linking the collective began to erode.[17] At the time, Bauman reflected on the consequences of the process on several different levels. In *Culture and Society*, they were fuelled by the question of the market assuming the function of a key to the decomposing socio-cultural structure (Bauman 1966a: 374–450; Brzeziński 2018: 77–94). In *Sketches in the Theory of Culture*, however, he presented them in terms of the potential beginning of a new stage in the history of Western civilization.

It is worthwhile in this context to introduce a lengthier statement of Bauman's, contained at the end of the chapter 'The problem of universals and the semiotic theory of culture':

> we live in an age that seems, for the first time in human history, to acknowledge cultural multiplicity as an innate and fixed feature of the world, one which gives rise to new forms of identity that are at ease with plurality, like a fish in water; and even boasts of the fact that it not only discovered but even accepted as a truly human state and mode of being both noble and dignified this indeterminacy of the human condition, as humanity's calling. Our era both multiplies the marginal regions of meaning and is no longer ashamed. Quite the opposite, in the mouths of its greatest thinkers it acknowledges them as its constitutive feature. (p. 117)

These words – written by the sociologist half a century ago – can successfully be placed alongside his later works on the role of ambivalence in contemporary culture (Bauman 1991), the decomposition of social and cultural structures (Bauman 2000) or the fragmentation of identity (Bauman 2003), etc. At the time, Bauman perceived these processes in an early form, but he suspected that they could give a rhythm to later socio-cultural changes. He perceived contemporary reality in liminal categories, directing attention to the fact that nearly all functions that for years, in his view, were carried out by culture succumbed to *de facto* suspension in the framework of the heterogeneous developing society. Writing about the 'liquidity' of the contemporary world, its growing pluralism, and the intensification of global ties (pp. 149–150, 163–164), he contemplated the role that culture would play in the future. It seems correct to assert that he was then laying the groundwork for his later works on modernity.


## CONCLUSION

In the later part of the text referred to in my Introduction above – Bauman's reflections on the subject of the metaphor of the 'message in a bottle' – that author wrote: 'sending the message into unmapped space and time rests on the hope that its potency will outlive its present-day neglect and survive the (transient) conditions that have caused the negligence' (Bauman 2005: 142). The publication of *Sketches in the Theory of Culture* – taking place half a century after the time of its creation – glimmers with this exact kind of hope. This is a book that is not only historical, but also a work with an essential meaning for contemporary humanities and social sciences. First, it is an important testament to the development of intellectual currents in the 1960s. Bauman's work introduces the reader to the debates that were taking place among scholars working on structuralism, semiotics, cybernetics, revisionist thought, etc. The author himself joined those debates in an active way, presenting very interesting solutions – frequently pioneering on a global scale – in the arena of cultural theory. Second, in this book there are many accurate anticipations of the development of socio-cultural processes. Bauman's reflections on the role of ambivalence, individualization or the global web of relationships are remarkably penetrating. What is more, the book corresponds elegantly to the analyses of the condition of liquid modernity by the same author. Third, this work can be read both as unveiling an aspect of the sociologist's work that was previously unknown, and demonstrating the continuities in his research interests. The reflection on the essence of culture and its transformations taking place during the last few decades was a constant topic for Bauman's work during his entire academic career (see Bauman 1992: 207).[18] *Sketches in the Theory of Culture* is not only the initial phase of his interest in this problematic, but also contains an array of threads that in later years would be developed by the author.

It is also worth emphasizing that all of Bauman's work is oriented as much towards an analysis of socio-cultural realities as to their changes (see Brzeziński 2015). In *Sketches in the Theory of Culture*, this question is also laid out clearly. The author sets himself against the vision of the passive individual, who is completely subordinate to existing structures and institutions: 'Man is not only the creation of the world, but also a creator', he wrote; 'In the fact that he is a creation, there is nothing specifically human. Humans are constituted as human only when, and to the extent that, they act as creator, operator, subject' (p. 168). These words are representative of Bauman's thoughts at every stage of his creative work. He continuously encouraged a critical approach to the status quo, transcending existing realities, and also undertaking activities whose goal was the transformation of existing realities. This was expressed by placing social, cultural, and political imperatives created by modernity alongside each other, in an effort to liberate the hope of overcoming them. The historical reading of *Sketches in the Theory of Culture* – as a work prepared for print directly before the March events – takes on a particular meaning in this context. Bauman wrote: 'If we do not accept uncritically the values that existing culture is adapted to creating and spreading, when we perceive the essential flaws in the dissemination of values that a given culture adheres to in its ideology, we have the right to subject the dominant system of culture to critical analysis and offer a counter-proposition of another system' (p. 244).

Today, the message of the book has, in the sense considered here, an essential meaning. An array of the ideas it sketched out as predictions about the future were presented as challenges that present-day society will need to confront. In this analysis – conducted by Bauman for many years – liquid modernity comprises a *de facto* materialization of his earlier fears. Both then and now, he presents a challenge to his readers to actively participate, with the goal of conquering these difficulties. It is worthwhile in this context to once again cite the fragment of his response that I have made into the compositional frame of this text:

> The 'message in a bottle' allegory implies two presumptions: that there was a message fit to be written down and worthy of the trouble needed to set the bottle afloat; and that once it is found and read (at a time which cannot be defined in advance) the message will be still worthy of the finder's effort to unpack it and study, absorb and adopt it. The message in a bottle is a testimony to the *transience of frustration* and the *duration of hope*, to the *indestructability of possibilities* and the *frailty of adversities* that bar them from implementation. (Bauman 2005: 142–3)

## NOTES

1 This research was funded by the National Science Centre in Poland on the basis of the grant awarded after obtaining a doctoral degree, based on the decision No DEC-2014/12/S/HS2/00391.
Dariusz Brzeziński is affiliated to the Institute of Philosophy and Sociology, Polish Academy of Sciences, ul. Nowy Świat 72, 00-330 Warsaw.

2 I would like to express my gratitude to the staff at the Ossolineum Publishing House for their permission to undertake the archival search.

3 Fragment of 'Report on writing off the loss of the honorarium and costs of publication' from 9 May 1968, located in the editorial files for *Sketches in the Theory of Culture* (card catalogue no. B-196).

4 It is worth pointing out that the reviewer of *Sketches in the Theory of Culture* – Stefan Żółkiewski – was removed from his post as secretary of Division I of the Polish Academy of Sciences as a result of the March events (Eisler 2006: 439).

5 The same decision by the Minister of Higher Education – Henryk Jabłoński – on 25 March also led to the dismissal from their posts at the University of: Bronisław Baczko, Leszek Kołakowski, Stefan Morawski, Maria Hirszowicz-Bielińska, and Włodzimierz Brus.

6 In the copy of the proofs was half of the chapter entitled 'Economies, culture, and typologies of societies'. It was recreated on the basis of the article 'On the matter of the urbanization of villages' published in *Culture and Society*, 3 (1964), after adding an expanded – surviving in full – introduction. The chapters entitled 'Cultural determinants of the research process' and 'Three observations about problems of contemporary education' were recreated on the basis of texts published under similar titles in *Studies in Philosophy*, 4 (1966), and *Pedagogical Quarterly*, 4 (1965), respectively. The final chapter in the book was published earlier as an article entitled 'Two notes on the margins of mass culture' in *Culture and Society*, 1 (1965). According to documents contained in the editorial file for *Sketches in the Theory of Culture*, it was to bear the title 'Masses, classes, elites: semiotics and the reimagination of the sociological function of culture', and so it has been titled in the book. Some of the papers used in the book were translated into English at the time (Bauman 1966a; Bauman 1967a), but they have all been newly translated for the purposes of this book.

7 Of the six chapters preserved in their entirety in the proofs, two of them – 'Towards a semiotic theory of culture' and 'Man and sign' – were created on the basis of articles published earlier in academic journals (the first in *Culture and Society*, 3 (1967) under the title 'Sign, structure, culture', and the second in *Sociological Studies*, 3 (1967) under the same title as here). In their case, the changes undertaken in the process of preparing the book for print were negligible. It is also worth noting in this context that fragments of the first and fifth chapters of the first part of the book were published in English in the articles 'Marx and the

contemporary theory of culture' (*Social Science Information*, 3 (1968)) and 'Semiotics and the function of culture' (*Social Science Information*, 5 (1968)).

8 Translator's note: Where possible, the original English citations have been supplied. In cases where they could not be located, I have translated Bauman's translations back into English.

9 A list of the works Bauman wrote before emigrating can be found in Tester and Jacobsen (2005: 223–6).

10 Studies in this area were conducted by Bauman under the auspices of the Division of Historical Materialism at the University of Warsaw, under the direction of Julian Hochfeld, and the department that arose out of this division. The sociologist took on the directorship after Julian Hochfeld, when Hochfeld took his position at UNESCO.

11 Translator's note: Although the text was originally written in English, I was unable to locate this specific quote, so this is my own translation from the Polish translation.

12 Stefan Żółkiewski's review can be found in the Ossolineum, in the aforementioned editorial file for *Sketches in the Theory of Culture*.

13 In *Culture and Society*, Bauman presented a typology of human collectives, taking into account the range of their social and cultural differences. At one end of the continuum, he placed the society 'Hhhm', characterized by homogeneity in the field of social structure and an axionormative system; at the other end, the society 'Htht' – heterogeneous in both of these dimensions. The latter he also described using the term 'heterogeneous developing societies', having in mind the dynamic of changes taking place in them.

14 This view of Bauman's on culture very much calls to mind the classical formulation of this category in anthropology. Ann Swidler wrote about it as follows: 'It assumes that culture shapes action by supplying ultimate ends or values toward which action is directed, thus making values the central causal event of culture' (Swidler 1986: 273).

15 It is worth mentioning a short quote from *Culture and Society*: 'the sphere of goals, values, meanings, and patterns – all of the things that without regards to their origins beyond the individual are interiorized or can be internalized – we will include in this book in the concept of *culture*' (Bauman 1966c: 10). It is worth mentioning at the same time that, in the sociologist's opinion, adopting specific goals does not always have to be connected to the possibility of their realization, because structural factors may stand in the way. This is the basis of the conflict between culture and structure, whose genesis and evolution is the overriding subject examined in *Culture and Society*.

16 '[C]ulture is simultaneously a process of organizing, structuring the environment of the individual, and a way of correlating and ordering the individual's behaviour with the pattern of the surrounding environment', wrote Bauman in *Sketches in the Theory of Culture*. It is worth noting that most of the chapters comprising the second part of the book were published in article form before the publication of *Culture and Society*.

17 Bauman described this process in terms of the emergence of 'schismogenic mechanisms', in this way deploying a category introduced by Gregory Bateson (Bauman 1966c: 186–232).
18 In a conversation with Roman Kubicki and Anna Zeidler-Janiszewska, Zygmunt Bauman uttered the following – important to this context – words: 'It seems to me ... that for this entire time (and it has been nearly half a century, after all) I have been asking the same, or similar, questions, it's only that I wandered from one place to another in search of answers' (Bauman, Kubicki, and Zeidler-Janiszewska 2009: 56).

## BIBLIOGRAPHY

### Books and articles

Bauman, Janina, 1998, *A Dream of Belonging – My Years in Post-war Poland*, London: Virago.
Bauman, Zygmunt, 1957a, 'O potrzebie socjologii partii [On the need for a Party sociology]', *Myśl filozoficzna*, 2, pp. 3–26.
Bauman, Zygmunt, 1957b, *Zagadnienia centralizmu demokratycznego w pracach Lenina* [Questions of democratic centralism in Lenin's works], Warsaw: Książka i Wiedza.
Bauman, Zygmunt, 1959, *Socjalizm brytyjski: Źródła, filozofia, doktryna polityczna* [British socialism: sources, philosophy, political doctrine], Warsaw: PWN.
Bauman, Zygmunt, 1962a, 'Values and standards of success of the Warsaw youth', *Polish Sociological Bulletin*, 2, pp. 77–90.
Bauman, Zygmunt, 1962b, 'Social structure of the Party organization in industrial works', *Polish Sociological Bulletin*, 3–4 (5–6), pp. 50–64.
Bauman, Zygmunt, 1962c, 'Struktura władzy społeczności lokalnej [The structure of local social power]', *Studia socjologiczno-polityczne*, 12, pp. 7–30.
Bauman, Zygmunt, 1963, 'Antonio Gramsci – czyli socjologia w działaniu [Antonio Gramsci – or sociology in action]', *Kultura i społeczeństwo*, 1, pp. 19–34.
Bauman, Zygmunt, 1964a, 'Bieguny analizy kulturowej [Poles of cultural analysis]', *Studia socjologiczne*, 3, pp. 51–91.
Bauman, Zygmunt, 1964b, 'W sprawie urbanizacji wsi', *Kultura i społeczeństwo*, 3, pp. 51–70.
Bauman, Zygmunt, 1965a, *Kariera. Cztery szkice socjologiczne* [Career: four sociological sketches], Warsaw: Iskry.
Bauman, Zygmunt, 1965b, 'Osobowość – kultura – struktura społeczna [Individuality – culture – social structure]', *Studia socjologiczne*, 2, pp. 203–33.
Bauman, Zygmunt, 1966a, 'Two notes on mass culture', *Polish Sociological Bulletin*, 2, pp. 58–74.

Bauman, Zygmunt, 1966b, 'Kulturowe determinanty procesu poznawczego [Cultural determinants of research processes]', *Studia filozoficzne*, 4, pp. 107–18.

Bauman, Zygmunt, 1966c, *Kultura i społeczeństwo. Preliminaria* [Culture and society: preliminaries], Warsaw: PWN.

Bauman, Zygmunt, 1967a, 'Some problems in contemporary education', *International Social Science Journal*, 19 (3), pp. 325–37.

Bauman, Zygmunt, 1967b, 'Człowiek i znak [Man and sign]', *Studia socjologiczne*, 7, pp. 49–82.

Bauman, Zygmunt, 1967c, 'Modern times, modern Marxism', *Social Research*, 3, pp. 399–415.

Bauman, Zygmunt, 1967d, 'Znak, struktura, kultura [Sign, structure, culture]', *Kultura i społeczeństwo*, 3, pp. 69–95.

Bauman, Zygmunt, 1968a, 'Marx and the contemporary theory of culture', *Social Science Information*, 3, pp. 19–33.

Bauman, Zygmunt, 1968b, 'Semiotics and the function of culture', *Social Science Information*, 5, pp. 69–80.

Bauman, Zygmunt, 1968c, *Szkice z teorii kultury* [Sketches in the theory of culture], Wrocław: Zakład Narodowy im. Ossolińskich (incomplete editorial proofs).

Bauman, Zygmunt, 1969, 'The end of Polish Jewry – a sociological review', *Bulletin on Soviet and East European Jewish Affairs*, 1, pp. 3–8.

Bauman, Zygmunt, 1972, *Between Class and Elite: The Evolution of the British Labour Movement: A Sociological Study*, trans. Sheila Patterson. Manchester University Press.

Bauman, Zygmunt, 1991, *Modernity and Ambivalence*, Ithaca, NY: Cornell University Press.

Bauman, Zygmunt, 1992, *Intimations of Postmodernity*, London and New York: Routledge.

Bauman, Zygmunt, 2000, *Liquid Modernity*, Cambridge: Polity.

Bauman, Zygmunt, 2003, *Liquid Love: On the Frailty of Human Bonds*, Cambridge: Polity.

Bauman, Zygmunt, 2005, *Liquid Life*, Cambridge: Polity.

Bauman, Zygmunt, and Wiatr Jerzy, 1953, 'O roli mas w historii [On the role of the masses in history]', *Myśl filozoficzna*, 3, pp. 69–99.

Bauman, Zygmunt, and Keith Tester, 2001, *Conversations with Zygmunt Bauman*, Cambridge: Polity.

Bauman, Zygmunt, Kubicki Roman, and Anna Zeidler-Janiszewska, 2009, *Życie w kontekstach. Rozmowy o tym, co za nami i o tym, co przed nami* [Life in contexts: conversations about what is behind us, and what is before us], Warsaw: Wydawnictwa Akademickie i Profesjonalne.

Brzeziński, Dariusz, 2015, *Myślenie utopijne w teorii społecznej Zygmunta Baumana* [Utopian thinking in the social theory of Zygmunt Bauman], Warsaw: Scholar.

Brzeziński, Dariusz, 2017, 'Human praxis, alternative thinking and heterogeneous culture – Zygmunt Bauman's revisionist thought', *Hybris*, 2, pp. 61–80.

Brzeziński, Dariusz, 2018, 'Consumerist Culture in Zygmunt Bauman's Critical Sociology: A Comparative Analysis of his Polish and English Writings', *Polish Sociological Review*, 1 (201), pp. 77–94.

Eisler, Jerzy, 2006, *Polski rok 1968* [The Polish year 1968], Warsaw: IPN.

Gramsci, Antonio, 1971, *Selected from the Prison Notebooks*, ed. and trans. Quentin Hoare and Geoffrey Nowell Smith, London: Lawrence & Wishart.

Krajewski, Władysław, 1982, 'The March events of 1968 and Polish philosophy', *Praxis International*, 2 (1), pp. 106–10.

Kraśko, Nina, 1995, 'O socjologii zaangażowanej Zygmunta Baumana [On the engaged sociology of Zygmunt Bauman]', in Tarkowska, ed., *Powroty i kontynuacje*, pp. 22–37.

Swidler, Ann, 1986, 'Culture in action: symbols and strategies', *American Sociological Review*, 51, pp. 273–86.

Tarkowska, Elżbieta, 1995a, 'Koniec i początek, czyli próba antropologii społeczeństwa polskiego [The end and the beginning, or an attempt at anthropology of Polish society]', in Tarkowska, ed., *Powroty i kontynuacje*, pp. 9–21.

Tarkowska, Elżbieta (ed.), 1995b, *Powroty i kontynuacje. Zygmuntowi Baumanowi w darze* [Returns and continuations: a gift for Zygmunt Bauman], Warsaw: Wydawnictwo IFiS PAN.

Tester, Keith, 2001, 'Introduction', in Bauman and Tester, *Conversations*, pp. 1–15.

Tester, Keith, and Michael Hviid Jacobsen, 2005, *Bauman before Postmodernity – Invitation, Conversations and Annotated Bibliography 1953–1989*, Aalborg University Press.

Wiatr, Jerzy, 2010, 'Zygmunt Bauman i początki socjologii polityki w Polsce powojennej [Zygmunt Bauman and the beginning of a sociology of politics in postwar Poland]', in *Zrozumieć nowoczesność. Księga Jubileuszowa Zygmunta Baumana* [Understanding modernity: Zygmunt Bauman's Jubilee Album], ed. Andrzej Chrzanowski, Wiesław Godzic and Anna Zeidler-Janiszewska, Warsaw: Wydawnictwo Officyna, pp. 265–70.

## DOCUMENTS COLLECTED IN THE EDITORIAL FILE OF *SKETCHES IN THE THEORY OF CULTURE* (BO OK CARD NO. B-196), LOCATED IN THE OSSOLINEUM PUBLISHING HOUSE

Editorial documents – correspondence between the publisher and Zygmunt Bauman.

'Review of the typewritten manuscript of Zygmunt Bauman's book entitled "Sketches in the Theory of Culture"'; author: Stefan Żółkiewski.

# From the Author

The articles collected in this volume were written at different moments
– some before, some after the publication of *Culture and Society*.
Collecting them in this volume can only be justified by one circumstance: a shared goal that the author perceives in all of them. That
shared goal is to work out a theory of culture that would allow for
an understanding of human actions, their shared characteristics and
variety of forms, that would go beyond the closed circle of ethnographic and ethnological description or empirical statistical generalizations. It seemed to the author that semiotics, combined with a still
vibrant and relevant Marxist interpretation of social structure, provided
the proper elements for this kind of theory.

A clear goal does not guarantee its successful realization. Indeed,
the author is quite nervous to submit the products of his efforts to
the judgement of the reader. In the case of a critical assessment of the
propositions assembled in this volume, he will take comfort in the
knowledge that the importance of the stakes is such as to justify
the work – and the knowledge that even a failed attempt at tackling
a new and important problem can, after all, fulfil a positive role,
stimulating creative interest in subjects that have heretofore not received
sufficient attention. In the author's opinion, one such issue is an understanding of culture not as a disorganized catalogue of human creations,
not as an accidental inventory of unmotivated ideas, and not as an
aggregate of passive reflections of the object world – but as a system
of human praxis, constantly organizing the system that comprises the
human and the human world.

All of the sketches collected in this volume are an attempt to combine two theoretical perspectives, offered by semiotic theory and Marxist structuralism. They appear in different proportions, and this explains the division of the sketches into two parts, as described by their titles.

'Towards a semiotic theory of culture' presents preliminary efforts to interpret culture as a system of signs that actively organize the human world, reducing its uncertainty, rendering it predictable, an organized system of reference for human praxis. In 'Some research problems in the semiotic theory of culture', I try to describe the topics of study of 'initial research', which emerge in the light of this kind of cultural system. Another sketch, 'The problem of universals and the semiotic theory of culture', in keeping with its title, presents the problem of general, widespread schemas of organizing the world, illuminated in diverse forms in every concrete cultural system and in every functionally distinguishable field of culture. Here, we also see the problem of universals as an issue for theoretical generalizations, methodologically different from a procedure that is simply called 'empirical generalization'. The third sketch in the first part, 'Man and sign', is an attempt to utilize previously formulated propositions for analysing particular traits of human life processes that form, as with all other living things, a unity of procedure assimilating the environment to the organism and accommodating the organism to its environment.

'Cultural and extra-cultural organization of society' is a sketch that looks more closely at the relationship between culture and social structures, postulating that this relationship can be described in terms of categories of meaning. In the sketch 'Economics, culture, and typologies of societies', I examine – on the basis of the widely discussed contemporary phenomenon of 'rural urbanization' – the problem of the mechanism of determinism that unites the sphere of commodity circulation with the structure of cultural systems. The sketch 'Cultural determinants of the research process' examines more closely the influence of these determinants on the human cognitive map of the world. The final two sketches are devoted to the application of the theories of culture presented in this volume to contemporary pedagogical issues and to the analysis of the important contemporary phenomenon described as the development of mass culture.

The thanks that typically adorn an author's preface this time go to my colleagues from the Department of Sociology at Warsaw University – harsh and merciless critics of my work who are also genial friends, thereby supplying the two things necessary to create the proper atmosphere for intellectual work. Many of the ideas in the book that may find favour with readers are theirs. The flaws of this volume are not their fault – these can only be attributed to the neglect or stubbornness of the author. Particularly warm thanks go to Professor Stefan Żółkiewski, who first introduced me to and interested me in the semiotic theory of culture.

*Konstancin, February 1967*

# Part I

## Sign and Culture

# I

# The Origins of the Semiotic Theory of Culture, or the Crisis of Cultural Anthropology

One of the lessons to be learned from the popularity of the semiotic theory of culture in recent years is the eternal praxeomorphism of the human way of seeing the world. People imagine the world in the way they've learned to model it; they always ascribe to it the mechanisms whose hidden connections they have recognized by modelling them in practice and replicating them in experiments. People explain the correspondence between their experience of the states of 'entry' and 'exit' of examined objects with the help of models, which always dutifully personify the recently achieved state of technical-operational capability. This hearkens, to an equal degree, to Thales of Miletus, as to contemporary geneticists, who – following the birth of the idea of the hologram from the cradle of technology that produced lasers and masers – ascribed to genes a holographic nature, or to those psychologists like N. E. Golovin, who, shortly after figuring out the technique of 'scanning' in tele-location, presented the process of human thought as 'scanning' a field of information. Knowing the praxeomorphic tendencies of the human mind, we can easily find the connection between the technical successes of information theory and cybernetics and the perception of culture as a system of signs organizing information – in other words, structuralizing, 'self-organizing systems' of humans and their environments.

These reflections reveal the sources of inspiration for those seeking a modern theory of culture. But they do not explain the search itself. Why, after so many years of, if not an aversion to theory, then at least a lack of hunger for it, this sudden turn among anthropologists towards a general theory of culture? Why the sudden protest against an unreflexive accumulation of new descriptions of tribes, villages, and urbanizing suburbs to the already gathered hundreds of thousands of volumes of ethnographic documentation? An answer to this question requires a more careful examination of the situation that arose halfway through the twentieth century in human reflections on culture.

## CULTURE AS AN OBJECT OF RESEARCH

In the *Allgemeine Kulturgeschichte der Menschheit*, published in 1843, Gustav Klemm connected the idea of culture to the shape of a tree, if it were consciously cultivated by a person; to rubbing sticks together to make fire; to the custom of cremating the father's corpse; to decorative body-painting. In this way, more than 120 years ago, today's idea of culture reached its final form. Firstly, the concept emerged from a selective and hierarchical sense that accompanied the Greek *paideia* and the Roman culture of *animi*: rubbing sticks together or striking matches against the rough surface of a box, cremation or burial, a tree of rounded shape or the false dwarfism of a shrub – all of this was now culture, some kind of culture. Secondly, this concept, stripped of evaluative ingredients, was subsequently applied to all elements of the world, which thereby became imprinted with the stamp of human action – which wouldn't exist, if it weren't for humans. All subsequently formulated definitions of culture fit elegantly within these boundaries, drawn with a flourish. All of these definitions aimed to narrow the boundaries of phenomena defined as cultural – to excise certain less interesting materials from Klemm's universe.

Thus, Czarnowski's well-known definition banishes beyond the border of what is considered culture everything that in Klemm's universe of human signs is accidental, singular, uncommon. Znaniecki, in his definition of culture, mainly takes care to remove from its orbit everything that is not a reference to human values, namely the 'physical' aspect of phenomena that would otherwise be seen as cultural. Finally, Ossowski proposes to exclude from the idea of 'culture' all things – objectified creations, constructed, admittedly, by humans, but endowed with an independent, reified existence ('correlates of culture'). This last definition, kin to Clark Wissler's concept of 1916 (culture as a delineated complex of associated ideas), demarcates a realm of cultural phenomena that is most useful for semiotic perspectives. This conjecture highlights the formulation of a definition of culture of identical scope by James Taylor in 1949: 'Culture can be briefly characterized as a stream of ideas flowing between individuals through the medium of symbolic activities, verbal teaching, or imitation.'[1]

All definitions of culture have in common not only that the collective elements they describe provide in sum the assemblage contained by Klemm's definition. They also share the fact that they objectivize culture – beyond all discussion, it is a human creation, existing in people and through people as an object in and of itself, exterior to the individual, and therefore a potential object of study. Such an intellectual objectification of the cultural sphere, though it seems natural and obvious to us today, certainly did not stem from an innate capability of the human species, or from the particular 'nature' of cultural phenomena. It was, and had to be, the product of historical development. Marx wrote about people: 'As [man] neither enters into the world in possession of a mirror, nor as a Fichtean philosopher who can say "I am I", a man first sees and recognizes himself in another man. Peter only relates to himself as a man through his relation to another man, Paul, in whom he recognizes his likeness.'[2] The structures of 'private' human thoughts are internalized traces of human social interactions. Looking at one's individual mode of being as an external object, reified, could only happen as the result of practical contact with another form of being, objective by virtue of its sensual externality and autonomy.

Cultural contacts were thus the cradle of the concept of culture.

Because it was this way, we can expect that the 'discovery' of culture as having an objective existence is most likely in heterogeneous, expanding civilizations, existing precisely through cultural contacts that eventually internalized cultural diversity. And this is indeed how it was. Culture in the sense described was 'discovered' in the cradle of the civilization in which the above-mentioned features were at the highest intensity – in the Greco-Christian world. The extent to which the properties of a civilization-object characterize the perspective of civilization-subjects, remaining in the realm of physical contact, is evident in the 'cultural blindness/myopia' of culturally homogeneous pre-Renaissance Europe, compared with the acuity of vision of the Greeks, sensitive to all cultural differences. Margaret T. Hogden, the author of a fantastic study of sixteenth- and seventeenth-century European anthropology, notes with wonder the fact that, for the European Middle Ages, it was characteristic that:

> Pilgrims left behind a massive collection of travel literature, created by religious figures, soldiers, and secular people, and describing the causes of their undertaking voyages, and about what they saw on their travels. In all this writing, which emerged out of contacts with other people, they evinced very little curiosity about other people, or an utter lack of it, very little interest in other forms of life, and little reaction to cultural difference.[3]

On the other hand, Herodotus – a person brought up in a society that, because of its cultural diversity, I included in the book *Culture and Society* in the category of Htht – devotes his *Histories* primarily to one thing: a diligent inventory of everything in the daily life of others that is different from the Greek way of life, unique, uncommon. Here is an example (I, 35):

> Concerning Egypt itself I shall extend my remark to great length, because there is no country that possessed so many wonders [...] Not only is the climate different from that of the rest of the world, and the rivers unlike any other rivers, but the people also, in most of their manners and customs, exactly reverse the common practice of mankind. The women attend the markets and trade, while the men sit at home at the loom; and here, while the rest of the world works the woof up the warp, the Egyptians work it down; the women likewise carry burthens upon their shoulders, while the men carry them upon their heads. They eat their food out of doors in the streets, but retire for private purposes to their houses, giving as a reason that what is unseemly, but necessary, ought to be done in secret, but what has nothing unseemly about it, should be done openly. A woman cannot serve the priestly office, either for god or goddess, but men are priests to both; sons need not support their parents unless they choose, but daughters must, whether they choose or no.[4]

For Herodotus, an 'experienceable fact' is that which stands in opposition to the form of being that he has unreflexively become accustomed to; but the appearance of such a significant opposition removes the lack of reflexiveness from one's own customs, reifying them, transforming them into a potential object of inquiry 'from the outside'. In this way, every civilization is 'egocentric' – and, moreover, it is precisely through this egocentrism that the road to relativism through self-examination leads.

The result of this reflection born of cultural contact is ultimately the awareness that one's own way of life is but one possibility among many (regardless of whether it is considered the best one, or simply a different one). The possibility emerges of asking oneself where this otherness comes from, and why different people observe different customs.

We know the answer that can be deduced from the beliefs of people from homogeneous cultures – the answer that they would provide themselves, if their situation did not render the question incomprehensible. The answer is straightforward: customs are as 'innate' a human characteristic as skin colour or hair-growth patterns. They are 'given'; in religious mythology, one can add that they are given by

God. Even in Hesiod, the natural order and moral system are considered on the same logical plane and seen as clauses of the same divine decree. In order to arrive at a different kind of answer, to understand the human sources of culture and moral commandments, one would need to establish the idea of an ideal, a goal, the formation of reality in accordance with a specific plan, in the crucible of technical manipulation of nature. One would also need to experience various norms and realities. One would need to go through, in other words, the decentring of the system of contingencies called civilization and the collection of yearnings known as culture, which is the legacy of a simultaneous, though not parallel, heterogenization of society and culture. As Jaeger wrote (reducing the question to an academic reflection on technology): 'The Greeks did not think of human nature as a theoretical problem until, by studying the external world, especially through medicine and mathematics, they had established an exact technique on which to begin a study of the inner nature of man.'[5] This paves the way for Plutarch's famous allegory about the three ingredients of *agri culturae* and *culturae animi* (good soil, good grain, and a good farmer), which was contained in the etymological choice accepted up to today as an answer to the question about the origins of the human way of being. Such an answer was only provided fully consciously and meaningfully by European civilization.

Only European civilization grasped the process of cultural transmission from the side of educating, rather than learning. Cultural education happens, obviously, in all civilizations. According to the classification formulated by Margaret Mead in *Continuities in Cultural Evolution*, it happens through unreflexive empathy, imitation or identification. Nowhere, however, does the role of teacher fall to someone who has been a student in the process: the subject is the person who is learning; the person passing on the experiences ossified in culture appears in the role of helper, conditions external to the process. Sometimes, one tribe encroaches upon or even subjugates another. This conquest is not necessarily connected with missionary efforts or a desire to convert, as was characteristic of European territorial expansion. In practice, in the place of the native, who must learn a foreign language in order to understand a message necessary to his survival, appears the colonialist who must force the natives to learn, in order to be understood. The situation of colonial expansion, based on a conviction of cultural superiority, leads to a change of the focus in the educational process. The emphasis now falls on 'Changing people's habits, people's ideas, people's language, people's beliefs, people's emotional allegiances, involves a sort of deliberate violence to other people's developed personalities.'[6]

The model for the hierarchization of ethnic cultures is contained in the social hierarchies of class culture. The *arête* of nobility created the ideal of *paideia*. The division within society into 'better' and 'worse' customs provides concepts that were later applied to assessments of ethnically foreign cultures. A teacher employed by the wealthy becomes the prototype for a nation-teacher, not only of foreigners, but also of 'primitives'.

Taken together, all of these elements explain why it was only in Greco-Roman culture that the idea and occupation of ethnography, or the analysis of foreign cultures, perceived as independent entities that could be treated like any other objects of study and description, emerged. This does not explain, however, what – on the level of personal motives – was and is sought after by the European (in the ecumenical sense of the term) ethnographer, entering into ways of life different from his or her own. This alone does not determine one's relationships to foreign cultures. On the basis of the elements described, one could create both the colonizing and the Romantic attitude towards cultural difference. What determines the choice between these attitudes is an additional factor – the ethnographer's attitudes towards his or her own society.

## ONE'S OWN SOCIETY AND THE PERCEPTION OF DIFFERENCE

The questions that I have just posed cannot be understood on the level of generality that is proper to psychological laws. The concept of the ethnographer obstructs this – meaningless in reference to most known cultures, belonging only to European civilization. Ethnography as a field of knowledge, and as a career, appears only in situations where a civilization gains over another a decisive advantage of a non-cultural nature – economic or military – placing it in relation to another people in the same position as (internally) the aristocracy occupies in relation to the plebeians, utilizing in the process theoretical terms and practical proofs in order to demonstrate its own cultural superiority. Only in this case does the dilemma of conformity or nonconformity in relation to one's own society and its customs take the form of a choice between alternatives, between romantic or colonial. Both of these alternatives acquire meaning only when it has been accepted that one's own civilization is the product of a longer (not in the sense of abstract time, but in qualitative-historical) development, and so because of this is already at a 'higher' phase of development; that one's ancestors once had customs that are even today maintained among 'primitive' peoples, and the descendants of today's 'primitives', if nothing unexpected happens, will live according to our customs. This conviction was not the subject of conflict in our times, when the pioneers of European ethnography were sharply divided into two camps. The difference pertained to evaluations of development – by which our society surpassed that of 'primitive' peoples – as good or bad; and that evaluation derived from perceptions of the virtues and vices of our own society.

This pattern had a banal shape: a critical perspective on one's own society was connected to the idea of civilizational decline, crippling the natural and harmonious order of things. A yearning for innate harmony acquires a complete shape already in the *Essais* of Michel de Montaigne. The Enlightenment's Noble Savage is already a variation of a topic codified by Montaigne:

> There is nothing barbaric or savage in this people, unless one would term barbaric anything that departs from their own customs. Because in honesty there is no other measure for truth and reason as example and the image of our own fatherland: there are to be found the best religion, the best laws, the best and highest custom in all things. They are wild, in the same way that we call a sheep wild, which nature produced and developed; when, in essence, we should rather call wild those that we condemned through our ideas and turned away from their natural way of being. In the former we find a lively and true collection of useful and innate virtues and properties; in ours, we have degraded them, turning them to the needs of our own spoiled tastes [...] We have freighted the beauty and bounty of nature with the work of our own minds, we have smothered it; so everywhere, where it shines forth in its purity, a strange shame is inflicted on our empty and wanton desires.

'Savages' inhabit a nation:

> where there is no marketplace, no knowledge of the sciences, numbers, no names for bureaucrat or political power, no servitude, wealth or poverty, no contracts, inheritance, no occupation, no respect for lineage other than tribal belonging, no clothing, no agriculture, metal, use of wine or wheat. Even the words that would refer to lies, betrayal, delusion, greed, jealousy, slander, forgiveness, are unknown.[7]

The list of virtues of the 'man of nature' was created from an act of accusation directed against one's own society.

Admiration for the development of civilization contained, for a change – without regard to the political affiliations of the author – a condemnation of primordial customs. From the perspective of the ideology of progress, the primordial (or simply the non-European) turned out to be synonymous with the 'backward' or the 'undeveloped'. This pronouncement was connected to a broad range of moral assessments. At one end of the spectrum was William Strachey, the author of *The Historie of Travaile into Virginia Britannia* of 1612. In his view, the atrocities committed against the inhabitants of Peru, Mexico, or the Antilles were actually beneficial, because their own lives were far more horrific. Or John Wesley (1703–91), who asked, outraged, whether Laplanders, Greenlanders, or Samoyedic people could be seen as being as civilized as our sheep or oxen? To compare hordes of savages to our horses or other domestic animals was to pay them a compliment! This view would later be adopted by the representatives of the 'white man's mission'. At the other end were the ideologues of 'help for the backward' and the spread of civilization. Their voices were increasingly heard in direct proportion to the rise of the military and political power of the 'savage' – an important argument for civilizing them.

We have tracked the divergent paths of European ethnographic thought up to this point, where they reach a fundamental crossroads. With the passage of time, as is typically the case in the development of society, the separate paths became institutionalized – and from then on, in order to start down one of them, it was no longer necessary to repeat ontogenetically the experiences that motivated them, that once served to create this or that way of perceiving the 'other'. Today, one can become an ethnographer in the same way that people become engineers or linguists: by choosing a career that, because of the perks it offers, has been deemed preferable. Only the occasional 'greats' feel compelled to reflect on their decision, explaining and examining its reasons and unconscious lessons. When they do this, they return stubbornly to a still-living structure, the relationship between my culture and other cultures, seeking a 'social motive' for the existence of their own career:

> It is no accident that the anthropologist should rarely have a neutral attitude towards his own group. If he is a missionary or an administrator, we can infer from this that he has agreed to identify himself with a certain system, to the point of dedicating his life to its propagation; and when he practices his profession on a scientific or academic level, one can very probably discover in his past certain objective factors which show him to be ill-adapted to the society into which he was born [...] There is no way out of the dilemma: either the anthropologist adheres to the norms of his own group and other groups inspire in him no more than a fleeting curiosity which is never quite devoid of disapproval, or he is capable of giving himself wholeheartedly to these

other groups and his objectivity is vitiated by the fact that, intentionally or not, he has had to withhold himself from at least one society, in order to devote himself to all.'[8]

The same applied during the time of Montaigne and Wesley, as today, in the time of Lévi-Strauss, who wrote these words.

But one thing has changed: the European stopped believing in the obviousness of his world. Or, rather, the European's world ceased to be obvious to him. There is nothing strange about this. A world that is fluid and changeable – one in which today so decisively gives the lie to the day before, so that no one could ever believe that tomorrow could confirm the truths of today – cannot be obvious. Experiencing the historicity of existence – that particular singularity of our version of civilization – ultimately undermines any realizations about the existence of any kind of value strong enough to subordinate the course of human events unto itself. In the beginnings of historical thought, such values were passionately sought after, only for us to refute or be disenchanted with them later on. The only insight that remained was about changeability/mutability itself, as a principle of being; it rooted itself so deeply in European thought that ethnographers, striving to reclaim the 'ahistoricity' of homogeneous civilizations, had to do violence to their own way of thinking. There are authors today who believe – and who support their beliefs with impressive evidentiary materials – that the same common sense that bids them investigate the existence of human society, 'analogous to the growth of an organism',[9] goes back to the time of Thucydides, and thus has had plenty of opportunity to become an unreflexive premise.

This same common sense has, in our own time, been put to the test. The conviction that the forms of human existence are ever-changing remains strong to this day; we strive to extend it, diligently collecting evidence for it – also for civilizations, whose existence gives the lie to it. But the biological analogy to predetermined, genetically encoded stages of development, the analogy of the caterpillar – which already contains within itself the chrysalis and the larva, which is a dormant butterfly – has ceased to satisfy us intellectually. We cannot believe that every society must pass through a fascist stage – so we believe instead in the testimony of archaeology, which demonstrates that not every civilization has a phase of cliff paintings or massive stone sculptures. Our society, which forces every generation to experience the crisis of values of the previous one anew, has made us sceptical of any axiomatic absolutes – even of those whose tracks we have not yet come across. So nothing is obvious to us anymore – and we cannot speak of the 'biological necessity' of social development. The term 'primitive', referring to a society other than our own, increasingly becomes a descriptive term and loses the historico-philosophical garb that it once had. We note the discrepancies between the paths of logic and the social laws of the vision of the world. When 'other' societies were still following immanent, independent paths of development, we saw them as being frozen in earlier phases of the road leading to our own way of being. When really – partly forced by our cannons, partly enchanted by the glimmer of our material goods – those 'other' societies accepted our model as being at the top of the ladder that they were climbing, our vision of the world lost its ladder-like shape, and the scattered rungs came to form a mosaic of diverging paths. Disdain for one's own model played no small role. Montaigne's line triumphed, albeit in a completely new form.

The work of Bronisław Malinowski and Ruth Benedict provided the intellectual materials for this triumph and determined its contemporary form. The internment in the Trobriand Islands of this subject of the Austro-Hungarian empire, whom the outbreak of war found at an ethnography conference in Australia, was the accidental fuse leading to the explosion of a cache of dynamite that had long been collecting under the rickety construction that was a single line of evolution. Placed, of necessity, on the outside, among a very un-European society, forced to master its language and participate in its everyday life, Malinowski was the first European ethnographer to perceive an 'other' society not as a disorganized collection of traits more or less different from European models, but as an independent, logically consistent whole, each piece understandable only in the context of the rest. Based on what Malinowski saw and wrote, Ruth Benedict created a new vision of the organization of the human species, as a collection of clay cups, from which each group of people drinks the water of life in their own way. It didn't matter, that she – along with her teacher Boas – didn't approve of Malinowski's methodological ahistoricism and his 'individual functionalism'; without Malinowski's revolution, there would be no 'culturosophy' from Ruth Benedict, and these circumstances are decisive for the affinities that create the stitches weaving together intellectual discoveries in the chronicles of human thought.

The result of the transformation discussed here was, firstly, the replacement of a purely vertical dimension by a horizontal one – and a linear geometry of time by a planar one. Lined up, until recently, in single file on a vertical ladder of development, the 'other' cultures suddenly found themselves side by side. The synchronic suddenly gained value, which it could not have when it was seen only as a passing moment within a stream of transitory forms. This new vision had its own egalitarianism, in accordance with the newly postulated notion of human equality; thus, already within this acceptance was lurking, often subconsciously, a protest against the functioning of one's own culture, which did violence to this postulate. Secondly, the meaning of revolution was expressed in the simultaneous replacement of the deterministic image of the world – a probabilistic image, a line graph – with a tree. Our world became one of many possible worlds, decidedly less likely than 'other' human worlds; this premise of the 'culturosophical' revolution brought its intellectual product into contact with the most modern philosophical premises of other disciplines, and therefore lent it splendour and persuasiveness, emerging from its accommodation to the general intellectual climate of the epoch.

The destruction of intellectual constructions cannot happen without any costs, however. They also had to be paid, for the demolition of the evolutionary model for organizing knowledge about culture.

## THE NAME OF THE CRISIS

The cost was the crisis of anthropology. The inevitability of this crisis was already contained in the revolutionary thought of Malinowski. When this crisis was to occur (when it was to be consciously recognized as a crisis) depended only on the momentum of ethnographic studies. And this momentum, thanks to the interference of cultural 'otherness' in the vital interests of Eurocentric civilization, was massive in the last half-century.

The meaning of this crisis can be described as an accumulation of a large store of potential information, which, however, could not be utilized as information – could not be transformed into 'information for us' – because the structures that it described were unknown. We have many forms that we understand must be signs; but we do not know how to decipher these signs. We don't know the code that they are a part of – bah, we don't know where to locate the reality within which they fulfil the function of a sign.

To put it more plainly – Malinowski's example created the impetus of an unprecedented production of endless descriptions of 'other' societies, organizing information about these cultures in a closed system within the frameworks of these societies. The researcher's ideal was to attain maximum coherence of the model, to penetrate beyond the level of perception – which is still permeated by the categories that the researcher brings to it from their own culture – to a structure of analysis internal to that cultural system. This was the general postulate that was instrumentalized in various ways: either, as in 'pure' functionalism, the perceived elements of culture were interpreted as serving the needs of individuals and collectives; or – in keeping with the demands of Thomas and Znaniecki – what was sought above all else was what these elements are, for the people making use of them (from such elements Radcliffe-Brown constructed his concept of social structures). The difference of opinions pertained – if we consider it from a broader perspective – to techniques of interpretation, but not to the primary goal of anthropological study. The ideal in both cases was the same: the standard anthropologist was the kind of person who forgot as much as possible of what their own culture had taught them, and, for that reason, was able to understand the most about the culture that became the object of study. This postulate, however – as soon became clear – placed before anthropology as a discipline, and every individual anthropologist, the antinomy of Frank Cushing.

Frank Cushing aspired to become a great ethnographer. He succeeded in achieving the requisite ideal completely: he was initiated into the Priesthood of the Bow of the Zuni. He became a great Priest. The result was that he ceased to be an ethnographer. At the crossroads, which was supposed to lead to triumphing over conflicts in multicultural communication, he found (not Cushing, to be clear, but those who studied his life) the end of all communication. For the blasphemous effort to return to the time before the Tower of Babel – it turns out – one pays with the loss of any ability to speak.

Luckily, only very few ethnographers proved as determined and successful as Frank Cushing in realizing their methodological aims. The divergence between research ideals and realities became the daily bread of ethnography. As is typical in such cases, reflection on methodology became taboo. The less theory, the less self-analysis – the better. Only very few returned to epistemological questions. When they did, they were rarely able to achieve much more than reheating old dreams of empathy. P. J. Bohannan raged over the 'cardinal error of ethnographic and social analysis': that it '[raises] folk systems like "the law", designed for social action on one's own society, to the status of an analytical system, and then tries to organize raw social data from other societies into its categories.' Such a cardinal error is 'raising the folk systems of the Romans or the Trobriand Islanders to the level of such a filing system for data which may not fit them'. In relation to institutions and legal concepts: 'We must realize that the same general type of material can be classified in several ways. It is, in the long run, the folk classifications that are important to social anthropology, not the "presence" of torts or contracts which are both folk and analytical concepts in another society.'[10] Critics like Bohannan were fans of the slogan 'forward to the past' – a return to the pure postulates of Malinowski. They believed in the possibility of their realization; they did not doubt the rightness of the heuristic. Once again, they demanded practices according to which the typical ethnographer – without reflection, to be sure, and quietly – would step away from the pressures of local realities. Consciously or unconsciously, they thereby worked to contribute to the state of ethnography that was increasingly seen as being a crisis.

This state, according to Walter Goldschmidt, was characterized by two primary directions of research: 'the detailed internal analysis of individual cultures which generally endeavors to establish interrelationships between diverse sets of institutions – best exemplified by the investigations of Malinowski and generally called functional studies; and (2) the comparison of institutions or structural features among a group of societies (either delimited or worldwide) showing the distribution and covariation of such features'.[11] The dead end that the combination of these two directions led ethnography into arose from a dilemma contained *in nuce* in the stance formulated by Malinowski and Boas, and thereafter accepted by most cultural researchers:

> Malinowski was most insistent that every culture be understood in its own terms; that every institution be seen as a product of the culture within which it developed. It follows from this that a cross-cultural comparison of institutions is essentially a false enterprise, for we are comparing incomparables. Yet the internal mode of analysis can never give us a basis for true generalization and offers no means of extrapolation beyond the local time and place. Indeed, it leaves us clearly in the hands of the Boasians, to whom each culture is merely a product of its own history. If we are to avoid the stricture that anthropology must be either history or nothing, we must find a way out of this dilemma.[12]

Many heterogeneous elements play into the perception of the state of contemporary anthropology as a crisis.

1 Despite the convictions of many ethnographer-practitioners (persistent because, among other things, not subject to self-examination), Malinowski's postulates are far from being realized. In the best case, ethnographers stop themselves, as Lévi-Strauss put it, 'halfway' between their own culture and the other, and, despite their aspirations of being immersed in the culture they study, they actually fill a role that they wrongly dissociate from, and which is the only role that truly justifies the existence of ethnography: the role of cultural mediator or translator of foreign languages. They fill this role regardless of their fantasies about their calling, and, when

they realize this, they experience it as transgressive, as something they must justify or explain. Escaping from the crisis at this point requires removing the moral stigma from behaviour that is widespread and unavoidable

2 The realization of Malinowski's postulates, though never complete, is sufficiently active as to give ethnographic descriptions of culture a form that renders the translatability of information about cultures practically impossible – or, at the very least, significantly more difficult. In intention and genesis, Malinowski's anti-evolutionarism was filled with the spirit of democracy and egalitarianism: in practice, the realization of his ideas led to the shattering of the image of the human species into distinct, non-communicating enclaves, and to such a stark highlighting of differences that the notion of a unified *Homo sapiens* was moved into the shadows, or even called into question. The (justly) criticized concept of linear evolution was not replaced with any other principle of a unified form of human existence. This evoked understandable protest and fervent searches for 'cultural universals', which, however, as Stanisław Ossowski wisely pointed out, turned out to be 'pre-cultural' universals – biological/physiological categories – or a wholly uninformative inventory of the areas of interest of the ethnographer, as in the case of Murdock's famous list: all people somehow organize the sexual relationships between men and women, all people form some kind of judgement about some kinds of crimes, all people have some preferred cuisines, etc., etc. In the second case, we are dealing with – to use the fantastic allegory of Bronisław Baczko – a typical broken vending machine, which constantly returns the very coin that one feeds into it. What is most important, however – the so-called efforts to integrate 'disciplinary' universals – is in essence merely an inventory of different measures of individuation, which is evidenced by Murdock's practical efforts to analyse one of these 'universals' – the system of kinship.

3 In order to save the idea of a unified human species under these conditions, we must go beyond the realm of anthropology *sensu stricto*, performing an operation of reduction, reaching for a psychological foundation for human action. The inevitable conclusion to be drawn from the application of the methodological propositions of Malinowski and Boas is the conviction that culture is that which differentiates: if something exists that unifies, it is the bio-psychic constitution of the human species, the neuro-physiological mechanisms, modified by culture only in its external-object expressions. If one could bring no other objections to this thesis, there would still be the one sufficiently problematic for anthropologists,

the 'a-culturalism' of the psychological means of 'cultural integration'. The awareness that psychologists are able to construct their experiments in such a way that the results of their research can be grasped in universal categories is poor consolation for anthropologists. From this fact, nothing, or almost nothing, emerges in answer to the question of whether, within the layer distinguished analytically as cultural, there exist – alongside differences – phenomena that are shared, attributes of the human as a cultural creature? And within what categories should such phenomena be modelled?

We live in an epoch of practical integration of world culture. It appears that – to the extent that the state characterized here, which we are calling the crisis of anthropology, does not change – ethnography could find itself in the rearguard of a world in which 'world history' was merely an analytical concept.

## CLAUDE LÉVI-STRAUSS, OR THE NEGATION OF THE NEGATION

If we are to believe *Tristes Tropiques* – which is just as much a tractate on the beauties and sorrows of the ethnographer's task as it is an autobiography – Claude Lévi-Strauss, student of Mauss and admirer of Saussure, embarked on his apprenticeship in cultural studies trusting in the wisdom and efficacy of the widely agreed-upon rules of the craft. He believed – as others believed – that the task of the ethnographer was to recognize 'otherness' as otherness, in its internal, 'private' logic, not tainted by the intrusive thought cultivated by the rhetoric of the foreign civilization. Ethnographic understanding could be accomplished only through direct physical contact with 'others' – in terms of space, by getting closer to the 'others', the ethnographer also grew further from his or her own culture, not only physically, but also intellectually. There was a silently accepted assumption that the relevant physical closeness guaranteed, or at least made more likely, a mental closeness.

Inspired by this conviction, Lévi-Strauss undertook his peregrinations to the 'source of the human'. The Indians, in their primordial, pre-civilized purity, were to present a clear image of this source, as opposed to their more civilized brethren. Unfortunately, those who still lived near the metropolitan centres of Brazil had not preserved much of their legacy. From the outset, it emerged that physical contact destroyed the object of study; as is typical in these cases, the process of research proved to have an influence on the object of study. There is no research as pure reflection: every study is an action – its object, after being studied, is different than it was before. Thus, Lévi-Strauss set off on an adventure to ever further reaches of the Brazilian interior, towards ever more savage otherness, to a purity that was less and less touched by civilization.

Kadiueo, Bororo, Nambikwara, each was a stage of farther distance from the centre of civilization, another stage in approaching a 'pure human'. But there were still too many impurities; if there was archaism, it was derivative, forced, degenerate, the leftovers of the civilizing process. Until finally (o, joy, gods be praised!), the situation that every ethnographer dreams of: the Tupi-Kawahib, a tribe lost in the depths of the interior, a tribe, that no ethnographer had ever encountered before, and – maybe – would never see again; a human in a chemically pure state, a neolith of the twentieth century, frozen in time, waiting for the discerning eye of the ethnographer, to unfurl before him the secrets of the fundamental basis of civilization. And here, at the end of his travels, on the verge of a great secret, after tearing away the curtain covering this 'holiest of holies' of the ethnographic religion, an epiphany takes place, the recognition of a mistake, and in its aftermath – conversion:

> although I had set off on the adventure with enthusiasm, it left me with a feeling of emptiness. I had wanted to reach the extreme limits of the savage; it might be thought that my wish had been granted, now that I found myself among these charming Indians whom no other white man had ever seen before and who might never be seen again. After an enchanting trip up-river, I had certainly found my savages. Alas! They were only too savage [...] There they were, all ready to teach me their customs and beliefs, and I did not know their language. They were as close to me as a reflection in a mirror; I could touch them, but I could not understand them. I had been given, at one and the same time, my reward and my punishment. Was it not my mistake, and the mistake of my profession, to believe that men are not always men? that some are more deserving of interest and attention because they astonish us by the colour of their skin and their customs? I had only to succeed in guessing what they were like for them to be deprived of their strangeness: in which case, I might just as well have stayed in my village. Or if, as was the case here, they retained their strangeness, I could make no use of it, since I was incapable of even grasping what it consisted of.[13]

Subjected to intellectual sublimation, the experience of failure resurfaced as a critique of the way that young people were programmed in the ethnographic environment. The tension created by the failure was released in the discovery of the antinomy of Frank Cushing. This discovery is the key to everything that Claude Lévi-Strauss, the great revolutionary of cultural self-knowledge, created thereafter.

The outlines of a new, revolutionary programme appear in the concluding fragments of *Tristes Tropiques*:

> While it is true that comparison between a small number of societies makes them appear very different from each other, the differences diminish as the field of investigation widens [...] [We must seek] to find the unshakable basis of human society. To this quest, anthropological comparison can contribute in two ways. It shows that the basis is not to be discovered in our civilization: of all known societies ours is no doubt the one most remote from it. At the same time, by bringing out the characteristics common to the majority of human societies, it helps us to postulate a type, of which no society is the faithful realization, but which indicates the direction the investigation ought to follow.[14]

This type is located at the level of neolithic culture. At this level – Lévi-Strauss relies on Rousseau here – there emerges a complete, not yet degenerated in its manifestations, 'human nature', which, according to Rousseau – as against the claims of Diderot – is not something pre-social, but something that cannot appear outside of society; the possibility of socialization is already inherent in human nature. 'The actualization of humankind's potential features takes place through their objectivization in society, in the form corresponding to the appropriate sphere of inter-personal relations – language, order of law, etc. [...] Generally speaking – "we truly become human only when we have already become citizens".'[15] To know the nature of humankind, it is enough to know the most primordial form of human socialization, at the stage when the 'cold', mechanical, cyclical social mechanism has not yet transformed into the 'hot,' uni-directional, entropy-creating steam engine.[16] Here, precisely, is human nature, and it only – or primarily – becomes manifest in human institutions: myths, ceremonies, systems of kinship – in these symbolic organizations, that are shaken up and reconstructed anew, like a kaleidoscope, with ever the same fragments of the human soul.

The effort to recreate this human nature is *La pensée sauvage*, a book about the thought of savages – like the pansy, growing wild before being cultivated by civilization. Before that, there was *Anthropologie structurale* – a volume of studies, efforts to use a new methodology, apply a new theory. Instead of physical proximity, which – as was made clear in *Tristes Tropiques* – interferes with attempts to attain intellectual closeness, rather than making it easier (epistomologically: physical contact destroys the object sought out for intellectual contact; psychologically: Lévi-Strauss' reaction to meeting the Tupi was a new version of Corneille's *Cinna*), there was the postulate of intellectual closeness while maintaining physical distance. Thanks to language, abstract ideas, thinking, people can mentally create the structure of the world – without destroying the object that this structure is meant to reproduce. It is necessary to cast off the idea of empathy from traditional ethnography: why should the researcher surrender the best, most accurate methods of modelling structures produced by his own civilization in order to penetrate the depths of a primordial thought that has not undergone similar self-reflection? What had been an embarrassing sin for ethnographers, which was worthy of critique when it was an unintentional departure from consciously accepted ideas, ought to be a programmatic postulate. The true structure of the primordial way of being, that crucial content, hidden from the sphere of phenomena accessible by experience, is not available to the consciousness of people who do not use modern methods of structural analysis. Being aware of these methods, the researcher may render the unconscious conscious, the sensory conprehensible. In *Tristes Tropiques*, Lévi-Strauss discovers the contradictions of the social structure in the skewed geometry of the ornamental tattoos of the Kadiueo. In *Structural Anthropology*, he finds an explanation for the obsessively emphasized oppositions in the system of kinship. In *La pensée sauvage*, he extrapolates what had previously been an assumption on thin pretexts, a theory of totemism: an explanation of the fact that one clan is the clan of the bear, the other of the eagle; and the explanation is to be sought not in the mythic associations between the clans, and, accordingly, between those of the bear and the eagle, but in the isomorphism of the two oppositions – clan A : clan B :: bear : eagle. Beyond the phenomenal sphere lie not so much individual or collective needs, as structures. Structure is the essence of culture. To understand culture is equivalent to understanding a shared structure behind all the specialized technological spheres of human activity. But the structure of what, exactly?

The structure of human thought; the spirit of the human, as Lévi-Strauss explains in *Le cru et le cuit*, and as he will repeat in *Du miel aux cendres*. If ethnography is a description of customs and institutions, anthropology is not the study of institutions, customs, but of the structure of human thought that is manifested in them. The model of society in all of its parts is the direct expression of the structure of thought (and beyond thought, maybe, the mind) (*Totémisme aujourd'hui*). This structure is essentially identical for the entire human species. What differs is only its objectified expression. Every expression is, however – and this can be tracked – the product of transformation, conducted on an elementary level. To make visible these transformations is the task of the anthropologist.

But Lévi-Strauss was, after all, seeking the shared basis of human civilization, and he found it in neolithic thought. On this level, we can certainly speak of an identical structure of thought in all cultures, and because neolithic thought remains even today the basis of our daily life, the shared structures are in evidence even in modern societies. On this domain, concrete thought dominates, achieving understanding without sacrificing particularity, located *au niveau de perception*, connecting isomorphic structures with signs that are intellectually accessible, suggested by experience, recognizable in that experience: totemic structures are an excellent example of this process. Fundamental thought links these structures according to the laws of intellectual grammar, which it is not conscious of – much like uneducated people are not consciously aware of the laws of grammar in language, although they use them successfully in speech. What is chosen to play the role of cultural sign depends on ecological and historical conditions, or on contingencies; but the structures, into which these signs are placed, exist – practically and theoretically – in finite amounts: there are exactly as many of them as can be built through combinations of a certain, small number of simple binary oppositions, accessible in the neolithic stage of the organization of the human environment. Culture – whose varieties and independent existence ethnographers under the influence of Malinowski insisted on so stubbornly – is precisely the choice of some portion from this collection of possible structures. Thus, it is necessary to say, properly speaking (this emerges particularly from the methodology employed in *Mythologiques*, in which the myths of 'various cultures' are examined as a product of reciprocal transformations), that the commonality of the human species is based in the finitude of the collection of meaningful signs, among which different cultural systems can select – always using, however, similar principles of construction, which allows for each structure to be examined as the transformation of another structure, although one that stems from a society with which it cannot be suspected of having physical contact, either now or in the past.

Lévi-Strauss always emphasized that this way of thinking about culture was strongly influenced by – at least in his case – the successes of structural linguistics. It was linguistics that worked out this 'most up-to-date method of analysis', which our civilization ought to use to analyse foundational thought. More rarely do we consider another fact: Lévi-Strauss, creating his idea of anthropology and its tasks, remained under the strongest influence of those portions of structural linguistics that attached very little meaning to semantic questions, assuming that the full analysis of a language system could be conducted without reference to the sphere of meaning. When we track the development of Lévi-Strauss' theories – from *Tristes Tropiques* to *Mythology* – we come away with the sense that the influence of those portions becomes ever more clear. Ten years ago, Lévi-Strauss said that the function of structural oppositions, and not the oppositions themselves, is the task of the anthropologist to understand, rather than the linguist. In *Mythologies* very little is said about functions – all of his attention is concentrated on structures and their transformations. The author is clearly avoiding the question: if the structure of myth has meaning, what does it mean? He gives a perfunctory answer to this question: structures give each other meaning; he does not give the question greater weight. In his view, then, we arrive, in the case of the structural construction of human culture, at one of these 'ultimate facts', of which we can ask 'how?' but not 'why?'. That is, simply, the structure of human thought. Perhaps this is based on the structure of the brain – but that is no longer a question for anthropologists. There is no need to inquire about it any further. So what happened to the function of structuring operations, which the anthropologist was identifying in the first place?

## WHAT NEXT?

It is increasingly difficult to answer this question from Lévi-Strauss' later works. In regards to the ultimate facts, there is no way to inquire about function. Even more: it is impossible to ask about their justification in relation to any other facts: their reason for existence is the very fact of their being. Thus, one cannot ask about their function, or about their meaning.

If the old conflict about materialistic or idealistic interpretation of the human still has meaning in contemporary humanities, this is where it can be found. Accusing Lévi-Strauss of epistemological idealism would have no basis. It is enough to look around and see how carefully he analyses South African bees, the melipona, and their strange honey, produced from everything except the nectar of flowers, in order to understand the position occupied by their honey in the structure of thought, and the categories that it represents in that structure; or the conscientiousness with which he studies – in order to understand their symbolic role – the traits of the particular species of animals utilized in totemic systems; or the accusations of a lack of principle directed at literary scholars (in an interview given to *Les Lettres Françaises*) who purport to use a 'pure' structural method to analyse literary texts: in order to understand the structural analysis of myth, one needs a foundational knowledge of ethnography, biology, botany, etc., but to analyse a literary work, created and functioning within a society of an entirely different kind, one needs knowledge of history, economic facts, and many other 'traditional' things – the hope of literary scholars, that structuralism would free them from the requirements of traditional erudition, were in vain. It is enough to look at a few of his statements about his theoretical perspective in order to see the 'materiality' of his epistemology in the most modern sense of the term. The problem looks different when considered from the perspective of sociological ontology: what is an 'ultimate fact' in the world of human affairs?

For Lévi-Strauss, it is the construction of human thought, the way of building intellectual structures, recreating or projecting alternative modes of human existence. For Marx, this ultimate fact is the actually existing human: an active, acting, human, who creates and consumes goods, and actively organizes his or her human world. When one undertakes this kind of philosophical decision, asking about the function of structures acquires meaning once again. It cannot be asked – increasingly, it cannot be asked – on the basis of Lévi-Strauss' philosophy. For Marxist philosophy, it is a basic underlying question.

How can Lévi-Strauss' work provide a richer answer to this question? Primarily through the structural method of making sense of cultural phenomena; acquired from structural linguistics and developed for use in anthropological works as a process of separating cultural phenomena into oppositions, revealing, within them, a structure isomorphic to them. One need only uncover the structure, and make a decision as to which plane of human existence to locate it in. In other words, in order to avoid the dead end into which Lévi-Strauss' philosophy leads the researcher – nonetheless, simultaneously without losing anything of Lévi-Strauss' methodological discoveries – it is necessary to figure out which reality it is in relation to that culture – this specifically human aspect of active life – fulfils the function of a sign.

From the perspective of an activist and materialist Marxist philosophy, the function of culture is based on reducing the uncertainties of the world. Culture (much like – according to Pierre Boulez – all creation) is based on the transformation of the unpredictable into the necessary. Cultural choices realize an unlikely possibility – along with art, they record a choice: they make that possibility, in the moment when the choice was made, a likely one. Culture is thus the creation of information, a process of extracting information from a person's internal and external environment. On the one hand, it is expressed in the active elimination of the possibility of certain occurrences, and thus in increasing the predictability of an environment; on the other, it depends on signalling the structure of that environment – thus, in enabling the choice of behaviours adequate to that structure, and thereby making it possible to uncover the information contained in that environment (by making its signs into a recognizable code). Thus, culture has functions of both information and control. The differentiation of a mental dimension of ideas, mediating the relationship between an organism and its environment, creates the possibility of separation, and thus of a reciprocal dissociation between these aspects. A sizeable portion of information contained in the environmental structure is potentially unsignalled and unextracted – whereas, on the other hand, within every sign system it is possible to find many oppositions that are 'beyond what is necessary': signs that have not yet found their functions. But a culture that exemplifies 'good functioning' is an arrangement in which this dissociation does not happen.

Assertions about the functionality of a given phenomenon are elliptical, until we add which arrangement it is functioning in reference to. We can examine functions of culture in regard to entire collectives (societies) that defined the limits of indeterminacy in their world in this particular way, rather than another one. We will be interested in the broadly social tools used in the processes of accommodation-assimilation: the correlation between the structure of society and the structure of possibilities contained in the 'natural' environment, the resources of socially accessible technology (or the varieties of repertoires of behaviour in regard to nature) and also the social resources of knowledge (or the meaningful oppositions that can be distinguished) about the actual world and a possible world (this kind of perspective encompasses, alongside other disciplines, also art and ideology). We will also be interested in modes of organization, the assimilation of this part of the natural world that this particular civilization has chosen as its environment (transforming the landscape, making one's world thermostatic by rendering indoor climate conditions independent of incidental fluctuations of the weather, etc.). But when we ask about the functioning of culture in relation to the individual, it rapidly emerges that what, from a social perspective, was an accommodating, 'internal' aspect of culture becomes, from the perspective of the individual, the subject of processes of assimilation, and thus something external. The individual's environment is composed, above all else, of other people: those other people stand between the individual and the goods necessary to satisfy her needs, playing the role of obstacles

– or of transmitters who will provide access to those goods. The problem of the accommodation of the individual is primarily that of attaining an isomorphism between the structure of individual behaviours and the structure of the human collective that forms the environment of that individual. The mechanism serving to solve this problem is the process of becoming acquainted with culture (in the process of its transmission and education) and its interiorization.

If we now combine these two perspectives – the individual and the social – it turns out that culture is simultaneously a process of organizing, structuring the environment of the individual, and a way of correlating and coordinating the pattern of the individual's behaviour with the pattern of the surrounding environment. In relation to the individual, culture is an extension or development of a capacity for adaptation common to all living organisms: the association of specific behaviour with particular stimuli. The most important quality of this mechanism that is specific to humans is that, in their case, these stimuli (signals) are most frequently determined by human action, they are themselves products of culture. In the case of the individual, the 'structure' of the environment and the 'structure' of the individual behaviour are not autonomous systems with independent determinants, and in any case they do not have to be – and in the worst case, they are only partially; they might be, and typically are, realized with the help of the same groups of mechanisms. The symbolic structure of the cultural system is in some sense a projection (though always incomplete and inexact) of both the structure of personality and the social structure.

Insofar as, in the case of the natural environment, the primary goal is 'discovering signs as such', so the components of the environment that are created by human activity, which are predominant in the general structure of the environment, can exist only in the case of 'marking' reality. Essential distinctions relating to the access to goods are incomparably richer in human society, and – what is most important – they are not correlated with innate human differences. For their directive function to be effective thus requires the introduction, into social reality, of a large number of various artificial oppositions of signs. In the same way that a spear extends the length of naturally short human arms, variations in clothing and accessories, ways of moving, etiquette, places of residence, and ways of eating serve to supplement the natural semiotic poverty of the human body. In the case of some of these oppositions, the semiotic–directive function is the only valid reason for their existence. For others, the function of satisfying needs (individual or collective) interferes with the semiotic function, making an unequivocal analysis more difficult, as in the case of the dual functions of food, clothing, shelter. The task of the anthropologist is to create an inventory of these multiple functions, to uncover the mechanisms (psychological, economic, social) that make the achievement of full correlation more difficult.

I have presented – in an extremely abridged form – the basic premises of a semiotic conception of culture and its social functions. In my view, these very premises demarcate the categories that ought to be deployed in unravelling the difficulties that have been termed the crisis of cultural anthropology. The development of these premises is the project of the other sketches in this volume.

# II

# Towards a Semiotic Theory of Culture

The postulate of 'understanding', as a particular feature of the examination of facts as human or cultural events, is not new to the humanities. In modern consciousness, it is connected to the names of Dilthey, Max Weber, Znaniecki. Without taking into account the differences between them – which may still be crucial to the history of social thought – all three thinkers located 'understanding' in the psychological sphere. 'Understanding' human action, to them, was equivalent to delving into the depths of the structures of thought of the acting person, or recreating the individual's 'cognitive map' of the situation – the goals that an active person strives to accomplish through their activities; the needs to which these goals remain connected. To 'understand' is, in other words, to understand the psychological 'external/ personal' determinants of human action. In Znaniecki's view, scholars of culture understand human actions if they find out what they are for the person who is acting:

> In contrast with the natural scientist, who seeks to discover an order among empirical data entirely independent of conscious human agents, the student of culture seeks to discover any order among empirical data which depends upon conscious human agents, is produced, and is maintained by them. To perform this task he takes every empirical datum which he investigates with what we have called its *humanistic coefficient*, i.e., as it appears to those human individuals who experience it and use it.[1]

However, Znaniecki decidedly opposes the solipsistic conclusions that such a position, at least to some ontologizing interpretations, could lead[2] – in his view, accepting the postulate of 'understanding' invariably leads the researcher to an intuitive conjecture about the subject of the experiences of the person acting, which is downright inaccessible, always only inferred, usually not without the participation of introspective experiences. This element of randomness, the irreducible ambiguity – inevitably present in 'analytical' or 'humanistic' sociology, and so decidedly foreign to the spirit of contemporary scholarship – alienated, and continues to alienate, most researchers of contemporary society. What is more, it contributes to alternative neopositivist or behavioural views that reduce the posulate of 'understanding' social facts to the sense that 'understanding' has granted to the study of nature – namely, to formulating general laws that bind empirical facts, intersubjectively observed as repeatable chains of cause and effect. This proposition tends towards concealing, if not negating, all differences between the research goals of the naturalist and of the humanist (distinguished, in this case, obviously, by the subject of study, and not the way of studying it).

It seemed necessary to reiterate these known issues because the following sketch will also treat an 'understanding' of social phenomena, but 'understanding' will mean something very different from that which we normally associate with the term, as it is used in deliberations about the goals of research in the humanities. The version of 'understanding' that we will be dealing with is not completely foreign to the postulates of analytical sociology. Quite the opposite, it is probably seriously, if not decisively, indebted to them for the awareness of the difference between the 'understanding' of the humanist and of the naturalist, and the awareness of the qualitative difference between the research goals of each, that the socio-cultural character of analytical facts presents to the researcher. It is also linked to analytical sociology by a distaste for behaviouristic reductions and for the tendency to enummerate or measure in studies of social facts associated with a neopositivist conception of sociology. But the notion of 'understanding' presented here is also opposed to the psychologism of analytical sociology. Assenting to the claim of a methodological distinction between naturalism and the humanities, it simultaneously seeks for the humanities a research procedure that would be both rigorous and intersubjectively verifiable; it strives to avoid sending the researcher onto – occasionally intelligent and informative, but always intuitive – voyages into the depths of the human soul. The version of understanding discussed here comes above all not so much from the straightforward relationship of 'actor–situation' as from the existence of society as a concrete, objective structure of social relations – a structure created unconsciously and existing not in the form of a 'cognitive map' constructed in the mind of the author of a diary, but created as the result of real, material human practice and existing in the sense that the elements of this practice act on and modify each other. This version follows, then, from the basic philosophical principles of Marxist humanities.

The problem of understanding appears in the context of a Marxist humanities not in the sphere of the relations between the psychic experiences and behaviours of the individual, but in the sphere of relations between human behaviours and the social structure, understood as a system of inter-human dependencies that are created in the process of the circulation of goods serving to satisfy human needs. Because we have been accustomed to 'structuralizing' into a system – which we call cultural – observable human behaviours, if they evince a repeatability of certain typical elements, so we can say that the problem of understanding in the version accepted in the following discussion pertains to the relationship between culture and social structure. In other words, we will be interested in the research methods that would allow us to 'understand' cultural facts by reference to social structure, and consequently would also allow us to discern that social structure, emerging from the given empirical facts of culture.

For simular reasons, the version of 'understanding' presented here is opposed to the philosophy detailed in the structural anthropology of Lévi-Strauss, particularly in the form that its creator gave it in his final work. Denying the importance of Lévi-Strauss' contribution to contemporary humanities, averting one's eyes from the stimulation that he provided to efforts of making the humanities more rigorous and scholarly in ways that would be proper to them, because in accordance with their subject, would of course be naïve. It is Lévi-Strauss who most loudly advocated for the humanities to assimilate the structuralist method, which was worked out in linguists thanks to the ideas of Baudouin de Courtney, de Saussure, and the members of the Prague Linguistic Circle; and it was Lévi-Strauss who perfected this method for the analysis of human thought. When it comes to social theory, however, to which I am proposing that this method be applied, Lévi-Strauss, as against some interpretations of his work, is far closer to the traditional mode of 'understanding' in sociology than that to which is of interest to Marxist theorists. If such a claim could arouse scepticism in the period that saw the publication of *Anthropologie structurale*, the text *Le cru et le cuit* renders it fairly obvious. This is how the author formulates the fundamental premises of his final study: 'I therefore claim to show, not how men think in myths, but how myths operate in men's minds without their being aware of the fact.'[3] And this is how he summarizes the conclusions of his findings, where he revealed numerous and mutually corresponding structures of meaning interfering in the very heart of analytical myths: 'And if it is now asked to what final meaning these mutually significative meanings are referring [...] the only reply to emerge from this study is that myths signify the mind that evolves them by making use of the world of which it is itself a part.'[4] Even granting the metaphorical nature of the above formulations – which Lévi-Strauss, a writer and philosopher, has a particular predilection for – it is hard to deny the impression that the author, armed with the structural method, attacks the very same problem that Znaniecki, rather than Marx, was grappling with. Lévi-Strauss longs to understand culture, penetrating (admittedly, in an incomparably modern and rigorous way) the structure of the human psyche. Methodologically modern, the anthropology of Lévi-Strauss, today, more so than ten years ago, is quite traditional in terms of the problems it examines.

There is no doubt that the modern way of framing the problem of 'understanding' culture owes much to the methodology of structural linguistics. The structural method shed new light on the long-discussed problem of 'meaning', revealing both the maximally objectified way it was analysed, independent of psychological interpretations, freed from the necessity of being enclosed within a closed circle of individual sensations or reactions. But the structural method, wonderfully suited to the research questions of linguistics (it is generally known what functions language serves; what requires study is the mechanism, thanks to which it can serve its communicative function), cannot in and of itself comprehend how it is used it for systems other than language – for instance, culture, in which case, as wisely noted in his own time by Lévi-Strauss, the research questions are precisely the opposite: the reciprocal relationships between phenomena are, generally speaking, known, but what is not entirely clear is their function.[5] The key to settling the problem of function, decisive for an understanding of culture, lies – generally speaking – beyond the reach of the possibilities of the structural method *eo ipso*. It requires drawing on a variety of other methodological and theoretical propositions, offered by a contemporary theory of signs, or semiotics, or by a theory of information and a cybernetic concept of system – without which the crucial structural relations can seem like 'the unconscious work of the soul'.

That is why we must precede our reflections with a discussion of these propositions.

## THE CONTEMPORARY CONCEPT OF THE SIGN

The most general definition of the sign can be formulated as follows: if object A 'sends' observer O to object B, then we can say that for O, A is a sign for B. In the above sentence, we see the term 'send', which is far from being operationally precise. But the use of this kind of general term was indispensable, so that a sufficiently broad definition could be created, which would transcend the controversies active in the contemporary theories of the sign. Even more broadly than in the similarly neutral expression of Tadeusz Milewski: signs 'are something that has meaning, not by virtue of what they are, but because they direct our attention to something else entirely, something that is often found altogether elsewhere, in a completely different area of reality'.[6]

A definition of the sign that would simultaneously be the most basic, and also broad, must contain the following elements:

1 It would assume the existence of a certain relationship between two phenomena.
2 It would assume the existence of an observer, to whom at least one of the above phenomena is at least potentially accessible via perception.
3 It would assume that the relationship described in (1) exists only 'through the mediation' of the aforementioned observer (which does not necessarily preclude the simultaneous existence of other relationships between the aforementioned phenomena).

However, only the relationship fulfilling the requirement of (3) is essential to the sign.

This, it seems, is where agreement among semioticians ends and the controversies begin, revolving around the interpretation of the nature of the 'sending' described above. In reference to this 'sending', we can raise two questions: (a) what kind of connection must exist between A and B for A to 'send' anything to B?; and (b) what are the necessary conditions for a relationship between A and O, for O to be 'sent' from A to B? For each of these two questions, there are a variety of responses.

Let us begin with question (a). The most radical answers essentially place no limits on the kind of relationship between the sign and what the sign signifies. A can, for instance, be the result of B. A burning forehead is a sign that an organism is feverish; smoke rising from a chimney is a sign that something is burning in the fireplace; wet pavement is a sign that it rained recently. Every result 'sends' one to its cause, and from this point of view we can treat all observable phenomena as signs, and an understanding of the world – as a deepening of the code, that allows one to decode their meanings, which in this case are the same as causes. Understood this way, signs are determined by meaning, and in order to understand them, the observer must 'uncover' this relationship of determination, and we are in the realm of biology, or phenomena perceived in forms proper to biology: these signs are the 'Anzeichen' of Husserl or the 'indexicals' of Peirce. We are not concerned with the fact that these signs do not have a 'sender' – or, at the very least, a sender who would produce them with the intention of communicating with someone about something. We interpret them as if the cause elicited the effect with the intention of conveying information about itself to an unknown addressee.

At the moment, we are not interested in the hermeneutic benefits that stem from accepting a similarly broad definition of the sign. It is enough that, overall, within this conception we do not find any distinguishing characteristics particular to the phenomena whose analysis is the domain of the humanities. That is why we will be more concerned with other ways of grasping the aforementioned relationship, excluding 'natural signs' (called 'symptoms' by T. Milewski) from the class of signs *sensu stricto*. This other perspective assumes the lack of a causal relationship between A and B – in other words, the kind of relationship that occurs in the case of cause-and-effect relationships. A informs us about B, not because it was evoked by B, or because the shape or other properties of B were something 'imprinted' on it. The informational function gives A a third factor, which is the observer – a person. In order to indicate the class of phenomena fulfilling the function of signs in the above sense, Alexander Zinoviev uses the idea of 'telling', which he defines in the following way:

> We will say, that in order to determine whether object $P^1$ corresponds to object $P^2$ is the same as achieving, with the accomplishment of certain conditions, which can be precisely defined, that following the choice of $P^1$ was the choice of $P^2$. Or, in other words: there exist conditions such that the choice of $P^1$ is followed by the choice of $P^2$.

And then 'If the particular function of object $P^1$ is precisely, that it appears in a relationship of correspondence with object $P^2$ (it corresponds to object $P^2$), then $P^1$ is a sign for $P^2$, and $P^2$ – the signified element for $P^1$.'[7] We observe the active, creative character of the process of determining sign functions in Zinoviev's account. We are not surprised by the author's assertion that 'the correspondence between objects is not determined in and of itself, but is decided upon by people'. In order for correspondence to exist, there must be a being

– a person or its model – capable of making choices. The act of choosing constitutes a sign, and simultaneously this singular, essential relationship, in which the sign denotes the element that it signifies. What is more, the less that any other relationship (even those that are semiotically non-essential) interferes with the direct relationship of compatibility between $P^1$ and $P^2$, the better $P^1$ will be suited to fulfilling the function of a sign, as long as it does not undergo transformation in the process of its realization, which could undermine its communicativeness.

It is worth mentioning that, in Soviet semiotics of recent years, we have seen many observations referring to this kind of active, processual nature of the sign. It is hard to say whether the decisive influence on a similar perspective was exerted by the traditional activism of a Marxist worldview, or the attraction of a cybernetic, controlling vision of the world. Characteristic, however, is the assertion of M. W. Popovich, that 'the goal is not to understand "artificial signs" as particular cases of "signs in general" (of the type "natural signs") but, if possible – the concept of "signs in general" (also including "natural signs") as a generalization of the concept of "artificial sign" or communicative sign.'[8] According to Popovich's proposition, the subject can become a sign, if: (1) there exists an interpreter, for whom the object is a sign (signal); (2) the observation of the sign (signal) is accompanied by the transformation of the information that it contains (the object has meaning for the interpreter, and can be understood by him or her).[9] In light of this kind of account, it is not so much that the world is a language, as that it becomes one as a result of people learning to extract the information contained in various phenomena. L. A. Abramian[10] goes in a similar direction, essentially identifying the sphere of the functioning of signs with that of directing:

> Directing is essentially a process of signaling. At least three factors participate in it: particular external changes; events, that signal these changes; the self-directing object, which receives these signals and reacts appropriately to their semiotic meaning. These factors comprise the fundamental elements of the system of object, which is the "substantive" basis of the semiotic process. They create the particular semiotic situation, outside of which the object cannot fulfil its function as sign.

Thus, we have a specific 'negation of the negation': first, we dismiss the aspects of the 'sign relationship' outside the human or the knowable in the name of the active role of the human; at the appropriate level of generality in this new perspective, we can, however, return to accepting 'natural signs' as objects of semiotics, but from a different point of view – one opposed to the initial perspective. In the final reckoning, the feature that differentiates the sign of a given subject is now only a function of the signalling–directive function with regards to the observer; the character of the relationship between the sign and the indicated element becomes arbitrary, so long as it exists, and is active, for that observer.

In this way, question (a) is merged, as it were, into question (b). From this last perspective it leads to the problem of when, and in what conditions, the observer becomes capable of extracting potential information contained within the sign. This problem is traditionally examined in the context of meaning grasped as a correspondence that takes place within the mind of the observer – and the majority of answers that one finds in the literature can be presented as modifications of the classic idea formulated in 1923, in accordance with the 'mentalistic' spirit of the age, in the following way, by C. K. Ogden and I. A. Richards: the object becomes the sign of another object, when it calls to mind that other object (characteristically, an essentially identical concept was formulated in 1964 by L. D. Reznikow[11]). With the rise of psychology, later variants of an answer were gradually behaviourized. Already in 1938, Charles Morris (in *Foundations of the Theory of Sign*) asserted that a structure of stimulation, which elicits a reaction in the organism that was earlier elicited by the same object, can become the sign of the object (and, again, we find a very similar definition in the work of D. P. Górski from 1962[12]). Finally, a version supplemented by the addition of pedagogical theory accepted in American psycholinguistics, the concept expressed by Charles Osgood[13] states: the 'not-object' becomes a sign of the 'object', if it evokes in the organism a mediating reaction, which (a) is a portion of a behavioural complex elicited by the object, and (b) elicits a clear self-stimulation, which mediates the reaction, that would not take place without the aforementioned association of the not-object with the object as a catalyst. The reader will associate this formulation with the expression that Lev Vygotsky[14] gave to 'psychological tools' (or signs) already in 1930: as distinct from technical tools, which operate on exterior objects, psychological tools act on the psyche. An external phenomenon becomes a psychological tool insofar as the behaviour is not directed towards it; however much it fills instead the 'role of the means, by whose help we direct and realize psychological operations necessary to complete the task'.

After these preliminary observations on the general concept of the sign, necessarily quite abridged and certainly unsatisfactory for a career semiotician, we may consider whether and which research problems can be illuminated by looking at culture from a semiotic perspective.

## THE MEANING OF HUMAN BEHAVIOURS

We have already indicated that the problem of the sign, meaning, and understanding were most thoroughly investigated in the field of linguistics. Humanities scholars are turning to linguistics for definitions of these concepts and for ideas crucial to the subject. This has unfortunate consequences: linguistics is limited in its interests to objects that specialize in the role of the sign, existing only as signs, and thus, at first glance, it takes us further from perceiving the sign function of objects that are not only signs. But it also has benefits: the nature of the sign is revealed more fully, unobscured, when the researcher's attention is directed to its purest forms, prepared from the results of other functional or genetic connections. This is why, even for the sociologist – who would like to see what new things can be said about human behaviours that are already well understood, if they are considered as signs with a meaning that lies on a different level of reality – what linguistics has to say on the subject of signs and meanings could prove very useful.

It is in language that the mechanisms of meaning and understanding are most clearly on display (these two terms essentially refer to the versions of creation and re-creation in the same process). This mechanism, as modern linguistics tells us, requires – taking it most generally – the existence of two structures that are isomorphic to each other[15] – isomorphic in the sense that the oppositions between the elements in the structure $S_1$ correspond to the oppositions between the elements in the structure $S_2$, although there is no genetic relationship between the elements of the structures in $S_1$ and those of $S_2$, and every structure is governed by 'its own laws'. If we accept that $S_1$ is a system of signs, and $S_2$ is a system of signifieds,[16] then the elements of $S_1$ are constituted by their opposition, within the 'paradigmatic' (the choice between alternatives that function in the same way, that are therefore interchangeable in a given position) and 'syntagmatic' (linear relationships with other signs, forming combinations of greater complexity),[17] with other elements of the same structure; thus, understanding them requires reference to the relationship between $S_1$ and $S_2$, or to the semantic level. According to J. D. Aspresjan's rigorous definition, the general stance that dominates linguistics today emerges from the assumption that the 'difference between any two lexical meanings, if it is essential in a given language, is reflected in essential structural differences. Thus, whenever we find a structural opposition, we can assume, that we have also discovered a semantic opposition, that is, an opposition between at least two independent meanings.'[18] One of the fundamental theses of modern linguistics is thus an idea about effects that are truly limitless – that meaning and understanding are a matter not of a relationship between single, individually taken signs, and a single subject or image, but of a relationship between a system of signs and a system of signifieds. The process of achieving understanding of the elements of system $S_1$ can only be achieved by grasping the arrangement of relationships between the elements, indicating their position in $S_1$ – which subsequently depends on discovering such a relationship between the elements of the system $S_2$, which are isomorphic to this arrangement (or, in Zinoviev's terms, 'corresponding'). We will see how essential these methodological directives are for understanding human behaviours in their semiotic function.

A crucial function of the system of signs that is language is communication, or the transmission of information. As Roman Suszko writes, in complete accordance with the contemporary framing of the problem, 'communication is a process with a social character, it is thus located within a certain group G of human individuals, who transmit and receive signs (signals) emerging from the organization of a certain system of signs'.[19] The communicative function is essential in the sense, as Martinet writes, that 'language can function on other levels insofar as it remains a good means of communication'.[20] Studying the communicative function of language and the mechanisms that serve to realize this function will exhaust, generally speaking, everything that can usefully be said about language. This does not mean, however – despite the often accepted, but logically flawed, converse – that the problem of communication in human society, and the study of tools of information-transmission, can all be reduced to the study of language *sensu stricto*. As Henri Lefebvre wisely observes, 'in practice, human beings communicate through a meaningful context just as much as, if not more than, through the language and the conversation that they participate in. Face, clothing, gestures (ceremonial or spontaneous), music, songs, and the like, play just as much of a role as language.'[21] (Let us add that, in light of the evolutionary perspective on the development of language within the species, the word seems to be the most recently introduced stenographic sign of other, more fundamental elements of signification; see 'Man and sign', in this volume). If this side of the question was much harder to perceive than the function of communication, which was obvious to everyone, this was because every thing and event that Lefebvre describes also has a function beyond the transmission of information: a closet serves to store clothing or pots, clothing to protect the body from cold, music satisfies aesthetic needs, etc. The attention of researchers was focussed most frequently on the second – the technical, as Vygotsky would say – function of things and behaviours of humans. In order to illuminate the function of objects and events, they were connected directly to an individual or collective need, invariably grasped as a certain state of tension disrupting the equilibrium of the human organism, or the organized collective of people, which the object or event would alleviate or prevent. The instrumentality of such thinking manifested itself regardless of whether the function was related to individual or collective needs, whether it was interpreted pluralistically or holistically. We find this type of thought in the definitions of Malinowski, describing the function as 'satisfying needs through actions, in which people are unified, utilizing products and consuming goods', and in the one that describes the function as 'the role of a given institution in the general framework of a culture';[22] and in Durkheim's assertion that: 'asking about the function of the division of labor is the same as seeking out the needs that it corresponds to';[23] and in the most holistic definitions, such as those of Radcliffe-Brown (a function is 'input of partial activity to the general activity that it is a part of'). This general activity creates a certain unity, which is achieved by virtue of the fact that 'all portions of the social system work together in a way sufficiently harmonized and internally coherent, that is without creating persistent conflicts, that could not be resolved or subject to regulation'[24]).

At the same time, as it seems, the terms 'technical tool' and 'psychological tool' introduced by Vygotsky should rather be grasped as descriptions of two functions that are qualitatively different, which can simultaneously apply to objects in the same collection, rather than as the names of two collections that are separate. As much, perhaps, as we can speak of things and events that are only psychological tools (words in a language – they can be seen as a technical tool only in incantations of the sort, 'Table, set yourself!' and other magical spells; magic in general, perhaps, could be interpreted as deriving the existence of a technical function on the basis of existence of the psychological function), it is much more difficult, in the human world, to find things that only have the role of technical tools. The same collection of clothing is simultaneously a psychological and technical tool. It can be explained in the context of the need that it satisfies ('in the winter we wear woollen things, because it is cold outside, and wool is a bad conductor of heat'), but it can also be understood in the context of information about something, which in clothing has no relation to its 'technical' function – but this information will be transmitted to anyone who looks at it and understands the code in which this information is expressed. This can be information about the class status of the owner, or about the owner's prestige, age, sex, job, or the role she or he is playing (hunting costume, equestrian outfit, ski wear, etc.), or of their friendly or hostile intentions. A similarly dual function is readily discernible in movements which serve to transport food into the mouth, the tools that we use to accomplish this, the way we address people we know well and those we meet by chance, etc. – perhaps, in all human behaviours and their material correlates. We can generally say that the role of 'psychological tool' or the means of registering and transmitting information serves, to a greater or lesser degree or proportion, all human actions and their correlates without regard to whether they possess any technical function.

From the above statement an important methodological conclusion emerges. Namely, the analysis of any set of human actions can be complete if and only if it is comprised of: (a) an explanation of the behaviours in their role as technical tools; and (b) an understanding of them in their role as psychological tools. None of these procedures, taken individually, is able to grasp any – or hardly any – human actions in their entirety. Some features of the action being examined will always remain 'redundant' – excessive, inexplicable, apparently unnecessary – from the perspective of variable sets carved out among the examined behaviours from the perspective of only one procedure. Some, but only some, aspects of clothing can be explained in light of the technical function of clothing. Others, but also only some, aspects become comprehensible in light of their psychological or informational function. Human actions are therefore two-dimensional: every time, they are a point of intersection between the technical-energetic and the psychological-informational planes. Every dimension has its own criteria of 'rationale' and they are governed by their own laws. Both dimensions must be the subject of sociological study. Society generally tends to be analysed, explicitly or implicitly, mainly as a system serving the production, circulation, and distribution of goods. A necessary supplement to this analysis is looking at human behaviours from a semiotic perspective – as a tool of transmitting information, as signs.

We come at last to the crucial question: if human actions are signs, what is the meaning of these signs? What structure, isomorphic to the system of human action, can be considered a system that human behaviours inform us of? Let us begin with a few examples.

A director and an employee both work in an office. If the employee wants to see the director, he asks for a meeting through the secretary who works in the director's office. If the director wants to see the employee, she tells the secretary to arrange a meeting. The director can also enter the employee's office without warning. This difference in actions cannot be explained through their technical function. If we assume that a drawbridge, in the form of a secretary, serves to protect the director from excessively overbooked time, then in order to demonstrate the technical rationality of the system, it would be necessary to demonstrate that the director's schedule is more full than that of the employee, which is not always possible. The difference in their actions becomes, however, comprehensible and rational if we consider its informational function: the difference in behaviours is isomorphic to the differentiation between the positions of the director and the employee in the office. It informs both sides about the character of their mutual relationship, and places them in the proper position with regard to each other, allowing them to orient themselves in the situation and to choose a technically rational means of action for it. The semiotic function appears even more clearly in the case of the difference between the number of stars on military epaulets, the server's apron and the bow tie, the carefully determined order of bows during a chance meeting on the street, and the broad variety of ways of executing this gesture, from nonchalantly touching the brim of one's hat with the ends of the fingertips to a body bent in half and an obsequious smile.

The informational function of human actions, much like all informational functions, depends on reducing the indeterminacy of the situation.[25] The amount of information contained in the communication is measured by the difference between the degree of indeterminacy that existed before receiving the communication and the degree that is present after it has been received. The more equally probable outcomes that a given situation could contain, the greater the amount of information provided must be, in order for the indeterminacy of the situation to be removed without any remainders. If there exist only two equally probable alternative states, there is only a need for one bit of information (a bit, according to C. E. Shannon, is precisely the amount of information that is necessary in order to make a choice between two equally probable, but mutually exclusive, possibilities); in the case of four possibilities, one needs two; in the case of sixty-four, six, etc. The conclusion that can be drawn is that the greater the indeterminacy of a social situation, the greater the amount of information about human behaviour that is proper to it that is needed in order to make possible a correct assessment. Our anxiety, difficulty, and hunger for information grow proportionally to the indeterminacy of a situation in which we find ourselves, proportionally to our inability to 'classify' it. We demand more semiotic elements from the stranger who stops us on the street than from a person whom we have encountered occasionally, and who has a stable position in our 'map of the world'. If this appropriateness does not manifest itself in direct proportion to the richness of the symbiotic etiquette, to the degree of indeterminacy of a situation, this is only because an additional, but still important, factor intervenes: namely, the complete specification of a situation is not equally important in every case, and satisfying all semiotic elements from the behaviour of one's partner is also a function of that importance. I discuss this problem at greater length elsewhere.

Broadly speaking, untangling human actions and their corollaries from the semiotic roles they are assigned allows us to choose the technical tools appropriate to a situation. And one unravels them from this role by removing the indeterminacy of the situation and 'constituting' it, as it were, in the consciousness of the acting individual. On what does it depend, what technical tools are rational in a given situation, or maximally useful and efficient from the perspective of needs that are to be satisfied through their mediation? This is based on the factors that objectively constitute the situation, such as the system of roads and walls opening or obstructing the path to the goods under consideration – in other words, from the social structure that indicates the mutual positions of the people standing opposite or next to each other in a given situation.

In brief, the behaviour of humans, insofar as it appears in the role of a sign, gives us information about the portion of the social structure that is crucial for the construction of a given situation – about the system of probabilities contained within a situation. Of course, it only informs the receiver for whom the code is understandable. Of the three fundamental types of signs distinguished by Charles Pierce – the icon, the index, and the symbol – human behaviours in their semiotic functions are closest to symbols: signs whose relationship to that which they signify is not dependent on 'any kind of similarity or a successive relationship or simultaneous appearance' of the sign and the phenomenon that it signifies.[26] Not perceiving this fact sufficiently explains the longstanding error of researchers into foreign cultures who tried to use an 'etic' as opposed to an 'emic'[27] perspective (an analogy of the difference in perspective between phonetics and phonology) – or they did not treat the customs they observed there as a code at all, and tried to 'rationalize' them by calling on individual or collective biological needs, or, finally, resigned, they acknowledged them as a visible manifestation of the innate irrationalism of 'primitive thought'.

These kinds of errors are not worth documenting here – every diligent reader of anthropological literature is sufficiently acquainted with them. It is worth looking closer, however, at a less easily perceived mistake, one that also emerges from valuing an 'etic' analysis over an 'emic' one, but something that has emerged not so much from the regular process of understanding the sign function of behaviours as from the interpretation of these functions from a framework of other structures that are foreign to it – usually from a framework of one's own, well-known structure of meaning. In other words, the mistake that we have in mind arises in cases where the researcher forgets that the meaning of the observed behaviour can be grasped only in the context where it has meaning – or in the co-functioning of two structures: the code of behaviour, which serves the circulation of information, and the social structure that serves the circulation of goods.

As an example of this category of error, we can consider the phenomenon, noted in all primitive societies, of the zealous surrendering of riches, where people at the top of the social hierarchy give away their fortune. This phenomenon bewildered researchers from societies where a similar behaviour would be grounds for having someone committed. Anthropologists undertook various ways of describing this puzzling spectacle, assigning it a cultural meaning that would be accessible to them and their readers; in order to do so, however, they wrongfully treated it as an element of their own code, and not as a component of an entirely different structure, that would only take on meaning within its framework. Some authors suspected that getting rid of one's wealth, seemingly 'irrational', is, however, a particularly refined, albeit roundabout, way of achieving individual material gains. This seems to be the position of Raymond Firth:

> many of the economic actions of primitive peoples, including their feasts and other large-scale consumptive efforts, appear to lack an immediate rationality. But they do in the long run meet the ends of material gain. Even where this is not so, rational conceptions have not been abandoned. Their scope has only been extended to embrace the social system, and not merely the economic system.[28]

A similar view is expressed by equally authoritative researchers of primitive peoples such as Melville J. Herskovits.[29] Back-breakingly convoluted constructions proved necessary to save the obviously anachronistic account of the meaning of facts, connected to the context of the market and social structures determined by the relationship to property that was well known to researchers but not to the objects of their studies. Other anthropologists were inclined to treat the prestige acquired by the generous organizers of feasts through the model of commodities circulating in the capitalist market, with functions of exchange and storage. Neither one was able to elude the traps that abound within a method that serves to examine the meaning of acts considered individually, outside of the structure that is semantically and contextually essential to them.

The fact of the matter is that the phenomena considered here could possess the instrumental meanings ascribed to them by Firth or Herskovits only in the case where they were rooted in a social structure in which 'economic choices are specifically determined by the relative value of the *goods* involved'.[30] Only then could we seek out the 'technical function' of the activities of the organizers of feasts in terms of the gains that they anticipate in exchange. Then, too, the situation in which the individual 'of higher standing' gives, and the one of 'lower standing' takes, could seem contradictory and contrary to common sense and would awaken concern in the researcher, defused with the help of the acrobatic hypotheses of the kind formulated by Firth.

The same problem will appear in another light when we remind ourselves that it is not the shape or external appearance of a behaviour that fulfils the information function, but the fact of its contextual opposition to another course of action; and when we further realize that the opposition at the heart of any comprehensible code is unchanging in relation to the signs themselves, which can be replaced by others, so long as the opposition is maintained; or that the 'materials' from which the opposition is 'fabricated' are in every society drawn from the materials available to it, and there is no reason to consider any one material 'innately more useful' to serve the sign function than any other. If we remind ourselves of all this, it will become clear to us that the differentiation of social positions does not, 'from the nature of things', have to be expressed as the higher position being associated with taking rather than giving, and vice versa. Such a view is comprehensible within a society in which the circulation of goods is regulated by the ownership of commodities, or by depriving other people of the rights to dispose of them. But is this also the case in a society in which there is no market for the exchange of goods, or private property – namely, in a situation in which one category of people gains access to goods only if they meet the conditions set by another category? Or in a society where the circulation of goods is regulated by institutions of universal access to all goods, regardless of who made or discovered them? Why are we surprised by the fact that, in such a society, hierarchies are made manifest by differences in giving, and not taking? Or that a higher position is in the same relationship to a lower one as giving is to taking, and not the other way around?

If X gives, and Y takes, X is 'nobler', 'better', more worthy of respect than Y. Y should honour, or be subordinate to, X, and consider X a worthier person. A generalized principle of reciprocity constitutes the code of conduct, whose meaning is a pre-market social hierarchy. H. I. Hogbin describes this situation in relation to a small village in New Guinea:

The man who is generous over a long period thus has many people in his debt. No problem arises when they are of the same status as himself – the poor give one another insignificant presents, and the rich exchange sumptuous offerings. But if his resources are greater than theirs they may find repayment impossible and have to default. Acutely conscious of their position, they express their humility in terms of deference and respect [...] The relation of debtors and creditors forms the basis of the system of leadership.[31]

In this way, the leaders, the people most respected and listened to with great humility, are those who 'eat bone and chew rock', because all of the finer things they give away without hesitation. Malinowski reports on similar situations. On the island of the Trobrianders, 'to possess is to give [...] A man who owns a thing is naturally expected to share it, to distribute it [...] And the higher the rank the greater the obligation [...] Not in all cases, but in many of them, the handing over of wealth is the expression of the superiority of the giver over the recipient.'[32]

Leach writes about the mountain people of Burma: 'In theory then people of superior class receive gifts from their inferiors. But no permanent economic advantage accrues from this. Anyone who receives a gift is thereby placed in debt (*hka*) to the giver.' A person of higher class is 'all the time under a social compulsion to give away more than he receives. Otherwise he would be reckoned mean and a mean man runs the danger of losing status.'[33]

Let us observe that the variety of codes serving to convey information about differences in social positions not only becomes visible when we look at primitive societies. The problem is worthy of separate and extensive treatment, but here we must note that, in our society, on different 'levels' of social organization (family, friend group, political group, mixed environment), entirely different behavioural oppositions are used to demarcate social hierarchies indicated by the situation. This fact places before us the still important question of arbitrariness or its lack in the choice of a behavioural language. We must investigate, to what degree, if at all, the 'signifying' structure determines the shape of the 'signifying' code.

## ARBITRARINESS AND THE DEGREES OF FREEDOM IN ACTION-SIGN

Looking at the system of human behaviours as a code actualizes the problem discussed by Plato in *Cratylus*: does language link form to content 'by its nature' (*physei*) or by consent (*thesei*)? One of Saussure's primary claims was that the sign (identical, in his framework, to Peirce's 'symbol') is arbitrary, meaning that 'it is not motivated, meaning, it is arbitrary in relation to the signified element, with which it is not connected by any innate tie'.[34]

This thesis is not accepted without reservation by contemporary linguists. First, is it said that linguistic signs are 'arbitrary' to varying degrees: 'poir' is a more arbitrary sign than 'poirier', 'icon' more so than 'iconoclast'. Second, it is pointed out – as has already been discussed in connection to the general theory of the sign – that a sign may not be determined by extra-linguistic phenomena, but it is absolutely marked by the structure of language itself. However, we are not interested in such reservations, but in the essential fact, raised by E. Benveniste[35] and C. Bally[36] – namely that, while the sign is indeed arbitrary in relation to the 'outside world' (every linguistic structuralization is to a certain degree a convention, one of many possible), that principle of arbitrariness cannot be transferred to the relationship between two aspects of the same sign – the form (*signifiant*) and the content (*signifié*). The form and content are not arbitrary in regard to each other: they are mutually constitutive, they become a sign only in their organic unity.

The relationship between the sign and external reality does not play an essential role in the problem before us. We are interested not in the epistemological problem, but in the cultural or sociological one. We are only interested in the social reality, and that reality does not exist beyond culture or independently of it. It does not exist outside of human behaviour. The problem that we are investigating is located within 'sociological semiotics', or in the realm of the relationship between the 'form' and 'content' of human actions, treated as signs – and thus, in the sphere where the principle of arbitrariness does not obtain, because what is at work here is not a passive 'reflection' but an active creation of reality, not simply the 'reflection' of the structure of a situation but the structuring of that situation. Because we are dealing with an active and creative process – with structuring, and not only recognizing structure (though both components can, in varying proportions, appear at the same time) – we have to assume the existence of some kind of mutual relationship between both aspects of the behavioural sign.

This relationship, obviously, cannot be grasped as 'similarity'. The researcher who would try to decode the 'language' of business or etiquette on the strength of an iconic or sign-like analogy to phenomena located in the signified realm would be on the wrong trail. The sphere of the signified – the sphere of the circulation of commodities – differs from the signifying sphere – the sphere of human actions – substantially enough that the term 'similarity' cannot be meaningfully used to refer to the relationship between them. That which determines the relative stability and unreplaceability of the sign is not 'innate', nor is it based on a relationship of resemblance to the signified.

There exists nonetheless a certain type of relationship between the sphere of the signifier and the signified (culture and society) that is in some sense 'natural', to which we can relate not so much the notion of similarity as the concept of 'congruence', used in geometry and set theory (in Wacław Sierpiński's formulation:

> the necessary and sufficient condition (for two sets A and B to be congruent to each other) is that there exists a one-to-one correspondence between their points that preserves the distance, such that if $a_x$ and $a_2$ are points in set A, and $b_x$ and $b_2$ are points in set B assigned to them, then the distance between $a_x$ and $a_2$ is equal to the distance between $b_x$ and $b_2$).[37]

Remembering that, in graphs, the edges connecting vertices can be interpreted as symbols of the relationships between individuals, as symbolized by vertices[38] (particularly in 'type k' graphs and marked ones[39]), we can replace the maintenance of relationships by the preservation of distance in the formulation of the congruence of systems. In this case, actually, we do not use the term 'congruence', as Saussure pointed out:

> We are prey to a serious delusion if we describe a given component [language – Z. B.] simply as the connection of a given sound with a given concept. Defining it in this way would mean that we separate it from the system of which it is a part, or that we believe that it is possible to begin with the components and build the system as a sum of these same components; when in fact, it is the opposite, we must begin with the entirety, in order to be able to obtain in the process of analysis the elements that it contains.[40]

In the quoted fragment lurks a still essential thought: namely, that the informational content of the sign is contained not so much in its direct relationship to the subject that is not a sign, but in its relationship to other signs of the same code. These relationships, we can add, correspond to the relationships between elements of the signified sphere, revealing the 'congruence' of both spheres. This calls to mind a specific type of icon, discussed by Peirce: diagrams, or complex signs in which the 'similarity' between the signifier and the signified refers only to the relationship between their parts. The respective relationships, created in a concrete social situation between the participants as a result of their actions, can be interpreted as 'diagrams' of the routes of the circulation of commodities, or as an adequate portion of the social structure. In some cases, this code of the diagrammatic function can be achieved by relatively simple means – through symbolism based on the similarity of relations. Jakobson, for instance, indicates that, in many languages, the plural is formed from the singular through the addition of a morpheme – however, we do not know of any languages in which it is created by the removal of a component; and similarly, in many languages, by adding a morpheme, we create various degrees of comparison in adjectives.[41] In reference to the code of human conduct, we could indicate the dramatic growth and increasing complexity of social etiquette depending on the social distance between the people involved.

It would be an oversimplification, however, if we considered such simple symbolism, a phenomenon that is rather rare, as a necessary condition of the 'diagrammatic' principle of construction of the code. Even consistent utilization of the diagrammatic principle leaves a lot of freedom in the choice of means of expression. In simple graphic diagrams, we can express the same relationship through coloured bars, parts of a line, or segments of a circle, and many other figures. The informational function of a diagram is not affected by these changes, as long as we maintain the relationship between the elements that we aim to express through the diagram. In very complex diagrams – for example, in the case of fashion and trends in clothing, differentiated by class, sex, or generation – we similarly observe an enormous scale of change in the arrangement of oppositions within the information function. From the perspective of the information function, nothing limits the fluctuations of fashion beyond the maintaining of essential differences – only the differences, however, and not the concrete form of dress or the gesture, play a semantic role, or convey information. The desire to hollow out specific differences, particularly important at a given moment, can occasionally be realized at the cost of occluding others that are less important in conveying information: the tendency observed today towards gradual reduction of differences between male and female clothing and behaviour in the younger generation serves an important semantic function – it sharpens the opposition between the 'adult generation', who carefully ensure a clear expression of gender difference in clothing; and thus this opposition has taken on a particular social weight as a result of historically conditioned features of the era.[42] Similarly, all privilege is only essential from the semiotic perspective insofar as it distinguishes the bearer from other people. It ceases to exert a motivating pressure from the moment when the commodity that was its object also becomes the property of people from whom that privilege was meant to distinguish the bearer. During the era of the birth and beginnings of television, owning a TV was, by right of opposition, a sign of belonging to the 'high brow'. Today, in an age where TV is widely accessible, that belonging is signified through the same opposition by not possessing a TV. Students of institutions of higher learning abandoned the special hats that they wore when schools ceased to acknowledge class privilege. Actually, it would be worthwhile to consider the clear differences between the semiotic mechanisms of feudal and industrial culture: the first relies mainly on the instrument of privilege, 'individualizing', as it were, the social structure; the second operates through categorical indicators above all – 'class-ing' the structure. Unfortunately, we do not have sufficient space to investigate this important problem.

So we come to the key matter for the analysis of the semiotic function of human behaviour. In order for any kind of thing – a sound, a movement, an object – to fulfil the function of a sign and reduce the indeterminacy of a situation that it refers to, it must distinguish itself from other things functioning in the role of sign. It is not so much that a code is a collection of signs, as that signs are elements of a code; they are only signs insofar as, and precisely because, they are elements of a system. As to considering this code as a system, it is not so much a collection of elements – and not only an arrangement of elements – as an arrangement of oppositions that differentiates those elements from each other. It is not the elements taken individually that fulfil the semiotic function, but the oppositions between them. Bowing to someone on the street would have no meaning if there were not passers-by to whom we would not bow; it is precisely because such people exist that bowing can serve its informational function – it distinguishes the subset of people that we are connected to through culturally normalized relations. The sign 'entry through secretary's office' would not be a sign, in the sociological realm, if one entered all offices through the secretary's office. Representatives from traditional British parties, typically arriving at the House of Commons in top hats, eagerly donned bowlers instead when the first working-class representatives began to appear in top hats as well. The dynamic of the profile of consumption of the 'higher classes' in contemporary capitalist societies is characterized by an endless flight from symbols that lose their distinguishing value as a result of mass production. This general rule was laconically and precisely described by A. J. Greimas: '1. The individual term-object does not possess any meaning; 2. Meaning assumes the existence of a relationship; it is the manifestation of this relationship between terms that is the necessary condition of meaning.'[43] And somewhat more metaphorically by Claude Lévi-Strauss: 'All distinguishing factors can be seen as functioning in their own right in a collective effort of meaning only in the character of an element that is able to replace, regularly or occasionally, other elements classified in the same group.'[44]

The above considerations refer to human behaviours only insofar as they inform us of the structure of a situation that exists independently of them and of their form. More specifically – they refer to human behaviours the more so, the greater the degree to which these behaviours remain in a 'continuously reflecting' relationship to the social structure: the more they only 'present an image', similar to a diagram, of the relationships that comprise the social structure, which came into being before them and without their influence. In other words, the arbitrariness of behavioural signs grows in relation to the degree to which the social structure is able to evade cultural regulation, and thus in the degree to which the active role of culture is replaced with passive information about the existing state of affairs. Of course, there is no situation in which one or the other role gains supremacy. But in one case, when all participants in a situation remain in direct and intimate contact, as in a group of friends or neighbours, we find the element of 'structuring' dominating in behaviour over the role of 'reflecting the structure', or of 'passively informing' about the structure, more than in the opposite case. To determine the proportion of each of these two roles would require a separate analysis. But we can generally state that the greater the creative, structuring role of behaviour, the narrower and less conventional is the relationship between the form of behaviour and its contents. Elsewhere, I have described this idea as the problem of 'compatibility' and 'separation of' culture and society.

## THE SEMIOTIC FUNCTION AS DETERMINANT

We already mentioned that human actions must be interpreted as referring back to two different 'rationalizations': the technical and the semiotic. Because, regardless of the significant difference between the requirements located within these two systems of reference, governed by their own laws, these are after all the same actions, uniform despite their functional dualism, despite the fact that they can be analysed on two mutually autonomous levels, and thus in each action, to a greater or lesser degree, a conflict between different demands can appear. The degree of freedom allowed by one function can come into conflict with the demands of another. As to the question of how much the interference of functions limits the scale of freedom of actions, we will clearly see this in the example of the kinds of actions that fulfil an exclusively – or almost exclusively – semiotic function in its creative version that 'structures social reality'. Max Gluckman proposes that these actions be designated with the term 'ceremony', having in mind 'any complex organization of human activity, that is comprised of forms of behavior that express social relations'[45] (in our view, it would be correct to speak of 'constituting' rather than 'expressing'; the wedding ceremony creates, rather than 'expresses', a new social relation). To the category of the ceremony belong all 'coming-of-age rituals', whose function depends on constituting a transition from one social role to another. The semiotic function of coming-of-age rituals explains the extraordinary diversity of their forms as described in ethnography – vastly exceeding the acclaimed variety of ways of hunting or farming. It also explains the plenitude, the expansion, of these rituals within primitive societies, whose various roles one and the same person can serve within the same environment (which makes it extremely important to make society conscious that a change of roles is taking place, as well as a change in rights and responsibilities), and a relative deterioration of such rituals in modern, complex societies, where the varying roles are played by people who are generally from various environments, as a result of which each environment only knows a person in one, permanently fixed role. That this is precisely the cause of the true disappearance of coming-of-age rituals is attested to by the maintenance of these rituals in cases where the individual is to have successive, various roles within a hierarchy without changing environments, and thus is to remain among people who know him or her in the previous role; an excellent example is the public defence of dissertations or habilitation in academic environments.

Behaviours specialized in the semiotic function also highlight the creative, structuring role contained in preservation of information. It is the ritual of baptism that makes the infant a member of society, the initiation ceremony that turns the youth into a man, the ritual of burial that removes a person from the realm of living, the coronation that turns the usurper into a king, and a touch of the sword that elevates the cadet into an officer. But whence comes the widespread drive, noted in all civilizations, to structure, to organize the human world, outfitting every situation and every social role with a tightly formulated codex of human behaviour and highly visible etiquette? An answer to this question requires a brief excursus beyond the realm of sociology and even semiotics. We must return for a moment to the intimate relationship between information and control referred to before.

In 1961, the University of Illinois organized a conference that remains representative, in terms of its participants, who were devoted to the problem of self-organization. The scholars gathered there, based on the materials published afterwards,[46] set themselves a very ambitious task: to address, in light of the new perspectives opened up by cybernetics and 'thinking' machines, the fundamental questions of the philosophical problem of the relationship between humans and nature. At the time, many ideas were formulated that offered an answer – though a highly philosophical one – to the question just posed. In an especially brilliant lecture, G. W. Zopf said, among other things:

> I cannot think of anything more cruel and stupid than a Nature which would create a child equipped only with logic. And I know of no thought more fertile than that, that large layers of adaptability (to a given, concrete world) are from birth built into every organism. The organism does not need to discover the most unchanging properties of the world or its most rigid boundaries – they are given a priori, embodied in the organism itself. Such properties, such as a facility for induction, preferring specific criteria of similarity, a tendency to a particular fragmentation of the world, are contained within the structure of a living machine. The machine does not examine all possible worlds – most of them, it cannot acknowledge as possible, and does not need to.

In the above claim, we find an idea that is still quite crucial: that the explanation for certain very general and widespread modes of human action and thought should be sought in the very fact of 'good adaptation' of the human species to this particular world that they live in, and not another one. As W. R. Ashby forcefully emphasized at this same seminar, referring to the studies of G. Sommerhoff, 'there is no such thing as a "good organization" in an absolute sense'. Every organization, beneficial under some conditions, may turn out to be 'bad' if circumstances change. Bah, even the very degree of organization cannot be evaluated in an absolute sense. An excess of organization can, in certain conditions, be just as much a sign of a poorly adapted organism as a primitive organization. If, for example, Ashby says, small meteorites continued to pass through the earth's atmosphere, the most well-adapted form of organization for a living substance would be an amorphous protoplasm, able to seep through a sieve and capable of flowing from one place to the next without opposition.

But we are most interested in one of the examples considered by Ashby. Is the fact of possessing memory, and the ability to learn, evidence of 'good' organization of a living organism? Let us say that someone utilizes a system of a 'lure' on rats: they throw tasty pieces of fat into a canal. The rat, an inherently suspicious creature, initially bites off only a very small piece. Discovering day by day new pieces of fat in the same place, it becomes accustomed to the sight and 'learns', ultimately satisfying its hunger without reservations. Only then is a poisoned piece of fat thrown in; because of its memory and ability to learn, the rat dies a violent death. And if the rat had no memory? Every time it would bite off only a very small piece of the bait, and would not eat the poison. Memory is thus the sign of good organization if one assumes that the outside environment is relatively just, and that certain situations are repeated – that certain states are generally followed by other clearly indicated ones. The organized, 'structured' behaviour of an organism is thus only a symptom of 'good organization' if the world in which the organism lives is itself organized and structured. We can accept that the facility for self-organization and structuring one's own behaviours that serves living organisms is the result of natural selection, in which the forms that utilized a structure isomorphic to the structure of their environment survived. A tendency to self-organization is manifested in this way as 'developed' in living organisms and playing a fundamental adaptive role.

The problem considered in Ashby's philosophical contemplation was treated experimentally by Soviet psychologists. A. N. Leontiev and E. P. Kripczyk undertook to examine experimentally the conditions for effective 'information processing' in people. The experiment was simple: they measured the speed with which people pressed buttons responding to signals given by the researchers. In the first version, they were interested in the relationship between the speed of the reaction and the 'average amount of information' contained in the signal (meaning that the amount of information contained was modified by changing the number of equally probable, equally possible signals). In the second version, they measured the speed of reactions depending on the 'individual information' carried by the signal (meaning that they modified it by altering the probability that one of two possible signals would appear – by manipulating the frequency with which a given signal would appear in a certain interval of time). It turned out that the graphs of reaction times had a completely different shape in each of these cases. The reaction time was extended considerably more with an increase in 'average amount of information' than with greater 'individual information'. The authors of the study came to the conclusion that the human organism is better able to handle situations in which it is confronted with signals of varying degrees of likelihood than when there is no basis to expect one signal more than another. In the opinion of the authors, this variety of reactions to identical situations in the purely numerical sense emerges from the 'active' ways in which people become acquainted with a situation; people grasp the structure of a situation and feel it out, 'arming themselves', as it were, against rare and unlikely occurrences – hence the comparatively quick reaction time to them.[47] People are thus much better prepared to behave in situations where the structure is clear (a structured collective is precisely a collective in which certain occurrences are more probable than others) rather than in amorphous situations.

Further light is shed on these ideas by the experiment conducted by E. I. Bojko.[48] Information about the selection of one out of sixteen signals was given to the subjects, first by simply indicating a concrete signal, and, in the second version, via coordinates: the row and column that the sixteen signals were divided into was given. From the point of view of measuring information, the first method is much more efficient (average information per symbol = 4 bits, 'redundancies' = 0) than the second (average information per symbol = 2 bits, 'redundancies' = 0.615). However, in the first version of the experiment, the reaction times measured were decidedly slower than in the second; furthermore, in the second version the subjects 'learned' much faster. This contradiction is quite instructive. For a theory of information, interested in the possibilities of communication through a given channel of fixed capacity, 'efficient' is the same as quick. It turns out that the human brain is constructed in such a way that it decidedly prefers precision, and unerring reactions. An excess of information, unnecessary from the point of view of a theory of connectivity, may have a decisive meaning for adaptation in the case of living organisms. In a maximally efficient mode of conveying information, correcting errors produced by 'noise' (or interference), or from flawed receptors, is absolutely impossible. And for the living organism, one error may prove to be an irreparable tragedy.

The experiments mentioned here clearly confirm Zopf and Ashby's hypotheses. A living organism is constructed according to the needs of a 'structuralized' world, and only in such a world can it prosper. It is naturally predisposed to acquaint itself with the structure of events around it. At least in the case of the human organism, this is not only an ability to 'passively mirror', or even an ability for cognitive discovery. Quite the opposite, it is a qualitatively new ability actively to structure the observable universe, bringing into order that which is unorganized, adapting its environment to its own abilities.

## CULTURE AS THE CODIFICATION OF THE SEMIOTIC FUNCTION OF ACTION

The human species, by virtue of its very existence, has similar problems to solve to those of other species: finding a proper balance between the set of opportunities concealed in its natural environment and the set of its own powers. Humans are distinguished from animals not by the type of existential problems they face, but by the way they solve them. This particular way is specifically human – it is the essence of human species-being, if that greatly overused expression has any meaning.

This particularly human way of solving existential problems is based on the fact that humans as a species form societies – in other words, they create their own external conditions, in which humans as individuals are to inscribe their existence. They create these conditions – organizing, structuring their world, transforming 'permanence', unpredictable homogeneity, into 'impermanence', a predictable heterogeneity; according certain possibilities a greater probability than others; rendering the conditions of their own being predictable by the very fact of acting in order to create and preserve them. All of this is accomplished by the human species, narrowing infinite contingency to a finite, economically constructed array of practical possibilities, and doing so by placing between every individual and his or her world a web of meanings, transforming 'that which is empirical' into 'that which is comprehensible'.[49] This particularly human method of solving existential problems is realized through action – through action, and not by simply doing things, which animals also do; through particular ways of behaving, whose function – in addition to satisfying the biological needs of human creatures – is also to organize the world or create an organized world, imposing a structure on an amorphous sphere of experience, producing a negentropy in a world touched by the growth of entropy. The human species is constantly removing the indeterminacy of its world, but it achieves this by actively organizing that world, and not simply by discovering a natural order granted to it by Providence or Nature. 'Actively' in the material and cognitive sense at the same time, because both of these aspects, remaining in a relationship of meaning, will discover their natural unity in the practical act of human action. 'The chief defect of all hitherto existing materialism – that of Feuerbach included' – as Marx wrote in the 1840s – 'is that the thing, reality, sensuousness, is conceived only in the form of the *object* or of *contemplation*, but not as *human sensuous activity*, *practice*, not subjectively'; 'Consciousness can never be anything else than conscious existence, and the existence of men is their actual life-process.'[50] Humans as a species do not only 'learn' to orient themselves in a world that is given, once and for all; they render this world that they enter an organized one, in which their orientation may be complete in a way that it cannot be in any 'natural' world. The human species creates a world suited for apprehending cartographically, and also creates a map of that very kind of world. It is left to individuals to acquire the ability to read that map.

This claim demonstrates the massive, creative role of culture in its semiotic function, less commonly raised than its technical aspect. Culture transforms amorphous chaos into a system of probabilities that simultaneously is predictable and can be manipulated – predictable precisely because it can be manipulated. The chaos of experience transforms into a consistent system of meanings, and the collection of individuals into a social system with a stable structure. Culture is the liquidation of the indeterminacy of the human situation (or, at the very least, its reduction) by eliminating some possibilities for the sake of others.

The basic tool for realizing this elementary function of culture is the model of behaviour. In order to understand fully the meaning of this broadly utilized but highly ambiguous term, it is worth calling to mind the two fundamental semantic oppositions that indicate its content. The first is the opposition 'pattern–law'. Sometimes this opposition is described as being between a 'norm' and a 'reality', highlighting the element of indebtedness in the concept of the pattern, as opposed to existential judgements (see, for example, the juxtaposition of 'existential' and 'normative' ideas in Parsons;[51] from the actual opposition, emerging from the perspective of logic, it is concluded – not entirely correctly – that there is also an opposition from a sociological perspective). We can, however, consider this same opposition in its applicability to human affairs from another perspective. A law is a sentence that informs us that the likelihood of a given event, if the conditions a, b, c...n are fulfilled, is $P = 1$. The pattern, however, informs us only that if these same conditions are met, $0.5 < P <$: that the occurrence of a given event is likely, but not necessary. It is likely that X in situation S will behave in the way $Q_1$: it is more likely than that X will behave in the way $Q_2$, $Q_3$, or $Q_n$. But behind those other kinds of behaviour stands some dose, though not a large one, of probability. The contrast between the law and the pattern is highlighted in proportion to the increase of the difference between 1 and P, and the decrease of the difference between P and 0.5. In the consciousness of a tribe relatively isolated from cultural contact, with a relatively closed cultural system, the difference between the law and the pattern would be hard to grasp. Essentially, in the consciousness of primitive people, the 'laws' governing natural events and the 'laws' governing human events were on the same plane. The concepts of fault and sin, clearly derivatives of an idea from a pattern stemming from the concept of law, appeared relatively late in human history, only as a result of a heterogenization of culture and intense inter-cultural contacts.[52] Until that time, departure from the pattern was treated similarly to an illness – as a violation of the natural order that must be eliminated, and whose elimination (the return of the old order) would not leave any remainders in the form of moral opprobrium, feelings of guilt, etc. This mixture of concepts in our civilization of sharply distinguished ones could be supported by this one fact that both the ideas, which we were inclined to call laws, from our perspective, as well as the ones that we termed patterns, actually served to inform us about a very similar probability of events.

The concept of a 'pattern' is overly bound up in an opposition to the concept of 'individual behaviour'. The pattern is never realized in its pure form, on its own, but always through some concrete behaviour. The action is richer than the pattern. It conceals, as it were, the skeleton of the pattern with a living fabric of individual personality, dictated by the character of the acting person and the unrepeatable situation. The relationship of the pattern to the action could be compared to the relationship between the phoneme and any uttered sound. It is hard to find two people who would pronounce 'r' or 'e' in an absolutely identical way. But if the person listening, a member of the same language group, understands the sound as 'r', it is only because they perceive behind the curtain of all individual traits the practical answer, a certain assemblage of differences, setting the phoneme 'r' apart from all other semantically important phonemes in the language. So long as the individual does not diverge from the pure phoneme so far as to cross the boundaries of understanding – the distinctive oppositions proper to the phoneme – the assertion of the sender, however many individual features it has, 'redundant' as regards the phoneme, will not fall into conflict with the model and will not lose its communicative function. The model of action is thus an 'action' in relation to individual actions (or, as Goodenough describes it, individual actions are 'icons' of the cultural model[53]).

If we now take into account both of these aforementioned oppositions, the pattern of action will appear to us as an assemblage of distinctive features, distinguishing the most probable actions of certain individuals of a given cultural collective in situations within the framework of a given cultural system of meanings. This definition brings into sharp relief the decisive role of patterns of behaviour in the structuring of the social world and the simultaneous reduction of its indeterminacy – the increase of 'negentropy'.

The emergence of a pattern of behaviour is always a choice among thousands of abstract possibilities, though it is rarely the result of a conscious choice. The emergence of a pattern is thus a decisive moment in the process of structuring human reality, in the process of rendering experience comprehensible. Let the world, structured in this way, appear to people as a fundamental reality in relation to their reality, later; the fact remains that this world, in this form that it appears to people, has been constituted by human actions, uniting in itself the signifier and the signified – and thereby mediating the relationships of 'individual–society' and 'human species – nature'. Nothing strange in the fact that, consciously and unconsciously, in pedagogical efforts and unknowingly, the members of a cultural collective return obsessively, and in infinitely many ways, to the hierarchy of a few simple pairs of oppositions, simultaneously constituting their thinking and their mutual relationships. Nothing strange that, in striving to uncover the internal structure of various fields of human action – as Lévi-Strauss does so penetratingly ('we can therefore hope to discover for each individual case, in what way the cuisine of a given society is a language, into which that society unconsciously translates its structure, without retreating, again unconsciously, from revealing its contradictions'[54]) – we continue to discover mutually congruent structures, isomorphic, endless variations on the theme of the same motif, born of the human destiny that is the eternal struggle to give meaning to a world that does not in and of itself have any, organizing the world rather than 'being' organized by it.

The human species is distinguished from other species by its 'cultural facility' (called, in other contexts, 'culture in an attributive sense',[55] an analogue to the 'faculté du langage' of Saussure or 'rieczewoj organizacji' of L. W. Szczerba[56]), the explanation for which we can find in the genesis of our species. This cultural facility is precisely the ability to structure the world by rendering certain eventualities more likely than others. The cultural system ('culture in a distributive sense', an analogue to Saussure's 'langue', the 'jazykowo sistemy' of Szczerba, or the 'jazykowowo standarta' of A. A. Leontiev)[57] is already the realization of this facility, the result of the selection of certain possibilities, realizing one possible way of structuring the world, among many. Above all this is the arrangement of selected models of behaviour, mutually complementary, but also equipped with the function of information, constituting the structure of the human world, while also rendering it readable. This cultural system is precisely the collection of references – external, but also internal, cognitive – that form the context in which an individual, a member of a given cultural collective, can act. Becoming conscious of this fact allows us to get beyond the vicious circle of the tedious controversy between 'choice' and 'determination'. 'A directed praxis' – as Stefan Żółkiewski writes – 'does not arbitrarily call into being, but makes use of already existing practices, it chooses among them. Cultural structures serve as an inventory of unconscious possibilities, which never exist in an infinite number.'[58] Only in this context does the meaning of individual human actions emerge, which become comprehensible as the realization of the cultural 'pattern', tied to other patterns within a cultural system, 'signifying' and 'signified' together, being the code of the human world and the information contained in that code.

# III

## Man and Sign

The human is the measure of all things ...

This discovery by the Sophists also allows us to understand the changing fortunes of human self-awareness, humanity's understanding of its own nature. The measure of all things is not so much the human as a certain type of anatomic/physiological organization, but the human as historic being, organized by social and cultural factors. These factors and their organization are subject to historical changes, and along with them the measure that humans bring to the whole – as well as to themselves – also changes.

The phenomenon of anthropomorphism is typically interpreted in a mechanistic way. There exists, as a given, a particular way that humans conceive of themselves, which is then used by people as a ready-made schema in their efforts to make sense of and understand information about other forms of life, supplied by their senses. The human and the world are two realms that are mutually independent – 'elevated, coming to an agreement with each other' – with each trying to fit the other into a tight net of its own laws and categories: in essence, however, the mechanism of anthropomorphism is much more subtle. By changing the world – Marx said – people change their own essence. Modelling the world, humans create their own worldview. It is not so much that humans are the measure of their world, as that the social practice of humans, simultaneously concrete and symbolic, is the measure of the human and everything else. A child playing with building blocks and an adult construction project serve the same purpose: broadening the net of categories by which the human intelligence can assimilate the world to its own needs and accommodate its needs to the already achieved structure of the world.

The simultaneously subjective and objective process of human practice indicates at every moment the conceptual framework through which humans may reflect upon themselves.

In 1637, the luminaries of European thought found out that:

> what above all is here [namely, the construction of the human – Z. B.] worthy of observation, is the generation of the animal spirits, which are like a very subtle wind, or rather a very pure and vivid flame which, continually ascending in great abundance from the heart to the brain, thence penetrates through the nerves into the muscles, and gives motion to all the members; so that to account for other parts of the blood which, as most agitated and penetrating, are the fittest to compose these spirits, proceeding towards the brain, it is not necessary to suppose any other cause, than simply, that the arteries which carry them thither proceed from the heart in the most direct lines, and that, according to the rules of mechanics which are the same with those of nature, when many objects tend at once to the same point where there is not sufficient room for all (as is the case with the parts of the blood which flow forth from the left cavity of the heart and tend towards the brain), the weaker and less agitated parts must necessarily be driven aside from that point by the stronger which alone in this way reach it.[1]

And, twelve years later, they could provide a more in-depth, precise description of this phenomenon:

> there are three things to be considered in the sinews, to wit, their marrow or interior substance, which stretches itself out in the form of little threds from the brain, the original thereof, to the extremities of the other members whereunto these threds are fastened; next, the skins wherein they are lapt, which being continuous with those that invelope the brain, make up little pipes wherein these threds are enclosed; lastly, the animal spirits, which being conveyed through these very pipes from the brain to the muscles, are the cause that these thredds remain there entirely unmolested, and extended in such a manner, that the least thing that moves that part of the body, whereunto the extremity of any one of them is fastened, doth by the same reason move that part of the brain from whence it comes: just as when a man pulls at one end of a string, he causeth the other end to stirre.
>
> Lastly it is to be observed, that the machine of our body is so composed, that all the changes befalling the motion of the spirits may so worke as to open some pores of the braine more than others: and reciprocally, that when any of these pores are never so little more or lesse open than usuall by the Action of those nerves subservient to the senses, it changes somewhat in the motion of the spirits, and causes them to be conveyed into the muscles which serve to move the body in that manner it ordinarily is, upon occasion of such an Action.[2]

Their great-grandchildren continued to discuss with great fervour these 'springs setting human machines into motion' in the intellectual salons of the Rococo, and the seemingly obvious assertion that 'the mind possesses muscles that serve for thinking, just as the muscles of the legs serve for walking'.[3] People were fascinated by the newly discovered possibilities of apprehending the world through strings, which would set other strings into motion, doors that would open to various widths, and tubes, where hot liquids flowed through the top, and cold ones through the bottom. This is how the world appeared to them, as well as their own persons. It could not appear otherwise – they had created it, up to that point, in such a way.

Later, in the deeds of human worlding, there came the age of electricity, and the human nervous system began to appear to people as telephone wires, with electricity running through them. The actual state of the subjugation of the world, if it does not completely determine the way that humans are perceived, at the very least indicates the rather rigid, hard-to-cross borders of their freedom. We are easily reconciled to the thought if we are to apply it to the aforementioned opinions proffered by fans of antiquity, barely recovered from the dusky corners of memory – according to those opinions against which we are armed with alternatives more authoritative, because more in accordance with our contemporary experience. The thought evokes resistance in us, when it bids us to relate it to ideas accepted today. This variability of our reactions is not at all mysterious. We simply lack a critical perspective towards contemporary views, that Archimedean point of leverage that would allow us to move the world as we see it. We see these views 'from the inside', and that system of references, through which its historical limitations could become visible, is unimaginable to us, just like the third dimension is to the two-dimensional caterpillars of Cwojdziński. It is not an accident that the phases of development of human practice and thought are demarcated by revolutionary convulsions and transformations.

## THE CONTEMPORARY FORM OF PRAXEOMORPHISM

Instead of speaking about anthropomorphism, as an innate tendency of human thought, we should instead discuss praxeomorphism. Our frameworks for seeing the world, and for seeing ourselves, demarcate an actually achieved stage of a phylogenetic process of assimilation and accommodation, whose content is the historical practice of socio-cultural humans. This thesis applies to the same degree to Cartesian visions as to those currently seen as the final and unquestionable word of academia, though in the second case it is not and cannot be similarly obvious. Today, pulling strings and opening doors has ceased to amuse us. In modelling the world, we can climb to a new level, qualitatively – assemblages that are self-organizing, self-controlled, or independent. No sooner than we began construction of such assemblages, we could look through their lens at the 'natural' ways of being surrounding us. This new perspective could not arise in any other way than from the shape of concrete tasks, at which we arrived in the development of our historical action. What G. W. Zopf said about machines can also be applied to all objects of human knowledge: the final test – whether a machine can serve this very function that we ascribe to them – must be 'operative': 'Machines will perform the demanded function only in the case where we enter the command that corresponds to that function. I will say it again: if I can interact with a machine most effectively by accepting the premise that the machine thinks, then it thinks.'[4]

Our stage of modelling is characterized by the construction of independent assemblages, or such arrangements in which the directive processes occur, which are moreover equipped with their own ways of converting energy and information, making it possible to modify the structure of the arrangement.[5] This kind of independent arrangement 'can be directed without an external organizer, it is its own organizer and directs itself in its own interest'. What is this 'own interest'? 'The self-direction of an independent system according to its own interests is nothing other than maintaining the structure of the independent system in a state of functional equilibrium as much as possible.' In other words, 'the essence of the independent system lies in the possession of a structure that resists the possibility of changes that would result in physical parameters of the system that would exceed the limits that would allow the system to maintain an ability to direct itself'. In brief, the goal of self-direction is self-direction. The goal of balance is maintaining balance. We do not find any fault with this reasoning, but we cannot, after all, refrain from the observation that our agreement with it is probably not unrelated to the overwhelming feeling of the world's 'purposelessness', which is a discovery of our epoch, and which, upon closer inspection, turns out to be a rather perverse version of the assertion that 'purpose' is a purely human category, and no one, aside from humans, ascribes it to either humans or the world.

I do not know whether the convergence in time of the Great Crisis and Walter B. Cannon's[6] book proposing the category of 'homeostasis' as a kind of key to understanding living organisms should be ascribed to accident. 'We come to the conclusion', Cannon wrote, at the time:

that the organism is not based, strictly speaking, on maintaining a certain balance in resistance to external conflicts, as rather on a constant transformation and balancing in the response to external factors. The organism is not a 'closed system' existing despite the rest of the world, but a system open at every point, remaining in a constant and necessary relationship to the environment.[7]

In America, J. M. Fletcher,[8] and in France, Jean Piaget,[9] proposed transferring the category of balance from biology to psychology as a key category serving to organize and explain psychic processes.

The idea of balance was, of course, not born in 1932. Cannon himself writes of his many predecessors, some from much earlier historical moments. Even if we omit the rather ambiguous analogies found in Hippocrates, Spinoza after all asserted that *conotus se concervandi*, and Herbert Spencer considered balance to be the purpose of evolution. But the old term took on a new meaning in our time. Already with Cannon, but more so with his followers, the more they delved into the cybernetic machines of our age (disseminating the way of thinking about the world discovered by Marx 100 years earlier – anticipating, as it turns out, the modern age), the more they brought to the fore the dynamic, dialectic meaning of the category of balance. As Piaget writes: 'balance understood in this way is not something passive, quite the opposite, it is something decidedly active [...] Balance is synonymous with activity [...] About the structure, we can say that it is balanced in a sense in which the individual remains sufficiently active, in order to counteract all disturbances of external compensation [...] The concept of balance contains the concepts of compensation and activity':[10]

> Life is [...] the constant creation of forms that are ever more complex, and the gradual achievement of a state of balance between these forms and the environment. To claim that intelligence is a particular accident of biological adaptation means to accept that it is essentially an organizing factor and that its function is based on the structuring of the world, much like an organism structures its direct surroundings.[11]

Thus, we are dealing with an entirely new way of grasping balance, one that is quite distant from mechanistic analogies – a concept equally tied, genetically tied, to a Marxist dialectic of praxis as to the experience of modelling cybernetic machines. This balance is simultaneously the result and the premise of activity. It is actually the second aspect of activity, serving only the activity of machines – both those that are 'born' and those that are 'built'. In building, we rather use the term 'structuring' than 'structure', 'organizing' than 'organization', 'adapting' than 'adaptation'. A balanced organism is essentially a system that has 'structured' its environment by selecting from it certain aspects essential to itself and its 'self-organization' at the same time, or 'accommodating' its own structure in such a way that it becomes isomorphic to the acquired structure of the environment. The organism, of course, reacts to external stimuli, but which traits of the 'physical' environment are stimuli that evoke a reaction, and what form that reaction takes, is determined by its 'internal' structure. On the other hand, the activity of the organism is determined by that internal structure, but the actual selection of the repertoire is determined by the structure of the environmental stimuli. And both the external and the internal structuring depend on carrying out the 'organization', or, as Ross Ashby writes, on instituting boundaries, selecting certain possibilities out of an unlimited collection of abstract possibilities, on rendering one sequence of events more likely than others. We could say that the difference between the self-organizing 'human' machine and the 'animal' is based on the fact that situational-organizational identity is achieved by the animal primarily by modelling its own structure, whereas the human achieves similar ends mainly by organizing its internal environment, by making it more structured, therefore more predictable. But both the human and the animal are organisms that form a totality with their environment, and for whom the processes of assimilating their environment and accommodating their own structure always comprise an inalienable aspect of one life process. As W. S. Tiuchtin writes: 'in neurodynamic states the reflecting apparatus produces structures (organized relationships) that are isomorphic with respect to the relationships (structures) in the sphere of things, and both orders of relationships are mutually related'.[12]

We take it as given that the set of events is organized – it has a structure – if the occurrence of certain events is more probable than the occurrence of others that belong to this set. 'Structured' totalities are, therefore, not homogeneous. The degree of their heterogeneity is indicated by the term 'information'. But the greater the heterogeneity of the situation, the greater its informational contents. The amount of information can be measured, subtracting the degree of indeterminacy which an entirely homogeneous collection would possess – and therefore one in which every choice would be equally probable – from the degree of indeterminacy actually possessed by the 'structured' entirety. Moreover, structuring is a process of increasing the informational contents of the set. The categories of 'structure' and 'information' remain in the closest possible relationship to each other; they can be defined by each other in turn.

It is no wonder, then, that the concept of structuralization as a mode of being for living organisms cannot make do without the supplement brought to it by contemporary theories of information, developed by Shannon on the basis of experiences emerging from modes of communication. Thinking in categories of information is making a resurgence today. Whenever one encounters a clear structure, it is about information. The structure of large portions of DNA is perceived as a genetic code; the structure of portions of RNA as a code of information accumulated in the memory. The experiences of modelling modern means of communicating information have no less influence on modern thinking than experiences with self-opening trapdoors had on Descartes' thought, and operating springs on the thinking of La Mettrie.

The modern grasp of an organism's life process mainly depends on absorbing the maximum amount of information about its environment and the structures of its organic processes that correspond to it. This process does not depend on passively imprinting the structure of external events, as in the case of a birch block that breaks into pieces under pressure from the blade of an axe. Quite the opposite – the side initiating the process, its subject, is precisely the living organism. It saturates the environment with information. It can do this in two ways: (a) discovering the structure of the environment; (b) giving the environment a structure by actively manipulating it. This aim can also be reached in two different ways: (a) phylogenetically, with the help of the inherited transmission of the maximally structured form of one's organism, which is not particularly susceptible to change; or (b) ontogenetically, through learning and acquiring new skills. These two sub-divided divisions should not be seen as material for the creation of a four-part classification of living beings. As studies of animal behaviour show, the way of being of every species represents all of the possibilities described here, but in highly variable proportions. Generally speaking (but only generally), we can say that both axes are oriented evolutionarily: the development of biological species from elementary protoplasm to human went – in both dimensions – from a decided majority of elements from (a) towards an increasingly larger role of elements from (b).

It is clear in the definition how an active manipulation of the environment can be perceived as the basic activity of the organism. It is not as clear in the case of 'discovering' the structure of the environment, whether phylogenetically described or ontogenetically acquired; we have become accustomed to intuitively treating such 'discovery' as the world imprinting itself on our mental organs. But, in fact, every organism discovers, makes itself aware of, only certain aspects of the environment. We can even say, falling into subjectivism – but only from a mechanistic perspective – that the structure of the environment is, every time, even in a purely cognitive process, a function of the same environment as the set of functional drivers of the organism. The thing is that the organism extracts from a potential collection only that information which is essential – from a functional perspective – for it. Mass observations of the behaviours of all species of animals have clearly demonstrated that they are characterized by more or less settled models of behaviours only in relation to: (a) other examples of the same species, (b) representatives of the species that preys on them, (c) representatives of the species that they prey on. As regards any other creature, animals do not have either inherited or learned stereotypes of behaviour; these other creatures might as well not be a part of their environment (in any case, they do not compete for the same food source) – they don't exist for them, they are unnoticed, they have no 'meaning' for them. The exploration of the world is always selective, subject to the organism's needs: endogenically directed, and not exogenically.

Acquiring information about the environment (regardless of whether through the onotogenetic or phylogenetic path) depends on connecting certain ways of behaving not so much with the object of that behaviour, as with the probability of the object appearing. A direct reaction to the object does not necessarily mean an 'informational grasp' of the environment; if the reaction only occurs when the appropriate object appears, in an unpredictable and absolutely accidental way, we cannot, based on the definition, speak of the 'structuring' of the environment. And the adaptive value of such a delayed reaction would be small; what good is the flight instinct when you're in the wolf's jaws? How much more valuable is this instinct when it occurs as a reaction to the odour emitted by the wolf's sweat glands? Thus, mastering information about the environment is based on creating a structure of behaviour adequate to the system of probabilities of certain objects appearing – namely, the ones important to animals.

In other words, it is based on creating a fixed relationship between observation and action, corresponding to the stable relationship between that observation and the likelihood of the object that is important to the organism appearing. If such a relationship is created, the aforementioned warnings become, for the animal, a sign of an important object. Mastering the information – the organism structuring the environment – is based on transforming objects and events that are functionally neutral in and of themselves into signs of objects and events that are functionally important. In light of this assertion, we can look at the efforts of psychologists investigating 'processes of learning' (both the classical one, as I. Pavlov called it, and the 'instrumental' one, examined by American psychologists such as Skinner, Tolman, Hull, or Lundin) as studies of ways of transforming meaningless events into signs; and at the research of ethologists in the style of Lorenz and Tinbergen as the study of an inherited 'system of signs'.

Any object or event that is the result of another object or event can be a natural sign, so long as the stability of the cause-and-effect relationship has been linked to the appropriate instinctive response in the behavioural repertoire of the organism. The scent of a wolf's skin is one such natural sign for the rabbit, the sign of the human for a mosquito is the warmth of his or her body, the sign of a fish for a duck that is hunting it is a lengthened shadow on the surface of the water. In this case, the semiotic function is clearly a side-effect of these entities: the wolf does not sweat in order to warn the rabbit, or the human in order to lure the mosquito. But in the animal world, these are the features that have a clearly specialized sign function. These are primarily the features that serve a communicative role in intra-species relationships. They may be fragrant substances, which bees use to mark out the path to a newly discovered source of nectar; or the chirping of a grasshopper letting other grasshoppers know that the jump it is about to make is not the sign of an approaching enemy and should not be taken as a warning signal; or the green ring around a duck's neck, whose display plays an important role in mating rituals, and without which copulation cannot happen. But these 'semantically specialized' traits can also be counted among 'natural' signs, in that their meaning is singularly, unalterably, and unconventionally tied and mounted to them, in a quasi-instinctive form in the psychic structures of members of the species.

Thus, animals, as members of the species or as individuals, transform into signs, uncover the meaning of, only those subjects that remain in some kind of innate relationship with events that are essential to them from the perspective of their life processes. Animals do not only adapt to their environments, but also cut the environment to their own measure. Instead of saying that 'the human is the measure of all things', we could rather say that 'every living organism is a measure of what it takes as its world'.

## SIGNS AND THE ANIMAL WORLD

The great French ethologist Remy Chauvin offers this sharply worded account of the contemporary way of understanding animal organisms: 'A neutral observer looking at the living world has a completely different perspective than someone from twenty-five years ago. It is a world of signals. A given species distinguishes only certain signals, that are contained in its world. Other aspects of the world as a whole remain completely unnoticed, or have no meaning.'[13]

Indeed, much had to happen for this semiotic perspective on the living world to triumph. Even during the 1820s and 1830s, Chauvin's view would have been unfavourably seen as heretical by the greatest minds of biology and animal psychology. After the naïve awe over the 'goal-oriented' quality of Nature in the style of Haeckl or Fabre in the nineteenth century, there was a period of several decades dominated by two views that competed with each other but were equally mechanistic in essence – simplified ways of thinking about life processes of the animal world. One way, mainly represented by McDougall,[14] used a straightforward schema of 'goal–reaction'; the animal sees the object that serves as its food, attacks, kills, and eats it; the animal sees the object to which it serves as food, turns, runs away. The animal always acts according to its needs. A cat with a full stomach, McDougall says, calmly allows a mouse to play at its feet. To which the ethologist Lorenz replied, years later: McDougall must not have ever seen a living cat or mouse. Another way, initiated at the end of the nineteenth century by Loeb and developed by E. Rabaud,[15] was characterized by a similarly straightforward formula: 'stimulus–reaction'. The blind mechanisms of animals are set into motion over and over by external stimuli, swept through life by an accidental collection of stimuli, like fallen leaves by a random gust of wind. Both schools expended no small amounts of energy on proving the absurdity of the opposing side – but, really, they were largely in agreement in their tendency to separate the life cycles of animals into isolated reflex arcs. We can ask to what degree this way of perceiving the animal world was a result of the way of observing it – mainly in laboratories, and through experiments, in which the researchers saw the animal's behaviours as a series of isolated reactions, because, for the experiment to function correctly according to Mill's rule of reasoning, both the stimuli and the reactions were removed from their natural context. It was American psychologists who perfected the use of this method. They took as a premise the existence of a general mechanism governing the behaviour of living creatures, and for long years they enclosed their research programme within a framework of creatively constructed labyrinths and paths traversed by starved white rats. There remained, however, one mystery (which these psychologists did not consider): to what degree did this false world, carefully created by the researcher, emulate the natural environment of the rat, to which the phylogenetic development of its species prepared it? And were the rat's behaviours in this artificial observed world an accident of pathology rather than a representation of true animal behaviours?

Ignoring these very questions gave rise to the beginnings of the school of ethology (which its adherent called 'objective'). Its founders were K. Z. Lorenz[16] and N. Tinbergen.[17] Both began by leaving their laboratories and embarking on a lengthy, thankless observation of animals in their natural habitats. They quickly realized that their suspicions were accurate. The behaviours of animals were hardly reminiscent of the endless peregrinations of hungry rats in their labyrinth.

The main conclusions from the school of ethologists is surprisingly in accordance with the contemporary stance of 'praxeomorphic' ideas about living organisms, and could be described in the following way: the environment is not a collection of 'stimuli' or 'goals' of animal behaviour. Together with the organism of the animal, it comprises a systemic, clearly structuralized totality. Every behaviour of the animal is a lengthy and complex process of the cooperation between organism and environment. Every successive element of the animal's behaviour tends to elicit a specific signal in the environment. It enters into what the stereotype defines as the next stage, if this necessary sign does not appear. Otherwise, a break in activity ensues.

Thus, the animal itself is the initiator of all of its activities. This scheme of activities, indicated by the structure of the organism, gives a rhythm to its actions and delineates the 'meaning' of elements of the surrounding world. The same physical entities can be signs of various objects, depending on which phase of the animal's activities they appear in.

> When a wasp hunts, the sight of a caterpillar will elicit aggressive action, and the use of techniques to paralyze the victim. But if we place an immobilized caterpillar near the nest at the very moment when the wasp is preparing to open it, in order to place another piece of food there, it will grab the caterpillar and push it into the nest without doing anything to immobilize it. If we put another caterpillar there later, when the mother is closing the nest, it will be used as material to close the opening. Even later, when the insect is involved in house-keeping, cleaning and carefully maintaining the area around the nest, the caterpillar will be tossed aside like useless garbage. Thus the same object can elicit very different reactions depending on the phase of action of the hunter, although a caterpillar will always be the source of the same stimuli in appearance, odor, touch.[18]

The wasp, like all other living organisms, is a measure of all things. This behaviour of a living organism gives meaning to the elements of the surrounding world, structuring this world, determining the signifying meaning of its components. According to ethologists, external stimuli 'only serve the role of a signal eliciting instinctive behavior',[19] and they can only play this role when they appear at a very specific moment in the behavioural cycle. Any round white object, regardless of its size or ellipsoid-ness, the roundness or cylindrical nature of its shape, will cause the brooding goose to try, with rhythmic movements of its beak and neck, to push it into the nest. A goose that is not sitting on eggs will not notice even a goose's egg lying beside it. Once set into motion, the schema of behaviour remains rigid and is brought to its conclusion, even if the stimulus that initiated the action, and that is ostensibly the purpose of the action, vanishes. If this round white object that had previously been shown to the goose is removed from its field of vision, the bird will calmly undertake 'in vain' the entire expected ritual for recovering an egg that has fallen out of its nest.[20] The stimuli that elicit and are released by the behavioural mechanism of the organism are mutually dependent on each other within a highly organized totality of 'organism–environment'.

Up to this point, we have discussed the relationship between the organism and its environment – and specifically with the part of the environment that is not determined, either by phylogenetic processes of forming instinctive structures in the organism, or by the ontogenetic process of enriching the repertoire of behaviours. If, however, the catalysing stimuli, which we have discussed, are located in the behaviour of another member of the species, then the behavioural mechanism described appears to us as a message in intra-species communication, or intra-species social organization; in light of today's imagining, we can consider both of these views to be synonymous. ('It seems very likely', says Ross Ashby:

> that we should describe 'maintaining' or 'organization' of parts as a state, in which there is 'communication' between parts [...] The transmission of information from A to B necessarily assumes the presence of certain restrictions, a certain correlation between events in A and in B. If for example during a given occurrence in A any one of several events can take place at point B, then there is no transmission from A to B and there are no restrictions placed on all possible pairs of states (A, B).[21])

Some bare minimum, at least, of communication appears in every animal species. Even those species whose members are typically solitary – keeping their distance from other members of the species (e.g. the albatross) – in certain stages of their life, participate in activities that require cooperation with other members of the species. One such activity is copulation, and ensuring the survival of descendants; another such activity is 'defending territory' from other members of the species; every member of the species structures its environment in the same way, aspires to the same elements, and is therefore a potential competitor for sustenance, mates, etc. Thus, any species not marked for extinction must have a built-in map of the important elements of its external environment in addition to a 'cognitive' one, a series of behaviours aimed at developing cycles of cooperation with other members of the species. For each creature, the stereotype must be so constructed as to comprise a consistent system, together with the corresponding stereotype of the other animal – a potential sexual partner or a potential competitor for territory. This means that every element of individual A's behaviour must be a semantically unequivocal stimulus for individual B, and vice versa. Only in this case can the cooperation of two individuals take the form of a stable sequence of the type $A_1 - B_1 - A_2 - B_2 ... A_n - B_n$.

The studies of Tinbergen on the behaviours of the 'social' stickleback fish, in which, as we know, the males build nests for the eggs laid by the females, acquired worldwide fame. Tinbergen claimed, above all, that the male sticklebacks carefully guarded their territory, chosen for the construction of the nest, from other males. If two males met, the behaviour of each was like a set of interlocking gears, set into motion according to the behaviour of the other. If the intruder bit, the host would also bite. If one struck a 'frightened pose', the other would do the same. If one fled, the other would give chase. The behaviour of the partner was always 'interpreted' unmistakably as a sign with a tightly restricted meaning, and the other would react to that meaning. Of particular interest, vividly reminiscent of human anxiety in cases of 'culturally ambivalent' phenomena, are moments where two males meet in situations where multiple meanings are possible: on the borders of their territory. Then neither is the host and neither is the intruder – or, rather, both are simultaneously hosts and intruders. Their behaviour in such a situation thus cannot form a consistent sequence. The behaviour of individual A does not produce the expected reaction of individual B and vice versa. The conflict between the urge to attack and the urge to flee finds expression in a functionally meaningless 'metastic action': both males begin to dig holes at the edge of their territory – a behaviour that is wholly inadequate to the situation, a behavioural mechanism designed for the construction of a nest.

'Territorial' behaviours are extremely widespread among animals. They have been observed among spiders, fish, amphibians, birds (the famous songs of birds are simply the males signalling the territory in their possession). 'A territory is usually maintained inviolate only within the species, and, therefore, species recognition is quite necessary. Unless animals of different species compete directly for the same items of food at the same time they usually ignore each other. A number of birds may live in a small tree, but generally not two members of the same species.'[22] These 'territorial' signals, usually via odour or sound, are put out by animals in a world that is full of scents and sounds. The simple conclusion to be drawn is that, firstly, the signals must distinguish themselves from their environment by being 'unnatural', unlikely in a given environment – they must set themselves in opposition to other smells and sounds in the environment. Secondly – and this is probably the most important – the mental organs and motor skills of the individuals of a given species must be particularly attuned to this type of opposition. Long and short vowels are in meaningful opposition in the English language, but, to a Polish ear, not accustomed to distinguishing between them, the first stage of learning the English language presents serious difficulties in grasping the different meanings manifested in this opposition.

In this way, we have arrived at the problem of signs and meaningful oppositions – this common denominator of both the 'signifying' character of intra-species behaviour and the signifying structuralization of the external environment. We can generally say that the evolutionary development of communication in the animal world proceeds primarily in two directions: (a) increasing the number of discernible and created meaningful oppositions; and (b) the appearance and expansion of the ability to continue increasing the number of these oppositions in the course of individual life (the appearance of a facility to differentiate between acquired signs – or, learning).

The wealth and plasticity of behaviours remain in tight correlation with the number of differentiated signifying oppositions (though any attempts to determine 'objectively' which of the two is the cause and which is the effect would be unfounded). Differentiating only two oppositions (for example, dark–light, sour–neutral) among protozoa could be tied at most to four variants of behaviour. The number of possible variants, as it is easy to count, together with the facility for differentiating among the meaningful oppositions, grows at a geometric rate. The more meaningful oppositions, the richer the complex of 'behaviours – structure of the environment'. Many experiments with mannequins clearly proved that only certain elements of the environment, sometimes very general ones, had signifying meaning for instinctive behaviours. The male stickleback fish will fight with any dummy of any shape as long as it has a red underbelly; but it will not fight, even with an exact replica of a male stickleback fish, if it lacks this red belly. If a kite that is long on one side, and short on the other, is sailed over a school of ducks swimming in a lake, the reaction of the ducks will depend on which way the kite is flown: if the long side is in the front, the ducks swim calmly on; if the short side is first – the ducks flee (reacting to the short necks of predatory birds). A freshly hatched chick will follow any large moving object that enters its line of vision, as if it were its mother.

The class of events that could serve in the role of stimuli for instinctual behaviours thus seems quite 'diffuse', and always includes, alongside events that are functionally essential, also nonessential occurrences. It would be hard to explain this phenomenon through the innate imperfection of sensory organs in animals. It has been possible, with various animals capable of learning, to teach them to distinguish between figures and shapes that they would not normally be able to in the 'wild'. Thus, we must accept a different solution: not everything that is offered up to the senses is 'chosen' as important by the animal; not all of the things observed by the senses has meaning, is a sign. Their way of organizing reality is always an abstraction – it assumes that certain features are overlooked, others highlighted. Such a selection is always the product of phylo- or ontogenetic cooperation between the organism and the environment. Given this, the 'idiocy' of the male stickleback, exhibited in the aquarium in natural conditions, was not necessarily so foolish. It is possible that the likelihood of something with a red underbelly that was not another male stickleback appearing in these conditions was so slim that developing a behavioural mechanism for other oppositions beyond 'red underbelly – non-red underbelly' would not be functional. Similarly, the appearance of kites impersonating birds of prey is, in the daily life of earthly lakes, rather uncommon, and certainly a matter of indifference to the race of ducks. Much like humans who answer the door every time they hear a knock, though the knock could come from a lion who escaped from the zoo. Admittedly, if escaping from the zoo and visiting people's apartments became a typical hobby for local lions, people would quickly learn to distinguish the scraping of a lion's paws from the assorted mass of sounds that one may hear at the front door (unlike ducks, who – possessing only the phylogenetic mechanism of producing signs – would probably pay with their lives for a miraculous, sudden extension in the necks of flying predators). The Soviet researcher S. A. Rysakova, in experiments on 'information processing' by humans, in one variant gave meaning to three out of eight possible signals that were all equally nonsensical (one signal turned on a red light, a second produced electric shocks, a third would destroy the device); it turned out that, in the 'meaningful' variant, the subjects mastered the ability to manipulate 3.5 times faster in some cases than in the variants 'without meaning'.[23]

The less that meaningful oppositions practically distinguish animal receptors, the less complicated – the more general – is the world of animal organisms, the more straightforward the structure and impoverished the repertoire of behaviours. The more 'unchanging', the less elastic is the 'organism–environment' complex. This means that organisms equipped with a smaller number of signs are 'less adapted' to their environment. What would be a grave fault in organisms with a more complex behavioural repertoire, for simpler organisms may be a hardly noticeable tremor in the wave of reality that is important to them. The life functioning of simpler organisms is dependent on the most general, unchanging characteristics of their external reality. For this richness of their own repertoire of behaviours, for the semantic complexity of their world, organisms with a relatively greater complexity pay with a greater dependence on the caprices of their environment. This hypothesis cannot ultimately be verified, but the enduring survival of primitive species that emerged in the Paleozoic era, in contrast to the kaleidoscope of short-lived and extinct and newly emerging categories of 'more advanced' species, is quite striking.

Probably for this reason, an important condition of evolutionary adaptation in organisms demanding more from the environment – organisms of such an internal structure that, on the strength of the law of isomorphism, they demand an environmental structure that is semantically more varied and richly equipped with signs – is a phylogenetic supplement, an instinctive mechanism for creative signals, with an ontogenetic mechanism: an ability to learn. For an organism with a complex structure of multi-layered behaviour, indiscernible fluctuations in the environment become important to their lives, even though they are meaningless for species with simpler structures. Thus, even minor changes to the environment are also important – and much more likely than global, catastrophic shifts, which could doom earthworms, with their general and comparatively few oppositions of the type moist–dry, light–dark. Evolutionary development, generally speaking, tends to ever greater numbers of semiotically essential features of the environment – though we must note, and emphasize, that this tendency is not of a singular nature: the elements included in the semiotic system are not identical in different species, which of course is observed when comparing the weakly structured sense of smell in humans with the 'spatial olfaction' of certain insects, or the proportion of aural signals to odour signals in primates with similar proportions in cats or dogs.

It has been demonstrated beyond all doubt in experiments that the ability to learn appears only in organisms that are equipped with a bilaterally symmetrical nervous system.[24] Beginning with this evolutionary level, the portion of elements acquired ontogenetically – learned – in the general balance of individual behaviours clearly grows, though not in a systematic way. It is symptomatic that the role of elements of learning is comparatively highest in the branches of the evolutionary tree that are characterized by the greatest variability and a 'species-genetic' dynamism.

In the most general view, we could present the process of learning as a process with two faces: (a) gradual elimination of reactions to signals not tied to objects that are meaningful to the organism's life from the repertoire of behaviours (the phenomenon of habituation, or 'getting used to'); and (b) a gradual introduction of reactions to signals that manifest their connection, or their temporal-geographic proximity, to objects that are meaningful to the organism's life into the repertoire of behaviours. The process of learning is thus a process of selecting signs, which must be precise in the very degree to which the various particular features of signs determine the probability of the events signalled by them, or to the degree to which the event signalled by the them is meaningful to the life process of the learning creature (in the second case, the process of learning operates on the principle of Pascal's wager: it would be unwise for the deer if it deliberated whether the scent of human skin that it perceives is a sign that the person producing the odour came to the forest for hunting or for romance). Similarly, the learning organism indicates endogenously the lineaments of this sign system, which will be the result of a process of learning; it brings to this process an innate feeling for those features of the environment that Pavlov called 'unconditional stimuli'. This collection of unconditional stimuli provides the selection criteria for the construction of the system of signs. And this collection becomes smaller with the progress of evolution, and limits processes of learning less and less. As the astute Japanese researcher Syunzo Kawamura observed, macaque monkeys instinctively only recognize their mother's milk as food; they must learn to accept other things as sustenance.[25]

Learning – namely, adjusting its repertoire of behaviours to the set of probabilities contained in the environment – the organism makes the environment more predictable for itself, 'structuring it', even when the modification of the material structure does not go beyond eliminating potential competitors from the territory. The process of learning is also the most elementary mechanism of this complex assimilating–accommodating process, a process that is isomorphic to the structuring of the organism and environment, which is the content of the phenomenon of 'organic life'. This mechanism becomes especially generative when it penetrates ontogenetic development.

## INTRA-SPECIES COMMUNICATION AND THE CREATION OF THE HUMAN

So long as the problems of an individual member of a given species are limited to identifying and chasing off an unknown male from its terrain, and finding, in the thicket of living creatures, a female ready to copulate, the assortment of communicative signs need not be particularly rich, and no ecological necessity will justify their growth. A qualitative change occurs only when the individuals of one species embark on a social life. The greater the role that contacts with other individuals of the species play in structuring their social life, the greater the role that signs specialized for the service of intra-species communication – the 'code' of the species – will play.

The one axis of difference in behaviours during contact with members of one's own species at the stage preceding the aforementioned qualitative jump is sex. It is enough, for the sake of intra-species interactions, for them to have the necessary clarity and singleness of meaning, to have very simple codes, operating through one or two oppositions, allowing for the differentiation between: (a) a member of one's own species and the rest of the world; (b) a member of the opposite sex and a member of one's own sex. No other distinctions are necessary, and would be a non-functional luxury from the perspective of organic adaptation – the institution of territorialism practically excludes all intra-species contacts of any other kind. Sometimes it happens that in a species that is diffuse in this way there will be the ostensibly paradoxical phenomenon of individualized personal contacts, primarily in relations between the sexes: on this backdrop, long-term or even life-long marital bonds are formed, in which the male can consistently identify 'his' female without error among all the other females; and, vice versa, a phenomenon that Kramer termed 'the birth of the individuum'.[26] This phenomenon can be explained, however, through the rather similar phenomenon of 'imprinting' an object, which explains why a freshly hatched chick can identify any large moving object as its mother. During mating season, the sensory apparatus of the male in this particularly 'individualized' species is primed to 'imprint' the first female he attracts. This type of individualization therefore does not have a lot in common with the process of distinguishing individual positions in differentiated behaviours, which happens on the basis of social organization.

The intra-species code is not much enriched in cases where the species has become accustomed to living in herds during certain times. By a herd, we understand an anonymous collective of individuals living in geographic proximity, using the same feeding ground, but not working together to satisfy their collective needs. A herd, in other words, does not constitute a 'self-organizing system' – according to G. A. Pask – it emerges when 'entering into a coalition would provide an advantage'.[27] Life in a herd does not give the participants entering into it any visible advantage in comparison to an eventual life alone: the amount of sustenance acquired is not increased. The individuals in the herd live alongside each other in space, but they are not together in a social sense. The enrichment of the code is also not substantial: it generally amounts to a signal warning of danger, but such a signal also appears occasionally among species about whom it would be hard to say that they live in a herd. An opposition of signs (usually by scent) that allows for distinguishing a member of one's own species from an intruder is also counted among general oppositions serving to identify members of one's own species (that are not connected to aggressive behaviours); it is only this sign opposition that acquires the role of determining between the alternative of 'friend–foe'.

The situation undergoes a significant change when the herd meta-morphoses into a 'proto-society', when matters of the redistribution of goods enter in, or assuring certain members privileges, generally connected to the emergence of 'patronage' responsibilities towards other members, and including things like sharing food with younger individuals not yet capable of acquiring their own food. Proto-societies (I pass over 'insect kingdoms', constructed on a different principle – an ontogenetic plasticity of certain physiological mechanisms; see the work of M. Lindauer[28]) can be created only among species whose neurophysiological systems allow for learning – because their central feature is a differentiation of roles, namely 'rights' and 'responsibili-ties'. In the realm of proto-societies, in addition to the differentiation of behaviour on the axis of one sex as opposed to another, or a member of the group and a stranger, there is yet another important level of differentiation: 'higher – equal – lower'. The semantic axis of 'higher–lower' is the simplest way of coding a social structure for the use of the individual. Although the roles in the proto-society can be differentiated in only a minor way – as is the case, for example, in the 'pecking order' among birds – from the perspective of every individual, taken individually, the entirety of the herd falls into two categories: 'higher' and 'lower', with the occasional addition of a third, neutral category. In this way, the complex hierarchies of proto-societies can be constructed with the help of two 'switches' in the behaviour of each individual. The 'leader' in such a society would be the individual who never needs to put her behavioural 'switch' in the second position. That it really is this way is proved by many studies indicating the existence of hierarchies in particular closed cycles of proto-societies: A is 'higher' than B, B than C, but C is 'higher' than A. The members of the proto-society do not differentiate their behaviour in response to complicated systems of class belonging of their interlocutors. They only remember the result of their own confrontations, which solidified the meaning of their particular relationships to the other members of the herd, and, from their point of view, structured the herd into a two-part whole.

We asserted that the appearance of the 'higher–lower' opposition was extremely important. Indeed, it presents a new quality in comparison to previously developed oppositions in intra-species communication. It comprises a transition from 'discovering' the sign nature of the environment – 'getting to know' its pre-given structure or including certain elements of that structure into an environment important to the species – to the active creation of environmental structure, an effort in the direction of 'introducing' unequivocal meaning and predictability to a collection of events that on their own are not unequivocal or predictable. Thus, we have in this opposition the birth of a mechanism qualitatively new in the deeds of evolution – a mechanism of practice that enacts the active organization of information.

Indeed, insofar as the axis of sex, and even of 'friend–foe', are based on 'innate', natural differences between individuals, it is only these differences that become important to the species – the axis of higher–lower introduces differences into the group that would not exist for the members of a herd, or 'objectively'. Placing individuals along that axis happens through practical action, through the battle 'all against all', which only then determines the relationship that individual members will have to the others. Hence the unequivocality and predictability of the environment which the proto-society is for its members, is not a phylogenetic given, and is not even acquired through learning – it is 'thrust' on the environment by the living collective itself. Reality is therefore organized – admittedly, according to a given phylogenetic schema, but it is, however, actively organized. One of the most essential species characteristics of *Homo sapiens*, which placed humans on the highest rung of development, is not, at least in its initial form, an entirely new phenomenon in the history of the species.

Following on the evolutionary development of the neurophysiological apparatus of the species, the possibilities of further complications in the proto-society emerge – different ways of organization, depending on more than one semantic axis. Relatively complicated relationships can be found in species of monkeys living in the wild. The great authority in 'primatology', R. Carpenter, distinguishes eleven different variations of behaviour among these species.[29] Admittedly, most of the differences he counts are founded on innate differences, not those that are acquired or imposed. What seems especially important, however, is Carpenter's assertion that a characteristic of each of the differentiated types of relationship is its susceptibility to modification, specialization, differentiation, or generalization acquired through a process of conditioning or learning. This plasticity of relations assumes the existence of a relatively rich semantic axis, of an active character that structures reality. This assumption would confirm the numerous observations that accordingly apprehend the tremendous role of processes of learning in the behaviour of monkeys. Kinji Imanishi[30] gives specific information about the emergence of a habit, accepted by the group, of eating candies and washing sweet potatoes in the stream, which is clearly developed through a process of learning (imitation). Multiple observations pertaining to the role of social contacts in the mastering of new skills by monkeys have been documented in laboratory settings.

Let us note one other very important quality of proto-societies of a higher order. Unlike herds that are hierarchized only 'individualistically', in the case of monkeys, the emergence of something like 'classes' is observed on several levels of hierarchy. Males occupying a 'lower' position than some members, and a 'higher' position than others, typically stick together, and in the case of an attack on one, they come to his defence.[31] This principle of construction of a hierarchy is certainly more complicated than the one found among chickens – it requires, perhaps, that the individual be aware of the entire hierarchy, and not merely his own position. It also cannot be constituted by the particular efforts of individuals, but requires some kind of collective effort, an undertaking of the entire society: the position of any given individual is decided through not purely his or her own efforts (the results of their own fight), but also the fights happening between other individuals. The social structure gains, in this way, an existence that 'transcends' the individual $n$ to some degree, it appears to individuals as 'objective', as established – and the 'socialization' of a mature individual becomes a mechanism that places him or her in the appropriate place within that structure. And thus we find here, in a blunt, primitive form, nearly all of the characteristics of a social structure encountered in groups of humans, together with the dominant feature of such structures: namely, that its contents are a regulation of the circulation and division of goods, and its constitutive factor, a system of signs (one would like to say 'cultural', if it were not for the lack of language), differentiating inter-personal behaviours in accordance with their position in the structure (and vice versa: the position in the structure is indicated by a collection of forms of behaviour, placing the individual in this very position; in small hordes of monkeys, similarly to the most primitive groups of humans, the 'adaptation' of structures of patterns of behaviour and structures of the circulation of goods is still in effect, and thus the question of what is original, and what is derivative, cannot be meaningfully posed).

This observation conflicts with the typical way of seeing the relationship between humans and other living creatures. This typical way of seeing is a rather vague 'intuition', emerging perhaps from a particular web of concepts predominant among humans; and the phenomenon, widespread in culture, whereby defence mechanisms suppress realms of ambiguity in order to maintain a situation where meanings of behaviour are clear; and the tendency, imposed by this defence mechanism, to direct the selection of confirming material, guaranteeing a 'self-confirming' result. The postulate of semantic unequivocality, operating with particular force for humans in the boundaries of 'human –non-human' (which is also the border beween the 'cultural field', which is governed by two-sided models limiting the unpredictability of behaviour, and the rest of the 'psychic field'), demands acknowledgement of the decisive gap between humans and their closest evolutionary relative; demands thinking in categories of 'either–or'. That is why we are inclined, 'by the nature' of our cultural way of organizing the world, to busily seek out specific properties of individuals and focus our attention on unique features of people, overemphasizing the significance of these findings. The debate over whether that which separates humans from other living species is quantitative 'only', or 'even' qualitative, is not, let us be honest, solvable empirically through the naïve positivism encapsulated in the 'superhuman' sense of the word 'empiria'. It is our cultural way of knowing the world that bids us acknowledge that 'even' qualitative traits, which – if they were located at other, less drastic borders of thought – would be recognized without resistance as 'only' quantitative. The tendencies of science are contrary to the innate drives of the cultural mechanism for organizing the world. The gaps between the threads in the web of ideas are the main source of energy for research and the development of knowledge, which always lead to the emergence of new categories, which cover not only the cracks, but also the borders, and marginal regions. Thus, it must lead to the production of semantically ambivalent regions, and therefore to such areas where culture in its primary function – the semantic unification of the world – is accustomed to guarding over a merciless taboo, producing feelings of the sacred, and fear.

In the entire era of human history that has been documented by written testimony of human thought, there lurk on the border of 'human–animal' misshapen freaks, bloodthirsty monsters, wonderous beasts, shrouded in the mists of god-fearing terror. They were needed precisely as a visible incarnation of cultural taboo, as the realization of the irresistible human tendency to manifest the impassibility, inaccessibility, of mental barriers. Pliny the Elder, and, in his tracks, Gaius Julius Solinus, creator of the most popular encyclopedia of medieval Europe, wrote about the terrifying Atlantics, that 'don't even have names' and curse the sun, and the no less horrific Troglodytes, living on vipers and dwelling in underground caves. The imagination of Isidore of Seville was even richer: the boundaries of the *oikoumene* in the Middle Ages were densely populated with creatures demonstrating beyond all doubt the hermetically sealed boundaries separating humans from the non-human. Isidore's *Etymologies* contain Anthropophagians, Cynocephalians, Cyclopes; monsters without heads, but with mouths and eyes on their chests; there are monsters without noses and some that pull their lower lips over themselves at night like a blanket; the Sciopodes have one giant foot, which they stand on for hours when taking shelter from storms.[32] Peter Martyr described in *De Novo Orbe* the discoveries of Columbus, seeking, first and foremost, confirmation for the claims of teratology. He diligently recorded occasions to locate the new kingdom of the Anthropophagians, who 'geld [children] to make them fat as we doe cocke chickings and young hogges, and eate them when they are wel fedde: of such as they eate, they first eate the intralles and extreme partes, as hands, feet, armes, necke, and head. The other most fleshye partes, they puder for store, as we do pestels of porke', and their young women 'they keep for increase, as we do hens to leye eggs'.[33] Bah, even in the time of Linnaeus, various iterations of *Homo monstrous* found their way onto the systematic table of lists of species alongside *Homo sapiens*. Linnaeus did not deny that the forms distinguished by him could develop; but it was development in an Aristotelian sense, that did not undermine cultural unity: every form developed, aiming for the ideal granted to it – and only it – through Nature or God. It was the more perfect, the more it was particular to it: individual and unrepeatable.

We should not be surprised that it was with a resistance far surpassing the normal stubbornness of academic conflict that common sense defended itself against the evolutionary ideas of Darwin. Fighting Darwin, the Church was defending not only theological doctrines, but also the durability of the fundaments of the human world; for a long time it could count on the support of human intuition, demanding clarity in semantic divisions, the univocality of the world's signs.

The innate tendency of cultural mechanisms cannot be overturned so easily. The place of Anthropophagians in social consciousness was quickly occupied by monstrous fossils, various pithecanthropes and neanderthals, non-humans, non-apes, similarly distanced in time from their own *oikoumene* as the Cynocephalians were in space, and just as ably serving the function of a protective barrier separating humans from that which is living, but not human. For a very long time, people with irreproachable academic authority such as Koreber expressed in writing their conviction that 'humans' appeared suddenly, in the gap between father and son: under the influence of purely biological mutations, a creature was born with a giant skull and well-developed nervous system, but it was dumb and loud and in the shape of a monkey – until one day a flash of genius illuminated the previously empty corners of the brain, and that is how the Human appeared in the world, master of all creation ...

Unfortunately, cultural taboos were driven out from even these defensive positions. With resistance, unwillingly, they had to retreat before the pressure of newer archaeological (palaeontological?) discoveries. Not so long ago, Chinese discoveries were hotly debated. The tools found alongside the bones of synanthropes must have arrived there accidentally, or must have been carried by 'real people' who undertook the difficult task of killing the monstrous synanthropes. It could not be that a creature as primitive as the synanthrope could, like a Human, undertake the difficult task of creating tools ... (recall how the great Carthailhac insistently attacked for many years – and to the applause of educated Europe – don Marcelino de Sautuola, the accidental discoverer of the Altamira Cave Paintings: palaeolithic monsters couldn't paint in such a way, it was too impossible to be acknowledged). Along came Dart's discoveries in Sterkfontein, Swartkrans, and Koomdrai in South Africa, which showed that the maker of tools was a biological form even more primitive than the synanthrope, generally unable to stand firmly on two legs and, in terms of mental capacity, much closer to an ape than to contemporary humans.[34] Verifying the discoveries made by L. S. B. and Mary Leakey in Olduvai Gorge in Tanganyika calmed a new wave of protests. It was proved, as, if it did not contradict 'what everybody knows', who would want to know? It was proven that all abilities and capabilities that we consider features of a particular class of individuals encompassed by the name of 'human' developed gradually, step by step; and that the development of culture had already begun in forms biologically distant from modern-day humans – much earlier, long before humans achieved their biological form of today. This discovery finally sanctioned (at least academically) looking at humans as beings that brought together and combined in their own way certain capabilities that – in earlier, simpler versions – were also useful to forms preceding them in the evolutionary sequence. And not only on a biological level.

One of the most important, most revolutionary consequences of this new perspective on human activities is the acknowledgement that culture, previously considered as a product of evolutionary biology, was a co-author of that evolution.

Perhaps the following example will make this creative role in the evolution of the biological role of culture more clear: the skulls of house cats, dogs, pigs, horses, and cows have the same relationship to their ancestors in the wild as the skulls of *Homo sapiens* do to those of *Homo neanderthaliensis*. They are smaller, with weaker musculature and smaller 'hooks' for muscle. These anatomical details became smaller without negative consequences as they ceased to be necessary for the organism's sustenance. Why did the features that made the muzzle a tool of battle cease to be important? Domesticated cats, pigs, and horses, much like the humans who tamed them, live in a different world from their wild ancestors: in a world that is much more 'regular', organized, cut more clearly to the measure of their needs, 'structured' according to their needs. Their organism and their world fit together, like the concavity of the foot with the bulge of socks. A well-muscled jaw and sharp pointy teeth were 'redundant' natural equipment, serving as compensation for an irreducible unpredictability of external conditions. As this unpredictability was systematically reduced, as a constantly repeated rhythm was imposed onto this world, the innate excess of biological equipment 'just in case' became increasingly irrelevant to adaptation. Thus, its reduction does not entail any tragic consequences.

If the ancestors of modern man had already achieved a level of proto-society, their 'external environment' was composed of two elements: the part with which communication and a consensus of action were impossible; and of individuals of one's own species, with whom one cooperated to acquire sustenance and defend against enemies. The task of 'organizing the external world' encompassed two tasks: eliminating the contingency lurking in the 'non-communicative' portion by actively transforming it, by giving it a material structure isomorphic to the structure of one's own needs; and increasing the predictability in the second part by establishing a stimulus–reaction sequence. The solution to the first task is technology; the second, models of behaviour. Both tools for organizing the world collectively comprise culture.

(Speaking of technology and models of behaviour, in both cases I am thinking of something that transcends the distinction, so important to logicians, between 'descriptive knowledge' and 'normative knowledge'. If culture is a system of signs, and a sign is simply the linking of a specific way of reacting to a particular object, then culture, much like the sign, is both 'descriptive' and 'normative' at the same time, and both of these qualities serve it simultaneously and in an inextricable way. Signs serve both to recognize, identify, objects, and to recognize, identify, the forms or predispositions of behaviour that are linked to them. Differentiating between patterns simultaneously serves to draw a cognitive map of the world; the oppositions between descriptive categories actively correspond to the oppositions between patterns. Both structures are isomorphic in relation to each other and both form inseparable sides of human practice.)

And, thus, the world, in which the Ur-human began life, before it attained today's biological form, was an artificial world, organized by culture. To this artificial, organized world, the most proper of all 'species-driven representations of the environment', humans adapted biologically. 'Tools, hunting, family organization, and later, art, religion, and a primitive form of "science", molded man somatically, and they are therefore necessary not merely to his survival but to his existential realization. It is true that without men there would be no cultural forms. But it is also true that without cultural forms there would be no men.'[35] Adapting biologically to the cultural world, the human became a slave of culture. It is the limitation that humans imposed on themselves, in placing it on their world.

## THE BATTLE OVER HUMAN UNIQUENESS

We ennumerate many things that 'only humans' ...

Only humans laugh. Only humans cry. Only humans think up other worlds, called religions. Only humans build sand castles in their imagination, called art. Only humans have values, in addition to needs, and conscience in addition to fear, and history in addition to the future. Only humans know that they will die... Only humans – Teilhard de Chardin says – distinguish themselves as the subject of their own internal coherence and values.[36]

All of this has some kind of common denominator. Today, we believe that the common denominator, the foundation of the particularity of the human species, the secret of its domination over the world and self – is language. Not simply the sign system, but language. The use of signs is attributed to all living organisms. Language is seen as the exclusive discovery and property of humans. But what is the difference?

Researchers describe many communicative signs, including acoustic ones that are used by monkeys living in the wild. A gibbon, temporarily separated from the group, upon returning will demonstrate its 'self-ness' and friendly intentions by enveloping its relatives in a quiet squeaking. The females of another species of apes will, when in heat, approach the desired male and violently vibrate her tongue in the oval opening formed by her lips. Both signals are clearly intentional and elicit a narrowly restricted reaction from the partner – they are, then, unequivocally 'understood'.[37] The acoustic signals of monkeys are comparatively rich. The Soviet researcher N. A. Tich distinguishes, for instance, among apes, the sound complex 'o-o-u' manifesting fear, the complex 'mla-mla-mla' expressing friendliness, 'c-c-c' an invitation to groom, 'ak-ak-ak' signalling danger and calling out for help.[38] These are probably the most developed communicative signals discovered in the animal world. But they are quite different from the system of communication of humans. Ernst Cassirer[39] points out one difference: all signals emitted by monkeys refer to their emotional state; none of them has an 'objective' referent. These are, according to the classification of Tadeusz Milewski, symptoms, rather than signs in a strict sense. They don't say anything about 'external' reality; they do not give information about an objectified relationship of meaning; they merely express a particular state of the organism expressing it, much like the reddening of a female baboon's buttocks indicates that she is in heat. But there is yet another difference. The monkey's system of acoustic signs has a single level, and it is closed and unproductive – much like our three-sign system of traffic signals. These signals cannot be added to, connected for the production of new meanings: we cannot illuminate the red and green lights at the same time, without introducing into the situation, instead of a new meaning, a state of utter chaos and a lack of meaning. Thus, the monkey's system is a one-way street, from which one can only cross over into boundless development by introducing higher levels of articulation. And this is a property of human language.

Cassirer says that human signs–symbols, unlike natural symbols, are designators, and not merely operators. Cassirer here grasps, perhaps, the decisive feature of the human sign system: its creative – productive in relation to the world – character.

All perception, not only that of humans, encompasses three equally essential elements: (a) sensations distinguished from chaotic surroundings, driven by external stimuli, sensations differing in some features and different from other components; (b) assembling the differentials of a situation in a certain classificatory system, contained in the neu-rophysiological apparatus of the organism – namely, evaluating the situation; (c) the collection of operations set into motion by the afore-mentioned evaluation.[40] This assemblage of operations can be rigidly and unequivocally connected to the evaluation, but it may be separated from it by a plethora of operations ensuring a certain number of degrees of freedom. Although the schema of observation in animals and humans can be described in a similar way, as presented above, we can also point to important differences. The 'evaluation of the situation' in the case of animals (but also in the case of babies!) is a subjectively biological evaluation. The classificatory system is decid-edly 'subjective', structured according to the state of the organism – 'threats', 'satisfying hunger', possibly 'pleasure' and 'pain'. The world does not divide into various, objectively existing things – and so the organism does not separate itself from it as an independently existing thing. There exists only a global universe of sensations, in which the connection between endo- and exogenous sensations is still immediate and organic. And, because it is so, neither the organism nor the external world appears as a potentially manipulatable object. For a dog, the 'master' is a complex assemblage of smells, touch, food; the dog does not react to a photograph of the master (unless it has been 'conditioned' to, of course). Humans, however, 'objectiv-ize' the world and themselves, and Piaget, with brilliant astuteness, unveils this complex mechanism, leading the infant, through strenuous efforts, to such objectivization. On the other hand, a human's assess-ment of a situation – and only a human's – is carried out in the mind, and not necessarily practically (not necessarily through the realization of reflex arcs); and it takes place through the utilization of a developed web of ideas, which clearly has an abstract character not bound by time, space, or image. Between imagination and conceptual thinking, there exists a qualitative gap. None of us can imagine 'a dog in general' that would not take the form of a possible position in space – lying down, standing, sitting, running. But all of us have the abstract concept of a 'dog in general'. Thus, even in the case of such a simple image, our observation is articulated in two logical categories, which relate to two abstract concepts. It is hard to overemphasize the horizons that are opened by such a structure of thought. But this structure is obviously secondary in relation to the structure of human sign systems, developed on a principle of two levels of articulation.[41] The linguistic categories do not 'reflect' ideas – they create them. In language, the human acquires the rules for active classification, organizing, giving the world unified meaning. In order actively to manipulate the world, the human must first 'objectivize' this world. But the subject-ness of the world is not a given, it does not appear to the senses in unmediated form; it is, in any case, in the form in which it appears to people, a complex product of conceptual operations.

On the one hand, we can treat the human mind as an extension of development of the desire, proper to all organisms, to balance assimilation and accommodation – to 'isomorphize' the structure of opportunities in the area and the structure of needs of the organism. We can look for adaptation mechanisms homologous to human intelligence in all organisms. From this general view, the problem undertaken by human intelligence and by the human species in general is nothing particularly new in the history of life. On the other hand, however, as Piaget says, 'if the categories of thought are in a certain sense preformed in biological action, they do not appear in the realm of biological functions as conscious structures, or even unconscious ones. If biological adaptation is a kind of material recognition of the environment, a range of further processes of structuralization were necessary, in order for this mechanism of pure action to produce conscious imagination and cognition.'[42] A human recognizes things in their sensory experiences with the help of words, uttered or thought. 'In order to ascribe, for example, actual dimensions to a small splotch that I perceive as a mountain or as an inkblot, I have to place it into a substantial and causal world, into organized space, etc., and thereby give it an intellectual structure.'[43] We can say that the sign system stands between every animal and its environment. It is not a trait particular to the human species. In the case of *Homo sapiens*, this system of signs, through a multi-layer articulation, among other things, has attained such development in terms of 'quantity', that it acquired a new quality: it became an actual mediator of the relationship human–world, making possible in this way the objectivization of both the world and the human individual.

In the case of animals, as well, signs are an aspect of action, a side, an element, of human activity. But, again, the unparalleled enrichment of these signs in the human species is connected to an enrichment that is unknown elsewhere, an increased variation of action. We saw before how what had previously been plain animal behaviour becomes differentiated with the addition of even one semantic axis. Human language – and the human cache of conceptual categories – is characterized by an incredible richness of semantic axes. This goes hand in hand with the possibility of a differentiation of patterns of behaviour that is not encountered anywhere else – shapes of human activity and human creation. Humans can differentiate in the 'external' world, thanks to their conceptual armature, nuances and differences that are so subtle that even the most incredible sensory apparatus cannot discern them. But with this we also see an ability to specialize in subtle ways, to extend one's activities and the traces they leave on the external world.

And what about tools? Is it not their creation that is the distinguishing feature of the human species? But yes, Marx's discovery retains its merit even today, and no modern trends or academic discoveries will undermine it. It is thanks to tools that humans can transform their material world, change its natural structure, eliminate some of its properties that will not be assimilated, multiplying others that are seen as good material for assimilation. Signs and tools – it is only these two elements of human culture that possess, thanks to their potential to multiply and differentiate, the marvellous property of accumulation, making possible both the growth of the human species, and the increasing complexity of its life forms – a transition from a primitive, 'omnipotent', internally undifferentiated culture to a highly specialized culture founded on a division of labour, practically boundless in its growth;[44] from mechanist cultures, functioning at the 'absolute zero of historical temperature', to cultures reminiscent of a steam engine, developing on a level of 'historical heat',[45] maximally dominating their world and producing in the process a lot of entropy ...

But tools, much like linguistic signs, are two signs of human praxis that cannot exist without each other. This praxis is the true distinguishing feature of the human species. Much like the other two inseparable aspects, it has the ability to increase exponentially, to stack, to accumulate. It does not only seek out the opportunities hidden in reality, but creates opportunities. It is the culmination of the active relationship that a living organism has with the world. In it, the modelling of the world by biological life has achieved its fullest form. But is it the final form?

## INSTEAD OF A CONCLUSION

The age of cybernetic machines, which, as we saw, led to a new perspective on the age-old problem of human nature, has also become a prerequisite for academic events that are perceived by some thinkers – and, above all, by immortal common sense – as a new attack on barely recovered feelings of the sovereignty of the human species and the idea of the unequivocality of its position in the taxonomy of the world. These events: the construction of machines described as 'thinking', which undertake many tasks ascribed to humans – except far more effectively than humans. Public opinion and its spokespeople protest with the same vigour as people once opposed the propositions of Darwin. This cannot be – for something that is not human simultaneously to be human. A new, terrifying sphere of cultural ambiguity arises: one which had been the site of taboo, evoking both our metaphysical fear and a sinful, irrepressible curiosity.

In 1950, the historic article by A. M. Turing appeared, in which this spiritual father of 'thinking machines' proved that it is possible to build a machine that would behave like an intelligent human – therefore, an intelligent machine.[46] In 1952, Ashby built a homeostat, which maintains in its 'external environment' a balance beneficial to itself. The speculatrix machine produced by Walter (1953) prowled its surroundings seeking food and shelter. In 1954, Walter and Deutsch constructed a famous cybernetic mouse, learning to ably navigate a labyrinth. Finally, in 1958, the model LT (Logical Theoretician) arose, whose author acknowledged that it solved problems in a way that was identical to a human being.[47] All of this took place to the accompaniment of endless discussion happening on both sides of the Ocean and Elbe, regarding whether a machine could think. Definitions of thought were strenuously sought out that would exclude the increasingly refined demonstrations of constructed electronic craftsmanship. After a year or two, if not earlier, it was necessary to find new definitions. Michael Scriven[48] saw experiencing emotions as the most important feature of humans, and happily concluded that 'we must force machines, to plow and work, to carry out and imitate, but not to feel pleasure, or mercy or pity for themselves'. Keith Gunderson[49] rescued the dignity of humans by pointing out that 'we cannot say of the phonograph, that it performed the piece on Saturday with a rare perfection, nor will the phonograph ever earn our encouragement'. Anatol Rapaport[50] critiqued computers, saying that they were not capable of extracting a commonality from situations of varied appearance and weren't capable of independently creating the norms of accepting a response. This is only a handful of responses, examples of the thousands of positions taken in literature on the issue.

I am not a cyberneticist, and am unable to assess the technical merit of these and many other accusations. I suspect that some of them are based on misunderstanding, whereas others contain gaps that are of a technical, and maybe even theoretical, nature. I am interested in an entirely different aspect of the issue – its cultural basis and its influence on our conception of the human.

Thus, the conflict, aside from the aspects of it already mentioned (fear of semantic ambivalence, whose inseparable sacral coating clearly appears in the apocalyptic fantasies of a world where machines rule mercilessly over humans, so popular today), has yet another instructive angle. It calls to mind the medieval debates on the question: is God so powerful that He could create a being more powerful than Himself? This debate cannot be resolved, and it depends on our philosophical position, whether we acknowledge both theoretically possible responses as testifying to the nothingness of humans or to their strength. Personally, I incline towards the second view, and that is all I would like to add to the very sensible opinion of I. B. Nowik: 'Although both sides of the debate about the relationship between humans and machines remain open, the most dangerous is the position that delineates in a dogmatic way the path of development for cybernetic machines, thereby closing off the path to new ideas and replacing the metaphysical dialectic with a game of "ignorabimus".'[51]

# IV

# The Problem of Universals and the Semiotic Theory of Culture

Classification and generalization are two alternative methods of organizing given materials of experience. The first method seems both more archaic and more primitive. It does not go beyond the level of experience; it does not add any new knowledge to that which is already contained in the protocol of the claims of the senses. It only allows for an abridged account of what would otherwise require a much longer list. The brevity of the inscription and transmission of empirical knowledge offered by classification is always relative. Firstly, logic does not indicate any boundaries to the amplitude and minuteness of classification. Because being in accordance with the givens of experience is not only a necessary condition of correctness, but the unique, objectively articulated 'guide' that directs the act of classification, a maximally correct classification would have to reach even the $(sub)^n$ class, which would contain only single objects; no 'objective' indicators could validate halting the subdivision of subclasses into further subclasses on any more general level. Secondly, every classification is undertaken on the basis of some chosen trait. Apples can be classified based on colour, size, sugar content, variety – and none of these classifications is 'in and of itself' superior to another; justifying its reason for existence, each of them must ultimately be based on the caprices of the researcher.

This does not mean, however, that classification is useless in the process of creating academic knowledge; quite the opposite, it introduces a necessary order into the chaos of empirical materials, and can be incredibly useful in the process of creating theories, so long as it does not grant it a larger role than it can possibly achieve – a role other than an individual stenography that is useful to an empirical level of understanding. The problem is that comparative studies do not set themselves more ambitious tasks than achieving a relatively clarified description of fundamental observations, if they do not aspire to anything more than replacing the class of statements of the type 'apple$_1$ is red', 'apple$_2$ is red', ... 'apple$_n$ is red' with the statement 'the class of red apples', and if the achievement of such a statement, or a collection of such statements, is mistaken for the achievement of a new theory of the studied phenomenon. To avoid doubt, we will acknowledge that the process of classification also contains the procedure of generalization; it is generalization on an arithmetic level, also not going beyond the level of empirical sentences, much like classification.

A generalization that would truly be an alternative to classification, which we mentioned at the outset, refers to the level of modelled constructions, or to the level of theory, supported on the level of sensory experience, but qualitatively different from it, and offering the kind of knowledge that is not contained in experience itself. The problem of cultural universals is the question of precisely this kind of generalization. This claim explains the difference between the concept of universals used in this study and the concept that is found in ethnological literature, and which found its fullest expression in a banal description created by Murdock: that in every society, people raise children somehow, and treat illnesses, everywhere people punish crimes, have some form of inheritance, etc, etc. Every such 'item' can be the premise of yet another classification, and, in this way, many generations of ethnologists have ensured an endless game, whose results can never be finalized, leading to a ceaseless transfer of flashcards from one drawer to another.

What if, instead, we go beyond the truly universal fact of the human species, and say that humans, in their activities, practically adapt the world to themselves and themselves to the world, imprinting the structure of their needs on the material and mental shape of their environment, and the structure of the world onto the shape of elementary schemas of their practical reason, their phylo- and onto-genetic development produces a general schema of a vision of the world, a schema simultaneously both subjective and objective, because it is in equal parts a product of the assimilation of the world and the accommodation of the mind? And what if, as a result of this assumption, we were to say that there exists, common to all people, comprising the particularity of their species, a schema of thought-action, imprinting on the structure of their systems of kinship and judiciary, the structure of medical care, and political systems, and all the other 'items' so diligently dissected and grouped by professional categorizers? If we also take as given that this schema – without regard to whether it is deployed consciously by its users – is the foundation of other functionally distinguished 'spheres' or 'institutions' of social life, receiving, thanks to it, the phenomenal, sensory, qualitative particularity of its needs, which it was elicited to satisfy? Accepting such premises and considering them from the perspective of the material collected by ethnographers and classified by ethnologists could open up truly new perspectives on research. One would like to say: immeasurable perspectives. Only then could we be swayed into grasping that which is general (not confusing it for that which is shared) in cultural material, terrifying in its heterogeneity; only then could we also be tempted by what is surely a central feature of studies of the human: tracing the isomorphism of culture and social structure, whose existence we suspect, but whose nature we can only speculate about. But we are, after all, discussing something nontrivial – about the shared principles of the construction of a normative vision of the world and an 'objective' image of the world, mental and practical organization of the human environment.

Awareness of the above goal justifies and simultaneously imposes the vastness of the field of research. Seeking out the elementary structures of thinking–action, or of human praxis, one ought to reach both for documents (oral and written) of human thought, and for material points of departure and products of that thought: methods of practically organizing the human world. Structuralization is the same as unearthing foreseeable occurrences and simultaneously raising them to the level of abstract possibility, rendering some possibilities more likely at the cost of others. A person – like a self-organizing machine, and possessing a specialized mechanism serving to process information, or to reduce the indeterminacy of a situation upon 'entry' – realizes these goals of structuring simultaneously 'on the inside' and 'on the outside', introducing order into the environment (assimilating it mentally and practically) and giving an isomorphic structure to his or her own thought (accommodating it to the environment). Both of these processes are mutually inter-dependent, resulting in common outcomes of acting on the structure of the world and the properties of the human machine of self-organization: a conflict over the primacy of the synchronic level makes no sense. The world of the human, and human thoughts, have an isomorphic structure, and that shared structure is also imprinted on both aspects of contact between human and world: on human action and on human thought. The site of cultural universals, as we understand them here, is thus culture as a whole. All of these manifestations of culture 'on the level of perception' can and should be acknowledged as empirical points of departure for constructing a model of universals.

At first glance, the task seems impossibly difficult. Indeed, it would seem that at least some ways of looking at the world are determined by the very nature of a person's organic qualities. This delusion stemmed from the presuppositions of a longstanding conflict – that still occasionally bubbles up from time to time – on the topic of 'innate ideas' or 'a priori categories'. It would seem, for instance, that to such ideas, imposed by the nature of the human organism, belongs the category of space, determined by the innate qualities of human sensory organs, which perceive only certain mid-range portions of the size of bodies or lengths of sound waves. But these are limitations imposed on individuals only on the sensory-motor level of their psychic organization. If people did not manage such things with their intelligence, the limitations of the receptors that humans were born with would suffice to explain 'universals' – except that they would not be cultural universals. However, the thing is that – as Piaget writes – 'the Euclidean space perceived by our faculties is only one among possible ones, which can be physically experienced. Quite the opposite, deductive activity and the organization of the mind is limitless and leads, in the field of space, to generalizations surpassing all intuition.'[1] Thus, it is not the construction of human receptors and effectors that, prior to culture, determines 'cultural universals', though it certainly demarcates the boundaries of the practical material from which they can be constructed – leaving, however, a space that is quite expansive, for the possibility of an entirely plastic adaptation of the species, or certain members of it, to the conditions of their own existence (and vice versa). In the gorgeous study by Pierre Francastela, *Peinture et société*, we find a bracing analysis of changes in the organization of space that took place from the medieval period to modern times, and were immortalized in European painting. Medieval paintings did not organize space: the placement of objects was not determined by their physical distance, 'objectivized', but by their distance from God. Regardless of their position in a physical sense, the figures of saints, as those who were closest to God, were the largest; after them were the clergy; and, at the very end, located in this hierarchy as the smallest, were secular lambs. The space of the painting was thus directly organized in relation to God as the point of departure and according to a principle that produced all forms of organization, including the spatial one.

The Renaissance discovered perspective: now space was organized consciously, from the point of view of the human, subjectively and objectively at the same time: the painter chose a point from which he observed objects, but nature, however, decided from what point of view those objects were to appear to him. The world was, from then on, a stage for humans, and not for God, and the individual – in cooperation with nature – created a way of organizing it.

How are Francastela's ideas related to the belief in the pancultural existence of categories of space? It is indeed difficult to come to a conclusion other than that even categories of space – the most obvious candidate, it would seem, to accompany the notion of an innate idea – is a cultural category. Perspective, in its Renaissance formulation, is not a feature of the world in and of itself, much like the sacral organization of space of the Middle Ages also is not. Both ways of perceiving space are the product of an actual study of the cooperation of the world and human consciousness in a practical, active, assimilating–accommodating process. From that process, as from an empirical point of departure, one ought to begin by searching for cultural universals, maintaining at the same time complete neutrality in the conflict about the idea of nativism or innate ideas. Even if such innate ideas have influence on the shape of cultural universals, it is only in such cases, and to the extent that they have been included as advantageous for adaptation in human praxis and have not been overcome. And thus their existence, or lack thereof, does not impact our investigation.

Let us consider, however, whether the medieval and Renaissance ways of organizing space, in all this fragmented 'au niveau de perception' that so fascinated Francastela, did not have certain shared features, located beyond the level of sensory perception, on the level of internal structure – which could be recreated not through a simple protocol from sensory experience, but on a path constituted by generalizing models. To this question, we should probably give a positive answer. Yes, we can model the structure of our way of seeing the world that is equally present in both ways of seeing space, though it is present there only in the way that what is general is present in what is concrete. One example is the organization of the world by dividing it into concentric spheres: internal and external, and an array of spheres mediating the two. In the case of medieval painting, the figure of a practical concept of 'inside' is given by God: what is close to Him is what is internal. In Renaissance painting, the 'inside' is indicated by physical closeness, earthly, to my 'I' – to me, who, painting, constructs this image of the world. In the first case, the schema of concentric spheres is imposed on a world organized by eschatological values. The redemption of the soul is the primary goal of human praxis, the most valuable of sought-after goods: it too, personified by God, is located in the centre of the human sphere. In the second case, the hierarchy of values orbits earthly goods: humans, satisfying their physical needs, proper to their bodily forms of today, become the focus of the organization of space. But, in both cases, the schema of the organization of space is similar. What determines its structure?

It is human practice, embodying the structures – isomorphic to each other – of the external world and the human mind. It is this practice, referring in various ways to various fragments of the world, through its own process of differentiation, that carves out concentric rings from the world, differing from one another in the cognitive– creative meaning that they have for the expansive, self-organizing human machine. The nearest ring is the sphere in which humans satisfy their day-to-day needs; it must give them a feeling of safety in the area of the most important needs, those that are decisive for existence. It is thus a realm of not only collection, exploitation, but also cultivation. It is to serve not only today, but also tomorrow, and the day after. People have a relationship of ownership and selfhood with it; the boundary between one's own person and this sphere are not entirely clear, altruism can be mistaken for egoism, and egoism for altruism; the benefit of this sphere is a clear indicator of its own success. Then comes the sphere which also satisfies ad hoc needs – but they are ad hoc, on a case-by-case basis. It is a forest, as it is seen by a farmer who occasionally goes hunting so as to diversify his menu. In relation to this sphere, the concepts of egoism, equal exchange, and private interest become meaningful. Here one encounters enemies, but also friends. This sphere is dominated by the desire to exploit, by immediate gain, without caring about cultivation. Here there is a clear separation between 'me' and 'them'. Behind it, in the background, looms the external sphere, lacking clear contours – not drawn clearly because they are essentially indifferent to my needs; nor are they particularly useful, or particularly unfavourable. Sometimes, by accident, something from that sphere might get snatched up, assimilated. These are, however, such rare cases, and in the general balance of life so inessential, that I feel no need to clearly regulate my stance towards this sphere, and its persistent lack of clarity as a result of this does not seem threatening to me...

Thus, it is probably human practice that imprints on human thought this schema of concentric spheres, which it later embodies once again, via feedback, whenever we undertake the process of domesticating, structuralizing some newly emergent life function, a new aspect of inter-human contact or the encounter between a person and the world. Would this be one of the sought-after cultural universals, one of the principles of construction of every system of culture and every differentiated 'field' of culture?

At this point, we should introduce the ideas of Edmund Leach, which – as it seems – provide proof of the wisdom of our thinking.

## EDMUND LEACH'S THEORY OF REALMS
## OF SOCIAL SPACE

There are few works in the anthropological literature that are as daring and intellectually fruitful as a short article by the English follower of the concepts of Claude Lévi-Strauss, Edmund Leach – an engineer, who, relatively late in life and as a result of several accidental occurrences, became interested in anthropology, acquiring international fame thanks to the originality and theoretical ambition of his concepts, and just as quickly becoming *la bête noire* of English ethnology as a result of a merciless battle against the tradition – sacred to all English ethnologists – of the descriptive styles of Malinowski and Radcliffe-Brown. I have in mind the article 'Anthropological aspects of language: animal categories and verbal abuse'.[2] In it, Leach juxtaposes 'realms of social space' (according to his terminology), distinguished by people on two different levels, differentiated based on two aspects of human interest: (a) their sex lives, (b) satisfying hunger (sustenance); and he uses a table, that we can present in the following way:

|   | 1 | 2 | 3 | 4 | 5 |
|---|---|---|---|---|---|
|   | Me | House | Yard | Field | Far away |
| A | Me | Sister | Cousin | Neighbour | Stranger |
| B | Me | My favourite household pet | Herd | Wild game | Wild animals |

Through minute analysis, Leach asserts that $A1:A2:A3:A4:A5 = B1:B2:B3:B4:B5$. In other words, that the relationship between the successive terms in the two categories are isomorphic in relation to each other.

Thus, a sister is not perceived as a sexual partner. A beloved cat or dog is not treated as a meal – though, much like a sister is 'objectively' a woman, so a poodle is 'objectively' meat. A cousin is not perceived as a potential wife, but is a more common and appealing partner for sexual relations, and sometimes the object of pre-marital sexual initiation (Leach bases his conclusions primarily on customs typical in English culture, but in ethnographic literature we can find many examples of a broader dissemination of these principles). According to Brenda Z. Seligman, although exogamous rules that exclude close relatives from the field of potential sexual partners can be seen as an expansion of the sphere of obligations internal to families prohibiting incest, their social role and emotional weight are completely different.[3] According to Meyer Fortes' account of the Tellensi in Western Africa, they believe that even the thought of incest with one's mother is unlikely, and sex with one's sister would be humorous – no mature person is capable of such a funny behaviour; but a 'sister' from one's clan, who is biologically distant, though she cannot be chosen as a wife, is extremely attractive as a sexual partner – the more so, Fortes adds, because sex with her has a light tinge of illegality. Neighbours are a collection of potential candidates for marriage, but otherwise relations towards them vacillate along the axis of 'friend–enemy'. 'Strangers', distant women, are practically not women at all. Only very rarely does it happen that they appear in the role of women. As for animals – the herd serves for food, but individuals marked for eating are generally deprived of sexual identity via castration. Wild game is consumed in a sexually unaltered state, and, much like the relationship to female neighbours, we remain in a relationship of friend or foe towards them. Distant wild animals do not appear on our menu – either we are disgusted by their bodies and do not see them as potential meals, or we eat them rarely, only on very special occasions.

Spaces distinguished in the sphere of satisfying hunger and satisfying sexual urges are juxtaposed by Leach with the series 'Me – House – Yard – Field – Far away'. The names used here, suggesting concepts connected to physical distances, should not be, as it would seem, taken literally. The relationship between the physical 'far away' and a socio-cultural 'far away' is certainly not one of identity, something everyone would agree with; but aside from that, it is certainly not so obvious and uncontroversial as it may otherwise appear. Thus, on the one hand, Jordan M. Scher, expressing what are essentially general opinions, says that only in a modern, complex society can there appear a 'stranger who is neither acquaintance nor clearly enemy, that is, the passing pedestrian'[4] – someone who is physically close, while also being quite distant culturally. On the other hand, Margaret Mead says that it is only the experience of one's own superiority, strengthened by the practice of colonization in civilized peoples (and therefore complex societies), that created the attitude of proselytizing, which maximally removes the borders of which people are considered strangers, and whose cultural status is ambivalent. It is a centripetal tendency common to primitive people, making impossible the thesis of the superiority of one's own customs, that makes it so that they can easily live alongside peoples whose 'cultural distance' is tolerated without hesitation, and confirmed in the claim that 'We [human beings] do it this way, and they [other people] do it differently.'[5] Unravelling this question does not have greater relevance for our problem – we merely point it out. For our goals, it is sufficient if we make ourselves clearly aware that the terms used in the above sequences should be understood similarly to names used in other sequences – as subjective–objective symbols, referring to cultural meanings, and not to the properties of the things themselves, which can be described in physical terms.

Much more essential from our point of view is the divergence between 'realms of social space' distinguished by Leach and the spheres we proposed above, differentiated by internally distinguished human praxis. This divergence, it seems, can be easily remedied. Space 5 in Leach seems rather clearly to cover our external sphere; space 4, our intermediate sphere; that leaves spaces 2 and 3. In our opinion, they both fit with the characteristics we have ascribed to the internal sphere. These characteristics are most fully in evidence in everything that we learn from Leach about space 3; space 2, however, is a typical 'border' sphere (between 'Me' and space 3), which emerged as a result of the merging of 'overflow' from both neighbouring spaces. Similar liminal spheres could easily be distinguished, even between the remaining spaces or spheres, though they do not play as important a role in human existence as the border region described by Leach. It is important, however, that the characteristics of border spheres are derived from the characteristics of neighbouring spheres, and are not independent. Border spheres have certain specific, still important meanings, which we will discuss separately. For now, let us merely indicate that, when we try to apply Leach's concept to other spheres of life, besides those discussed by the author, the heuristic utility calls for precisely three, and not more, concentric spheres. Although – let us emphasize this strongly – the space within each sphere is also organized and the cultural meanings located 'on the left side' of the sphere might not be identical to the meaning of elements located 'on the right'. The thing is, however, that specific places inside the sphere differ from each other only in a quantitatively expressible intensity of general characteristics of spheres, where places located in different spheres differ qualitatively.

Let us reach to the domain that is sociologically decisive to the discipline, to these very cultural institutions that regulate the circulation of goods, that condition that is the *sine qua non* of the existence of human collectivities. In this highly important, vital, not in the least marginal sphere of social life, we can easily distinguish three different cultural principles, fantastically suited to three concentric rings and their defining characteristics, as given in the previous section.

The first principle is the institution that Marshall D. Sahlins described in his time as 'generalized reciprocity'. It is based on the fact that humans give without thinking about the gains that are to be made by doing so; they give without thinking of a return; giving is not consciously thought of as 'getting rid of', as loss. Perhaps even the term 'recprocity', even with the modifier 'generalized', is in this context improperly used. In any case, the element of reciprocity does not penetrate to the level of consciousness and does not act as a motive for behaviour. A farmworker who throws himself under a train to save a horse is an excellent embodiment of the functioning of 'generalized reciprocity'. Maybe the amount of goods given and acquired as a result of the functioning of the principle of generalized reciprocity is balanced in the long run, but this circumstance has no justifiable motivation. There are rather different motives at work here: an extension of the concept of 'I' onto people, to whom one gives, perceiving the act of using goods by them in the same way as one perceives the act of using them by oneself. A father giving his earnings for the support of his family does not generally do so thinking of the gains he will get later from his son or daughter. A person sharing their last penny with a dear friend is not necessarily doing so out of a calculation and the thought of ensuring themselves assistance in the case of future need. The principle of 'generalized reciprocity' is difficult to empathize with in our market-driven world, which immeasurably broadens the intermediate sphere at the cost of the internal one. But plentiful ethnographic material confirms beyond all doubt its presence and the immense role it plays at certain stages of social development; all attempts at presentist interpretation of the facts connected to it – undertaken by 'economic anthropologists' such as R. Firth, and aiming to prove at any cost the existence of a capitalist reckoning among the locals, lurking under the pretences of 'irrational' generosity – call for equilibrium-izing processes towards stubborn factual material. We will provide a fragmentary ethnographic documentary below.

The second principle is better known to us from our own experiences of the institution of mutual reciprocity (balanced). Here it is about the idea of a kind of 'giving' that is accompanied by the expectation of an equal return. More specifically, we give item $D_1$ only if, and only insofar as, it is a necessary condition in order to acquire in exchange $D_2$. If $D_2$ could be acquired without giving up $D_1$, we would gladly take advantage of the opportunity. Thus, if we give $D_1$, it is only because we are in a situation where we are forced to, where it is the only way for us to acquire the desired $D_2$. The principle of mutual reciprocity thus cannot function spontaneously – unlike generalized reciprocity. It must be supported by an element of coercion in the form of equal strengths of the owners of $D_1$ and $D_2$, or powers of subordination, continually requiring of both sides certain norms of exchange and containing the resources necessary to force both sides to respect those norms. The effective functioning of principles of equivalent reciprocity thus requires in essence the existence of some kind of extra-cultural, external tools of regulation. This is also connected to a game of competing strengths over clashing interests; it occurs in conditions of a dynamic balance, achieved through the levelling of respective vectors of strength in opposing directions. Let us return, as a conclusion, to the observation that the extremely widespread, and clearly described by ethnographers, institution of 'gifts' (after the offering of which there regularly occurs, though not necessarily immediately, a reciprocal gift from the receiver) can be presented as an intermediate form between generalized reciprocity and balanced reciprocity.

Finally, the principle of exploitation – appearing most fully in robbery, wartime plunder, the predatory use of no-man's land, hunting game animals to the point of extinction, but taking a 'more civilized' form, based simply on taking without giving. As a rule, it is a marginal directive, not very important in the balance of the process of satisfying needs, sporadically employed in culturally and socially unregulated contact with the sphere of 'strangers' (with the exception of individuals and groups seen as pathological, and therefore those for whom the internal sphere is anomalously narrow, and the external sphere encompasses in practice the intermediate one). But it also happens that it has more long-term uses in relations between fragments of the same society (in cases of one-sided giving). Utilizing the principle of exploitation, arising for the needs of servicing the sphere of 'strangers', and producing as a result of its force the concept of strangers, regularly produces a clash between two ideological perspectives: assessments of existing relationships, by those who give, as those between strangers; and the efforts to present these same relationships, by those who take, as a case of generalized reciprocity (though occasionally the takers accept the existing state as one of strangers and they fortify this strangeness with a system that is quasi-state-like, developed by an adequate ideology).

Let us look more closely at the ethnographic documentation of the three concentric spheres of social relations, constituted by the three principles regulating social relations described above. The ethnographic data actually pertain to only two of the spheres (the internal and the intermediate) and to their external structure. There is little information about the external sphere; ethnographers are generally interested in the typical, rather than the sporadic.

Thus, among the Kung tribe three clearly different forms of 'exchange' emerge: among close relatives, things are shared without any form of accounting; among more distant relatives goods and foodstuffs are offered without hesitation, but with an expectation that they will be reciprocated in equal measure; and finally, with the neighbouring Bantu, there is regular trade.[6] In New Guinea, the inhabitants of villages by the sea share among themselves without any restrictions. But they trade with the people from villages farther inland. They feel something akin to shame about this: they never conduct business transactions in the village, they go somewhere else for this purpose, on the road leading inland. A store belonging to one of the locals is located 50 metres away from the nearest village building. When Busama, an inhabitant of a seaside village, receives a rope bag from one of his fellow villagers, he gives him in exchange a gift worth twice as much as what he would have paid a merchant. The people say: 'A person is ashamed to treat someone close to them like a merchant.'[7] Among the Tungusic peoples, the clan offer each other reindeer; but in their interactions with people who are not members of the clan, a reindeer is an object of trade.[8] The Kuma practise what we called 'generalized reciprocity' among a small sub-clan: within the clan as a whole, there is the exchange of gifts; but outside of it, the principles of trade prevail, though they also vary depending upon whether one is dealing with regular trading partners or a random buyer. In the first case, they agree without argument on the established value of the goods; in the second – they bargain furiously. It is not irrelevant to add that the local term for a person one trades with literally translates as 'I-together I-eat'.[9] Among the Siuai in Oceania, we can distinguish three economic sectors: full sharing within the family circle, extensive mutual assistance between relatives and the residents of the same village, and a system of trade with people from other villages. A person living in a village in Tikopia is delighted if a relatives asks for something as a gift, and gives it without hesitation, with true joy. If this person needs something, they will turn without hesitation to a relative. If, however, the Tikopian intends to request something from someone who is not a relative – from 'an other person', as they say in Tikopia – they prepare food, filling a large basket, and placing a piece of fabric or even a blanket on the top. Only when equipped in this way do they turn to someone with a request. They usually do not encounter rejection. We see something similar in Malinowski's writing about the Trobrianders, Evans-Pritchard about the Nuer, Firth about the Maori, Henry about the Pilaga. We can assume without risk that, in the discussion of this issue, only the technical–material difficulties make a complete induction impossible.

In all of the societies studied by anthropologists, an internal circle clearly differentiated from the external and intermediate spheres has been identified; its contents are not identical in different tribes – sometimes it only includes a small family, sometimes it stretches to encompass an entire tribe spread over a large terrain – but it is always government by the relations described by Margaret Mead, writing of the Arapesh people of New Guinea:

> If there is meat on his smoking rack over the fire, it is either meat which was killed by another – a brother, a brother-in-law, a sister's son, etc. – and has been given to him, in which case he and his family may eat it; or it is meat which he himself has killed and which he is smoking to give away to someone else, for to eat one's own kill, even though it be only a small bird, is a crime to which only the morally – which usually means in Arapesh mentally – deficient will stoop. If the house in which he is living is nominally his, it will have been con-structed in part at least from the posts and planks of other people's houses, which have been dismantled or temporarily deserted, and from which he has borrowed timber. He will not cut his rafters to fit his house, if they are too long, because they may be needed later for someone else's house which is of a different shape or size.[10]

The image that emerges from the lessons of these ethnographic testimonies overall points to the following truths:

1 There exists a clear differentiation of rules governing relations with: (a) 'one's own'; (b) people with whom one regularly interacts, but only for the purposes of satisfying specific, selected needs; (c) strang-ers, with whom all contact, even if it is for some reason essential, is occasional, accidental, one-time only. These three types of people comprise three global and concentric spheres, into which human practice divides its social world, remaining in the realm of the 'psychic field' of the individual.
2 The contents of each sphere may be extremely varied. What is more, particular spheres may expand or contract in response to cultural or social changes. However, they always maintain their distinctiveness.
3 The division of the social world into these spheres is conducted largely from the point of view of the degree of the 'information economy': the more 'external' the circle, the lesser, more fragmented the liquida-tion of the indeterminacy of the situation, guaranteed by culturally sanctioned models of behaviour. This situation remains in accordance with the fact of non-identical weights of the various spheres for accomodational–assimilating life processes of the organism.

4 Every sphere contains heterogeneous elements. The boundaries between spheres are always to some extent arbitrary; in essence, they are composed of their own spectrum of attitudes. More internal regions of a given sphere typically differ from more external regions of it, though generally not to such a degree as the adjacent regions of neighbouring spheres. These regions are typically the 'weakest point' of cultural regulation, the region of the sharpest conflicts, tensions, antagonisms, and the source of psychic discomfort (like all indeterminacy, for that matter). It is this important phenomenon – which comprises, in our opinion, a further cultural universal of immeasurable importance – that we must now consider more carefully.

## UNDEMARCATED MARGINS IN A DEMARCATED WORLD

All classification is a victory over chaos, says Lévi-Strauss.[11] Distinguishing amongst elements in the world of things and giving them names, humans transform 'continuity' into 'discontinuity', rendering the world accessible to an organizing perception and an organizing action. The realization that individual 'things' have an objective existence, in distinction from 'that which is general', which exists only in the human mind, is a primitive-materialistic delusion, raised to the level of ontological principle by nominalism and reification, and born anew in the common-sense perception of a world already organized and informationally arranged by culture. 'Sensory perception ["sensory experience"]', writes M. W. Popovich, 'provides just as little information about what is individual as about what is general. Only in encountering a system of classification of a higher order of abstraction ["a secondary system of signals"] do sensory images take the form of images of individual objects, that is, elementary empirical data. The intellectual meaning of impressions is thus enriched by the thinking.'[12] 'In order to perceive individual concrete things as real objects', says Piaget, 'it is necessary to supplement what one sees with what one knows.'[13]

The key to classification offered by culture precedes the knowledge of things – it is the prerequisite for noticing them, the condition for orientation in the world. Thanks to it, humans can function in comprehensible and predictable surroundings, achieving the degree of minimalization of the indeterminacy of a situation that is needed to achieve necessary and expected effects in the environment.

This function of the cultural system of meanings is generally clear today and does not require more extensive discussion. Leach's accomplishment, however, is that he brought attention to an aspect of the mechanism that serves to realize this function of culture, and generally has not been considered.

Language alone does not suffice for securing a complete 'marking' of the world. If the concepts given names in language divide the world into discrete things, it happens only rarely that 'individual beings' carved out in this way exhaust that which is being divided; that which is finite can never exhaust the infinite. Between named things, there remain gaps – regions unnamed, unmarked by culture, not offering clear perceptions, incomprehensible, not divided into known and easily distinguished stimuli, clearly associated with equally known 'personal' reactions. A culture that would accept the coexistence of demarcated, known regions with such unknown, unmarked ones would poorly execute its function as a tool liquidating or reducing the indeterminacy of the world. That is why, in realizing the semiotic function of culture, language must be bolstered by other tools, specializing in eliminating regions of indeterminacy. This other tool is – and here we come to Leach's contribution to the semiotic theory of culture – taboo.

> It teaches us that the world is made up of 'things' distinguished by names; we must train our perception to recognize the discontinuity in the environment [...] This second type of perception trained in the above way is achieved through the simultaneous use of language and taboo. Language gives us names to distinguish things; taboo forbids us from acquainting ourselves with the portion of the continuum, that separates things from each other.
>
> Of course – what is repressed becomes particularly interesting. Avoiding the fact that all studies are aimed at 'discovering' those parts of the environment that are located at the border of what is 'already known', we also observe the phenomenon, described in different ways by anthropologists and psychologists, based on the fact that whatever is taboo is not only the object of particular interest, but also anxiety. Whatever is taboo is sacred, valuable, important, powerful, dangerous, untouchable, disgusting, unmentionable.[14]

The ambivalence of attitudes connected to taboo is, of course, not Leach's discovery. His accomplishment, however, is to connect the phenomenon of taboo with the mechanism of realizing the semiotic function of culture.

It is initially difficult to grasp the size of the class of phenomena that are explained by the particular role of cultural domains, which we propose to call the unmarked margins of a culturally demarcated world. The concept of a margin provides a unified explanatory key for phenomena previously considered in distinction, grasped separately, at a distance, deprived of a common denominator of 'empirical generalization' – for phenomena for which there have heretofore been sought extremely various generating mechanisms, rather than them being portrayed as differing from each other only epiphenomenally as a result of the same cultural universal.

Let us return, however, to this way of understanding the genesis of the margin. The way to understand it, proposed by Leach, is in its own form overly broad and requires greater precision. It is necessary to distinguish between two phenomena that are completely separate, in terms of their cultural situation. It is hard to imagine that the domains that are unnamed – and therefore simply unknown and unknowable, as it would seem from what we know about gnoseological mechanisms of human knowledge – could be a subject of 'particular interest'; in any case, it seems doubtful whether this 'particular interest' and 'particular unease' must always accompany each other and always signal the same, common, cause. People are afraid of the dark, which they cannot penetrate with their vision, whose contents they cannot master; people become nervous when they find themselves on unknown terrain, where they do not know what they might encounter. These are examples of a certain category of situation, in which the common denominator is a lack of meanings adequate to describe the experienced state, making it impossible to foresee the sequence of events. It is hard to say, however, whether such situations are meant to be particularly attractive to people. It is not an accident that they are generally the terrain of the most intensive cultural expansion, which aims to liquidate them, to manage them completely with information. The traits of academic research indicated by Leach, as well as the discovery of torches and lightbulbs, are identical examples of such a conquest.

From the above examples, the regular 'blank spots' on the cultural map of the world should be distinguished as being a completely different category of phenomena, to which it is appropriate to apply the term 'margins'. The blank spots cannot be a cultural universal. They are always a transitional event, temporary, and, most importantly, relatively easily removed in practice; it would otherwise be incomprehensible why one would resort to taboo in order to manage them. Margins, properly speaking, are something else entirely. They are a chronic phenomenon that is decisively unmovable, constantly encroaching on the daily life of humans, characterizing the cultural field to the same degree as its relative organization. Although it seems to us that phenomena deserving to be differentiated and individually named as margins are those regions whose primary characteristic is not a lack, but actually an excess, of cultural meanings. Included in cultural meanings, they are fully accessible to human observation, identifiable, and can be grasped through the senses or the imagination. But they also do not have a singular meaning, and, more specifically, they simultaneously have various meanings, and those meanings are mutually contradictory. They are therefore not so much marked, as excessively marked. They achieve this excess, which blossoms in a truly Hegelian way into an indeterminacy of a higher order, an unresolvable, nagging, anxious task of reconciling what cannot be reconciled.

Thanks to developments in structural linguistics, today we are familiar with the mechanisms that make it so that 'signs signify'. We know that individual elements not opposed to anything do not possess any meaning; that in order for a relationship of meaning to appear at least two elements existing in opposition must be present, which can only then fulfil the function of signification. A sign is capable of causing us to differentiate one object within the plane of 'that which is signified' only in a case when it is opposed to another sign within the plane of 'that which signifies'. Without opposition, there is no relationship of meaning. Because it is so, in order to possess the capacity for information, or to reduce the indeterminacy of the situation, the semiotic system must above all introduce clear distinctions on both planes that can be grasped both intellectually and by the senses. The differend is the elementary building block of any semiotic system. The greatest discomfort of a person not knowing a given language comes from the 'blurring together' of sounds in an ear untrained in differentiating between them in this specific language, which within the framework of a given system play the role of semantic oppositions.

Thus, in the process of classification by culture of a constant, chaotic world, alongside the possibility of leaving certain realms empty, 'gaps' between meaning, there appears also the phenomenon of 'blurring together' of meanings, or of them spilling over onto neighbouring realms. Between every clearly distinguished category, non-commissioned officers and officers, there appears the unfortunate ensign, the subject of many dramas and mournful ballads, whose status in life is characterized not by his not belonging to any of the neighbouring categories, but by the fact that he belongs to both at once. It is this situation that is both suspect and alluring because of its indeterminacy – worthy of contempt and hidden admiration, and also fear. Every ensign has painfully experienced the innate ambivalence of this situation on his own skin.

Speaking more generally, the situation of the margins presents itself to us as a result of the 'spilling over' of cultural categories onto neighbouring regions. The result of this overflow, occurring from two sides at once, is that spaces in which meanings from other situations that are mutually opposed to each other appear between the categories – meanings to which the dominating culture gives a character of opposition. This repeated indeterminacy of the situations of the margins seems only to justify the use of taboo to convert or save the intended singularity of meanings and translate the intensity of psychic experiences connected to this phenomenon. Culture responds to such foundational indeterminacy with efforts to acquire knowledge; in the case of repeated indeterminacy, the efforts to learn are not medicine – the phenomena of the margins cannot be practically or intellectually assimilated. Thus, the threatened unequivocality of meaning of the cultural field must be saved through the use of repression and taboo, to the degree that it can be – and the physical elimination of the margins (an effort that is frequently renewed, but always futile, as evidenced by, for instance, the changing fates of the institution of the ensign; the empty spaces created by the elimination of certain categories of the margins are immediately occupied by new categories, previously not perceived as marginal; the existence of margins is an inseparable attribute of a culture's particular way of realizing its semiotic function). We will apply the concept of margins to the phenomenon of interferences between neighbouring cultural categories, and not to the gaps between them.

Accepting this premise, we stop accepting the accusation of irrationality, generally directed at us by critics of religion under the heading of the ritual of the Eucharist; if it even is irrationality, then it is an irrationality deeply rooted in the mechanism of the semiotic functioning of culture. What could be more normal than to direct the most intense feelings, that mixture of fear and admiration, towards phenomena that have dual meanings by their very nature, like the Host – simultaneously the work of human hands and the Lord's Body, a place where two elements, defined in their opposition to each other, collide? Or maybe the very fact of using the taboo term 'irrationality' to describe a similar situation is evidence of a similar, deeply rooted tendency in us to repress phenomena that entail contradictory meanings? We cease to be surprised by the fact that, in Christianity, the cult of the Virgin Mary and the Son of God overshadowed the adoration of the immaculate heavenly Father or the Holy Ghost. There is nothing secret in the categorically unified nature of those beings, no multiplicity of meaning, that could resurrect positions that the culture reserves precisely for marginal situations. Another matter entirely is a flesh-and-blood woman who brings God into the world. Or the son of man, who is also God. We cease to be surprised by the phenomenon, common to all religions, of significant emotional intensity, of locating the most fervent sacral feelings in images or statues of gods, about which it is known, of course, that they are the work of human hands, but which are also included in the sphere of godliness. To reach, for a change, to an entirely different field of culture: the difficulties connected to the cultural assimilation of the concept of social property become clear. It is an idea located at the intersection of two opposing concepts, stimulating behaviours of opposing principles: 'mine' and 'not mine'. Social property is both mine and not mine; at the very least, it does not belong to me in the same way that the handkerchief in my pocket does. Because it is mine, I can behave with it in ways that are sanctioned by culture for things that are mine: I can tear up, throw away, or give someone else the handkerchief. Because it is also not mine, I am not allowed to do so. Social property thus simultaneously elicits feelings of aggression and fear, inclining us to link it to values and capabilities that are great, powerful, and redemptive. In older times, the hills and forests being social property, 'someone's' and 'no one's' at the same time, gave them an aura of holiness, creating the sense that they were the seat of the gods. The immanent multiplicity of meaning contained in this concept is irreducible. Various forms of taboo, adapted to the cultural climate, are thus the only remedy.

But the largest accumulation of marginal phenomena, which also play the largest role in culture, occurs at the intersection of the spheres 'I' and 'not-I' and at the intersection of the spheres 'mine' and 'stranger's'.

Let us begin with the first intersection. The government of Uganda managed to convince citizens of the need to dig deep latrines and cover faecal matter with soil by saying that it would render the excrement inaccessible to sorcerers. S. M. Lambert, an American doctor practising on the Solomon Islands, remembers the panic among the locals when he took a stool sample from one of his patients. After much persuasion, the locals agreed to give stools for analysis, under the condition that they would be allowed to stay until the end of the examination, and later safely bury the rest of the excrement.[15] These are the first two available examples of the phenomenon of universal culture. All the parts of the human body that could be separated from the rest, which are simultaneously 'me' and 'not-me', are surrounded by taboo, which on the one hand demands that they be seen as indecent, disgusting, shameful, and on the other, bids them be ascribed a remarkable power, which justifies their universal use in magical practice. I skip over the terror that is spontaneously evoked by the sight of a hand, leg, or head separated from the trunk. But, on a daily basis, we encounter the persistent taboo connected to human faeces and urine, sweat and spit, clippings of nails and hair.

The ambivalence born of taboo on the borders of the sphere of 'I' and 'not-I' emerges most forcefully in the case of parts of the human body, but it also turns up, although in a diluted form, on a broader terrain. We did not like to allow other people to make use of objects that had been in contact with our own bodies long before we bolstered this instinctive aversion with the rational justification of 'avoiding bacteria'. But the semantic field of 'I' reaches even further; in some measure, it covers the entire sphere distinguished by Leach as the realm of 'home', and what is acknowledged by us as a marginal sphere, subordinated to cultural meanings assigned both to 'I' and to the sphere of 'mine' in general. We now understand why our sister is not, to us, a woman, nor our brother a man; why a domesticated dog or cat is not meat; why we feel disgust towards a house mouse, but not towards its wild cousin the field mouse. We also understand why we are inclined to allow only the people we are close to into our home kitchen or bathroom. And maybe this also deepens our understanding of the remarkable intensity of emotion that we feel towards people encompassed by the domain of 'home' (or, at least, by the universal expectation of such intensity, and the disappointment we feel when such intensity is not to be found), and the complete elimination, in this domain, of the difference between altruism and egotism.

The second highly socially significant area of taboo is, as we mentioned before, located at the borders of the realms of 'mine' and 'stranger's'. The realm of mine can be treated as a creation of the cultural concept of 'I'. It is a region in which we identify, in which we are at home, in which we not only exploit, but also cultivate. What remains after we carve out the sphere of 'mine' is the creation of the cultural concept of 'not-I'. It is something that is marked by its opposition to me, by contradicting that which I know and think about myself. The appearance of an object that connects those two cultural characteristics brings to life an indeterminacy that cannot be eliminated. It is the region of what is, almost by definition, unpredictable, in regards to which we are defenceless; we do not know how we should behave in order to bring about the demanded series of events; we lack an unequivocal model of behaviour; the region clearly evades our control. We are enraged and terrified at the same time.

Colloquial wisdom provides an endless stream of examples of this situation. We know the disgust and repulsion that saturate terms like 'parvenu', 'nouveau riche', 'cosmopolitan'. The concept of 'enemy' elicits our hatred; the concept of 'traitor' – also our loathing. A heretic is always a graver enemy than someone of another faith. Every political side, as a rule, most fervently fights those groups that, taken 'objectively', are closest to them. The slogan 'who is not with us, is against us' has its deep justifications, as does the amount of energy released by this slogan: it is only necessary to prove, and maybe even to cause as a result of some action, the singular meaning of the situation that is postulated by this slogan. The margin is not a sphere that makes impossible the 'objective understanding of a situation'. This was demonstrated quite clearly by the experiments of Hovland and Sheriff: a group of 'judges' who were deeply involved as pro- or anti-black were asked to classify sentences as either pro- or anti-black. Both subgroups proved unilateral in their assessment of the unequivocal sentences. However, the more ambiguous sentences were without hesitation classified by each group as belonging to the opposing side. Similar results were produced by the studies of Hovland, Harvey, and Sherif on modes of classification by an auditorium filled with people for and against prohibition, after limited discussion on this controversial subject.[16] If this concerned only a regular difficulty in understanding, and if straying from the 'objective' state of things was simply the result of an error stemming from ignorance – the errors would go both ways. The one-sidedness of the direction of the 'errors' indicates beyond all doubt the existence of another factor – not the usual difficulties connected, for example, to complicated algebraic equations. They indicate the functioning of the cultural institution of taboo.

A particularly drastic case of the intersection between 'mine' and 'stranger's' discussed here is the category, widely discussed in the literature, of 'marginal people'. This category has taken on significant weight today, when the violent processes of marginalization all over the world are creating categories of people representing 'new culture' in 'old societies' – by nature, things that are ambivalent, meaning-wise, in the light of both of the cultural systems at whose intersection they are located.

> A typical example of someone moving outside an older world and failing to enter a new is the Busama storekeeper, a native named Yakob. He is unsuccessful alike as a member of the encircling kinship society and as a Europeanized business man. The people disapprove of him so strongly that they always scolded me for talking to him. They were never indignant if I spent an hour or two associating with criminals, but they used to criticize me severely when I bought a tin of cigarettes from him. 'He's a black man who wants to behave as though he were white, and you oughtn't to encourage him', they used to tell me.[17]

The author of an erudite text devoted to marginal people, Everett V. Stonequist,[18] divides the subjects of his research into 'racial hybrids' and 'cultural hybrids'. Elżbieta Neyman recently offered a decidedly richer classification of marginal people.[19] But, aside from the differences that divide and justify efforts to classify them, people of the margins are united by an overarching shared trait: they have a multiplicity of cultural meanings, and in an irreducible way. This ambivalence in their cultural meaning, which cannot be eliminated, ceaselessly pushes their surroundings to try to repress or annihilate them, and pushes the people themselves to a constant but futile conformity directed to a more alluring cultural possibility, or to leading protest movements as a less alluring category, or to accepting their position of chronic multiplicity of meaning and isolating themselves from the rest of the world in the fortress of a cultural system that is externally consistent, and constructed from its marginal position. The miserable dual situation of 'Eurasians', Anglo-Indians, was described by G. M. Williams:

> They are subject to ostracism both by the English, as by Hindus. They themselves look down upon Hindus, with a bitter hatred, because they see their Hindu blood as cursing them. They are drawn toward the English and court them, miserably. When speaking of England they always call it the 'fatherland', though they may never have been there, and they constantly strive in vain to break through to British environments.[20]

The position, pregnant with endless conflicts and tensions, that the particular mechanism of the realization of the semiotic function of culture imposes on people of the margins is the indicator of the special role that this category plays in the development of cultural systems. Being the least balanced, most weakly organized element of these systems, it also concentrates the most dynamism, and simultaneously contains this weakest point, in which the traditional cultural structure is most easily broken. As Stonequist writes, the 'marginal man is the key-personality in the contacts of cultures. It is in his mind that the cultures come together, conflict, and eventually work out some kind of adjustment and interpenetration':

> Because of his in-between situation, the marginal man may become an acute and able critic of the dominant group and its culture. This is because he combines the knowledge and insight of the insider with the critical attitude of the outsider. His analysis is not necessarily objective – there is too much emotional tension underneath to make such an attitude easy of achievement. But he is skillful in noting the contradictions and the 'hypocrisies' in the dominant culture. The gap between its moral pretensions and its actual achievements jumps to his eye.[21]

Let us try to summarize this portion of our reflections.

1 In the process of realizing the semiotic function of each culture, aspiring to informationally organize the whole psychic field, there must be 'discrepancies' of meaning, that take on one of two forms: either (a) 'cracks' between categories, resulting from a lack of cultural information or (b) a marginal region, with a multiplicity of cultural meanings, emerging as a result of the 'spilling over' of two insufficiently disconnected neighbouring categories.
2 The defence mechanism of cultural systems towards shortcomings of type (a) is based on the mobilization of exploratory efforts; and towards insufficiencies of type (b), on the utilization of the institutution of taboo, efforts aiming towards cultural repression or physical annihilation.
3 Among all categories of marginal ambivalence, a particularly exalted and universal role in cultural systems is played by margins emerging from the intersection of the spheres 'I' and 'not-I' and the spheres of 'mine' and 'stranger's'.
4 The margins comprise the weakest (least conservative) elements of cultural systems, the most able to absorb change, and releasing the greatest reserves of dynamic energy. If it were possible to create a culture without margins, it would doubtless be the most stable culture in all of history.

**AFTERWORD**

I have barely touched on the topic of cultural universals. Because this topic is not one to be resolved in an article, but in a lengthy study. But perhaps I have succeeded, regardless of the scarcity of results presented here, in demonstrating that it is worth the risk to try to find these universals by a different path from organizing apples according to colour, size, etc., and coming to the conclusion that 'all apples have colour' and 'all apples have size'. This other path is the analysis of the necessity contained in those very cultural functions – the function of meaning, subordination, the structuralization of the world, and the transformation of unpredictable chaos into a finite collection of possibilities with a calculable probability that they will take place; a necessity contained equally in the precise operation of the mechanisms of realizing this function, and in the unavoidable imperfections of their operation. Maybe universals discovered in this way make possible classificatory efforts that are superior, because intellectually productive and consciously leading to synthesis.

Let us observe: cultural universals inform us of ambitions, tendencies, nameless motivations, indicating an unconscious cultural effort. They do not speak – in reference to a system as dynamic as the cultural one, they cannot speak – of nameless and calcified forms, about eternal forms, filled with more or less exotic contents. The 'spherization' of the cultural map is a tendency, and the aimed-at form of culture but a form that is never fully attained; the full arc of classification is always distanced from reality, and because of this is fluid, always unfinished, never final. The margins of meaning are to an equal degree the Achilles' heel of culture, and its eternal fate. Cultural systems constantly run from the margins and are simultaneously endlessly creating new margins, eliciting new semiotic efforts – and so on, into eternity. The universals of cultural systems are also universals of their dynamism.

One objection comes to the lips of everyone who has lived in the second half of the twentieth century. Because we live in an age that seems, for the first time in human history, to acknowledge cultural multiplicity as an innate and fixed feature of the world – one which gives rise to new forms of identity that are at ease with plurality, like a fish in water – and even boasts of the fact that it not only discovered, but even accepted as a truly human state and mode of being both noble and dignified, this indeterminacy of the human condition as humanity's calling. Our era both multiplies the marginal regions of meaning and is no longer ashamed. Quite the opposite, in the mouths of its greatest thinkers, it acknowledges them as its constitutive feature.

We still do not know and cannot know whether this qualitatively new phenomenon in the history of the human species signals a new level of cultural evolution, being a permanent and irreversible accomplishment, or if it is only the symptom of a transitory crisis, born of the crucible of the culture that is the most cosmopolitan since Roman times. The category of people truly well adapted to the semiotic multiplicity of meanings of the world, chronic revolutionaries who are not secretly yearning for the recovery of the lost singularity of meaning (not creating in their fantasies an alternative to such singularity), is still no more numerous than the category of the psychopathic victims of the tensions born of such ambivalence. Empirical evidence is too scarce to support this or the other decision, the period of time overly narrow to come to a conclusion. The problem of the cultural ambivalence of our era is itself ambivalent in meaning. Maybe for this reason it is so stubbornly attacked from all sides in philosophical discussions, and by all the social movements of the era that we are living in.

I would not hesitate to acknowledge this problem as the most important riddle for the diagnosis of our times – as the *sine qua non* condition of all future efforts, and all efforts connected to the future. What is this innate tendency of the citizen of the twentieth century to a multiplicity of meanings? A sickness or a maturity? The illness of a senile age? Or maybe an opportunity never before seen in history? Maybe a new revolutionary leap in the historic adventure of humanity, whose role in the creation of culture bids historians of the future to look at the Neolithic revolution with a wink and a nod, as a minor episode?

The efforts to answer this question create one of those situations in which the work of philosophers merges with the fate of humanity.

# V

# Some Research Problems in the Semiotic Theory of Culture

The cybernetic point of view, as has recently been often discussed,[1] calls for every object of inquiry to be perceived as a 'black box', or as an object, that discloses to an observer only its 'inputs' (physically accessible external pressures) and 'outputs' (equally accessible observations of the physical 'behaviour' of the object). That which connects the inputs with the outputs directly – meaning, in such a way as if the observer did not exist – is not physically accessible to the researcher. But if the observer is a researcher or, even more, an experimenter, she or he can connect the studied object through 'feedback' into one system of interconnected elements. Then the researcher acts on the object, observing in its output the results of his or her activities; these observations influence his or her decisions, which lead to new actions on the inputs of the studied object, etc. In the course of this process, the researcher penetrates 'the depths' of the object of interest, intellectually grasps physically inaccessible connections between input and output. These connections are perceived in a different way from states of entry and exit. Observing the entry and exit provides a 'protocol' of the sensory experiences of the observer. On the basis of this protocol, the theoretical work of the researcher begins, aiming to model the 'essence' of the examined object, its internal structure. The task that confronts the researcher is based on 'recoding' the information contained in the protocol into information about the 'constructions' (now occasionally referred to as the 'constructs'). These constructions – models created by the researcher, but limited in their arbitrariness by the data of the given protocol – they do not have, and cannot be, 'similar' to the arrangement of feedback which 'actually' connects the input and output of the examined object. It is sufficient for them to be isomorphic in relation to this arrangement. The sought-after isomorphism manifests itself when the model constructed by the researcher-theoretician 'behaves' in the same way as the examined object – namely, when the model reveals to observation a similar correspondence between the states of 'input' and 'output' to the studied object.

In this way, according to the well-known view of Herbert A. Simon, 'all theories are analogies and all analogies are theories'. To construct a theory is to build a model that would behave analogously to the studied object. Of course, this does not mean that the model must be a 'replica' of the object, a physical recreation of the material object. Quite the opposite, we most frequently encounter a symbolic model of the object which utilizes not material elements, but ideas, concepts, abstract symbols. But, without regard to their character, models should, aside from carrying out other useful functions, describe and facilitate an understanding of complex systems or events.[2]

If we accept this conception of theory, popular in academia today, then founding a programme for the study of culture must begin by determining what constitutes, for the researcher of culture, this 'black box', which determines the boundaries of his or her theorizing.

The study of culture is, beyond all doubt – at least in large part – the study of human behaviour, or, more narrowly, the study of the cooperation of human individuals. It is precisely in this cooperation that events are realized, which studies of culture attempt to analyse and make sense of through theoretical models. The most straightforward schema of a similar cooperation can be written in the following way:[3]

Individual A          Individual B

S ⟶ r . . . . . . . . . . . s ⟶ r

'S' in this schema indicates the field of stimuli acting on individual A; 'r', the reactions of the individual to those stimuli – reactions equipped, in truly human fashion, not only with the tools that Vygotsky classifies as 'technical', but also with those that are 'psychological' – in other words, with certain signs, referring to meanings accessible to all individuals knowing the code that these signs are elements of. This sign-level 'r', after being decoded, becomes the stimulus 's' for individual B. To this stimulus 's', individual B reacts in manner R.

In the above schema, as can easily be understood, the space (S–r), similarly to the space (s–R), delineates the boundaries of the 'black box' for the psychologist. S and 's' are treated by the psychologist as the inputs of the object being studied, and 'r' and R as outputs. If they have theoretical ambitions, they strive to model the region of mechanisms that they do not have direct access to, connecting the stimulus to a reaction. If our psychologist persists in their animosity towards theory, and fully satisfies their ambitions through the production of observational protocols, or, eventually, in abridged descriptions of them (so-called empirical generalizations), they are freed from the difficulties caused by the influence of the mysterious black box of individualism on the results of the experiment, with the help of the secretive 'IV' (intervening variable), which acknowledges only a quantitative dimension of existence. The re-zoning of this IV onto the subject of nature is not so different from the resigned claims of Melvin H. Marx: 'All behavior must be, of course, mediated through a certain type of psychological function; ignoring this fact is fully justified, but this does not negate the fact that some kind of process or mechanism lies behind the Intervening Variable. The important thing is that none of them has been defined; examinations of this problem are dominated by the tendency to think about IV in categories of 'some kind of process, which is necessary to define the relationship S–R.'[4] These psychologists see the mysterious 'intervening variable' as a necessary evil, as a palliative placed on resistant material, far distant from the ideal that would make a non-theoretical paradise possible. If only – as Kenneth W. Spence expressed it in his own time – together with the systematic change in the environmental conditions of X,

> we found a simple function connecting the values selected by X with the corresponding values R – we would not have a problem, because we could precisely describe the principle connecting them. Unfortunately, however, things rarely appear so straightforward, particularly in psychology. After repeated presentations of conditions $X_1$ it is highly likely that the reaction will take on a different intensity, or that it will not be possible to graph the relationship between two sets of experimental values. At this very point we introduce hypothetical constructions and say that the reacting variables are determined in part by $X_1$ and in part by some additional factor, or additional factors $I_a$, $I_b$ ..., $R = f(X_1, I_a, I_{b...})$.[5]

It is hard to dispel the impression that the 'problem' Spence describes is not so much the theoretical model as it is the maximally sparing way of describing the givens of experience, which has a limited predictive power. Other psychologists – who take into consideration that, in the case of individuality, they are dealing not so much with an object passively 'imprinting' external pressures as with, at the very least, a self-organizing machine – are distrustful of the possibility of devising a method for describing the mechanism of this machine without using a model. That is why they yearn to go beyond the level of 'empirical

generalizations', which does not really go beyond the sphere of possibilities already contained in the collection of protocols, to achieve
the level of a theoretical construction that would illuminate new perspectives for understanding the object and acting upon it. Thus far,
the models constructed by these psychologists belong in one of two
broad categories: animistic models and neurophysiological ones.

Let us return to the study of culture. Our image presents, alongside
the black box of the psychologist, also the black box of the researcher
of culture. It is the region between 'r' and 's'. That which we call
culture – without regard to the varying definitions that we encounter
in the literature – is located in this very sphere. The fact that the
behaviour of individual A is a stimulus for individual B – and a
stimulus that cannot be reduced to its physical shape, but refers to
the meaning encoded in a code comprehensible to both partners, and
conventional – is precisely a basic cultural fact, an 'atom' of the field
of inquiry of the researcher of culture. Thus, both for the psychologist, as for the researcher of culture, the point of departure is human
behaviour. But the researcher of culture begins where the psychologist
ends, and ends where the psychologist begins.

The empirical point of departure for the researcher of culture is
the oft-observed fact that, within the framework of a particular group,
the behaviour of one individual elicits specific behaviours of another,
and the form of these elicited behaviours is not dependent on the
physical form of the behaviours that elicit them, but is invariant in
regards to certain common elements connected to various behaviours
that elicit them, with varying physical characteristics. These shared
elements are not of a physical nature: they are the meaning of the
behaviours, a meaning that can be expressed via various, mutually
interchangeable codes: by the linguistic code, a code of gestures, of
clothing, of the organization of space, tone of voice, etc. Untangling
these mutual semantic elements can be done by using Mill's Rules of
Reasoning in a purely experiential way. We are still in the realm of
experimental protocols. Our researcher of culture is still an ethnographer, aspiring to produce empirical generalizations.

The anthropologist becomes a researcher of culture only when they
progress to the level of constructing models that reproduce the internal
structure of the system – which is not straightforwardly given, or
accessible to sensory experience – thanks to which the behaviour of
A becomes that which evokes the behaviour of B, and the behaviour
of B, that which is evoked. She or he thus models the system of meanings and the mechanism of meaning-making, and, by doing so, constructs the system of culture. This system is to individual interactions
as language is to individual speech acts, and the tonal structure to

individual melodies. It is completely encompassed by that which Ferdinand de Saussure said once about the relationship of language, one of the subcodes of culture, to its empirical symptoms – speech:

> What, then, is linguistic structure? It is not, in our opinion, simply the same thing as language. Linguistic structure is only one part of language, even though it is an essential part. The structure of a language is a social product of our language faculty. At the same time, it is also a body of necessary conventions adopted by society to enable members of society to use their language faculty. Language in its entirety has many different and disparate aspects. It lies astride the boundaries separating various domains. It is at the same time physical, physiological and psychological. It belongs both to the individual and to society. No classification of human phenomena provides any single place for it, because language as such has no discernible unity.
>
> A language as a structured system, on the contrary, is both a self-contained whole and a principle of classification. As soon as we give linguistic structure pride of place among the facts of language, we introduce a natural order into an aggregate which lends itself to no other classification.[6]

Does culture, understood this way, objectively exist? It exists in the same sense that language does, or any theoretical construct, that connects 'inputs' and 'outputs' with a realm of facts, identical to the inputs and outputs of a black box that are accessible to the senses. Although not provided directly by experience, it reaches deeper than sensory experience, it penetrates to the 'essence' of the event, allows us to perceive intellectually that which the eyes cannot see – a dynamic structure that explains the movement of events observed in experience. In a similar way, the realm of consciousness that Freud added to the ingredients of individuality rendered clear behaviours seemingly senseless and inexplicable, and the Marxist model of the dialectic between creative energies and the relations of production made comprehensible the play of mass interests and antagonisms.

Every anthropologist, probably, strives towards theoretical models of culture understood this way, though they strive in different, often mutually conflicting, ways. Because, too, a collection of axioms does not in and of itself determine all the properties of the constructed model. The description of the model cannot be distilled by counting out empirically attainable parameters, defining their limits – if it could, we would be dealing with empirical generalization, and not a theoretical model. Within the limits determined by the parameters set by experiments (collections of inputs and outputs), one can build various models, and referring to empirical facts is not a sufficient (though it is a necessary) criterion for the choice between them. There must, therefore, be additional criteria, skilfully chosen from deliberations on the subject – but also, after exhausting the options, it may turn out that more than one model is left on the battlefield.

I would like, in the following study, to propose not so much models, which ought to be the result of theoretical study, as paths leading to the eventual construction of such models. The propositions contained here emerge from the concept of theory discussed above – its relationship to the givens of experience and its role in research. They also emerge from the possibilities that are opened up as a result of looking at culture from a semiotic point of view (see the article 'Sign, structure, culture'). In my view, taking on this perspective (not necessarily as the only possible one, but as one possible one) also indicates a plan of research, by pointing to problems that anthropologists have, until recently, not taken on to a large degree. It is these kinds of problems that I am talking about. That is why I omit, in the following discussion, the current of research that found its fullest expression in the work of Lévi-Strauss, and in Polish scholarship was most thoroughly, and with great erudition, presented by Professor Żółkiewski.[7] This current of research, insofar as I understand its potential correctly, is most powerfully applied to building models that are generated by the enduring accounts documenting the process of thought, from 'texts'; it is thus most attractive to scholars of literature, art theorists, everyone who works with the products or correlates of spiritual culture. This current did not, it seems, develop in the direction that was signalled in the early works of Lévi-Strauss, primarily in his phenomenal analysis of the elementary structures of kinship, with time turning more attention to the application of the structuralist method to traditional Diltheyesque problems. In the following reflections, I am more interested in the new – or nearly new – problems that emerge when we strive to construct theoretical models on the basis of fundamental acts of cooperation, accepted as the 'black box' of the anthropologist. But, even limiting our studies in this way, we cannot be sure that the paths indicated will exhaust all possible approaches. Delineating them is rather an illustration of the generative potential of these premises than an inventory of their actual potential.

## ON THE POSSIBILITY OF A GENERAL THEORY OF SYMBOLIC BEHAVIOUR

It is surprising how rarely efforts are undertaken in the humanities to construct a general theory of symbolic behaviour (or of cooperation mediated through symbols), and thus a theory encompassing into one whole the verbal and non-linguistic 'subcodes' of a semiotically considered culture. Already, in 1908, W. B. Pillsbury was writing that: 'We come to the conclusion that "meaning" encompasses practically everything. We see meaning, when we look; we think meaning, when we think; we express our progress in terms of meaning, when we act; as it seems, we do not acknowledge anything except meaning.'[8] Fifty years later, Kenneth L. Pike also asserted that – aside from his own – 'I am acquainted with no other major attempt to show how verbal and nonverbal culture could be integrated into a single theory.'[9] But the assertion that language is merely one of the subcodes – even if the most communicatively specialized one, and therefore the most semiotically perfected one, but nonetheless, merely one of the subcodes that humans use to express culturally agreed upon meanings to each other – no anthropologist denies this assertion. At the same time, however, in the course of the last few decades, there have been several major steps in the direction of a theory of language, when in the research on other, non-linguistic subcodes we continue to find ourselves essentially at the level of describing the basics of empirical experience.

The suspicion arises that behind the growing chasm between the developments of the theories of a linguistic subcode and the stasis of theoretical studies on other subcodes lie deeper causes than a standard dislike or unconsciousness of non-linguistic subsystems of symbolic culture among researchers. Perhaps we should seek the causes in the fundamental inapplicability of theoretical methods developed in linguistics to other subcodes of culture? Perhaps this fundamental inapplicability of theoretical methods stems from the particularities of the physical nature of acoustic language? This would be an incredibly crucial cause, given that the infamous methods of structural linguistics, at least up to the moment when Chomsky formulated his 'generative grammar', developed, and in many circles continue to develop, under the auspices of analysing this very structure of the linguistic code. At first glance, it seems that nonverbal behaviours are much less regular than speech, and that extracting regular structure comparable to those found in the phonology of Roman Jakobson, is in their case quite difficult, if not fundamentally impossible. Simply transferring methodological insights from structural linguistics onto other varieties of symbolic behaviours, seeking out corollaries to 'morphemes', 'phonemes', and 'differends' in the world of gestures or ceremonies, does not seem attractive to many researchers. Today perhaps more so than twenty-some years ago. If, among the Prague circle, the linguistic problem of the relationship between language and the non-linguistic sphere of social reality was practically central for the structuralists, and their sensitivity to the general cultural context of the phenomena they examined was truly great, then at the level of the glossematics of Hjelmslev we find a postulate of the absolute isolation of 'linguistic reality' from all other spheres of social reality, leading to the logical dead-end of Saussure's postulate of 'studying language on its own grounds'. We come away with the impression that the more refined structural methods become in terms of understanding the properties of language – understood as a singular, closed system – the less applicable its methods become for building models of other cultural subcodes. However tempting it is to find analogies in linguistics, they must be resisted, if one does not wish to succumb to amusing, but not fruitful, manipulations, just as susceptible to disappointment as those that attended former enthusiasms in the humanities for physicalistic imitations. The hopes that are so popular today, for integrating humanities with the structural methods developed by linguists, seem to be suitable for application only in a very limited sense: that very general aspects of this kind of thinking proper to structural linguistics will be accepted, but these are features that pertain more to 'structure' than to 'linguistics'. Such extremely general features are contained, for example, in the following assertion by E. Benveniste:

> The basic principle [of structuralism – ZB] is the assertion that language creates a system, whose parts are connected by relationships of coherence and dependence. This system organizes elements, which are articulated signs, mutually differing and dividing from each other. Structuralist theory claims that the system is primary to these elements, and it arrives at the structure of the system through the relationship between the elements, both in patterns of speech and in formal paradigms.[10]

This sentence contains enough postulates to express a common direction of theoretical pursuits in the area of various subcodes of symbolic culture, thus spurring hope for integration, but there are also sufficiently few of these postulates here to avoid hampering efforts aimed at devising particular methods that are especially suited to the properties of particular subcodes.

Thus, the 'fundamental principle' of structuralism leads to the following postulates: (a) we must strive to build a theory for constructing a consistent system of dependencies; (b) the meaning of every element of the system is indicated by the position that it occupies in the system; (c) the fundamental fact that we must begin with is the empirical role that these elements can play in actual events (cooperative acts); but these roles are also indicated by the positions these elements occupy in 'linear' and 'transversal' cross-sections of these events. Practically, if we want to relate these postulates to non-linguistic forms of transmitting information, the first difficulty to be conquered is solving two problems that are far from clear: (1) what ought to be considered an 'element' of the non-linguistic subcode?; or (2) what is the nature of the relationships that comprise the structure of this subcode? These two questions constitute a programme for the initial phase of research, which could eventually lead to a general theory of symbolic cooperation.

One possible answer to these two questions can be found in the work of the aforementioned Kenneth L. Pike. In his research, the appeal of linguistic analogies was quite strong. The author admittedly goes so far in searching for analogues to phonemes or differends in human behaviour that we could say that he does not go below the level of 'morphemes' – he remains more on the level of structural semantics than of phonology. He himself asserts that he wishes to bypass, at least in the first phases of developing his theory, the problem presenting the greatest difficulty – namely, deciding on the 'smallest elementary elements' of a non-linguistic informational subcode.

Pike takes, as a point of departure for his theory, an observation of great importance: that there exist contradictions between the fact that 'a behavior event is often a physical continuum with no gaps in which the movement is stopped' and the fact that 'human beings react to their own behavior and to that of other individuals as if it were segmented into discrete chunks'.[11] From the physical perspective, human behaviours have a 'wave-like' nature, but from a semiotic perspective they have a corpuscular nature. From this perspective, non-linguistic acts are not fundamentally different from linguistic acts. Every person knows well from their own experience that, when they want to understand something said in a language they don't know, the greatest difficulty they face is separating an incomprehensible stream of speech into individual words. Pike assumes that these culturally determined meanings of particular, physically inseparable fragments of behaviour allow the receiver to distinguish between them, just as understanding language is the pre-condition of differentiating particular words within a stream of speech. If language, in its dual, wave-particle nature does not present an obstacle, when its individual elements must be extracted, it also should not put off the cultural researcher who strives to imitate the methods of linguists.

Having arrived at this conclusion, Pike develops the linguistic analogies further. As we know, for linguists, any element that can be replaced by another one in the space that it occupies in a linear statement, sentence, or word, without changing the entire structure, can be treated as an individual element of that level. Such an element, along with others which can replace it in this role, create a class defined by its identical linguistic function. Pike then carries this methodological assumption over to studies in non-linguistic activities. Similarly to the way that the fluid movements of a tennis player are indistinguishable to a layperson, but to a specialist can be easily perceived as forehands, backhands, lobs, volleys, etc., and with similar ease divided into classes, where they are alternatives, mutually replaceable – so, in all other repeatable, institutionalized forms of behaviour, the researcher of culture can finally distinguish 'positions', or those places where various alternative elements can be inserted, and 'classes', or collections of these alternative elements that can be slotted into those spaces. These 'positions-classes', as Pike calls them, would be the elements taken as individual components within the framework of the analysis of symbolic behaviours, and from them one could construct systems. The structure of these systems would create, as we can and should deduce, relationships similar to those studied by linguistics – and thus, syntactical schemes, linear relationships (syntagmatic), and transverse or class ones (paradigmatic).

I have presented Pike's extensive theory in a merciless and unfairly abridged version. It is difficult to dispute the generative nature of this research. Indeed, it opens up an extremely broad programme for studying meaningful human behaviours, which could be technically and materially quite attractive. This brings to mind the possibility of the widespread use of a technique, developed in its own time – admittedly for other research needs – by the enthusiasts of Taylor's version of 'principles of scientific management'. It is hard to determine in advance how such studies would enrich our knowledge of humankind.

It is necessary, however, to state clearly, so as to avoid misunderstanding, that what Pike is essentially proposing is not so much a theory of culture corresponding to an actually accepted structuralist theory of language, as a way of presenting non-linguistic behaviour that is similar to the way that contemporary structuralists perceive language: it is a proposition to codify 'language' on the basis of non-linguistic behaviours. But 'language' is understood here not in terms of its function, as a tool of information, but exclusively as a structure constructed in a certain way. This certain way is precisely what fascinates Pike. One has the impression that all of his efforts have been undertaken with the goal of demonstrating that one can apply the same methods to other subcodes. Pike does not admit the thought that the same information functions can be performed by different subcodes in various ways; that the principle of construction of the structure of language might be only one of many ways of solving the problem of the task of structuring social reality and information; that what connects the various subcodes of symbolic culture might be a shared pool of information that they serve to transmit, and not a shared principle of construction. But these are all doubts that cannot be resolved a priori. Perhaps the studies proposed by the ideas in Pike's theories will ultimately show us that the path they set out is not a dead end.

Another proposition – more original, because less tethered to linguistic analogies – is to be found in a very interesting work by S. F. Nadel.[12] Nadel describes his work as a theory of social structure. However, he also says that 'people belong to a society in virtue of rules under which they stand and which impose on them regular, determinate ways of acting towards and in regard to one another', and, if he also says that A r B – or the sentence 'A stands in a particular relationship r to B – is equivalent to the statement A (a, b, c…n) : B, where a, b, c,…n are 'modes of behaviour',[13] then, accordingly with the distinctions that I drew in *Culture and Society*, I believe that the real subject of his investigations is the structure of culture as a system, and not social structure (by this concept, I refer not to the models of behaviour, but to the conditions for realizing these models – conditions defined by the system of dependencies that result from the production, distribution, and consumption of goods).

I cannot describe Nadel's entire, expansive theory; I want only to draw attention to its basic principles of construction, to the direction of its investigations, which offers a genuine alternative to the direction proposed by Pike. For Nadal, the elementary element of the structure of the cultural system is not an element of action, but a physical element (albeit one that is differentiated not by a physical, but by a semantic, principle), a role. A role is a collection of features of a given individual, features inherited or imposed by fate or acquired as a result of the individual's own efforts; what is most important in the characteristics of this collection of features is its property of being connected to an acknowledged, culturally prescribed way of behaving towards other people in their contacts with the person who plays that role. Nadel seeks, on the level of experience, certain unchanging forms of behaviour, which we could call models; from the variety of models, he draws conclusions about the variety of roles accepted in the framework of a given cultural system. On the level of construction, however, he seeks dynamic, mutually determining relationships between roles. A very sympathetic feature of Nadel's theory is this dynamic of roles, arising from its processual nature. Nadel writes:

the option made by an actor in the course of his role performance, which determined the subsequent development of the role, is likely to be itself determined by the previous responses he encountered on the part of his co-actors. Thus we must accept something in the nature of a *mutual steering process* whereby the performance of one role guides or conditions the performance of another [...] the roles linked in the steering process *posit* or *implicate* one another, for if $P_1 \square (a...1/s)$ there must be a $P_2$ such that $P_2 \square (1/a...s)$; $P_1 \square P_2$ and *vice versa*.[14]

Nadel thus extrapolates, from the premise that the information function contained in human behaviour is based on the structuring of the situation of cooperation, that this structuring takes place in the process of the cooperation of two or more partners. With such a schema, we can assume that the cultural system, the sought-after theoretical model, is precisely this kind of system of mutually relativized roles in a practical cooperation that sets out the 'meaning' of each role and simultaneously sanctions a given sequence in their activities. The behaviour of individual A becomes a signal indicating the cultural identity of A and designed to elicit the appropriate behaviour in response from individual B – the behaviour that the cultural system common to A and B has rendered the most likely. In the framework of a given shared culture, a finite selection of roles that is accepted by this culture is chosen from a seemingly infinite universe of abstract possibilities and an equally finite selection of practically possible situations. Actual acts of cooperation further reduce this catalogue of possible situations, finally liquidating the indeterminacy of a situation.

Nadel does not take lightly the problem of the ways in which these roles are constructed. From the perspective of one, individually taken feature, humans belong to a certain class of individuals (class in the logical sense), connected simply by the fact of possessing these features. A role is something more complicated – one of these aforementioned points of interpenetration of classes, which are designated as important by a cultural system, and to which this cultural system assigns particular meanings and a specific model of behaviour. A recurring problem for research is to decide which of the abstractly possible points of interprenetration of the classes are 'perceived' by a given culture and granted a special function, and which are dismissed, not distinguished by any particular cultural institution. It is also an interesting research problem to recreate the phylo- and ontogenetic dynamic of these choices made by culture. But within culture there may also be combinations that are even more complicated than roles: an accumulation or 'personal unions' of roles. In this field, culture also makes a choice, sanctioning one connection of roles but rejecting others. But it is not these aspects of the 'internal construction' of the elements of a cultural system that seem to be the most important of those inspired by Nadel's theory. It is rather the informational-controlling view of the structure of the cultural system that makes Nadel's theory the most modern and in accordance with the tradition of the development of research, as opposed to the seemingly more refined propositions of Pike, referring to a method that its French adherents succeeded in making the fashion of intellectual salons.[15]

## THE PROBLEM OF A SYNCHRONIC ANALYSIS OF THE 'CULTURAL FIELD'

One of the possible models of a system of culture is as a structure, constructed as a system of oppositions and mutually complementary roles. This model would remain in a relationship to the model of social structure, understood as a system of dependencies between members of the population, which, because of their relative isolation and autonomy, could be seen as a social totality. But this is not the only way of organizing roles in a structural model. Another way, equally important to research, is as a 'spatial' organization. This requires introducing the concept of a 'cultural field'.

All space is organized by relationships of distance. Cultural space is organized by relationships of cultural or informational difference. At the heart of every society, the intensity, the informational saturation, of contact between every individual and other individuals belonging to the same collective is unequal. Some individuals are joined to every 'ego' by vital, comprehensive, and multi-functional ties, whereas the 'ego' only interacts with certain others because of clearly defined, temporary – even if important – goals; with certain others, there is no expectations of satisfying any of its essential needs – it realizes in a general way that they exist, but here the informational contact ends. This typological differentiation of cultural and information contact constitutes around each individual their own 'cultural field', which could be represented graphically as a series of concentric circles around this individual (it does not need to be added that the size of these circles would not express either physical distance or what is called 'social' distance – namely, the distance between their positions within the social hierarchy). These circles would also differ from each other in the degree of 'informational content' – in other words, with how far the culturally determined models for reducing the indeterminacy of a situation that arises from the encounter between the 'ego' and anyone from one of these circles extends. Measuring this reduction (or measuring the content of information contained in these models), one could – *in principio* – rather precisely define the boundaries of these circles.

The number of circles that we will divide the cultural field into is of course a function of our decision as to the typology of the models. For reasons that we need to clarify, it seems that the goal is the differentiation of three elementary circles: a central circle of individual patterns ($K_o$), a central circle of patterns of roles ($K_r$), and an external circle of categorical patterns ($K_k$).

The individual patterns possess, relatively speaking, the greatest capacity for information; in limit cases, this capacity reaches its essentially theoretical limit, eliminating without remainder certain abstractly possible behaviours for the sake of other, actual ones, and guaranteeing complete predictability of a sequence of behaviours. The individual patterns regulate cooperation in a small environment, composed of intimate connections, internal contact, in situations that are maximally diverse, presenting an occasion for various behaviours with different goals. This set of circumstances demands from the pattern that is intended to serve such an environment that it be maximally multisided, exhausting all eventualities, and at the same time transparently constructed, indicating a narrow and not-conflicting hierarchy of goals, means, and norms of behaviour. If the members of this small collective adhere to an equal degree to an identical individual pattern, their cooperation is maximally organized – certain variants of behaviour become maximally unlikely; for this reason, people perceive the situations contained within $K_o$ as those of maximum comfort; having the sense – which is, after all, confirmed – that their behaviour $Z_1$ will evoke the expected behaviour $Z_2$ from their partner, they perceive the situation as being completely subject to their will and control. They dominate it, they can modify it at will, they know what they are supposed to do in order to produce the transition to the state that they aspire to. This feature of $K_o$ explains most fully the fact, repeatedly confirmed in research, that the more intimate a group, the more emotionally safe people feel in it, the more important the role it plays in life as an antidote for a mysterious, highly contingent, and unpredictable world resistant to human will.

The informational capacity of the patterns of roles is much smaller. If this pattern eliminates indeterminacy, it is only in a strictly defined collection of situations, generally driven by some specific goal, encompassing activities subordinated to a specific need. A situation regulated by this pattern is unequivocal in meaning for the partners only to the extent that both do not undertake activities unconnected to the above goal or indifferent to the above need. In $K_r$ there is much less freedom to manoeuvre than there is in $K_o$. The partners must be on guard to not 'break character' – if they do, they will find themselves face-to-face in a culturally unregulated situation, therefore an unpredictable one, in which the form of behaviour $Z_2$, elicited by behaviour $Z_1$, is unknown. Similarly, when it comes to the behaviour of the partner, only a very specific fragment of the repertoire of his behaviour, the only one that is contained within the role, has for our 'ego' semiotic value – is a comprehensible cultural code, is a transparent invitation to clearly delineated activities. If the partner ventures beyond this repertoire – we are helpless and lost. The command to 'take care of business and leave', plastered on the walls of companies, is not only intended to protect the official's time.

The circle $K_r$ has another important feature, which becomes visible when it is confronted with $K_k$. The pattern of roles, which informationally defines this circle, is in relation to the 'ego'. This means that identifying any individual from $K_r$ as fulfilling role r automatically brings about the entry of the 'ego' into the role of 1/r – and vice versa. This can be formulated in another way: the individual enters into the role of r, if the 'ego' adapts to the pattern assigned to the role of 1/r. The relationships binding the 'ego' to the individuals belonging to $K_r$ are a collection of complementary roles: of the type 'passenger–conductor', 'client–salesman', 'petitioner–official', 'director–subordinate'. Without taking into account everything that we know about extra-cultural mechanisms that assign roles of this type, in each concrete situation both of the partners has some degree of freedom in manipulating it. It is this fact that gives its activities a form in accordance with the pattern ascribed to role r, setting into motion a chain of behaviours, causing the positioning of the partner in the role of 1/r. The director can essentially expect that the partner will assume the role of subordinate only if his own behaviour is in accordance with the role of director. Obviously, the converse thesis is less obvious. Extra-cultural views intervene here, located in the circle of the distribution of goods and access to them, delineating the actual influence of the partners. We could be tempted to classify different roles according to the degree of freedom of manipulating the situation that the people involved have. But some degree of freedom is possessed by the participant in any role, and in any role the 'ego' perceives $K_r$ as a partially manipulable circle, subject to their structuring efforts, though to a lesser degree than $K_o$.

The category patterns have the smallest capacity for information, relatively speaking. I am not even sure if it makes sense to use the term 'pattern' in this context, because it is associated with prescribed forms of behaviour. A category pattern does not offer any indicators as to the desired behaviour of the 'ego', and also does not have a lot to say about which of the behaviours of the partner are most likely. It merely allows for this or that individual to be placed on the cognitive map of the human world, included within a particular category of the type 'millionaire', 'capitalist', 'worker', 'Jew'. Sometimes it connects a given category to a murky stereotype, projecting onto the individual some of the positions taken by the 'ego' towards people from that category, but leading to the emergence of enduring patterns of behaviour only in cases where the 'ego' enters into more lively and regular contacts with this person, which generally leads to this person passing from sphere $K_k$ to $K_r$, or even $K_o$. In general, however, people belong to $K_k$ insofar as they exist on the margins of the 'ego's' awareness, not ingratiating themselves into his intimate life, or into activities associated with the satisfaction of particular needs. An extremely important feature of categories is that they are not fundamentally relational to the 'ego'. They appear to our 'ego' as having an objective existence, whose qualitative definition is not dependent on his will or behaviour. Their qualitative distinction does not stem from their own nature, like the distinctiveness of stone or wood, and it can be subject at most to a researcher's classification, but not creative structuring. The information contained within the category patterns has thus a character that is maximally passive, derivative; it allows the subject to be identified and serialized – but it says nothing, or almost nothing, about how to actively give it the form it seeks.

Summarizing the above reflections, we can assert that, in the process of crossing from $K_o$ through $K_r$ to $K_k$, we observe a progressive diminution of the active, structuring element of information contained in the patterns, and the increase of a passive, derivative element. This is not, however, the only variable that changes its value in linear fashion as it moves from internal to external circles of the cultural field.

Let us point out, for example, that, proportionally to the increasing 'passivity' of the model, its 'rigidity' increases: the slimmer the portion of the situation extracted by the pattern from the mysterious depths of indeterminacy, the more narrow the portion of terrain that the pattern controls, that the 'ego' can rely on in seeking out its own mode of being; the more strict and absolute the demands of the pattern, the more narrow the scale of acceptable oscillations, the more modest the resources of accepted variation on the subject prescribed by the model 'phoneme' of behaviour. The 'ego' is able to recognize the same individual pattern in highly various, extremely individualized forms of behaviour; it is able to impose this pattern on partners using extremely diverse repertoires of their own alternative behaviours. The amount of freedom contracts greatly in the case of roles, in order to be at the bare minimum and not leave any room for individualization in the categories. That is why, when the effort to avoid error in the choice of a pattern is for some reason particularly important (for example, in the army), reason dictates that it not be dependent on individual abilities to eliminate the noise produced by individual traits or characteristics, and that it use clear identifying signs that do not leave any doubt as to the nature of the category or role. The further from the centre of the cultural field, the lower the tolerance of the patterns for the noise from particular individualizations.

To this cause, too, we should probably ascribe another aspect that emerges in relation to the degree of movement towards the edges of the cultural field: the increase in formality demanded of the 'ego' by the patterns. The further from the centre, the more etiquette – the more modest the repertoire of culturally regulated behaviours, but each of them is minutely defined, and in great detail.

Distinguishing three concrentric circles at the centre of the cultural field seems to be heuristically useful precisely because it illuminates the truths presented here. They are the very aspects that constitute the distinction between the spheres, variables used to construct the model of the field (as long as we do not forget that this model, like all models, is an abstraction, an approximation, an assemblage of selected features of 'reality'; the borders between the circles are essentially fluid, and individuals constantly move across them from either side, sometimes – because of different aspects of the ties linking them to the 'ego' – they can exist on both sides at once). But once the model has been constructed, we can be tempted into the empirical claim of a correlation between particular circles and the distribution of various other essential features of the cultural system. It brings out, for instance, the relationship between the circles distinguished here and the dissemination of positions that are allowable, market-related, and neutral – perhaps the expectations tying the 'ego' to $K_o$ support themselves with a generalized principle of reciprocity; and the same as what is expected in $K_r$ – only with a much weaker sense of reciprocity. It would be interesting to study the interference of different mechanisms of distribution of respect in particular circles within the field. Finally, a subject that seems to be the most essential for further research is the relationship between cultural and social regulation of cooperation in particular circles. It seems that in $K_o$ the regulation of practical behaviours (not only positions and stimuli) has an almost entirely cultural-informational character; but the farther from the centre of the field you travel, the greater the role that is played in the shaping of actual behaviours by relationships that go beyond an individual's awareness and energies. Along with this, the likelihood rises of experiencing contradictions between 'what should be' and 'what is', a pattern and the practical possibility of its realization. Nevertheless, this thesis requires much more detail and discussion.

## RESEARCH PROBLEMS IN THE PHYLOGENESIS OF MODELS

Up to now, we have been interested in a synchronic cross-section of the cultural field. Hence the static character of the image under discussion. But the structuring of the cultural field is not nearly as inert as it may appear. It is internally dynamic by its own nature: the circles influence each other, the way that culture inhabits one circle is not independent of the way that cultural patterns are distinguished within another one, and the way in which meaningful oppositions are set up there. The guarantee that different cultural circles will act upon one another is the fact that the ego is the link between them, that they all lead to the ego and are in some way constituted by the ego.

At this moment, we will need to concern ourselves with this kind of dynamic balancing of a synchronically cross-sectioned system. We will be interested in the diachronics of the cultural field in the first of its two aspects – the phylogenetic. We will be particularly interested in the question of whether and how, on the basis of a synchronic look at the cultural field, we can reconstruct its 'species' history (this means the history of the schema of the field, which a given system imposes on all of its participants, leaving them freedom only to slot other people into particular spheres). And how can we, if the various givens are co-existing or known from various historical schemas of the cultural field, present them as stages in a particular sequence of development?

Marx's postulate linking historical and logical methods is well known – the creation of such chains of development, as would fulfil both a historical dictate of correct chronology, and a logical one of the emergence of successive phases from previous ones. This postulate expresses a genuine ideal of all efforts that are not neutral regarding the dimension of time. Every researcher, however, who has tried to construct any kind of evolutionary sequence, knows very well how difficult it is to realize this ideal. The difficulty stems both from the fact of diffusion – the social contacts between societies that are never truly isolated from each other – and from the fact of 'genetic currents', which means that, insofar as these societies are indeed relatively isolated, incessantly accumulating their own cultural and structural-social mutations, they never repeat those mutations that took place in other times in other societies in all their essential details. Under these conditions, 'historical priority' does not have to be the same as 'logical priority' – and vice versa. We generally know, however, how these practical difficulties can be resolved. It would be possible to recover historical and logical value for one and the same sequence simultaneously, if it were constructed with a knowledge of the mechanisms that transformed form $F_1$ into form $F_2$. And if this were known to enough of an extent that it could be stated with certainty that, although it is not definite that the existence of form $F_1$ means that form $F_2$ must appear, be it sooner or later, it is known that, if form $F_s$ exists, then it must be the case that in some earlier phase, form $F_1$ existed as well. If, furthermore, the knowledge of this mechanism allows us to present forms $F_2$, $F_3 \ldots F_n$ as equally possible alternatives that are – however mutually exclusive at the moment of their appearance – developmental mutations of an original $F_1$, then we can resolve the earlier question connected to it about the eventual co-stadial nature of the systems containing the forms $F_2$, $F_3 \ldots F_n$.

The practical means of realizing these theoretical postulates can again be found in the resources offered by structural linguistics, or rather in the specific feedback between the achievements of the synchronic theory of language and the ways that historical linguistics approaches its task.

Since the days of Baudouin de Courtenay, it has been asserted in historical linguistics, on the basis of collected comparative material, that there are languages in which there appear the set of sounds $Z_1$ and the set $Z_2$, and languages in which there are only sounds from $Z_1$, but there are no languages in which there are the sounds from set $Z_2$, but not the set $Z_1$. On the basis of this claim, it has been assumed that the sounds from set $Z_2$ emerged in the process of the evolution of sounds from set $Z_1$. Discovering the mechanism of this emergence would provide a logical argument for the historical primacy of languages equipped with only the set $Z_1$.

Roman Jakobson[16] discussed this idea recently. He indicated that we know nothing of the existence of languages that possess aspirated consonants, but not unaspirated ones. Apparently, there are no languages with aspirated consonants, but without unaspirated; there are no languages with soft consonants without the corresponding hard ones, etc. This validates the hypothesis that the forms b, d, and g are later than p, t, k; the forms ph, th, kh are later than p, t, k; the forms b', d', g' later than the forms b, d, g. What is more, we can also formulate the hypothesis that all of these later forms emerged from the corresponding earlier ones. The existence of the earlier forms does not need to imply that, with the course of time, the later forms will also appear, but the existence of the later forms is sufficient basis to conclude that at some stage the earlier forms were present, even if they later vanished.

To confirm the above hypotheses, we need to discover the mechanism for the aforementioned transformations, based on the materially accessible slice of the history of language. If this can be done, it will be possible to recover effects that could not be overestimated in the form of a collection of two criteria frequently set in opposition in the typology of languages: the historical and the logical. The distance between these two perspectives is evidenced by Tadeusz Milewski's hypothesis that it is possible to discern a collection of phonemes (p, t, k, i, u, a, m, n, s, r, l)[17] that, appearing in all languages of the world, serve as a fundamental point of departure for all languages, starting from the point – we could say – that different languages of relatively isolated human collectives, using the same mechanisms of transformation, selected different subsets from a repertoire of alternative mutations that were theoretically possible.

We find a very interesting proposition describing the sought-after mechanism in the work of W. W. Martinov.[18] Martinov presents alternative ways that certain neighbouring forms 'roll into' derivate forms. For example, *dio*, after lengthy usage, can produce, as it did in Russian, a soft *d* (as in the word *d'orn*), or, as it did in German, a soft *o* (as in the word *dörren*). Martinov describes his hypothesis in detail, not on the basis of the translation of phonemes (he only uses phonemes to exemplify his already-developed theory), but on the basis of signs. We will present an extremely abridged sketch of this theory, referring readers interested in the details to the original.

Every semiotic sentence can be presented symbolically through the pattern SAO (where S – subject of action, A – action, O – object of action). S and O occupy marginal positions in the sentence, A – the central position. Let us take as an example the sentence: 'The train (S) brought (A) letters (O).' We can now narrow the spatial-temporal meaning of the above sentence by supplementing the central position with an indicator, which on the basis of its function we could call a 'temporal feature' or 'actualizer'. We can, for instance, build the sentence: 'The train (S) brought from Warsaw (A) letters (O).' 'Brought from Warsaw', of course, refers to a class of actions that is far narrower than those represented by 'bringing' in general. But this actualizer can also be shifted to a marginal position; then it will become a 'stable feature', or a modifier that appears in the position of the sign, as can easily be seen if we formulate the sentence: 'The Warsaw train (S) brought (A) letters (O)', or 'The train (S) brought (A) Warsaw's letters (O).' The phrases 'the Warsaw train' or 'Warsaw's letters' are new signs, properly speaking, which in certain conditions can 'roll over' to the extent that their original form will become difficult to discern – as, for instance, in the case of the 'television receiver' (as opposed to the radio receiver): 'television'. From this, it seems that the processes of the emergence of new sentences and processes of creation of new signs are tightly connected to each other and mutually condition each other. Martinov summarizes this with the following claim:

> The process of transformation from actualizer to modifier as a result of transferring it from the central position into a marginal one is simultaneously a process of the creation of a new sign, in that [...] the connection between a sign and its modifier is always potentially a new sign, just as, on the other hand, the connection between a sign with an actualizer is always potentially a new sentence [...] New sentences are born in a process of the constant creation of semiotic sentences. What is needed for the creation of a new sign in the cradle of a semiotic sentence, is that one of the actualizers be repeated enough times.[19]

The reader must be intrigued by the clear convergence of Martinov's studies with the phylogenetic questions about the cultural field laid out at the beginning of the chapter, or, rather, with the generalization of the scheme characterizing the system of culture.

Indeed, we can place particular elements of the sentence schema SAO in the following way: indicators of position (which for particular circles of the cultural field are people, roles, and categories) under marginal positions, inter-personal cooperation in the central position. Then the schema SAO presents itself to us as a general pattern for the cooperation of two individuals – an empirically accessible element of every cultural system. Now, using Martinov's theories about the dynamics of our schema and its mechanism with the appropriate terminological substitutions, we arrive at a theoretical framework for studying the phylogenesis of the cultural system. In order to discover the mechanism leading to the emergence of new positions (roles, categories) from old ones, we need to track the 'appearance' of a univocal initial pattern, tied to the increasing complexity, and resulting fusion of the derivatives, modified in different ways, for various cooperative contexts. We can expect that then, instead of one situation of SAO, we will come to the creation of two situations differentiated within culture: $SA_1O \rightarrow SA_1O_1$ and $SA_2O \rightarrow SA_2O_2$. The 'actualizer' in the pattern contains in embryonic form the 'modifier' position, or potentially new positions. This process can proceed in this way or in the opposite direction: the doubling of one of the marginal positions or the 'splitting off' of derivative positions from one of them invariably leads to the appearance of a new catalogued pattern of behaviour in culture. In this way, we arrive at the conceptual categories and basic elements of a research strategy for the systematic understanding of phenomena that are widely noted – general and simple functions crumbling into increasingly specialized and complex ones, or a corollary process of the similar refinement of roles and categories.

We were mainly seeking a way to recreate the phylogenesis in a reductive process, deducing developmental phases of the schema of the cultural field on the basis of an awareness of an actual synchronic cross-section.

It is in this very task that the propositions worked out in linguistics can be the most beneficial. The methods of structural analysis in semantics, developed by L. Hjelmslev[20] and A. J. Greimas[21] show how, in the meaning of one sign, by searching through all of the oppositions in which it plays a differentiating – i.e. meaning-producing – role, we can arrive at a catalogue of all of the 'semes', or the fundamental elements of meaning, that comprise the meaning of the given sign. Let us recall that we can only discuss the opposition of two meanings in a sensible way if those two meanings refer, from our point of view, to a certain shared level of signification. We can thus assume, that these 'semes' represent the original forms of our sign, or their modifiers. With the assistance of these 'semes', we can recreate the process of their formation by the increasing complexity of the actual schema of the cultural field.

Perhaps an eventual goal of various comparative studies will be the distinction (on the basis of what T. Milewski did with phonemes) of a certain elementary assemblage of cultural 'semes', both the most straightforward ones, because they are not further divisible, and the most fundamental ones. They would be a point of departure for all schemas of the cultural field, developing in various directions, created under the influences of both the endogamously increasing complexity of social functions, and the intricate processes of diffusion of culture and social contacts. It might turn out that this fundamental assemblage will produce three, similarly irreducible semantic fields: (1) older–younger, (2) same-sex–opposite-sex, (3) friend–enemy. Maybe it would seem like this very simple society, constructed from a combination of the most modest of possible assemblages of the semantic axes, could be presented as an arrangement of 'homogeneous' roles, but not simple ones: the accumulation of elements of laws and responsibilities that comprise future roles *in statu nascendi*. It might turn out that broadening the human collective that is connected through the process of the creation and circulation of goods – from groups of a few dozen people encountered among the Shoshone or Semang people, or among even more distant societies – would be one of the most essential developmental catalysts for separating out roles previously accumulated, in this way adding new semantic axes to the construction of cultural systems: the larger the collection of people that the 'ego' must encounter in the process of realizing its life functions, the greater the number of 'semes' it needs in order to orient itself in a situation, to meaningfully eliminate the indeterminacy of all situations that it might find itself in (crises of meaning, destruction of cultural systems, were historically always correlated with moments of a sudden expansion of social horizons, a violent encounter between two or more cultures, that had each, in their own way, been semantically self-sufficient up to that point). Perhaps it would lead to the formulation of some kind of law that would allow us to predict when this separation of the original position and the original model into the later positions and models would take place, and also demonstrate which variables determine this necessity. Probably, the capacity of any role is finite (only then a role must be essentially culturally meaningful, or contain an essential load of information) and, after a certain limit is crossed, there must be a splitting of roles into component parts. I think that the list of research questions and possibilities connected to the problem discussed here has not in the least been exhausted.

I would like to draw attention to one of the proposed uses of the schema suggested by research. I am thinking of the developmental processes of certain social subsystems, in the case of which historical hypotheses can be more easily verified than in the case of global societies. I am thinking in particular about organizations. In most cases, these are comparatively young organisms, often developing in the course of one generation's life, characterized by a relatively short cycle of development. They are thus an excellent object of research of mechanisms of pluralization of positions and patterns; they also serve well as examples for observing 'in action' the highly important phenomenon of 'pushing out' certain positions from the circle of roles into the circle of categories based on when they exceed certain (what?) limits of the subsystem. Perhaps using the theoretical framework proposed here for the examination of the known phenomenon of a chronic tendency of organisms to spread and bud could shed new light on the unusually important process today, which is unfortunately frequently analysed through the framework of theories of bureaucracy and in light of somewhat detectivist philosophies of history.

## RESEARCH PROBLEMS IN THE ONTOGENESIS OF THE 'CULTURAL FIELD'

The difficulties associated with a phylogenetic study of the cultural field pale in comparison to the problems faced by the ontogenetic approach, and this is because of the lack – up to now – of interest in the processes of realizing a general 'cultural facility' in the process of individual development. Of course, developmental psychology possesses tremendous resources; but it is interested, as we know, in the general development of psychic functions in children or the mechanisms of formal processes of learning without taking into account what the concrete object of study is. In both cases, psychologists' studies do not consciously uncover the process of the development of an individual's cultural field in conjunction with innate predispositions of the organism (the 'faculté de culture') and the schema transmitted in the process of upbringing. Anthropologists are very interested in this problem – but usually from the perspective of methods of teaching, educational institutions, the process of apprenticeship. Both because of the massive amount of material assembled in observation by psychologists and the no less impressive wealth of information from anthropologists, we can certainly extract a lot of information for our subject with very little work to reformulate the material contained in the literature. But we want to construct a new body of material that is centred around the questions driving our research, in relation to which the materials collected under somewhat different auspices could serve a supplementary role.

The point is, in brief, to grasp the phases of development shaping the cultural field in individual development. The problem is to some degree analogous to the questions of a child acquiring facility in using language. And, again in linguistics, and similarly in the framework of ontogenetic problems, very promising studies have been carried out linking the 'logical' and historical methods of grasping the problem. The most characteristic of these tendencies is Noam Chomsky's proposition of 'generative grammar'. Chomsky, though in partial opposition to the main tendencies of contemporary structural linguistics, proposes to reconceive the ways of organizing syntactic grammar accepted today in such a way that a new theory of grammar will bring to the fore its dynamic, creative character – demonstrating how sentences are 'generated' by a mixture of 'arbitrary' lexical material in 'arbitrary' frameworks of structural grammar. Realizing this logical method should, according to Chomsky's intentions, connect to the actual process of 'generating' sentences as it happens in the development of a child.

> A general theory of linguistic structure of the sort just outlined would, in this way, provide an account of a hypothetical language-learning device and could thus be regarded as a theoretical model for the intellectual abilities that the child brings to language learning [...] It seems to me that the relative suddenness, uniformity, and universality of

language learning, the bewildering complexity of the resulting skills, and the subtlety and finesse with which they are exercised, all point to the conclusion that a primary and essential factor is the contribution of an organism with highly intricate and specific initial structure.[22]

And, again, we could relate these words, with the appropriate changes in terminology, to the problem of 'learning' culture in general, and the cultural field in particular.

Studies on processes of children's language acquisition are quite advanced. In Polish literature on the subject, it is worth highlighting the work of P. Smoczyński.[23] Soviet researchers have devoted a lot of attention to the subject, and their results were recently summarized quite effectively by A. A. Leontiev.[24] If a non-specialist can express an opinion on the matter, their results suggest that Chomsky's efforts will be successful. It turns out, among other things, that in the process of children learning language, there are clear stages of 'syntagmatic phonetics' and 'syntagmatic grammar' – in other words, stages in which children acquire the structure of words or sentences, although they have not yet mastered the adequate acoustic or lexical material, and they fill the structures they have mastered with random material. Is this a process specific to the process of language acquisition, or a 'built-in' mechanism the organism has for understanding the world in general? I personally don't know which answers to this question are commonly accepted, but I am inclined to the view that juxtaposing studies of language acquisition with the results of efforts to apprehend a general structuralization of the human world as offered by the system of culture would allow us to come to a more precise answer to this question.

Undoubtedly, the emergence of the cultural field, structuring the part of the accessible consciousness of the world that is encompassed by codified patterns of behaviour offered by culture, is an element of a larger process – the emergence of a psychic field in general, and thus of a cognitive structuring of the whole world as it exists for the 'ego', or the consciousness accessible to it. This broader process is the realization of the function of intelligence that, as Jean Piaget writes, is innate in humans – not limited in its possibilities of structuring the world and the self to 'deductive activities and the organization of the mind'.[25] During individual development, this innate ability encounters ready-made offerings of culture. What happens next? Does the process of socialization essentially lead to the passive adaptation of the human organism to the portion of knowledge and habits that are trained into the memory? Is this not a case of human capabilities in an active process of creation, in accordance with nature? Piaget bases his comments on systematic and detailed observation of how the organism accommodating itself to the world is inextricably linked to its assimilation of the world, that these processes have their sensory-motor and psychic aspects, that the driving force of the whole process is spontaneous, 'assumed' as it were in the structure of the organism – that a child from its first moments is a subject generating intelligence, and not an object being shaped by it from the outside.

> In opposition to inorganic beings, which also remain in a state of equilibrium with the world, but do not assimilate their environment, we can say that a living organism assimilates the entire world, simultaneously accommodating itself to it, because all of the movements that characterize its actions and reaction to things are organized into a cycle that is defined both by its own organization and by the nature of external objects. We can thus consider assimilation in the most general sense as the embodiment of a certain reality in this or that cycle or organization. In other words, everything that answers to the organism's needs is material to be assimilated, a need is the expression of an active assimilation as such.

In the case of humans, this function is undertaken, and taken to its greatest heights, by the intellect that other species lack; but it is 'simultaneously a formal organization of concepts, which it uses, and the adaptation of these concepts to reality, taking into account the fact that these processes are mutually inextricable'. In conclusion, 'assimilation comprises, from a functional point of view, an elementary fact from which we can begin analysis, independently of the actual interdependence of mechanisms'.[26] This assimilation is based on the mental embodiment of one subject in another, on the achievement of the isomorphism of the structure of the external world and the organization of the mind of the 'ego'. If biological assimilation and straightforward assimilation are, as Piaget says, egocentric – they lead to a normal inclusion of elements of reality in the organism of the subject – this mental assimilation is 'objectivized': it does not annihilate the subject, but objectivizes it, exteriorizing in the process its own mental structure, in this way achieving the coordination of processes of accommodation and assimilation. This mental process – intellectual assimilation of the world during (or, rather, by) the simultaneous organization (accommodation) of the subject, aiming at the isomorphism of both structures, is the content of the development of individual intelligence; it is certainly also the content of the ontogenetic process of the cultural field. In the second case, what is incredibly important are the circumstances, which Piaget could not take into account, because in the fragment of the text quoted he was examining the emergence of intelligence in the 'presymbolic' phase, or during the period when the child does not yet use language, this crucial transmitter of culture: what is crucial is the existence of a social environment, and, within it, the presence of an offering of culture, which in this decisive stage of socialization mediates between processes of assimilating the world and the self-organization of the object.

The co-functioning of the axes assimilation–accommodation, located in the developing mind of the human individual, with the schema of the cultural field, offered by the environment of maturation, is the sought-after theoretical framework for the analysis of the gradual differentiation of the child's behaviour according to the addressee of the action and the situational character of their own position as determined by context – differentiation connected simultaneously to forming connections between particular behaviours and their social correlates in a lasting way. Entering into this material accessible to experimentation, and making use of the web of ideas proposed here, we can arrive at a theoretical model, presenting the role of the encountered cultural system in organic assimilation–accommodation processes of individual development.

## RESEARCH PROBLEMS IN THE DEVELOPMENT OF CULTURE

We have already mentioned the duality of the relationship between cultural signs and social structure. The relationship has the character of creation–reproduction: signs simultaneously 'structure' the situation of cooperation and make present to the mind its hidden, already determined structure. Particular signs differ in the intensity of this or that function. Particular social arrangements differ in the amount of signs of one or another function. These two circumstances give meaning to the construction of two functional types of ideal cultural signs: signs that create positions ($Z_{pt}$) and signs that derive from positions ($Z_{pp}$).

In this context, 'position' will refer to the space occupied by the individual in the system of social energies, or in the arrangement of inter-personal relationships referred to as the social structure; this space decides the individual's access to various goods, whose creation and distribution is the content of social processes. If, between some social position P, occupied by an individual at moment t, and some collection of signs $Z_1, Z_2, \ldots Z_n$ there exists a relationship

$$P^t \rightarrow (Z_1, Z_2, \ldots Z_n)^{t+} \tag{1}$$

then the collection of signs described will be defined as 'position-derivative'. If, however, the relationship takes the form

$$(Z_1, Z_2, \ldots Z_n)^{t-} \rightarrow P^t \qquad (2)$$

then the collection of signs described will be defined as 'position-creating'. In other words, the ideas discussed can be introduced with the help of the following definition:

$$Z_{pt}{}^{t-} \rightarrow P^t \rightarrow Z_{pp}{}^{t+} \qquad (3)$$

In the case of (1), it is only by occupying the position of P that the usage of the signs semantically linked to this position is possible. The function of these signs depends primarily on informing other human individuals, with whom one is dealing in a given situation, and giving them the choice of behaviours adequate to this fact. With the assistance of the signs $Z_{pp}$, the individual organizes the field of stimuli that operate in this environment (under the condition, of course, that the environment is composed of people understanding the code through which $Z_{pp}$ are expressed). In the case of (2), we are dealing with the opposite situation: it is precisely by acquiring in some way the signs $Z_{pp}$, outfitting oneself in them, that the individual comes to occupy position P. In the process, the individual assumes that acquiring the aforementioned signs and using them is also accessible to individuals who currently do not occupy position P.

The distinction introduced here is to some degree the semiotic correspondent of the distinction known to sociology between 'assigned' and 'achieved' positions. The existence of assigned positions always assumed that there exists a certain collection of signs $Z_{pp}$ that can only be used by people occupying a given position $P_p$. In the collection of dependencies forming the position $P_p$, there also enters among other things the dependency (which can be described as 'private possession of the sign') which does not allow for the usage of signs $Z_{pp}$ by individuals who do not occupy position $P_p$. In a society in which assigned positions predominate, there exists a tendency to encompass all cultural signs in a monopoly of categories. In a class- or caste-based society, or a slave-holding society, or a feudal one, there was a well-known tendency to organize all signs – clothing, household, symbols on armour, etiquette, means of transport – to assigned class–caste positions. The modification of signs that have a position-creating character, accepted only within the limits indicated by position-derivative 'types' – and thus under the condition that they do not cross the borders set out by the position-derivative function of the sign (it is worth recalling here the undeniable connection linking the particularities of the semiotic function of culture in class–caste societies with the medieval understanding of development as 'perfection of type'). Departures from this rule, emerging from the development of market relations, or the 'exchange of signs', was greeted with concern and anger, which found clear expression in this response from Sebastian Petrycy of Pilzno:

> If someone is to build a home, it is to be built beautifully and creatively [...] It should be built according to his position, without climbing higher. The nobleman, if he is wealthy, should build a home larger than the burgher, the voyevode, even larger than the simple nobleman. A King should have an awe-inspiring, powerful castle: powerful for its defense, awe-inspiring in its size, its height, the richness of materials, from cut stone, marble, alabaster, in order to display his mightiness to all, which would inspire respect and fear [...] An excess of appetite is found in the lower orders, in mean people, like the burgher towards the nobleman, or the villager towards the nobleman, the craftsman, the merchant, the tanner – in relation to people from cities, who are more honest. Whereas a miserly person cannot properly assess their wealth: acquiring some small sums, he builds a palace, imagines a bower, builds patios, lays out carpets and hangs expensive paintings – as if he were the greatest, in the city. We cannot praise this, because it is not in accordance with his state, but from the heart, done out of spite, which is an ugly quality.[27]

The correspondence between our differentiation and the dichotomy 'assigned position – achieved position' is not complete, because often positions that count as achieved are equipped with position-derivative signs. Generally speaking, a sign Z is a position-derivative sign of position P, if between Z and P there exists a one-to-one correspondence. Only in this situation does the detection of Z allow us to accept with a probability equal to L, that the individual equipped with this sign will occupy position P. A singular relationship of correspondence is generally achieved by a forced exclusion of individuals not occupying position P from the collection of those who can make use of sign Z. Examples are all uniforms and regalia. You cannot become an officer by acquiring an officer's uniform. However, the sight of an officer's uniform allows us to assume that the person wearing it is certainly an officer. Position-derivative signs are thus excluded from free circulation; among the conditions required for acquiring them is the condition of occupying a specific social space. And that is the true marker of the class of position-derivative signs.

If an indispensable attribute of position-derivative signs as an ideal type is their inaccessibility to people not occupying a particular position in the social structure, this emerges from the fact that, as long as the social structure remains unchanged, particular position-derivative signs can serve their differentiating function, and therefore their information-orienting one, for an endless amount of time. As long as there is a one-to-one correspondence with particular positions, they will not age, they will not 'use up' their sign function. In their semiotic situation, it is not assumed that there will be a need to change them, or replace them with new signs; in other words – there is a lack of semiotic stimuli for the development of culture. Quite the opposite – the semiotic function applies brakes to cultural development, delineating a firm boundary of acceptable innovations. And vice versa: including the condition 'occupying position P′' among those which are necessary to acquire sign Z, while maintaining the semiotic relationship between sign Z and position P, will necessarily lead to the amount of individuals who acquired sign Z quickly outgrowing the capacity of the structural position P. And therefore the sign $Z_{pt}$ will be devalued in its sign function, losing its position-creating power sooner or later; it loses it when it ceases to be a distinction, when it is spread too thin, when the particular indicators of the sign become a norm. In the semiotic–social situating of signs $Z_{pt}$, there are messages about their variability, the endless transformation of their form. The enduring differentiation of social positions is the source of an endless need for differentiating signs; and the widespread accessibility of these signs (widespread in the sense that it is indicated by changing collections, among which there is no variable for 'occupying the very positions that the described signs indicate') means that no sign can serve a distinctive function for very long. In other words, position-creating signs are the fuel for the development of culture.

The widespread division of historical cultures into stagnating and developing can, in the light of the above reflections, be presented as a division into:

a) cultures in which the right to a sign emerges from the right to occupy a social position; or
b) cultures in which the right to a sign is prior to the right to a social position.

We advance the hypothesis that the degree of development of a given cultural system is a function of the relation between this system and the social structure it serves – of whether, within the culture, position-creating signs dominate, or position-derivative ones. Artificial barriers to the movement of cultural elements, imposing a positional monopoly on cultural goods, always leads to cultural stagnation. And, on the contrary, the 'democratization' of cultural goods, and possibly unfettered access to signs, are in themselves a constant stimulus for cultural development (despite those who seek, in tendencies to uniformity that always exist in mass culture, signs of cultural stagnation).

In conditions of the democratization of culture – and only in such conditions – two endlessly conflicting processes take place:

a) absorption of ever-new cultural goods–signs by the 'norms' of mass culture;
b) the creation of ever-new goods–signs taking from 'absorbed' signs the function of differentiating signs.

The result of these processes is a constant 'growth of the level' of mass culture, the cultural 'norm', and the enrichment of the repertoire of accessible cultural signs. The innate tendency of democratic culture is its 'openness', in distinction to cultures in the dominant position, in which there dominates a tendency to a closed system.

The manifestation of this tendency is still one more phenomenon that we can describe as the proliferation of codes. The plenitude of cultural signs exceeds the systemic possibilities of a single code, spawning numerous specialized codes from this main branch, serving for the exchange of information between highly limited groups of people in one particular sphere of their social activities. Because, however, the users of every specialized code, through their social activities, enter into contact with groups using other specialized codes, there generally exists the need for a universal code – something akin to medieval Latin, except democratized – into which information expressed in specialized codes could be translated, thereby providing them with a comparable meaning. Perhaps the impression of 'non-systematicity', of the 'amorphousness' of contemporary culture, which is so often expressed in analyses of the present, stems from the fact that such a universal code essentially does not yet exist. There are efforts, undertaken in many societies, for the monetary system and its material correlates to play the role of a universal code. As of yet, these efforts have not met with complete success, which, among other things, should be ascribed to the lack of isomorphism between the monetary system and the majority of specialized codes, characterized by – in distinction from the monetary code – synergy. There has been, however, the spontaneous diffusion of a very imperfect universal code in the form of a particular 'quiz culture' comprised of remnants of signs that are not singular, but are treated as one-dimensional and equal simply because they are removed from the context of the codes proper to them, and thus temporarily deprived of meaning. Despite its imperfections, participation in the 'quiz' code is – given the lack of other universal codes – the unavoidable fate of everyone in the present, without regard to whether they aspire to any specialist code, and, if so, which. The dilettantism of the quiz is an unavoidable attribute of the proliferation of specialized signs and – let us add – the advance of information to the role of the main signs of culture.

The position-creating character of signs, leading to a 'lack of readiness' of the social condition that the individual encounters, steals up on the individual the responsibility for describing their own social position. Hence the rush to individualization as a widespread motivational necessity (and, because it is so widespread, it brings mass egalitarian effects). The rush to individualization in this or other forms is known to all socio-cultural systems. In systems based primarily on position-derivative signs and indicating restrictions on the free movement of position-creating signs, it tends to be closed, which we already referred to, in the framework of 'types'. Mannered perfectionism replaces innovation, and creativity of innovators is exhausted in the causalism of critics. In conditions of democratic culture, a meaningful portion of the aforementioned limitation (in any case, in those fields in which the primacy of position-creating signs is guaranteed) is removed, and the toleration of innovation greatly increases.

For many years, psychologists (among them D. E. Berlyne, K. C. Montgomery, M. Glanzer) have been demonstrating through experiments that for living organisms the novelty – the atypical, unexpected character – of a stimulus has a strong motivational force. When the 'novelty' does not meaningfully depart from what is known, it evokes positive motivations, manifesting in 'discovering behaviour', 'research'. When, however, it departs too far from the habitual, expected structure of stimuli, it evokes negative motivations – fear and flight. The phenomenon is relatively easily understood in light of what we know about the organizing, structuring role of information in relationships between living organisms and the environment, and the dialectic co-existence of processes of assimilation and accommodation. In the field of psychology, drives are still explained through the use of specific theoretical constructs, called 'internal tendency to closeness' (Holt), 'clinging' ('audience' – Berlyne), or 'chronic discrepancy between the level of activity and the level elicited by a sudden stimuli' (S. S. Fox).

The fact that the motivational power of a new stimulus is clearly connected to the level of 'novelty' or 'atypicality' allows us to advance the following hypothesis:

a) a 'new' stimulus will evoke in living organisms an ambivalent position, positive–negative; it can be presented as a combination of two positions, positive and negative, that are taken in response to the simultaneous action of two stimuli, positive and negative;

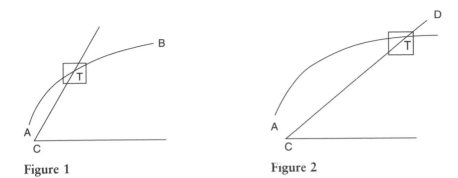

**Figure 1**                    **Figure 2**

b) a mutual relationship between two contradictory components of
   the ambivalent position can be presented similarly, as did Miller
   and Dollard for modelling reactions to the simultaneous responses
   of 'rewarding' and 'punishing'. This gives us figures 1 and 2.

In these drawings, the horizontal axis indicates the increasing degree
of 'atypicality' of the stimulus, the line AB – the intensification of
positive motivation, which we call the 'impulse' – and the line CD
– the intensification of the negative motivation, which we will call
'repulsion'. The rectangle labelled with the letter T shows us the
regions where 'the intensity of impulse and repulse become equal',
or an ambivalence experienced with particular acuteness. The curve
marking the growth of impulse as a function of the degree of 'atypicality' of the stimulus is equal in both drawings. We assume that only
to a vanishingly small degree is its shape modified by structural-social
changes. If it is subject to changes, they are rather caused by idiosyn-
cratic factors: the type of individual differences, a temporary state of
the organism, etc., which is only very indirectly dependent on aspects
of a 'structural' nature. The placement of the line expressing the
change in the intensity of repulsion as a function of the novelty of
the stimulus is completely different. The shape of that relation, tightly
connected to the intensity of punishment for departure from the norm,
is clearly dependent on the character of the socio-cultural context
that the individual is situated in. The difference between figures 1
and 2 illustrates the relationship between stagnating cultures (dominated by position) and developing ones (dominated by signs).

   The above assertions call upon us to consider more closely the role
of the spaces labelled 'T'. These are spaces of cultural taboo, usually
constructed on the psychological phenomenon of ambivalent positions.
The overlap between anthropological and psychological descriptions
of ambivalence is genuinely striking. The attitude towards taboo is a

mixture of curiosity and fear, deification and disgust, desire and repulsion. The containment of objects evoking similar attitudes through cultural bans that are enforced, guaranteed by social control, pushing them to the margins of the permissible cultural field, serves – taking the thing functionally – to delineate the boundaries of permissible innovation. Taboo forms the boundary lines of the space in which the innate impulses of the organism are not suppressed. Considered semiotically, it marks the border of the terrain of acceptable cultural variability.

The difference between figures 1 and 2 essentially leads to the decision of where on the scale of novelty the region of taboo will be located. This is the measure of a culture's tolerance of innovation. We can generally accept that the further you move this position on the scale of novelty, the broader the region left to cultural variability, and the more hospitable the conditions are for the development of culture.

The results of these movements are not of a cultural, but a social-structural nature. The problem of the position-creating or position-derivative character of cultural signs, from which we began in our analysis of the meanings of a culture's capacity for development, goes beyond the framework of purely cultural phenomena; it is located on the sphere of relationship between culture as a system of signs, and the social structure as an arrangement of dependencies that these signs signify. An analysis of the conditions of development or stagnation of a culture always refers to the problem of social structure. We do not delve into it in these reflections, whose goal was merely to signal a few hypotheses as to the cultural and psychological mechanisms mediating between social structure and innovation or cultural stasis.

# Part II

## Culture and Social Structure

# I

# Cultural and Extra-Cultural Organization of Society

Cybernetics, highly trendy and quite respected today, has bolstered the eternal tendency of human thought to dichotomize their vision of the world. Dichotomism is a characteristic of immanent arrangements, whose transformations are examined by cybernetics. Entry and exit points of systems, and the elements that comprise them, are even: alongside an entry or exit point of energy, there is an entry or exit of information – and in this way, every arrangement has a dual structure, or rather two structures. The elements are connected through a web of energy feedback, but also through a web of information feedback. Any transformation of an element or arrangement is the result of an interaction between an energy transmitter and an information transmitter.

The roots of theoretical research into this methodological dualism certainly lie in very ancient traditions of philosophical reflection on the human world; this reflection is every day reaffirmed by every person in their experience of the world, which is dichotomous in its general structure. Every person experiences on a daily basis the fact of their own will, desire, strivings, which are experienced as recalcitrant, resistant to confrontation with 'reality'. The signals of the first ingredient of the experience come from 'the inside'; the signals of the second, from 'the outside'. Reflecting on the experience, a person projects their image onto two screens – an internal and external one. The product of this projection is the perception of every action as an intersection of two mutually dependent structures, not entirely translatable, each possessing an independent existence, in its own way 'substantial' (in the Platonic sense; not to be confused with the materialist one). Thus, in the elementary experience of the discrepancy between what should be and what is, signification and being signified, the will and its exterior embodiment dwells eternally in the living wellspring of the gnoseological dichotomized view of the world. Because the two screens are a given, the elements projected onto them can be structured in various ways, depending on the choices of the organizing directive. If we are interested in the structure of human behaviour, we will speak about the dichotomy of motive and situation, going from the act of the individual to a hypothetical structure called a position (in one direction) or the situational determination of the situation (in the other). If we have broader aspirations for our research and want to understand the construction of the social world, we will organize the contents of our screens into structures of consciousness and social existence. On the next, ontological level of generality, our dichotomy takes the form of a relationship between thought and matter. Yet other variants of structuralization are also possible. If we undertake a mental re-projection of the 'internal' screen 'onto the outside', the dichotomy will appear to us as the relationship between base and superstructure. A re-projection from the inside will illuminate the dichotomy of essence and existence. There are many variants, if we consider that the autonomy and mutual dependency of the two screens were the primary topics of philosophical reflection, at least in the circles influenced by Greek culture.

The cybernetic vision appears to us in the light of these reflections as a new variant of the intellectual universalization of elementary experience. It is a product of the reorganization of the contents of this experience from the perspective of complex systems. The correspondence of entry and exit, the expression of these correspondences through a singular function with a finite amount of variables is, in the study of complex assemblages, analysed from the perspective of the correspondence of systems of information and energy circulation. The singular functioning of the arrangement requires the total correlation of both webs of energy. If we use the old language of philosophy, it requires a complete agreement between what should be and what is, norms and the possibility of realizing them.

Let us postulate treating human society, or a relatively isolated and self-sufficient collection of people with complementary drives, as precisely such a complex assemblage: we should seek out two intersecting assemblages of energies. We find a clear analogy between the expenditure of energy and the production and distribution of various goods conditioning existence, and the capability of individual action in humans and their various groups. A similarly clear analogy appears between the expenditure of energy and the creation and dissemination of various signs and models, orienting the individual or collective intention to act. Accepting both analogies, we can treat both society and people as a complex assemblage of a dual nature, or as an arrangement with two structures.

One arrangement appears as a collection of situations defining access to goods. The system 'society' remains in a relationship of inclusion to the system of 'individual'; the field of assimilationary processes of the individual is the same terrain, which from the perspective of the system 'society' is a field of accommodating procedures. The aforementioned situations, into which individual life processes are inscribed, are located in this field. Culture is an attempt to unify this field, to organize and structure it by means of introducing and interpreting information. The purely abstract theoretical model of culture, fulfilling this function in an excellent way, would assume the complete identity of the individual-assimilationist directive (patterns of behaviour) with the socio-accommodating directive (institutional requirements, or – as Parsons writes – structural-functional ones). A large portion of contemporary American sociology accepts this theoretical model and the indicator of a social norm, treating all empirical departures from it as 'deviations' (transgressions). It is silently accepted that information – or the domain of the question of socialization and interiorization – is the one field in which the organization of the human collective in societies is realized; if this organization fails to function in some way, it is necessary to seek out the causes for the disruption of socializing and accommodating processes. In these cases, we are dealing with a purely cultural model of society. It occludes independent factors of economics or the political systems as the markers of a situation, to which culturally prepared information is applied for exploratory–controlling purposes.

Meanwhile, in all known societies – more so in heterogeneous than homogeneous ones – the field and power of the cultural regulation of processes are limited. The limitation of cultural regulation emerges when the structure of knowledge and expectations, or the pattern of information, ceases to be isomorphic in relation to the external structure of the situation, or in relation to the arrangement of opportunity, defining the accessibility of goods that are the object of action. This situation always exists when – as in our type of society – cultural expectations are more homogenized than the opportunity to fulfil them. The result is a disjunct between the informational postulate and the energetic possibilities, and thus between the cultural model and the motive of action – a situation that Lévi-Strauss described as the excess of meanings without defined objects, and the excess of events without meanings.

This disjunction appears to people in a dual form: (a) as a discrepancy between what is known and what is desired; and (or) (b) as culture's failure to serve its informational-controlling role, or as a 'fuzziness' of the situation of action, a hunger for knowledge, goals, and values. Both forms have their source in the conflict in the relationships of correspondence (isomorphism, adaptation) between processes of accommodation and assimilation. Processes of individual accommodation organized by culture (socializing–interiorizing process) do not lead to the creation of structures of thought and behaviour enabling assimilation to the environment: this evasion of the world from human control is called alienation. Both of these processes of disjunction form the motivation for – on the one hand – research efforts (the intensification of individual-accommodating processes) and – on the other – an active organization of the world (intensification of individual-assimilating processes, which in their results turn out to be social-accommodating processes). The product of these motivations are on the one hand the 'projected worlds' of art and ideology, and on the other, the technical manipulation of the natural world and the political-legal manipulation of the human world.

Generally speaking, the role of culture in regulating life processes (as one principle of regulation) decreases in accordance with the weakening of information between the actor and other participants in the situation of action. It is the largest in intimate circles, personal ones, which can be served by a single code of signs and meanings, with a sufficient capacity for information to reduce practically to irrelevance the indeterminacy of all possible situations of interaction. It is the smallest in cases where the access to goods, which is the goal of action, is dependent on people from collectives whose cultural system does not possess points of intersection with the cultural code of the actor. That is why the aforementioned disjunct may not be completely felt by people moving in one particular circle of a single culture that is relatively self-sufficient in energy for their entire life. It is felt particularly strongly in urban environments, and exponentially multiplied in an age of great geographic mobility and extra-social communication. The discovery of the class system became possible only at the moment when the intensification of inter-class transmission of information led to the cultural unification of culturally constructed models of behaviour serving to maintain the difference between the collection of opportunities correlating with situations involving an access to goods, marked by class position. There is nothing strange about the fact that it is in this epoch that we find the greatest pressure to innovate, generating maximal dynamism both of the cultural system (systematically anticipating the process of appearance of new structural oppositions through the creation of new signs, or the swiftness of cultural products getting 'used up' in their role as positional signs) and in the social structure.

The informational-controlling function, as already discussed, serves the function of culture. But it is not always fulfilled – a fact that the one-sided cultural version of sociology neglects. The fact of this function being unfulfilled is the strongest stimulus of cultural production. The instinctive, phylogenetically constructed, subconscious fear people have of the dark, of a dense forest, or fog, ably demonstrates the drive people have towards clear demarcations, predictability, and thus to the 'informational saturation' of the scene of action. Culture is a constant effort to differentiate what is uniform – imposing a structure onto a world that does not have one, or whose structure is unknown. This effort is undertaken on two fronts: constructing a structure of signs, and practical structuralization of the system of signified elements. In primitive thought, both fronts collapse into one, and this is probably the most characteristic feature of *la pensée sauvage*. An individual becomes a member of a tribe not because they were born into it, but because they participated in rites of initiation. A person departs for the world of the dead, not because the physiological processes in their body have come to a halt, but because the funeral ceremony has taken place; a biologically living person, on whom such a ceremony has been performed, will also die biologically. In our society, people become a married couple not by sleeping together and having children, but because they have undergone the appropriate 'transitional ritual'. In modern thought, the consequence of experiencing the inadequacy of cultural information on the difference between what is 'objective' and what is 'subjective' is that the two fronts have separated from each other, as cognition and production have been separated, along with motives of action and the rule of law.

That is why in today's society, more so than in any other, when we describe human behaviour, we are not allowed to explain it by reference to variables of individual motivation (or interiorized traces of the cultural system). Describing, for example, people's behaviours during election season, we do not gain direct knowledge of the 'political culture' of a given society; the behaviour described is an accident of situational pressures that do not describe an isomorphic structure of interiorized patterns (that are therefore felt to be primary) and internalized norms, which again do not correspond to the opportunities contained in the external structure (and are therefore experienced as unfulfilled longings, an injustice – giving rise to frustration or aggression, either sadistic or masochistic). The subjectively experienced conflict between what should be and what is in these cases is the result of the projection of the objective conflict between the cultural and extra-cultural organization of society onto the individual screen. This extra-cultural organization – and here lies the root of the conflict – is regulated by the particular interests of certain segments of society – the hegemonic class – and is based not so much on the difference in values and motivations as on the difference of opportunities tied to particular social positions. This is what leads to the fact that, for many people, many patterns lack the possibility of realization. When patterns – by virtue of their inadequacy to a situation – lose their controlling power, what steps into their place is the force of necessity in the form of political–legal limitations. The legal–political arrangement, working in concert with the economic one, serves the same function, generally speaking, as the cultural system: its task is the limitation of the collection of abstract possibilities by maximizing the likelihood of some and eliminating others. But it realizes this function in a different way from the cultural system: it does not turn (or at least, it does not have to) that which is necessary into that which is yearned for; as a rule it is usually the opposite – a permanent tension between desire and necessity. A state of 'dysfunction' of the social structure in relation to culture arises – a state Marx described as alienation. At the wellspring of this state is the violence of a particular set of interests over others, called class dominance. The consequence of this state is an intensification of the transformation of both the cultural system and the social structure – an unending pursuit of the adequacy of both that is unachievable insofar as the variability of each is subject to independent factors.

## THE UNIT OF ANALYSIS: THE SOCIO-CULTURAL SYSTEM

Researchers of so-called primordial or primitive societies for a long time described their structure and function in purely cultural categories: on the basis of information received from their informants, they tried to recreate and make sense of the native world of meanings and patterns, and then to present the cultural system as a true image of the society. This procedure is no longer seen positively. It turned out, in the results of detailed analysis, that primitive societies, much like our own, experience a discrepancy between what should be and what is, that the image of inter-personal relationships that is constructed in the minds of people entangled within them is one thing, and the actual arrangement of relationships is another. Most likely the decay of systems under the decomposing influence of market relations of energy and models of competition has advanced so far everywhere that today there is no group of people anywhere on earth such that a description of their culture would exhaust everything there is to say about its structure, and where the traditional methodology of anthropology would not lead to a false image of reality. But we are not consumed by the fact that anthropologists might, in relation to certain categories of human collectives, have utilized a research perspective wildly inadequate to the analysis of our type of civilization. Most likely, the primitive societies themselves possess such properties as would make the wrongness of that perspective less obvious and inflammatory. The discrepancy between the systems of information and energy is not so sharp there as in our version of civilization.

This hypothesis remains in agreement with everything that we know about the genesis and emancipation of humans from the animal world. The collective, social existence of human individuals is nothing new when considered alongside animal species; what is decidedly new, however, is the emergence of an independent system of information, or the specialization of certain directives in their informational role. We should accept – according to logic – that in some stage of the prehistory of human communication, information appeared exclusively, or almost exclusively – as happens in insect societies – as an aspect of transmissions of energy specific to the species and untranslatable; and that, in the next stage, a different collection of 'material' for information emerged (speech), but contained within this event was the possibility of a fundamental autonomization of culture that was still realized to such a small degree that it was possible to speak of a full symmetry between both aspects of the social structure.

This kind of hypothetical situation of full symmetry of 'a complete agreement between culture and society' occurs, from a theoretical perspective, when: (a) in every situation, both of the partners involved can do what the information they possess inclines them towards; and (b) nothing and no one inclines them to do something different. In other words, the condition of such symmetry is the unidirectionality of the vectors illustrating the pressures put on the behaviour of any individual by the 'external situation' and 'interiorized patterns'. The American psychiatrist Kurt Goldstein constructed such a hypothetical world for use by injured and mentally disabled soldiers: the conformity between the situation and the expectations or principles connected to the requirements of the situation did not allow for internal disjunction, conflicted experiences and choices. In the world constructed by Goldstein, there were no – to use the terms formulated by Lévi-Strauss – 'things without meaning or assigned objects'.

For reasons that I will present later, it seems likely that Goldstein's artificial world approaches our hypothetical model much more closely than any historic or prehistoric societies. But it is also likely that so-called primitive societies are closer to the aforementioned model than our society, and that we can present the course of human history as a progressive separation of culture and society. Our hypothetical model does not depart overmuch from the knowledge that we possess, thanks to anthropologists, about small and mutually isolated and self-sufficient societies, free from cultural contact and encounters with groups from other cultures. It does not seem accidental that such societies are distinguished by a remarkable stability: fulfilling cultural expectations strengthens faith in internalized models, and using these models strengthens, in turn, the feedback loop of energies to which they are functionally applied.

In the context of this totality, questions about the 'primacy' of culture or society are difficult to answer. Both directions of thought are equally justified. One can, for example, reasonably assert that energy circulates through channels indicated by cultural models, though on the other hand it is known that mental conditioning of cultural patterns owes its strength to a dependency on social energies.

In the most general terms, we can say that the socio-cultural system is the more stable, the more that the following conditions are met: (a) all of the elements that are connected energetically in the framework of the system, are also linked by information; and (b) the contents of information transmissions are in accordance with the contents of energetic transmissions, meaning that the elements of the system can behave in such a way as is required of them by the informational directives (patterns and knowledge), and they want to behave in such a way, as is required of them by the energetic dependencies (position in the social structure). At the wellspring of the changes, we find an inadequacy of information and energy. In everyday sociological language, we can speak of the inadequacy of pattern and motive and the possibility of its realization in a situation, or of external pressure and internalized roles. Such an inadequacy is all the more likely and more frequent, the more starkly the following phenomena occur (each individually or all of them together): (a) the system of social energies approaches the model of a market without participants, regulated by laws of supply and demand, or the principle of value and economic force, and not principles of utility and traditional reciprocity; (b) social energy (the circulation of goods) goes beyond the collection of elements that are informationally connected; (c) informational energies (the communication of values and models) goes beyond the boundaries of the collection of elements mutually dependent energetically. The market, as opposed to a non-market circulation of goods, or socio-cultural contacts, creates a situation contributing to the inadequacy of the traditional collection of models and variables of the situation (or the opposite – new models and traditional situations served by old models), which in turn gives the change in the cultural system, or the change in the social structure – or both changes – an adaptive meaning.

Here then, and not in the properties of any of the states of any human collective, lie the wellsprings of socio-cultural variability, and the existence of people in a form that includes the dimension of historical time. It is curious that the same conclusion, in essence, was arrived at by major cultural researchers in the model of Margaret Mead or Ruth Benedict, because of the confrontation of the resources of anthropological discovery, as by philosophers – the phenomenological analysis of human existence. Existence is neither terrible, nor unbearable. It is us, negating it, who then deem it terrible and unbearable. It is one thing to experience suffering, and another to consciously experience suffering – and yet another to gaze at suffering experienced in this way from the sidelines, as an object subject to manipulation, and to imagine the state that would eliminate such suffering. As Sartre wrote:

> so long as a person is immersed in their historical situation, they are unable to see the gaps and flaws of a particular political or economic system, and not, as is stupidly said, because they are accustomed to it, but because that system encompasses their entire existence, and they cannot imagine, that things could be otherwise [...] It is only when a different state of affairs becomes imaginable, that a new light falls on our sufferings and difficulties, only then do we come to the conclusion, that they are unbearable.[1]

This 'different state of affairs can be imagined only when socio-cultural contacts render it accessible, either as experience, or as idea. In complete agreement with Marx and Lenin (*What is to be done?*), Merleau-Ponty wrote: 'My objective position in the process of production is never sufficient to awaken class consciousness in me. The exploited existed, before revolutionaries appeared [...] Resistance is thus not the product of objective conditions; quite the opposite – the decision of the workers, that they want a revolution, transforms them into the proletariat.'[2] The sum of human atrocities and sufferings, despite the complaints of pessimists, decreases with the passing of centuries and development of civilization. And the amount of protest, rebellion, revolution is, after all, increasing.

The incredible variability and liquidity of the contemporary world can be ascribed to the fact that the three prerequisite conditions listed above have all been fulfilled at once, and to a degree heretofore unprecedented. And they were fulfilled not only in the context of particular individual 'societies' (as we colloquially use the term today, to refer to collectives of people organized into states), but also in the 'Great Society', a term Graham Wallas used half a century ago to describe the phenomenon of people, for the first time in human history, tied in one gigantic web of energetic and informational connections. The goods created by humans are now reckoned on a global scale, and access to goods is determined by relationships going far beyond the boundaries of one nation, however large it may be, and the new cultural brokers (the term used to indicate individuals specializing in information transmission) are transformed into a global collective, serving the multiple directions of information flow beyond the boundaries of region and environment. The modern world is thus the arena of chronic and many-sided cultural contacts, an endless reshuffling of the boundaries of energy and information systems, and a notorious discrepancy between the sphere of information and the sphere of energy. It is not an accident that the problem of the disjunction between what should be and what is, and the relativism of all normative systems, today are the most consuming issues and create the biggest problems for contemporary thinkers. They are a marker of the world's movement towards a second, heterogeneous pole, where the other end of the axis was the previously described hypothetical socio-cultural structure.

Here are a few selected dimensions of this process:

The specialization and autonomization of human needs. Institutionalizing themselves in a mechanism of satisfying these needs in various organized structures. The relative autonomization of these structures. Their 'one-sidedness', their singular aspect – in the sense that they do not balance out the totality of necessary goods and information and they are not, for each of the individuals contained within them, the only structure within which the individual is contained. And thus a growing inter-dependence of these structures. But a mutual inter-dependence realized by contacts with nature, mounted in a 'programme' of these structures, rather on the principle of a model of faculties than on an obligatory 'instinct'. The growing number of points of intersections between autonomous structures – points which must enter into mutual contact, influencing each other spontaneously or in a planned fashion. The constant growth – elicited by specialization – of the informational isolation of these structures: an isolation that renders them informationally similar to 'endogenous populations', thus to populations in which progressive mutations result in an individual 'genetic current' separate from others. But, simultaneously, the constant growth of energetic links between these same structures – which is a result of constant, separate collisions, and

separate information systems. I am inclined to summarize these par-
ticularized tendencies by describing them as manifestations of the 'law
of uneven development of structures' – uneven development, which
makes the heterogeneous arrangement into an endless process of internal readaptation, transforming internal 'misfits' and a lack of balance
into the rule. I would also be inclined to see, in the de-correlations
of processes of autonomous development and the mutually inter-
dependent structures, the deep wellsprings of an intriguing changeability
of the world and of the socio-cultural arrangements contained within
it. Arrangements, each of which is composed of many structures that
do not form a system within the sphere of energy, or in the cultural
one; the de-systematization of culture leads to its being treated as a
collection of information, and not an arrangement, and thus into
what is often called 'mass culture', in distinction from cultural systems
that can be ascribed to functionally defined global social systems.

Among all of these autonomizing structures, there is a particular
collection to which I would like to devote a little more attention. I
am thinking of the collection that is composed of the humanistic
sociological disciplines. The direction of the development of human
collectives is set out not – or not so much – by its own needs, or by
the particular traits of their function, as by the properties of the
socio-cultural arrangement in which the direction is mounted. The
market exchange of goods transforms into market goods even
the most intimate features of human personality. The contemporary
autonomization of functionally distinguished structures also constituted
into similar structures the descendants of former humanists. New
social situations guaranteed new humanists a remarkable heterogeneity of ideas and a kaleidoscopic multiplicity of schools, quickly blos-
soming into various structures called disciplines, each with their own
particular trends and 'genetic currents'. These new structures, once
separated, paid for their right to autonomously define their own innovations by the narrowing of the channels of communication with
other branches that emerged from the same trunk. For the humanities,
this price was both excessive and ruinous. For naturalists, a common
language is not such a crucial matter. It is enough if they can communicate with specialists and practitioners engaged in creating and
disseminating goods, using the knowledge of scholars to squeeze out
new portions of energy from nature. With the 'average person' – the
non-specialist – the naturalist communicated by providing him with
instruments, in which the information acquired by scholars is mounted
in the form of mechanisms. In order to use these instruments, the
'average person' does not have to input new information into them
– he does not need to know the laws for the flow of electric currents

in order to use a vacuum cleaner. The naturalist perceives a need for communication with the 'average person' only when appearing in the role of popularizer, to satisfy an extra-energetic need of human curiosity that is ultimately marginal to their professional interests. Humanists find themselves in a completely different situation. Not everyone who is included among humanists is there by virtue of formal divisions and traditions: there exist simultaneously two principles of defining the humanities – the traditional, subject-based one (the humanist is the one who cultivates knowledge about humans), and a potentially more reliable one, a methodological-functional one (the humanist is the one who, in cultivating knowledge, treats their objects as the objects of conscious human action, and is interested in their informational content, which is constructed by humans – for whom a human can be seen as an object, and not a subject); thus, the situation discussed is different only for humanists in the sense of the second, methodological-functional criterion. As to those who are counted among humanists only on the strength of the first criterion, for them the problem of communication with the 'average person' manifests itself similarly to how it does for the naturalist. It is not an accident that, from a methodological-functional point of view, they are naturalists. They examine humans, but humans perceived as things, as objects, and not as the subjects of action, as systems reacting to stimuli external to them. Their function is determining states of 'entry' that most certainly produce the called-for 'exit' states. Their natural audience is less 'average people' than practitioners deciding which exit states are desired, and manipulating entry states. It is important to achieve and maintain a common language with those practitioners, and the humanists work hard at this. The situation is truly different only in the case of humanists distinguished by the second criterion. Their social function is strengthening that which destroys the singularity of connection between entry points and exit points of human server-mechanisms – that which renders worthless the probabilistic functions assigned to describe these correlations. These functions are realized in the strengthening of factors of will and freedom of choice, achieved by the enrichment of the informational resources of human 'arrangements'. And, thus, the humanist, in distinction from other scholars, can fulfil their social function only when they have contact with a 'non-specialist' through the medium of informational links. Ease of communication, and the messages being comprehensible to both sides, are necessary conditions of the justification of their existence. The progressive division of the humanities into numerous autonomous structures is therefore dangerous, because it calls that communication into question. Before this division happened, the humanities as a whole belonged to one environment, characterized by a lively internal exchange of information. What is more, this environment did not create a 'population informationally endogenous' – it created a totality only together with the broader circles of the 'public', for whom the productions of humanists were intended. Let us recall the Rococo salon, in which Diderot, Holbach, or Helvetius operated; the rooms at rue Taibout or rue Taranyi, where the Saint-Simonistes met; the lively environment of revolutionaries, gathering in Marx's London apartment. Let us compare them to any department of a modern research institute, where the employees encounter the 'public' only through the medium of polls and determined pollsters, otherwise moving only in their own circles, measuring their worth only through the opinions of their colleagues in the field, writing only for specialists similar to them, and caring about the ease of communication only between experts. In the context of the constantly swelling dimensions of contemporary humanities, the field of reference of any concrete humanist is shrinking at a terrifying rate. The rift in contact with 'non-specialists' is ever more difficult to repair in a situation where new canals of information between specialists within the humanities are themselves constantly drying up. Today, it is not only the 'humanist' who perceives a rift in communications with 'non-specialists' – a 'total humanist' is today a practically empty concept, whereas 'partial humanists' have an increasingly difficult time understanding each other. As a result, none of them utilizes the knowledge that a 'non-specialist' naïvely expects from 'total humanities'. It is hard to predict all of the consequences of this fact. I am inclined to see it as the threat of a growing dominance of energetic links, 'external dependencies', over informational energies, and over the conscious cultural choice, in determining the direction of the development of heterogeneous systems and the human behaviours they contain.

## THE UNIT OF ANALYSIS: THE HUMAN INDIVIDUAL

The information–energetic dichotomy can also be examined in the system of references in the collection 'human individual in its social environment'. Here – in my view – dwell theory's lessons for a dichotomous vision of the world. It is precisely in the human individual, if they mentally 'objectivize' their experiences and render them the subject of reflections 'from the side', differentiating in them two qualitatively different ingredients that also, because of their mutual irreducibility, are projected onto two variously located screens. One screen, located inside the individual, terms it 'will', 'conscience', 'impulse'; the second, located outside the individual, though not necessarily outside of the body (we can say: outside the informational layer of one's own 'I'), names it 'necessity', 'situation', 'internal pressure'. The dichotomous image of the world is, from a gnoseological point of view, an exploitation of the human way of experiencing their own existence. Because the dichotomous vision of the world is already given, we can seek the assemblage 'individual in the environment' as one possible arrangement of references for organizing it.

The point of departure for a Marxist approach to an analysis of this assemblage is the premise that the mode of being for a human in the world is action: 'We set out from real, active men.'[3] It is in action, and only in action, that man makes the world his own, makes it accessible energetically and informationally, transforms it into a 'world of his own', into the human world. Action is always a consumption of information and energy. Thanks to this, it disposes of information emancipated from actual situations of energy, in their own way substantial, existing independently of portions of energy present in the situation – in action, man does not only appear as the object of events, as a passive material on which external operators imprint themselves. To the linking of energy and information that is the action, man adds something 'from himself' – which was not in the situation itself. Man is not only the operated-upon, but also the operator. Man is not only the creation of the world, but also a creator. In the fact that he is a creation, there is nothing specifically human. Humans are constituted as human only when, and to the extent that, they act as creator, operator, subject. Human individuality manifests itself in this: that man is the carrier of information and for this reason he can treat everything that is not the 'I' as a receptacle of energy waiting to be moulded.

This humanistic vision is directly opposed to the positivistic one dominating in the humanities today, particularly in social psychology and behavioural sociology. (The following observations are not in reference to the research results of these schools of thought, which are quite rich and generative, but to the particular philosophy that some thinkers try to 'build up' or 'build onto' this research.) According to the accurate description of Gordon W. Allport, '[p]erhaps the simplest way to characterize the positivist view of man is to say that he is regarded as a *reactive* being. What he does is determined by outer forces or by inner drives. Like traditional natural science, positive psychology sees movement as caused and determined by pressures. Man is like inanimate objects (including machines) and like elementary organisms.'[4] In other words, positivistic psychology (and sociology) postulate perceiving a human as a kind of system, in which the entry and exit states are connected by a discoverable, singular function. Perhaps this function contains many variables – and if we are not yet able to describe them, it is because we are not yet familiar with a large part of it; the difficulty is purely a question of measurement, or methodology, and can be resolved with the aid of purely technical procedures. Positivistic humanities treat themselves as a discipline in the model of the natural sciences and that is why I consider this postulate to be exceptionally important. Frank T. Severin reveals the roots of this view:

> Human acts must be the product of inexorable natural laws similar to those controlling the behaviour of atoms; if it were not so, a rigorous science of man could not exist. If man were able to exert even a minimal influence over events in his life, accurate prediction of behaviour would be impossible even in theory. Psychology as a science must have for its subject man who is as 'lawful' as inanimate objects.[5]

Let us add: the subject of psychology as a discipline serving the purpose of manipulation. In this function, the essential *raison d'être* of psychology (and sociology) is measured by the degree of accuracy of predicting mass behaviours of humans under the influence of particular and manipulated determinants.

One can object to such a representation of the philosophic tendencies of positivistic psychology by saying that it strives not to predict the concrete behaviours of an X or a Y, but to determine the statistical probability that a concrete X or Y will react to stimulus A in manner B. In order to clear up any confusion, let us fully clarify the difference between the sentences, ontologizing our problem. The probabilistic modesty of positivists is of a methodological nature: we are speaking of probability, not necessity, because we construct our statistical model out of selected variables; if we worked out a model encompassing all possible variables (and the number of variables is finite, thus the task is theoretically possible), we could speak of necessity. The probabilistic grasp stems from the state of the research, and not the object of study. A human's behaviour is in itself singularly determined; it is only our knowledge of it that has a probabilistic character. Our perspective is different: we assume that the surprises littering every set of predictions, even the most conscientiously calculated ones – and appearing all the more, the more active the mass of people is – stem not from flaws in calculations, or temporary gaps in the state of research, but from a fundamental incalculability, the irreducibility of human behaviour to a collection of determinants specified in a positivistic manner, composed of internal forces and external pressures. Human actions are not only reactions, but also procreations. If, for the sake of analytical procedure, we exclude from human actions everything that can be singularly assigned to specific determinants directed towards the external personality (entry), something will still remain. Something new, that did not 'enter' into the system from the outside: that remained on the inside, that is the creation of the person. This something makes a person's behaviour only partially predictable, like the behaviours of any 'self-organizing system' – which is not only an object, but also a subject – in relation to its environment.

In other words, the particular feature of humans, acquired as a result of evolution, is the ability not only to receive and transform information – which animals are also capable of – but also to create new information, which had not existed in any previous form and is not only a product of cutting up and recombining information acquired from the outside. In order to function in this way, a human must possess (and indeed does possess) not only the ability to think, but also an ability to 'think about thinking', or reflexivity, whose subject is not only the informational content (not just that which the information describes), but the information itself, the fact of possessing it – experiencing, becoming conscious of it. It is a particular grasp of this 'second-degree system of signals', 'signals about signals', that was generally described by Pavlov, when he wanted to warn against a simplistic extrapolation from his experiences with dogs, against reducing the human psyche to a collection of reflexes. I wonder whether we could say that the human mind – or, rather, human reflexes – comprises its own 'higher order system', for which commands, which appear as information to the lower order, are energetic commands. These hypothetical systems of a higher order possess the unique capability of self-regulation, invention, negation, imagination – everything that, when observed from the outside, allowed Mumford to use the term 'playfulness'. Their existence means that human responsibility for their own actions stems from freedom of choice (humans are not responsible for peristalsis, which they clearly have no influence over), and is not only an illusion, upheld for justifying legal norms; a human can, but does not have to.

The spontaneously or consciously positivistic image of the world assumed passivity, seeing the explanation as evidence of determinism, seeing its function as fulfilled. Caught in the tight trap of its own vision, it vacillated between a psychophysical parallelism and a primitive monism, in both cases resigning itself to failing to understand its own images. At the one end of the spectrum, wonder awaited, always accompanying the 'synchronized clocks' of Geulincx; at the other, a depressing, though introspective, 'only', an acknowledgement of the fact that the release of adrenaline into the blood is, after all, something different from the experience of anger. For psychic comfort, positivism referred people yearning to 'understand' its claims to philosophy or theology – in any case, outside its own confines.

From this perspective, cybernetic thought offers a proposition of truly new horizons. It contains a vision of an active world, a world in action, a world in which the opposition between subject and object, so painfully felt by people in an age of splitting between the two, transcends the dialectic. Cybernetic dichotomism has nothing in common with psychophysical paralellism. It does not speak of any 'parallel' between mind and matter. Grasping the unity of both components of the dichotomy, it is closer, instead, to classic Aristotelianism, seeing form and material as inseparable aspects of being, as two faces of the same thing. Because of this, perhaps, cybernetics has emerged as a philosophy of the world as seen from pulpits and directors' chairs – its image of the world is a drama of action, creation, change; as in Marx's philosophy, so in the dry cybernetic models of the antinomy between subject and object, creation and being created, life and 'being alive' are carried out in action and transformation. Every transformation is a joining of information and energy, these new versions of thought and energy. It is a human transformation, known to the individual from the inside, from autoreflection, now extrapolated onto the world, and in this act of extrapolation rendering the world human without any remainders, anthropomorphized, though in a fundamentally different way from what was once done by religion.

Treating the dichotomy of 'culture–society' as a human analogue of the dichotomy 'information–energy' allows us to make sense of our knowledge of the social world in categories of the antimony of subject and object and the endless overcoming of this antimony in human action. In its deepest intentions, it is surprisingly in accordance with the activist philosophy of Marx. It is simultaneously significantly in contradiction with the philosophy of positivism and its sociological and psychological applications, in which there was a lack of viewing the human as subject. In the research programme contained in our propositions, the emphasis shifts from the problem of 'being determined by' to 'determinining'. Determining is furthermore grasped as action, process, a creative consumption of information and energy. The presence of a creative act in every human event means that it evades the positivistic perspective – that it can only be partially contained in a schema with a finite number of measurable variables. That which remains beyond the limits of the positivist schema is a fighting and active human, endlessly engaged in choosing, evaluating, organizing the world. Who is not only an endpoint of energy vectors but also a point of departure.

# II

# Economics, Culture, and Typologies of Societies

Presentism, emerging from the cultural determinants of the horizon of research, is an innate predisposition in the human mind, and it demarcates the way in which a person perceives the sensually and intellectually accessible world, in both the past and the present. The image of this world is always shaped by conceptual categories offered up by culture. Because this is the norm, it is difficult to speak of a mistake or cognitive error. This is why it is difficult to fault contemporary social sciences for stubbornly trying to relate the problem of 'economy and culture' to human societies as such, and not perceiving the historicity of the question. It is difficult, today, in the midst of the spatial and temporal domination of the market, to imagine a society in which the economy could not be divided 'from the inside' from the rest of social life – and if this division was ultimately made by introducing conceptual categories from the outside, then it turns out that the economy is so melded with the totality of social life, that any effort to create a visible boundary between them must end in failure or lead to a visible deformation of the true state of things. At the same time, before economics and sociology could discover and confirm their mutual autonomy, economics had to distinguish itself from the rest of social life and present itself as an independent and powerful dynamic factor. This happened when the heretofore inseparable life process in which the production, distribution, and consumption of goods were only aspects of a general mode of being that were indistinguishable 'from the inside' fell apart into roles played in different places, among various people, according to various codexes of behavioural models and under the control of different spheres of influence.

This process created oppositions structuring the diversity of human situations, which could be and had to be signalled by isomorphic oppositions in the world of signs, in the dimension of the semiotic function of cultural ideas and culturally acknowledged patterns of behaviour. The process of a gradual degree of particularization developing throughout history and the simultaneous pluralization of social positions, and the patterns of behaviour tied to them, was both the necessary and the only condition giving meaning to the problem of 'X and Y' and 'X or Y' in which the symbols of X and Y express components of the entire process of satisfying needs.

One of the problems of this kind, the problem of 'economics and social structure', became a 'phenomenon for cultural meaning' when the roles of the seller and the buyer were freed from institutional constraints of other viable social functions and became located in the person-less, anonymous sphere of the market, in which human individuals entered only in the role of sellers or buyers. The first step towards this situation is the commodification of certain goods necessary for satisfying basic human needs. This situation is not manifested fully until the next step is complete: until the human ability to create commodities itself becomes a commodity. Only then do the roles of seller and buyer become the lot of all individuals, and there ceases to exist a separate portion of the social system that would not be subject to its influence – that is, the influence of the structure of economic life.

If we accept these ideas, supported by plenty of ethnographic evidence, we must also accept that the problem of mutual relationships and mutual dependency between the economy and patterns of human behaviour can only be sensibly posed in the case where a significant number of goods spend a significant portion of their time on the way from producer to consumer in a market situation; and the greater this portion of goods and this portion of time, the more 'reasonable' our problem becomes. However general and widespread the problem we are discussing would seem from the culturally determined perspective of our research, it makes sense only in reference to portions of known societies – those that tolerate only a marginal role of the marketplace and relegate professional merchants to 'social pores' (according to Marx's term; let us observe, tangentially, that the semantically ambivalent situation of the merchant – 'straddling the border between insider and outsider' – was the premise of the frequently encountered cultural 'taboo' connected to his occupation, and a cause of the fact that, for a long time, ambivalence in conditions of 'outside' and the weak development of markets was maintained; the role of merchants was typically entrusted to people who were sufficiently different for them, through their own character, to take on the role of being a clear sign of difference. History provides almost too many examples – let us recall the Phoenicians, Syrians, Armenians, Jews, Lombards, Parsis, Greeks, who generally played this role of a taboo sign in foreign environments, beyond the realm of their native societies). It is in these societies that the production, distribution, and consumption of goods melts into an undifferentiated mess of social life in general. They are a 'way of life' rather than elements of social action that can be reasonably distinguished and organized into a separate analytic structure.

The process of going from 'indivisible totality' of social life to autonomy of institutional structures of economic life is a lengthy and gradual process (if you exclude the violent and catastrophic change taking place in pre-market societies as a result, for instance, of the market manipulations of economically advanced colonizers), in which it is difficult to distinguish sudden jumps or clear steps. Instead of using attractive dichotomous divisions, it makes more sense to speak of the 'relative dependence' of the economy in one phase, and the 'relative independence' in the second phase.

## METHODOLOGICAL PREMISES

It has become increasingly trendy in recent years to seek out and use a uniform, and also potentially quantifiable, variable, allowing for all the knowns of society to be grasped from the perspective of economics, in one smooth, continuous line. Most frequently, purely economic, statistically described and easily measured variables are used, such as 'per capita production', 'per capita income', etc. They are used so frequently that simply repeating them is taken as proof of their unquestionable cognitive merit. The classification of known societies – if we decide to use these variables as criteria – becomes simply a matter of determining, not without some degree of arbitrariness, a certain number of statistical classes. These purely quantitative and absolutely 'nonsociological' variables decisively push out institutional and structural criteria that were so widespread and uncontroversial during the times of List, Hildebrandt, or Bucher (not to mention, of course, Marx, who was decidedly in favour of structural typology and was the person whose influence decided its legitimization in research). Using institutional–structural criteria was based on a straightforward and obvious assumption: that in all societies goods must be produced, distributed, and consumed – and that the way that these processes take place (hence the qualitative question) determines one of the fundamental differences between societies considered as socio-economic systems. In this way, schemas emerged that were evolutionary to the same degree as statistical classes were for those who favoured statistical–economic measurements (often unconsciously), but they try to answer not only the question of 'what changes?', but also 'how does it change?', and even 'why?' – in other words, the questions: who are the actors in the historical process, and why do they behave in this way that sets society into motion? It is true that List or Bucher perceived all previous economic systems as rungs on a single ladder, leading unequivocally to contemporary forms – 'highest', 'most devcl-oped', 'most progressive'. But they at least acknowledged the qualita-tive differences between these prior systems. They were weighed down by a fully presentist distortion of perspective, proper to all singular evolutionary schemas, but they were at least free from the fault of blurring the temporal boundaries between significantly different ways of life or shutting their eyes to the revolutionary role of the market and private property. The same cannot be said, unfortunately, of fans of purely statistical measurements.

In a manifest or subconscious way, their concepts are based on a philosophical vision of the world that is simultaneously (a) more evolutionary in the linear sense than the sharply criticized theories of nineteenth-century 'armchair philosophers'; (b) – which is paradoxical – also ahistorical: human society develops, rather than perfects itself, in accordance with St Thomas' concept of an 'internally unchanging type'; the history of humanity is nothing other than the constant increasing proximity to a model, embodied completely in the contem-porary system of a gigantic market and mega-corporations. Humanity is always pushed along this historic–ahistoric path by the same human instincts of profit, gain, personal benefit. If these eternal motives are not manifested in behaviour at some moment, this becomes a 'problem' to be examined and explained. The very presence of the aforemen-tioned motives does not require explanation – it is transhistorical human nature; (c) adapted to controlling, administrative, manipulative ideology: problems of social changes and development are reduced to a collection of leading questions: accessibility of capital, its invest-ment, the calculation of gains, allocating workforce, improving rela-tions of input to output, etc. Tradition, habit, custom, etc., are considered only as 'obstacles' and 'brakes' on the road to the one rational figure of rationality; (d) subordinating that which is social to what is economic – if not in the historiosophical sense, then at least in the analytical, logical one. 'That which is social' becomes simply an aggregate of dependent variables, organized according to the appropriate economic indicators and owing their meaning only to these statistical associations. Even if the 'active role' of a sociological element is acknowledged, it is generally only in the context of 'halting' or 'benefitting' economic growth.

I am not an economist and I can assume with a clear conscience, with full respect towards a field of study unknown to me, that the premises I lay out here, however they may shock a sociologist, present abstractions acceptable to a discipline that seeks primarily to solve contemporary problems and does not trouble itself with understanding human existence. I also accept that, for the purposes of research goals that the adherent of non-sociological statistical measurements set themselves, the premises described are heuristically useful and even uniquely generative. They are if the point of view described here penetrates through a kind of feedback loop to the social sciences that have a different structure of goals and tasks. What happens when this point of view is accepted by ethnologists such as Firth or Herskovits, I have discussed already elsewhere.[1] What, in the case of economists, is a generative premise for research, in their case is an unforgivable error for a researcher who has assigned him- or herself the goal of understanding human action. This error causes us to turn our eyes away from the situation that the system of kinship, to which the exchange of goods is subordinate in a pre-market society, is not so much an 'obstacle' in the development of economic activity as a powerful motive-creating force. Except that it is not so much motives that contemporary economists could assume a priori – the motives of gain and increasing personal wealth – but motives of mutual assistance and solidarity, motives tied to the cultural homogeneity of the life situation, guaranteed by the self-sufficient and small society of people.

In sum: forced by the nature of their discipline to consider a decidedly broader sphere of social and cultural issues, sociologists in their research perspective must take into account the fact that in various societies it is not only 'per capita income' that is different – but also the way in which economic activities are factored into the totality of social life. This aforementioned differentiation is also tied to the difference in motivations that govern economic behaviours. For both reasons, economic–social systems differ from each other qualitatively, and not only quantitatively. Every sociological attempt to classify the qualitatively different types must contain an analysis of not only the 'purely economic' aspects (if they even exist), but also the seemingly irrelevant social and cultural causes, considered not only as obstacles, but also as playing a creative, active role. If the frequently discussed role of determining economic factors is indeed a fact, then it depends, among other things, on the fact that certain economic modes create the conditions for subordinating economics to socio-cultural factors, and other forms subject these factors to an absolute and all-penetrating dictatorship of economic values and institutions.

I wrote all of this not, however, to polemicize with the superficial 'economization' of sociology. In distinction from the ethnological school that Firth dubs 'economic anthropology', contemporary sociology is not in danger of discounting the socio-cultural factors in the questions that it studies. The danger, if it exists, is of the opposite kind: in some – at least – contexts, the purely cultural factors are overly reified, their connection to the social structure – or to the sphere of the production, distribution, and circulation of goods that are necessary to satisfy human needs, whatever name we choose to call it by – is forgotten. The danger is based on perceiving cultural patterns and values only in the categories of 'attractiveness', 'imitation', 'psychological motives' – without taking into account the deeper underlying conditions, located in the social structure. Keeping our eyes on this danger, I have prefaced my remarks with this reflection – explaining how I understand the role of economic–social factors – to serve as a warning against going too far in the other direction, always a danger for any polemicist.

I want, however, to concentrate on matters that are closer to the sociologist's craft – thus, not so much on a polemic with the absolutism of the autonomy of economic life as on a discussion with the absolutism of the autonomy of culture. The perspective that I would like to propose is the following: all cultural models, alongside their technical function (that is, referring directly to satisfying the needs of human individuals and collectives), also serve a semiotic function whose meaning depends on the transmission of information about the structure of the situation of human action, on making the situation 'unequivocal', reducing its 'indeterminacy' of the situation. This reduction of ambiguity is achieved by the selection of one abstract possibility that is contained in potentia in a situation, and rejecting others. However frequently we happen upon different models of behaviour in response to a conduit of a person acting or as an addressee of her behaviour, so we can expect that this differentiation serves a semiotic function, and is informationally significant – this means the semiotic expression of some essential opposition differentiating a situation of human action about which we are speaking; that, in other words, the *raison d'être* of the observed cultural differentiation is the corresponding differentiation of positions – and along with it the real opportunities – contained in the social structure, and characterizing the situation of people acting in relation to these various models. We can also accept that, if the urgently observed differentiation of patterns disappears at a given moment, this is also a signal that the oppositions in the social structure that previously served as its *raison d'être* are themselves disappearing or dwindling. In this sense, we can say that the structure of cultural models remains in a relationship of signification towards the social structure; that the social structure is, in relation to the cultural system, a 'base', 'infrastructure'; that explaining the causes of the changes in the collection of cultural models can admittedly be done, remaining only in the locked circle of cultural phenomena, but understanding them, or grasping their meaning, their semiotic function, can only be done if we analyse the relations between them and their infrastructure – the system of social relations – demarcating the access of particular individuals to goods, and thereby shaping the material dimensions of their situation and the structure of the probability of opportunities for their typical situation. If some cultural difference that initially seemed glaring no longer does, then the situations of the people whose difference from each other was previously defined by that distinction have become similar; if, however, in some previously homogeneous cultural category, differences have begun to appear, we can seek out oppositions important to the analysis of the altered structure of the circulation of goods in objective features distinguishing these cultural subcategories. Those are, generally speaking, the methodological premises whose utility I would like to advocate for.

A good illustration of these methods could be the problem of cultural changes that is widely examined and discussed among us, which took place in our country after the war under the influence of industrial changes and socialism. It is a good illustration – because the problem is well known to all sociologists – and that is also why the differences between competing dimensions of theoretical interpretation can be seen all the more clearly in light of them.

Let us now proceed to the analysis of what we know and what we think on the subject of phenomena that are generally grasped as the 'urbanization of the village'.

## INFRASTRUCTURE OF CULTURAL CHANGES

Up to now, we have typically described the process of 'urbanization' as a macro-social process; a country or one of its terrains could urbanize; it was said to have urbanized when the proportion of residents living in urban conditions grew and the terrain became saturated with cities. Thus, when we now speak of 'village X urbanizing' or say that 'investment Y influences the urbanization processes of neighbouring villages', we must be thinking of something else. But what?

Semantic intuition bids that we accept that whenever we speak of the 'urbanization of villages' we are thinking of a relationship along an axis, on one end of which is the city, and on the other, village society; and that, in this relationship, the active side is the city, and the village is an object that it acts upon. But if we stopped at such a weak, very liberal understanding of a term that interests us – fitting in essence into any economic, political, artistic, and traditional influences directed at 'city–village' – then linking the urbanization of the village to processes of transformation in the village environment that we observe in Poland over the last twenty years would be untenable. Because the village, from the moment that it became the village – many centuries before socialism, capitalism, and even feudalism – was shaped by and changed under the continuous influence of cities. From the moment that the boundaries of ancestral communities expanded and 'society' (or the human collective under whose auspices the entirety of human needs, and the ends of all social efforts, were housed – in the words of Oskar Lange, 'a collective without marginal elements') became a collective broader than the common ties of kinship of a tribe, the village was second alongside the city, equal and tied energetically to the entirety of the form of human coexistence. The existence of the city, as Redfield strongly emphasized,[2] is assumed in the definition of village and peasantry. The village cannot be seen in the same way as the primitive tribe, which is self-sufficient in the sense that it does not require the existence of any other human collective; an 'isolated', 'closed' society of a village is perhaps heuristically useful, but it is, however, abstract and a construction more or less divorced from reality. In early tribes, maintaining the cultural situation in the face of an urban–agricultural revolution, the totality of life activities melds into one integral 'way of being' and none of the activities essential to the satisfaction of the life needs of the society and its members is autonomous in relation to the others in such a way as to become independent from tribal culture. The traditional village has many remnants of such tribal integralism, but even the most 'traditional' of villages goes outside of its own borders in at least some portion of its activities. The market, by means of which a portion of the peasant's products falls outside of the society's use and a portion of the peasant's needs is satisfied through goods that are not the products of that society; and a political and cultural elite that introduced into the peasant society ideas and cultural values born outside of its confines – these are two (certainly not the only) bridges joining the peasant society with the 'larger world', connecting it in an enduring way, being thus an immanent component of the 'essence' just as much as those components that render it similar to a pre-urban, tribal society. Both in the synchronic and in the diachronic dimension, the village is 'incomplete' without the city. In the synchronic dimension, it cannot satisfy its needs entirely through its own efforts, and, in the diachronic, it does not have its own history, but is the product of a process, in which urban and rural currents constantly merged with each other and acted upon each other. Thus, all villages – the European, the Indian, the Mexican, the Bolivian – are called by Redfield 'half-society', and its ways of being, 'half-culture'. If we only care about the fact that the village is connected to the city and the city acts on the village, then nothing fundamentally new has taken place in Poland in the last twenty years.

But, given that we hear of the 'urbanization of the village' in relation to recent transformations, something stronger must be meant than an understanding of the relationship between city and village. What this understanding is can be gleaned by examining a list of the topics that appear in research devoted to 'urbanization of villages'. Urbanization is discussed in relation to the disappearance of certain Polish forms of communal life typical of the older villages, and their replacement by new ones – when, for example, the processes of producing goods become separate from the household economy, when the activities of the farmer take on features of a profession, when department store furniture appears in peasant homes, and brand-name clothing on village streets, television antennas sprout on village roofs, or sports teams are formed. It is mentioned sometimes directly, sometimes implicitly when the author assumes that the phenomena referred to are a result of 'the village adopting cultural models created in the city', or even the result of 'cultural transmissions' whose sender is the city, with the recipient as the village. In brief, it is about the village becoming increasingly similar to the city (or rather to the model of the 'ideal city') – and this already assumes a certain theory of cultural diffusion as a process based primarily on the 'imitation' of 'more attractive' models.

What is actually taking place in Poland and is discussed under the rubric of 'urbanization of villages' can be much more sensibly described in categories used by Soviet sociologists: as 'the erasure of distinctions between the city and the village' or in terms of the emergence of mass culture, or – as Antonina Kłosowska, following Macdonald, proposes – in terms of the 'homogenization of culture'. The thing is that these processes are not taking place between abstract models of the 'ideal city' and the 'ideal traditional village', but in historically specific Polish cities and villages, and are therefore happening both in the city, and in the village. And, as we will try to show, they happen as an effect of processes that are neither exclusively urban, nor exclusively rural, and which touch both types of human collectivities – though, of course, in the city they happened much earlier than in the village. But, in order to be convinced of this, we must exit for a moment from the sphere of customs, cultural norms, and forms of cohabitation or systems of psychic ties.

The ability of cultural elements to spread across territory is notorious; tomes have been written about the travels of tools, rituals, ideas. Diffusion is one of the fundamental factors of history, culture, and cultural instruments of the evolution of the human species as a whole. Certain elements of culture, like tools and technological ideas, are more easily spread, encountering fewer obstacles and more easily assimilating into different cultural totalities; others, connected more directly to the satisfaction of vital needs, and more with the developed system of political and ideological ties, collide with insurmountable obstacles in the form of particular interests. The spread of any cultural elements is not mechanical and dependent merely on whether two cultures have encountered each other, or whether the contact was sufficiently intimate, or whether culture A knew about the discovery of culture B, etc. The automatic imitation that is typical of the contagious psychosis of a crowd is not a good explanation for the mechanism of diffusion. But it is also not a good explanation for a model of rational thought, soberly weighing the virtues and flaws of cultural elements in order to ultimately select the more 'efficient' element instead of a less efficient one. If the imitation of the rationale of efficiency was a sufficient explanation for the mechanism of diffusion, we would be left only to wonder why, with today's means of mass communication, we are not yet experiencing the benefits of a general human culture, and why Malaysian rice farmers differ from farmers in Ohio. What is more, we have to wonder why, in pre-War Poland, in which there existed, after all, numerous urban centres and even industrial ones, and in close proximity to them – in terms of available means of transport – even more numerous villages, somehow no one was talking about the 'urbanization of villages'. Not every city, speaking generally, 'urbanizes a village'; feudal cities, for example, not only did not 'urbanize' villages – quite the opposite, they encouraged their traditional elements.

Meanwhile, the key to explaining cultural diffusion has long existed – it was carved out by the hands of Karl Marx before the term 'diffusion' was first used to describe cultural phenomena. If the pre-Marxist tradition of an urban theory of society separated economic activities from all social ties and meanings beyond naked motives of gain, Marx tied the economic sphere to the rest of social life anew; he illuminated the rich connections to politics, customs, morality, beliefs, art, becoming in this way – despite certain unwilling interpreters – the true author of the contemporary concept of 'social totality', the method of multi-dimensional analysis based on a vision of multiple aspects of social reality. Contemporary anthropology – discovering anew the limitations of a model of 'single aspect', 'pure' economic activity in an 'ideal market', and the factual multiplicity of systems of reference for the analysis of any social behaviour – develops in essence in the earlier-formulated thought of Marx. But the holistic quality of Marx's thought, which calls for the examination of society as a totality of social energies, with properties not identical to the sum of the properties of its members (and thus is in direct opposition to, for example, this view of Ralph Linton's: 'cultures are, in the last analysis, nothing more than the organized repetitive responses of a society's members';[3] or Ruth Benedict's: 'no civilization has in it any element which in the last analysis is not the contribution of an individual'[4]), and of culture as a system of energized patterns of behaviour, does not produce the banal claim that, in research, it is necessary to 'take into account various factors'. Marx's holism internally structures the social totality and the system of culture correlated to it, allowing us to separate out infra- and ultra-structures; without for a moment negating the multiple directionality of social energies, it allows us to differentiate in the social process the conditioning and conditioned systems, events and their premises.

In Marx's view, the arrangement of social systems in the sphere of satisfying basic human needs – that is, needs, which must be met in order to survive – is this kind of infrastructure in the total process of cultural evolution. Speaking more precisely – it is the set of relations (dependencies) between humans that determines the way that goods are acquired to satisfy those needs. If we now call this system of relationships the 'economic system', we can, following Leslie A. White, differentiate two of its logically possible and historically distinguishable types: (a) a system whose determinants are social energies between people as human beings; and (b) a system in which the determinant is the relationship between goods as objects.[5] What differentiates the two systems is, in the first place, the existence or nonexistence of the market. Not the exchange of goods, but the market, with its typical depersonalization of inter-human contacts and the way it reduces the role of people to that of agents serving the circulation of goods – and drives people into that role.

Tribal society did not entirely know the market, or it encountered it only sporadically; feudalism knew the market, but only a portion of the population was pulled into its orbit – for the remaining portion, only a marginal part of their needs was satisfied by participating in market circulation. That is why in feudalism, economic activity – at least for the peasantry – was still to a large degree an aspect of social ties, contained within the boundaries of a society that was so tight-knit as to make it possible for those ties to be a totality. Its persistence in this form was the result of a lack, or lack of development, of the broader market – or, in other words, economic activity ceases to be an aspect of ties between people and becomes a product of relationships between goods in proportion to, and under the influence of, the development of the market, the transformation of goods into commodities. This process has not reached its culmination in Poland because of capitalism. Its rapid conclusion in the course of the last twenty years is the infrastructure of phenomena that have been termed, not entirely adequately, 'the urbanization of the village'.

The process being discussed – the process of transition from the first to the second type of economic system, the process of 'marketization': satisfying human needs, directing the path of goods from production to consumption, through the market – is happening in Poland not only in the village, but also in the city, and it is not so much of urban origins, as 'industrial' ones; it stems from the rapid development of industry and its accompanying phenomena – among others, one we have not noted: the growth of need for wage labour. Separating processes of production from household economies, reducing the economic function of the family, the professionalization and the growing division of labour, splitting personalities into collections of specialized roles, the growing meaning of partial ties or impersonal ones – we see this in both the village and the city, not only as a symptom of 'becoming city-like', but as a result of the pre-industrial, in most cities and villages, transforming into industrial organization of society, though, in the cities, this process precedes that in villages.

## 'MARKETIZATION' OF THE PROCESS OF SATISFYING NEEDS

The 'closed' nature of the feudal village was not so much a function of its 'village' character as the fact of a significant part of its activities, aimed at satisfying needs, being excluded from the mediation of the market. We can say that the village was 'closed' – it created a relatively isolated society – insofar as the process of satisfying its needs took place without the mediation of the market; all the more so, the smaller the portion of necessary goods that was acquired outside of the market. The village managed without the market not because the peasant preferred to make do without it; and not because the peasant wrongly calculated, irrationally, and therefore produced goods on his own at a greater cost instead of buying manufactured goods at a lower price; and not, finally, because reasons of prestige and pressures of communal norms demanded that he turn his back on the market – but simply because that market did not exist, or was too small to be able to absorb what the peasant had to offer. In order to buy, first it was necessary to sell; with the lack of a market, the peasant's products were not commodities, thus they did not have prices, thus they could not be sold. But the lack was not only of a market for goods: there was a minimal labour force on the market, therefore the labour power of peasants was not a commodity, thus an object independently produced by them 'did not cost' more, although it required a greater expenditure of energy than if the same item was produced by a professional craftsman using more efficient means – it was calculated from the point of view of satisfying needs 'more cheaply'; his behaviour could be called economically irrational only in the case where the labour force, wasted on the production of creating the aforementioned goods, could easily be sold on the market, and in exchange for the sum acquired the peasant could get this thing and even keep the change. But with a lack of market need for labour power, this was not the case, and this fundamental potential commodity, which is possessed by a significant portion of indigent peasants (similarly to the mass of urban poor craftsmen and merchants) was not a commodity, and the possibility of entering onto the market in the role of consumer was not given. We can be convinced that it is not so much the socio-economic formation that is tied to this as the absorptive capacity of the market, by the experience of the contemporary homemaker, who is not always doing her own laundry instead of sending it to the cleaners, or baking her own cake instead of buying it at a bakery, out of a love for household tasks; her activities are less efficient than those of cleaners and bakeries, but, from the perspective of the household budget, her behaviour is completely rational economically, because her labour power, used for laundry and baking, could not be 'sold' – it does not have a price and 'does not cost anything'; doing the laundry at home becomes, from an economic point of view, 'pure savings'.

The role of the market as a factor in historicizing the analysis of economic activities was pointed out by Witold Kula.[6] It is difficult to overemphasize the importance of his research for the historicization of the concept of economic rationality. He indicates that the feudal market is 'not only narrow, but also in the highest degree, to use Keynesian terminology, imperfect'; that, as a result of this:

> figuring economic decisions based on calculations of a capitalist type, for example, pricing goods and services that are neither acquired nor exchanged according to the prices governing them on a given market, is, in examinations of pre-capitalist epochs, not only anachronistic behaviour – in that it interprets human actions according to the principles proper to a different era – but it also poses certain internal risks.

This is because

> factoring monetary elements, which entered into processes of production without passing through the market or exited production not headed for the market, according to their market prices, is based on several blatantly unrealistic premises: 1) it assumes the existence of relatively unified market prices for each of these elements, with labour power at the forefront; 2) it assumes that all articles and all kinds of labour power have an economic value and price, which allows that value to be measured; 3) it assumes that the entrepreneur, the organizer of economic activities and the owner of the means of production always have the possibility of choice; that a given article can be sold on the market in exchange for its market price, or that the article can be used in processes of production. This last decision is undertaken only in cases where there are grounds to expect greater gain from its production.

The phenomena presented as symptoms of the 'urbanization of the village' can be treated as a function of this kind of process of the market 'perfecting itself'. The result of this is ever more frequent decisions being made about the sale of articles that previously had been used in processes of domestic production, and also about acquiring on the market articles for consumption that were previously made at home. The growing frequency of such decisions is precisely the result of the market 'perfecting itself', a result of the transformation of ever greater masses of articles into commodities with a real sale price – this process is in turn the result of the development of industry. It is this in a dual sense: growing industry severs ever greater numbers of people from creating products for their own direct consumption with their own hands (primarily food) – it expands the need for products of agriculture and animal husbandry; and, secondly, it transforms into a commodity the greatest resource of the village populace – its labour power – thereby executing a meaningful transformation in the content of the concept of 'rationality', in reference to calculations of the peasant economy.

All of the things generally counted as features of a 'non-urbanized' or 'traditional' village society – the melding of production into household economy, the particular closeness of family ties, the lack of developed division of labour, etc. – can be treated as a collection of institutions adapted to satisfying human needs in conditions lacking a market, both in the village environment and in the urban one. And the persistence of those features, going well beyond feudal times, can be seen as a result of the longstanding stability of their foundations in Poland.

During feudal times, the peasant's contacts were negligible, the market was nationwide, and the more international one existed only for the great property-holders; the market possibilities of the peasant were limited by the capacities of the local market, whose dimensions were determined by the distance that a peasant's cart could cross twice in the course of a single day. And even to this market, the peasant came only when he needed to acquire a very specific item, to acquire goods that he could not make himself – salt, iron tools (when possible, wooden ones were used) – and in order to pay feudal tithes. From this comes the paradoxical phenomenon that, in periods of high prices for wheat, the peasant sold less of it than when the prices were low.[7] In a certain sense, the 'sale' of labour power was also outside of the market in cases of share-cropping. As Jan Rutkowski determined, compensation of farm workers in feudal service 'was composed of three fundamental aspects: housing, sustenance, and clothing, and the monetary reward was earmarked above all else for the purchase of clothing'. From the analysis of the components of the fortunes of a vassal, or someone forcibly pulled into monetary circulation, it emerges that barely 17 per cent of this wealth contains items that one may suspect were acquired from the market.[8] Nineteenth-century documents attest to a similar situation. One of the records of an audit of government-owned property in Będziń county from 1841 states that peasants 'sell their product for the highest price at the market in the city of Siewierz and with the money earned from it they satisfy their needs, they are involved in no other speculations other than agriculture'.[9] Julian Chmura cites examples of authors from the first half of the nineteenth century who write that:

> a feature of [...] feudal economies is the lack of monetary circulation [...] For using the ground the peasant pays the serfdom; the farm-hand and the virgin are paid with grain; for help with the harvest the lord of the manor gives a few bed of potatoes; everything pays and is rewarded in its own kind. Very little is paid in money, nobody knows how to use it, they bury savings under a tree or hide it up in the attic to be lost and forgotten.

'Our peasants [...] are able to work hard and make anything they need at home, and aside from buying salt, iron, and clothing [...] can make anything that they need.'[10] Let us recall that the meagre dimensions of the labour market were attested to by the minuscule number of factory workers, which in the second half of the nineteenth century, according to generally agreed-upon measurements, did not greatly exceed 50,000.[11]

The development of industry in the Kingdom in the second half of the nineteenth century transformed the village – freed from debt to the lord, but also from the protection and care of the lord and the manor, it became 'a reservoir of cheap (very cheap!) unqualified labour power'.[12] The supply of this resource greatly exceeded the demand, hence its low price on the market and the extremely broad range of situations in which the peasant – despite the existence of industry – 'calculated on' using his own labour power in a way that was far less productive than it would have been on his own farm.

As we know, however, this development of industry did not last very long. Inter-war Poland hovered around the level of industrial production from 1913, which testifies to a certain stagnation in industry, and also in the market of labour power. According to Mieszczankowski's calculations, in the years 1921–38 barely 1,080,000 people moved from the villages to the cities, alongside a natural population growth in villages reaching almost 5 million; this means that the wage labour market was not able to absorb the growth in numbers of people from the villages (what is more, as Mieszczankowski observes, even this modest stream into the city 'had in its size a lumpenproletariat character'[13]). Using the most 'liberal' – because subjective – definition of 'superfluousness', as 'a state of the subjective feeling of the need for seeking work outside of the farm', a group of researchers from IGS calculated the number of superfluous hands for work in Polish villages between the years of 1934 and 1935 as 2.5 million; but, of course, the number of 'superfluous' people, if a wage labour market that was perfectly capacious were suddenly to come into being, would be much higher. As the group ISS rightly observed in their study *Młodzież sięga po pracę* [The youth seek work]:[14]

the superfluity, arising gradually, is not perceived as unemployment: depending on the available labour resources, the farm adjusts – also gradually – its methods and organization of work, so that an excess of free time is never felt; one works in a less efficient way, undertakes tasks that could be spared if care was taken or better tools were available – but time 'is used up'.

The owner of even a puny portion of land did not have a choice – put work into the farm unproductively or sell his labour power. The decision was made for him by the lack of a labour market.

The results of stagnation – or rather of the shrinking of Polish industry – were investigated at a village in the Rzeszów region by Jerzy Michałowski; he came to the conclusion that:

> we can observe ever more clearly the phenomenon of the village sealing itself from contact with the outside world. That naturalization of agriculture, the contraction of a circulation of credit, the increased productivity of cultivation and many other factors led to the situation that the village was ever more independent of external factors, transforming itself into a practically closed system, with an ever-shrinking point of intersection with the surrounding world.

A significant natural growth 'devoured' without remainder the consequences of the departure of a portion of the rural population into the cities in the olden times of better economic prosperity – and the village retreated rather quickly to the conditions typical in feudal times that are essentially natural to the farm.

> If once, in Polish feudal times, land was counted not in acres, but in villages, because what was decisive was not territory, but the labour power it contained, then today we are at a similar point – we must count the villages, because even the territory, fertility of the soil, and the sum of economic effects from a given area determine to what degree the ultimate economic goal – satisfying needs – will be achieved. What is decisive is not the labour power it possesses, a power that is dead in today's conditions, but the density of consumers [...] How often we encounter in the fields a hired hand who spends the entire day tending a single solitary grazing cow or chasing 2-3 geese. Perhaps the result of a larger than normal number of hands at work has increased the care taken with each task, but it has also undeniably qualitatively deteriorated into extremely demoralizing conditions. This is, it seems, a psychological moment that will avenge itself later on the organization and productivity of work that happens even under better conditions.[15]

The excess of consumers burdening each hectare of land meant that the owner of each hectare based their decisions not on the maximum financial gain but on the maximal satisfaction of elementary needs (which, of course, in general conditions of hardship in the village had to remain an unattainable ideal). The village turned its back on the exchange of commodities – the market transformed a minuscule portion of its resources into goods – and voiced only the smallest of demands on the market. According to Michałowski's observations, of the 18 people who visited the village store during the hours of the greatest traffic, only 3 paid in cash (for a total sum of 1 złoty, 5 groszy); the rest paid in kind. In two villages with a total of 5,000 inhabitants, during July of 1934, the total purchases were one scythe, six buttons, one aluminium cup, and 10 dkg of nails; and the total earnings of the companies in the Central Union of Polish Industry from these two villages was 5.35 złoty.[16] Obviously, it was not the same in every Polish village; the villages in the regions of Poznań, Pomerania, or Silesia were much more advanced on the path of market production.

I have cited known illustrations of known facts; I gave them because they are often omitted in the context of the analysis of the cultural changes in the postwar period called the 'urbanization of villages'. At the same time, it is this collection of facts that characterizes the infrastructure of cultural changes called the 'urbanization of villages', if we are not only interested in symptoms, but also their causes.

The cultural differences between the industrialized city and the village that fully invested in natural agriculture had their basis primarily in the fact that the inhabitant of the city functioned in the framework of a market, the inhabitant of the village, in a world in which nothing on the path from work to consumption went beyond the boundaries of the total system of ties. That is why the model of economic thought, the model of rationality, and the behavioural motivations of an inhabitant of the industrial cities are much closer to the ideal model of *Homo oeconomicus*, though even the latter, obviously, is not fully identical to him, because *Homo oeconomicus* is a part of an 'ideal market' that has never been fully achieved. The peasant remained a peasant, the townsperson, a townsperson: for the peasant, the world polarized into the opposition 'village–city'. His culture was information only about his difference from townspeople.

## 'MARKETIZATION' AND CULTURAL CHANGES

'In the corvée', observes Marx, 'the labour of the worker for himself, and his compulsory labour for his lord, differ in space and time in the clearest possible way.'[17] In the mind of the serf, the feudal rent

in whatever forms it takes is always what he gives the lord, what he must share with the lord. That is why the battles of feudal serfs were generally fought over whether to completely eliminate the undesirable participant in the share of produced goods, or to significantly limit his 'portion'. Rebelling or supplicating against folwarks based on feudalism, the serfs did not demand a folwarks based on wage labour. 'Folwark without serfdom, before the development of the labour market, did not at all lead to the development of a folwark based on wage labour. To the contrary, it was a revolutionary idea of doing away with the folwark altogether [...] Folwark without serfdom was a potential program of the serfs for eliminating folwarks altogether.[18]

Regarding feudal rents, the serfs were not fighting in the name of capitalist wage labour, but in the name of closing the circle of production–consumption anew, in the name of integrating straightforward natural reproduction – in the name of preserving the products and labour force for the family farm. The thinking of serfs in these conditions was organizing around the satisfaction of needs, and not increasing gains; the members of the family were in the first place consumers, not producers; the 'producer' was the land, and it decided how many consumer goods would fall to each consumer.

In the lack of a wage labour market, deliberation over how to increase the earnings produced by one 'employee' made no sense. At most, one could think about increasing the production from 1 hectare of land. The upper bounds of that growth were defined quite emphatically by the objective conditions of the autarchic, non-market peasant economy. In order to analyse production in terms of the number of goods falling to each producer – in other words, for the term 'efficiency of work' (or an analysis which is the basis of 'rational calculation' in contemporary thought) to make any sense, there would have to first exist a situation in which there would be a possible choice between more or less efficient uses of labour power. As long as such a choice did not exist, the basis of calculation was not the seeking out of the most efficient (*ergo*, profitable) forms of economic activity, but the necessity of maximizing the satisfaction of needs for food of each member for the family – first consumers, and only later producers. From this point of view, the greatest reserves lay in the liquidation of subsidies for the sake of non-agricultural activities, burdening the family budget: for the landowner, the court, the church, the nation. The peasant comes into contact with the market only when he has to, in order to acquire the tools or consumer goods that he does not know how to make, or cannot make. In conditions of longstanding population growth (caused by a lack of migration) in the village, the supply of consumer goods is generally smaller than would be the required minimum for their survival; 'good demand' for agricultural products is thus not used for increasing the commercial activity of the peasant, but for improving the consumption of his family – while there is a simultaneous contraction of goods brought to market. During a weak development of market relations, we observe the same phenomenon in the city: 'In small-town stores entire families work, they work only part-time [...] the result of excessive difficulties in distribution is of course the marginal, quite low, almost zero, productivity of work'.[19]

On the second pole, we find the producers granted a limitless possibility of choice: the choice between more or less efficient (*ergo*, profitable) ways of using their labour power. An absorptive market for agricultural goods contradicts the principle that the 'best' use of land is extracting from it all of the goods necessary to satisfy all of the needs of members of the family; from this, the representation of agricultural production as only culture, albeit a profitable one, becomes meaningful, along with acquiring remaining consumer goods for money earned by selling products.

But the results of the broadening of the market for labour power become even more lofty; it is only after this has happened that thinking about production in the categories not of 'yield per hectare' but of 'yield per worker' or per hour of work becomes rational. The functioning of the market – particularly when it arises suddenly, as a result of rapid social changes – is, of course, not immediate: in a traditional village, economic activity was not distinguished from other social function – it was freighted with many meanings beyond the economic ones (for example, religious, social, status-related), and depriving it of these meanings takes time; researchers have repeatedly drawn attention to the fact that, for a farmer, raising a cow can have a meaning tied to prestige or position, even when it has lost its economic utility. Nonetheless, the emergence of a market for labour is the actual moment of transition. The entire cultural revolution of the 'urbanization' of the village is delayed and slowed down – but it is, nonetheless, a consequence.

Let us take as a starting point a phenomenon widely seen as falling under the heading of the 'urbanization of the village' – the separation of processes of production from the family farm, the home. With a lack of market alternatives, the home was a collection of consumers and producers at the same time; a member of the family was a producer in the family workshop automatically, or unreflexively, simply because they were also a consumer in the household economy. Even this calculation is essentially ahistorical; in the consciousness of the people involved, the roles of consumer and producer were not separate, they dissolved completely into one another in the social situation, completely determined by the size of the family and its land. And the basis of separating the workplace and the family farm can take place only with the separation of the roles of producer and consumer. It was the labour market that became the harbinger of such a division: it created the situation in which the fact that someone ate from the communal family pot did not mean that this person contributed to filling that pot by working the family plot. The lack of a market, its flaws, or the unattractiveness of the alternatives it offered, conditioned if not the creation, then at least the persistence, of this link between the household economy and the place of production, which Bogusław Gałęski, in a fantastic study on the general properties of social changes in villages, describes as a situation in which 'the destiny of a significant portion of created goods is being used by their producers and their families, and on the road from production to consumption they do not need to pass in one or another way through the mechanism of social acceptance; the work of creation again happens to a significant degree in the home economy'.[20] And the opposite – the existence of such a market gradually levels the results of the fact that the peasant economy produces foodstuffs; we can imagine a marketplace so perfect, and distinguished by a sufficiently attractive structure of prices for practically the entire economic production to go outside of the sphere of family consumption, and practically the entire family pot to be filled with products acquired at the market, and not created by the hands of those eating from the pot – in other words, that the typical situation is achieved, of the urban family long since pulled into the sphere of the circulation of goods, where the consumers are in the family, and producers outside of it.

The second symptom of the so-called 'urbanization of the village' is the weakening of family ties, so typical and obvious in older rural societies. The raw patriarchal nature of the traditional rural family crumbles – the harsh discipline of parents towards children, the extent of parental authority over the fates of descendants, contracts. Similar phenomena occur – sometimes in parallel, sometimes slightly earlier – in the 'urban' family. And in urban families, it varied; the afore-mentioned process took place earliest in the families of labourers, living exclusively from the sale of their labour power, and took place most slowly in families living off their property. In families of this last type, similar to peasant families, a particular closeness of ties stemmed not from the fact that the family possessed property, which was an object of desire for all members (and therefore caused them to inscribe the plans for their lives within the framework of the family and its efforts, fighting with each other over the rights to inherit and to curry favour with the patriarch in order to ensure a will and testament that was beneficial to them) – but from the fact that, aside from the family fortune, there were no possibilities for earning, or generally for achieving a social position that would be culturally sought after and desirable. The change in this regard for bourgeois families was ameliorated, but only to some degree, by the creation of a ladder of education as an instrument of an independent individual career, and large bureaucratic organizations as the channels of such a career, leading to ranks in position similar to those that were guaranteed by a large personal fortune.

For peasant families, what decided the change was the creation of a large market of wage labour in general. The land, still maintaining its attractiveness in light of traditional cultural values, ceases to be the only possibility – it becomes one of many, and the results of family insubordination cease to be as threatening as before, and fights for succession become more bitter than ever. It is not so much that the union of the place of production and the family economy lies in positions that are especially amenable to family tradition, as that there is no alternative, no choice, when it comes to options for making one's way in the world.

The third symptom of the so-called 'urbanization of the village' – 'professionalism', the professionalization of the work of the farmer – is also the product of a labour market. As Gałęski wisely observes, 'the basis of defining certain tasks, distinguished from others, as a profession, connects the activity of the individual to the rest of society, or, more narrowly, the exchange of the individual's work for society is realized in the form of value (products, services) which the individual gains as a result. This relationship forms the basis of the existence of a profession.'[21] The activities of the peasant participate in the social division of labour to the degree that they are an element of the society's structure of professions, in which they participate in such relationships, in exchange, in the market. So long as the peasant participates in exchange only through the products of his own economy – and thus his goods are not his labour power but only the results of its productive usage – his situation as the owner, or his place in the class structure, dominates in defining his general social situation above his position as maker, or his position in the structure of professions – and 'peasantness' is not so much a profession, as a possession. The peasant-owner becomes the professional farmer to the extent that his labour power becomes a potential product: it can be practically used to set into motion other tools, to work on raw materials, without connection to the fact of ownership – it can be sold as labour power. If in these conditions, the inhabitant of the village continues to work the land, then this activity can reasonably be regarded in terms of the division of labour – he 'chose this profession, and not another one'; though he is not actually selling his labour power on the market, it is an economic decision in the same sense of economic (assuming a model with a pure situation, this means considering the economic decisions without reference to their non-economic meanings) as the decision to get a job in a factory as a locksmith. The existence of a labour market gradually undermines the traditional way of thinking about work on the land as a function of ownership, gradually inclines one to consider even the fact of possessing land as a function of the farmer's profession, and pulls such changes into the activities of the farmer as are characteristic of labouring professions – such as attaining adequate qualifications and acknowledging education as an entry into the profession.

The fourth symptom of the cultural changes called the 'urbanization of the village' is the disappearance of the protective, defensive functions of the group – or, rather, of the prosperous members of the group – towards the inhabitants of the village. The function of mutual protection belongs to the elementary needs that must be fulfilled by every human society, and every human community possesses institutions better or worse organized to fulfil this aim. In the stages of cultural evolution in which society is organized into tribal communities, or when there is a federation of local societies, these functions are realized on a 'community' level and not a social one.

Everywhere in feudal, and even post-feudal (in England, for example, in the 1830s), Europe, the protective functions were performed by the court, the village community, the city magistrate, the parish. The feudal relationship was one of mutual obligation, and bourgeois ideologues demanding freedom had in mind the freeing of serfs not only from service to their lords, but also from the protection of their lord; the serfs more than once missed the feudal system from which they drew some feelings of safety, help in cases of catastrophe, protection from dying of hunger and utter indigence. Even in 1855, the peasants of Chlewisk complained that, 'under our previous landlord, all buildings were repaired and built anew with funds from the manor. Materials for walls, carts, ploughs, sleighs, household goods were given to us at no cost. Now everything is refused us. We were given healthy animals in exchange for overworked ones, which were put out to pasture. Now that does not happen.'

> It is true, that in the olden days we would go into debt, but we did not feel it as a burden, because we received from the manor all the wooden materials needed for tools and building fences, grazing for the herd, fuel, cutting grasses in the forests, exchanging overworked animals for healthy ones for free, constructing and repairing buildings at the manor's cost, without having to pay for any of it.[22]

The smaller the degree to which the peasants, through the medium of market relations, were connected to Society with a capital 'S' – that is, how long they looked to society, closed in the confines of the communal group, in the hopes of protection and insurance against fate – the more the heirs or wealthy neighbours filled the function, which early capitalist individualism commissioned to the industriousness of the individual-atom, and which, only today, after long struggles and battles, do institutions constructed on a macrosocial, state level of social organization begin to serve. The process of changing from protective institutions organized on a level of local society to such institutions distributed among general social organizations (divided by a period of painful conflict between social functions of protection) is thus – or maybe not simultaneously – the lot of the inhabitants both of the city and of the village. And it is a somewhat delayed result of the broadening of relationships of exchange, and the nets of economic dependency, from the local society to society generally – the fact, that society organized into a country, instead of the local region, became the level on which created goods are balanced against the need for them created by consumption. When the population of the village is pulled into the general social division of labour, it experiences this division of people into roles, so typical for the 'macronization' of webs of social relationships and the processes of particularization tied to it, specializing in social functions and the services of particular organizations that are called to them. With the mediation of each of its roles, then, the population of the village is pulled into the exchange of services and goods, which ranges beyond the confines of the native society. The relative independence of the individual from the group is shaped on this basis; observed in the boundaries of the group, cutting across the majority of its social ties, the population of the village then begins to seem like a collection of independent individuals, and thus becomes similar to the image that came into being in the minds of researchers observing the urban environment – in which, perhaps because of its size, it is hard to perceive 'the other end' of the threads of social relations, 'emerging' from particular individuals.

Finally, the fifth symptom – 'the penetration into the village of goods created in cities'. We probably do not need a lengthy demonstration in order to support the thesis that this phenomenon is the clear consequence of the already-described processes of 'marketization'. The peasants had not previously purchased goods made in cities – not because they did not like them, but because – firstly – they were not participants in the circulation of goods, so they did not have anything to purchase them with, and – secondly – if they could not sell their labour power for a reasonable price, putting their energies into producing a more primitive version of goods made in cities (and making them with a much larger – considering the matter abstractly – layer of costs, when we calculate the fictional 'price' of labour power that is essentially lacking in price) was not only 'economically more rational', but the only possible choice from the perspective of the needs that these goods were to satisfy. When, however, labour power did become a product and acquired a cost that could be paid, the situation changed: traditional sentiments might still explain choosing homemade clothing above department-store gowns in some cases, but from an economic perspective prioritizing tradition in this way became wasteful; for the energy and time put into making them at home, one could earn through the market an amount that would allow one to acquire goods of a similar utility, and other goods as well. Once one begins to think of the products of one's own hands as a commodity, 'commodity' thinking slowly takes over an entire sphere pertaining to the satisfaction of needs. Seeking the goods to meet these needs, the inhabitant of the village looks at the market and thinks not so much about how much time will be lost in order to acquire a particular necessary good, but also about how many and what goods can be acquired if time is spent in a maximally beneficial way (*ergo*, earning). In this state of things, the inhabitant of the village, similarly to the inhabitant of the city, groomed by the 'commodification' of inter-personal relations, is condemned to satisfy his needs through the mediation of the market. In regards to this fundamental fact, it seems secondary that the goods that one acquires are 'from the city'. It is simply that the factories that produce them are generally located in urban areas. Whence could the inhabitants of the village acquire such things if not 'from the city'? The important thing is that they get them from the market.

The processes described here are a base on which a phenomenon can take place, generally presented as the penetration of values typical of the city into village life. I am thinking of the distinguishing of institutions of free time, preferring certain kinds of entertainments, the hierarchy of ideals of successful living, etc. The values that we are discussing are rather tightly correlated with conditions of life in a market-based, plural society, bonded by the criss-crossing systems of organizational ties and the general social web of relationships, or economic interdependencies. Upon closer investigation, most of these values turn out to be new, not only for the residents of the village but also for most of the residents of the cities; their diffusion can very probably be most sensibly explained by considering the general social process of industrialization, the radical expansion of the labour market and the accompanying changes in systems of relationships and social ties. These values follow the path blazed through society by the tread of the industrial tractor. The tractor makes its way through urban environments just as much as rural ones – and that is why the thing we observe today (not, of course, without the influence, a conscious one, of efforts of mass communications, now located in a purely psychic sphere – which keep arriving in the village not as a gift from above, but as the result of an exchange of goods sold by the farmer in exchange for a product offered by the market) is the erasure of differences between the city and the village in the sphere of values, producing a single, homogeneous culture of mass industrial society.

## OTHER LESSONS REGARDING SIMILARITIES AND DIFFERENCES

If we move now from general considerations – maintained, despite local illustrations, in terms of the general principles of cultural evolution – and shift to matters that are specifically Polish, we must conclude that the processes referred to, taking place in our country under the conditions of a socialist economic-political system, are tied (in the general conditions in which they have been presented so far) not so much to a transition from capitalism to socialism, as to the final phases of the industrialization of society. Socialism brings into being the changes described here in some sense 'instead of' capitalism; speaking more narrowly, the changes described here, which in the West happen in the framework and under the influence of capitalist relations, took place in Poland only after the socialist revolution. It may turn out, from a historical perspective, that most places in the world will undergo this transformation under conditions of socialism, and not capitalism; this does not change the fact that the modernization of urban and rural alike, elicited by processes of commodifying interpersonal relationships and the general particularization of social life, will take place, as it seems, always, whenever a pre-industrial society transforms into an industrial one – without regard to which kind of social system gives rise to this metamorphosis.

The industrial–machine revolution can be credited with the total 'marketization' of the process of satisfying human needs, or, more narrowly, with directing the path of an individual's creative effort for the satisfaction of their needs through a broader social circulation and redistribution of goods. The result of this redirection (the term 'redirection' is perhaps better than 'marketization' here because it allows for the theoretical possibility of a redistribution without money) is also the widespread homogenization of the goods that serve to satisfy human needs: all environments draw these goods from the same market, served by the same mass-industrial series, and the process by which industry takes over the manufacture of goods also leads to the creation of a need for goods that cannot be made at home 'instead', and which one is compelled to acquire on the general market without regard to the actual economic rationale. Another result of this redirection is the particularization of social life and the specialization of social functions tied to the restructuring of society on the basis of intersecting arrangements of partial ties – and the transformation of people into petitioners of different specialized organizations (formed 'privately' or 'nationally') in order to satisfy various personal needs. Finally, the result of this redirection is also the spread, as the result of industrialization, of the homogenization of culture, based on the increased similarity of the conditions under which the satisfaction of personal needs takes place, regardless of a person's profession and ecological environment. All of these are, we can say, general truths, which meaningful industrialization will always bring into being, if it penetrates deep enough into the elementary life processes of society.

On the other hand, the introduction of planning on a broad social scale, or the elements of planning, into processes of the redistribution of goods (eliminating to a significant degree the role of competition and motives of gain as regulators of the production and circulation of goods on a general level of social organization), a characteristic of the socialist system cannot but influence the processes described here. In our previous reflections, we used terms like 'ideal market', 'perfection of the market'. We know that national planning introduces significant modifications into the functioning of the market and works against what economists call an 'ideal market'. What kind of influence does this have on processes of modernization in villages and the erasure of differences between cities and villages?

Witold Kula writes:

> Under socialism – we know this quite well from our own experience – market laws manifest themselves completely differently than in capitalism. The deficits of consumer goods manifest themselves for example, not in a general increase in prices, but in lines in front of stores and a gap between the state's price and the one on the black market. Elements of arbitrariness in the determination of price, especially of raw goods, lead to significant changes in the calculations of production facilities, the waste of certain raw materials (such as wood), a fictive profitability or a fictive lack of profitability. In conditions of a lack of free play of capital on the market, it is very difficult to bring the element of time and the determination of percentage to a 'common denominator'.[23]

It is obvious that this state of things must weaken the purity of the theoretical model of the percentage of the commercialization of the village economy. Here are a few preliminary modifications.

The lack, on the market, of certain essential goods, their inaccessibility, or high prices on the black market may lead to a situation where, even with a 'market way of thinking', it may seem 'economically rational' to produce these goods (or their corresponding substitutes) at home, and not only important in order to satisfy needs. In many cases, this can counteract the professional specialization of the production facility, tying the household farm with domestic production, maintaining elements of naturalism in the home. Another example: even in conditions of the larger society where there is a balance, in terms of a market that can absorb the labour force, notorious housing problems can lead to the mobility of workers being limited, which will generate local centres where the supply of labour power exceeds the demand, which will also mean, considered from the other side, that the effect of industrial investment on the 'marketization' of village labour power, and therefore on all the cultural changes that go with it, is limited to fairly restricted spatial boundaries, and thus processes of modernization take place very unevenly and at different rates in different places.

The system also serves in another way to modify the processes of erasing the difference between the city and the village. The high degree of organization of all aspects of life that is particularly common to socialist countries is not always the same in cities and in villages in Poland. Most of the inhabitants of large cities, without regard to their profession or level of education, are in a similar situation today, because they are functionaries of large organizations (this fact describes their basic source of income and social position) and in satisfying the majority of their needs they must appear as petitioners to similar large organizations. These two facts inscribe almost all of their life activities in the system of partial relationships (impersonal ones).

Things look differently in the villages, even today. Being able to own land means that the majority of residents of the village are in a position of relative independence in regard to the world of large organizations: it gives them relatively autonomous means of supporting themselves and allows them to satisfy some of their needs – which, in certain situations, theoretically speaking, could even become a significant amount – without coming into contact with such organizations. Among other things, the residents of the village, if they are not directly the functionaries of an organization (that is, if they are not farmer-workers or farmer-administrators) are not bound by the macrosocial system of protection and insurance. This fact spurs regeneration efforts or the galvanization of functions of protecting the group and works against the loss of numerous features of a closed local society. On the other hand, the mechanism broadly portrayed by Gałęski, of pulling individual peasant farms – while maintaining their property rights – into the macrosocial system of the socialist economy is nothing other than creating, on the basis of credit, contracts, purchases, related transactions, etc., points of intersection and dependence tying the peasant to larger organizations – and, thus, in a certain sense, making the social situation of the farmer similar (albeit not identical) to the social situation of the city-dweller.

In sum, it seems overall that the conditions in which urban mass culture is formed are based on the infrastructure of large impersonal organizations and the 'function-ization' of individuals with regard to these organizations; retaining properties is rather a factor working against the disappearance of differences between cities and villages, and in any case demarcates particular limits that make it impossible to complete this process. The differences can only disappear to the degree to that is conditioned by the redirection through the market of individual processes of production–consumption; and they are maintained only to the degree that is conditioned by the heterogenization of the social situation of the individual with regard to the dependence upon or relative autonomy from large, impersonal organizations.

I have barely touched on the broader problems considered by sociologists under the rubric of the 'urbanization of villages'. I had no intention of trying to systematize them or – what is more – to present a theory of them, competing with currently circulating theories. I only wanted to draw attention to the frequently overlooked, or largely unconsidered, infrastructure of the cultural changes described – to the narrow interdependence that conditions which of the changes takes place in this infrastructure. Highlighting these dependencies does not in any way undermine the importance of problematics such as changes in the beliefs or opinions of people in villages, differences between generations, the role of outposts of intelligentsia in villages, peasant-workers, or rural activists in transmitting urban customs and values to the village. But an analysis of the infrastructure of cultural changes is necessary to allow us to understand that a servant girl returning with her newly acquired wealth is not 'urbanizing' the village, and not only because she has a negligible number of companions.

In sum, I have tried to present here the following thoughts:

1 The cultural changes taking place in villages that I examine here are less a symptom of the 'introduction of cultural models from the city into the village' than they are of the erasure of differences between the city and the village, and the formation of a new, homogenic mass culture, to some degree new in relation not only to the village, but also to many pre-war Polish cities. In the urban-industrial-

market complex that is today's city, the active side of these changes is primarily the element of 'market-ness'; the action of the element of 'urban-ness' is effective only as a function of the actions of the former element.

2 The infrastructure which this new mass culture generates, and in regards to which it functions, is in the first place that of introducing the mediation of the market into the individual's path from labours of production to the satisfaction of needs.

3 Cultural changes such as separating the process of production from the home, the weakening of patriarchal family ties, the professionalization of production activities, the loss of functions of protection–insurance by local society, etc., are – sometimes delayed because of the traditionalism of institutions and educational processes – always the obvious result of the aforementioned changes in infrastructure.

4 The 'newness' of culture, both in the village and in the city, and its homogenization are among other things conditioned by the modernity of its material elements, including to a large degree the eventuality of the autarchy of the family in the satisfaction of its needs.

5 The tempo and consequences of the process of erasing differences between the city and the village (if we assume the adequacy and proper functioning of instrumental institutions) are all the greater, in our conditions, if there is:

a a fuller – that is to say, more internally mobile and absorptive – national market for labour power; and

b a higher market price for the labour power (it decides the terrain in which elements of the natural economy become economically irrational).

Decreasing the capacity of the labour market or lowering the price of labour can, then, on the other hand, exert a dampening effect on the processes of urbanization of the villages.

6 Important processes, which have run their full course, on the individual path of 'using labour energy to consumption' through the market can comprise an infrastructure conditioning the achievement of the first step in the process of erasing the cultural differences between the city and the village. Achieving the next step depends on further changes in infrastructure – that is, on the homogenization of the social situation of inhabitants of the village and the city with regards to large organizations specializing in executing particular social functions.

There is, of course, one more meaning of the term 'urbanization of villages': the village achieving 'urban conditions of life', in the sense of an urban scenery and an urban type of organization of space – brick houses, surfaced roads, gas, running water, sewage, sanitation, etc. But processes of 'urbanization of villages' understood in this way have not achieved significant results (in some cases, we can even speak of the 'ruralization' of city centres, if by 'village conditions of life' we understand the lack of the aforementioned elements). This process of 'urbanization' also requires the previously described changes in infrastructure, as well as significant advances in the degree of life and accumulation of earnings earmarked for communal purposes and 'collective consumption'.

# III

# Cultural Determinants of the Research Process

The reflections presented in this article are based on the idea that the essence of the socio-cultural process called 'research' is rendering comprehensible for people the bounty of socially acquired experience. Grasping the thing in somewhat narrower terms, we can say that research is the cultural – which is to say, informational – counterpart to the activity of production, which gives fragments of reality a meaning that is 'adaptive to energies' – namely, it gives them meaning from the point of view of providing society with energy. Research serves this function in the process of a conceptual systematization of chaotically acquired material of human experiences, just as production fulfils a role of organizing into a system of human needs the chaotic collection of human energy, collected outside the human organism. Grasped in a conceptual system, stimuli that were seemingly meaningless become information.

## THE RELATIVE AUTONOMY OF CULTURE

One of the most important features of the human species is the relative separation between webs of information and webs of energy. Taking into account the fact that every transmission of information is connected, however, to the transfer of some amount – even if only a small one – of energy, we can reformulate the above claim in the following way. For human society, it is characteristic that certain products are adapted to being specialized carriers of information, where other products and actions have maintained a role that is primarily one of energy. 'Informational specialization' is based on the fact that the relevant creation or action has an informational meaning, and the corresponding transmission of energy is negligible or does not exist for the partner of meaning. The roots of the specialization must be sought in the particularity of the human way of life, which is in turn the result of the biosocial evolution of humans.

In accordance with modern views on human evolution, the human species is an infantile form in comparison to its direct animal ancestors. This infantilization is based above all on the significant reduction of inherited biological resources – above all, on the almost complete lack of a repertoire of instinctive behaviours, adapted to a repertoire of the situations most likely, according to the way of life of a given species and the characteristic way that it satisfies its needs. Ashley Montagu describes it thus in his book *Anthropology and Human Nature*:[1] 'As a result of processes of natural selection, the direct ancestors of humans increasingly freed themselves from their instinctive behaviours – so that, when the human emerged, these behaviours essentially vanished.' Thus, in the course of evolution leading the human along, the process of natural selection privileged the biological 'not-determination' of the species, widening the sphere of freedom in response to the choice of action, the natural environment, and ways of exploiting it. 'In the course of human evolution, natural selection probably privileged an ability to learn, flexibility, an ability to adapt behaviour to changing circumstances' – it was not the development of some specialized abilities useful in some narrow set of conditions. Paradoxically, we can say that the most important of the features inherited by humans from their animal and humanoid ancestors is freeing themselves from the constraints of their biological inheritance. Of course, we are exaggerating somewhat here in order to achieve a paradoxical effect: in reality, a human is not entirely free from biological determination. Nonetheless, this determination is greatly weakened, or it has only slightly broadened the range of activities that are possible for a human based purely on their biological constitution.

When behaviour ceases to be a species-specific, singular response to a stimulus – when it thus ceases to be the case that change can only be produced by genetic mutation – models of behaviour begin to play an important role. The teleological regulation of behaviours by subordinating them to the appropriate pattern differs significantly from the automatic and instinctive determination of behaviour. An individual whose behaviour is determined by instinct, must behave in a certain way in certain situations. However, an individual whose behaviour is regulated by goals and by patterns of behaviour can behave in a certain way, but does not have to. That is why their behaviour is significantly less stereotypical, and adjusts more readily in response to the environment.

All patterns of behaviour are a type of information that the individual must acquire in order to appropriately organize certain types of behaviour in response to certain stimuli. That is why we can say that the ability to learn and to be educated – grasped as a facility to acquire and store information – is that particular feature of the human species that comprises the elementary condition of a cultural organization of society.

The capacity to learn is not an exclusively human trait (far more significant, in terms of setting humans apart from animals, is the ability to teach). Individuals of some species of animals are capable in the course of their life of increasing or modifying the innate repertoire of behaviours. Animals belonging to the categories that are marked by these abilities tend to be beloved household pets or to appear in circuses (behaviours necessary to these roles are taught to them by humans in this case, and not by other individuals of their own species). They acquire new abilities through grooming – through creating new automatic behaviours.

Of course, using sufficiently general terms, we can describe the learning of humans and of animals similarly; however, these are phenomena differing from each other in many significant ways. Teaching animals behaviours that are not determined by their instincts, and thus inherited, happens primarily by acting on them with stimuli characterized by the fact that the 'energy' side plays a significant role, though not the only one. The transmission of information accompanies the transfer of energy, but it is a 'side-effect' in relation to it. Purely informational stimuli (or those whose energy side is meaningless for a given animal) may incline or force the animal to adjust with a new form of behaviour far less frequently. The human capacity to learn is significantly different in this regard from an animal's capacity to create new responses that are conditioned, on grooming; a person develops new forms of behaviour mainly under the influence of stimuli whose energy aspects do not have particular meanings, and which in no other way are important for their lives in terms of energy.

Meanings separated from the things to which they refer, allowing them to be easily recorded and transmitted, stored outside the human mind, even outside the human body (for example, in writing), are the basic material, the 'substance', of culture. The autonomization of meanings intiated an endless process of cultural accumulation of human scientific achievements; without this autonomization, this process is unthinkable. The utilitarian value of material goods transmitted by each generation to the next one is comically neglible and unimportant in comparison to the creative power contained in the information that is passed on. It is this separation of meanings from the objects to which they refer, and the resulting conditioning of the relative independence of the cultural system from the collection of things, that renders the human being 'time binding'[2] – able to acquire, multiply, and create anew experiences out of materials from a distant past, or to transform the experiences of the individual into the accomplishment of the species. The contemporary person differs from their ancestors of 1,000 years ago not so much in the possession of brick houses and boxes on wheels, as by an incomparably greater collection of stored information and the abilities connected to it. The autonomized – in the sense indicated above – information circulating in society has begun to take on a life of its own, much like the process of collecting, working over, and transmitting it became something relatively independent from the process of acquiring, working over, and circulating material goods. Meanings separate from the things to which they refer can be subject to the transformations conditioned by what takes place in the same sphere of information, and beyond that, the processes of information have become potentially more important than what happens in society in the sphere of energy.

## THE STRUCTURE OF THE ACT OF RESEARCH

Humans use a bi-polar system of reference for the systematization of all acquired information: some of the stimuli are organized into a system called 'thought', 'inner self', 'essence', 'consciousness', etc'; the remaining part into a system called 'material', 'external reality', 'existence', etc. All information is grasped either as acquired from 'the outside' – that is, not controlled by the intellect of the subject, 'powerless', 'resistant', and not reducible to meaning that the intellect can take into itself – or as flowing 'from the outside', which means that it is experienced as something directly subject to the intellectual control of the subject. This elementary bi-polarity of the human image of the world has its own history – thus it seems reasonable, and justified by the historical material, to treat it as a certain historical acquisition. What is more, we can assume that it is a relatively new acquisition. I personally believe that the notorious, enduring dichotomy of the human image of the world can be treated as a form of intellectual reflection on the actual bi-polarity of the situation in which humans found themselves when the old unity of information and energy characteristic of early, homogeneous societies was torn asunder: both culture on the one side, and the social structure on the other

– 'what should be' on the one side, and 'what is' on the other – became separate and began to develop relatively autonomously. This dichotomy could arise when people began to have experiences that either did not hold meaning for them, or had free meanings, not inseparably tied to any particular physical carriers. I cannot undertake a deeper analysis of the conditions and course of this historical process here. I want, however, to take up the issue of how this fundamental dualism of the human image of the world influences processes of research.

Both sides of this dichotomy have the same roots. That which is called 'the self' is nothing more than a collection of information belonging to culture, chosen from the resources stored by previous generations and interiorized by the individual in the process of learning and socialization. That which is perceived by the individual as external reality also comprises a part of the world – a part, that the activities of this individual's ancestors distinguished and shaped into a certain whole, according to human needs of adaptation.

Our dualism is a temporary and fleeting, but also enduring – ever-renewing and constantly overcome – creation, and a premise integrated into human behavior.

That which we said above about all human action must be applied also to acts of research, because we are considering them from a sociological point of view. Every act of research is based on reconciling oneself to, finding a balance between, two uncoordinated pressures: 'from the inside' and 'from the outside'. As Lévi-Strauss describes it (in his reflections on magic), the situation of research is a result of humans finding themselves in conditions where 'the universe is never charged with sufficient meaning and in which the mind always has more meanings available than there are objects to which to relate them'; 'Torn between these two systems of reference – the signifying and the signified – man asks magical thinking to provide him with a new system of reference, within which the thus-far contradictory elements can be integrated.'[3] This third system of reference is science or magic, and so knowledge, if we use this last term in a more general sense, including in it both of the previous means of intellectually making sense of the world – types that are opposed to each other, according to contemporary popular thought, but that certainly do not allow themselves to be considered opposing from the point of view of their sociological function. Functionally, we can define knowledge as a system of information about: (a) how to divide disorganized, chaotically experienced mental experiences into wholes to which we can ascribe meanings that were previously worked out; and (b) which of the totalities, called things, phenomena, or events, created in this way should be assigned a specific kind of meaning. As we can see, both functions of knowledge lead to sketching out a certain 'map' of the universum, which comprises a necessary condition of every targeted activity. The functions of knowledge depend on transforming chaos into order, fluidity into stability, the occasional into the regular, the unexpected into the predictable.

The act of research depends on tying information previously collected, transmitted, and acquired with new, previously unencountered types of mental data. In this way, human learning is an endless process of alternatively uniting and destroying the unity of two groups of mental experience: the particular experience of a given individual and de-individualized (collective) experience. Both of these resources participate in every act of research, and are equally important and necessary. Both condition the end result – for example, acquiring new elements of knowledge. The analysis that does not appreciate, or even ignores, the role of culturally determined features of the mind and their influence on the final result of the cognitive act is unable to contend with the complicated structure of the learning process – it is limited to observing the one-sided relation between the 'subject' and the 'object' (treating the 'object' like a card, on which the pencil of mental experience draws the image of the 'subject'). There are numerous accounts by people that can only be fully explained by reference to 'the facts that comprise a given individual's situation': in practically every testimonial of a person, there is a role played by their cultural heritage, interiorized by the individual and transformed into 'internal' cognitive stereotypes organizing the world, evaluations, and choices. Culture helps to decide how a person thinks, how they perceive the world. People grasp reality by organizing the meanings made accessible to them by culture. Reality exists for people insofar as meanings made available by culture render it accessible. Dorothy Lee even defines culture as 'a symbolic system which transforms the physical reality, what is there, into experienced reality'.[4] Ernest Cassirer expressed the same thing in the following way:

> No longer in a merely physical universe, man lives in a symbolic universe. Language, myth, art, and religion are parts of this universe [...] No longer can man confront reality immediately; he cannot see it, as it were, face to face [...] He has so enveloped himself in linguistic forms, in artistic images, in mythical symbols or religious rites that he cannot see or know anything except by the interposition of this artificial medium.[5]

This culturally organized system of symbols, mediating every contact between the human mind and 'external reality', and participating in shaping its intellectual image, is given various names. Sometimes it is called the 'a priori element of knowledge', sometimes 'cultural bias', or even 'prejudice', and in other cases, the 'evaluative factor'. The names are various, but in the majority of cases the selection of terms expresses the author's negative attitude towards that which is not purely 'intellectual', impersonal, towards what is conditioned by the human character of the object, what does not properly fit in the utopian dreams of empiricists. This 'something' is ascribed the role of a deforming factor, falsifying knowledge – and this finds its conscious or unconscious expression in the use of terms like 'presumptive position', 'prejudice', 'bias'. In any case, the attention of researchers studying these issues is generally turned to whether the cultural determination of knowledge conditions the appearance of inaccuracy, errors, one-sidedness, obstacles on the path of seeking truth. Characterizing this type of view, reducing the role of culture in the process of research to 'bias' and 'limitations', the term 'positivist aberration' comes to my mind. It is hard to deny that cultural influences play a role in limiting understanding, but it is that very limitation that renders the human image of the world the measure of a historically concrete person. It is a remarkably faithful measure. Above all, closing one's eyes to the key, decisive, creative role that cultural materials play in shaping every fragment of the resources of information collected by people is even more dangerous and misleading. We cannot forget, even for a moment, that no mind could perform any kind of act of research without being properly equipped with models for organizing intellectual material – and all of these models have their source in culture. These models are shaped as a result of numerous acts of cultural selection. The similarity of intellectual images of the world is always to a certain degree a function of the similarity of cognitive models used, and the similarity of these models is always a function of the similarity of historical cultural legacies, adapted by the intellect using these models, consciously or unconsciously.

## CULTURAL DETERMINATION AND CULTURAL DIFFERENTIATION

The final sentence of the previous portion of the article allows us to introduce a very important distinction between 'cultural determination' and 'cultural differentiation' – two concepts that are unfortunately often blurred together, by both admirers and opponents of the perspective that research processes are shaped by cultural inheritance. It is true that every individual owes their 'mazeway', as Anthony Wallace called it, to culture: 'the organized totality of learned meanings maintained by an individual organism at a given time', 'the cognitive map of the individual's private world regularly evoked by perceived or remembered stimuli'.[6] It is not true, however, that the paths laid out in the mazeway must be completely different for individuals raised in different societies or in different parts of the same society. Speaking of 'cultural determination', I am thinking of culture understood as an attribute of all of humanity: I am thinking of the automatic system of information itself, described above – the system defining the characteristic properties of human life, independently of particular cultural forms. Only then, when we move from 'culture' to 'particular cultures' – considered from the perspective of their various features, and not from the perspective of what is proper to culture as such – is the problem of cultural determination transformed into a problem of cultural differentiation, both of processes of research and of images of the world. But that change in the concepts used means that the differentiating of systems of information becomes accepted as a cultural fact. That is why the key issue for us is determining to what degree using the term 'culture' in the singular makes sense – whether we are right when we consider known patterns of information as if we are dealing with collections that are relatively automatic, relatively isolated, relatively closed systems, differing from each other to such an extent that it makes sense to treat them as separate wholes. It is only this problem that requires further discussion. However, this is a question of the kind that cannot be solved without the help of empirical studies. So here I can only suggest a few hypotheses, which find rather strong support in the material of historical experience supplied by various times and places, so there is hope that they will be shown to be likely, if not proved, by future studies.

The boundaries of the cultural system depend – with the mediation of directed acts of cultural selection – on two variables: (a) on the boundaries of practical experience that is directly or indirectly adapted as a result of the dissemination of information and thanks to accessible or imposed cultural contacts; or (b) on social interests, emerging from the configuration of group situations – these interests render some information valuable for adaptation for one group or another, and others make it adaptationally worthless or even harmful. Speaking metaphorically, the first factor provides material resources, from which elements can enter into the arrangement of a given cultural system; the second makes possible the structuralization of disorganized and amorphous resources of information into a cultural totality. The first factor delineates the boundaries of accessible alternatives shaping a given cultural system; the second narrows that region to the factual framework of a given cultural reality, structuralizing the information resources into a collection of alternatives, among which a choice must be made. The combined influence of both of these variables explains why the accessibility of these resources of information is not a sufficient condition for the cultures of two different places to be similar or even identical. The same thing explains another well-known phenomenon in the cultural history of humanity: that societies with the same type of social relations sometimes create cultural systems that are vastly different from each other in many essential ways. The combined functioning of both of these variables also explains why efforts aiming to eliminate cultural differences exclusively by means of spreading information (for example, through the unification of education) are so blatantly ineffectual, both when it comes to differences emerging within one society and in differences between two societies. The achievement of a true unity within the realm of a broader system – meaning the elimination of boundaries between cultural subsystems and their connection into one, indivisible whole – requires something more than the freedom to utilize a shared cultural inheritance: it requires identical motives that direct the acts of cultural selection.

The mutual interaction of multiple discussed factors is manifested in all aspects of culture. The degree of conditioning by lack of cultural differentiation that the researcher must take into account also depends on which elements of the culture are the subject of analysis, because both the variability of people's practical experiences, easily supplemented by information acquired from the outside, and the variability of the degree of relative importance ascribed to this or that accessible information, depending on the configuration of social interests, are different in regards to various elements of culture. But an even more important thing, which is rarely taken into account, is that the boundaries between groups 'of varying social interests' should – at least in our heterogeneous society – be drawn in various ways, depending on which type of information interests us: the group whose members manifest the same position in regards to information belonging to category A can rapidly be a group torn asunder by intense and irreconcilable conflicts when it comes to information belonging to category B. Every modern society is not so much a totality, as a collection of pieces of many totalities, belonging to multiple intersecting structures; its pieces, fragments, remain in a dynamic balance thanks to certain univocal factors such as language, religion, political authority, laws – and, mainly, economic ties. Every fragment of society produces, in its own particular way, a differentiation between what is 'accepted' and what is 'rejected'.

In every known society, there exists a category of people playing the role of 'cultural brokers'. This is an important role. The people playing it are 'living channels' of information, upon whom its uncon-flicted and sufficiently wide diffusion depends – at the same time, they are the 'main carriers' of cultural goods. To this category, too, belong teachers and monks, troubadours and writers, chaplains and learned people. They always form a certain part of society, distinct in one way or another – a certain environment differing, in terms of cultural perspective, from the rest of their society, and forming an integral part of a certain world of 'human culture' that transcends the boundaries of particular societies: a broadly human oikumene, or at least a broader 'cultural sphere'.

'Cultural brokers', being members of particular societies but also members of a world of intellectuals that crosses such borders, comprise the primary channel for the tramsmission of culturally valuable infor-mation that flows between societies. To the extent that they are members of the same society, but shaped beyond particular societies, they have threads of mutual interests and they maintain their status in their 'native' societies. The high status of 'intellectuals transcending any particular society', acquired by a well-documented conformity to norms they agree upon, is in and of itself an important factor when it comes to ensuring them a high status in their 'native' society. This com-monality of the social system of references, goals, and motivations mainly pertains to intellectuals who study natural sciences, because the norms pertaining to their activities are strongly independent of what is particular in the cultural systems of their local societies, and simultaneously they are, in fulfilling their own roles, much less engaged in the conflict of interests internal to their own societies. That is why, in this field, cultural differentiation plays a lesser role – at least in the framework of a significant portion of our globe. This does not mean, however, that it does not exist in this environment. George F. Kneller was essentially correct when he said that 'The thermometer and the clock testify to the conviction that nature can and should be measured, that all such units of measurement are of equal worth, that life is governed by knowable and invariable laws, and that what can be observed and repeated is important.'[7] All of these convictions are cultural elements created, and then spread, by only one of these known cultural systems. However, when certain convictions become wide-spread, and those who believe them are also not conscious of the fact that other societies represent in this regard alternative cultural choices, then these convictions acquire an 'absolute' flavour and they are treated as attributes of reality in itself, and not as attributes of a particular research perspective.

It is easy to conclude that everything that has been said here on the subject of the natural sciences also pertains to the social sciences, which treat the objects of their studies as 'things', in the same way that those who study nature treat their objects when examining minerals and cells. There exists, however, another humanistic way of doing social sciences, which is based on treating people as the subject of action – not so much on a systematization of what is known on the subject of determining their fates through 'external laws', as on analysing the systems of their motivations, on integrating their external reality as a human projection. Because this is how the task of the social sciences is grasped, the mathematical construction of an expressed function between two variables – for example, between the level of income and a positive attitude towards the conservative political party – does not represent the end result of the process of research. Quite the opposite – it is the beginning. At this stage, the question of 'why?' is raised – and what happens next is less the result of performing a certain calculation, than of understanding a given phenomenon. When does human action become comprehensible – when do we have the right to say that we have understood it? When we have understood the motivations of the people involved, when we have explained how they perceive the situation, when we have affirmed the agreement or contradiction between the goals of the people acting and the pressure of 'external reality'. That is why, in order to progress from regular counting to a humanistic understanding of socio-cultural processes, what is necessary is a certain dose of Einfühlung, 'empathy', or what Stanisław Ossowski called 'feeling into' or 'internal experience'.

That is why, in humanistically conducted research on the social sciences, a much larger role is played by elements that are 'a priori cultural', and that which distinguishes the research perspectives of people raised in different cultural environments. This cultural 'weight' can, of course, be cast off, but the cost of entry to researcher paradise must be rejecting the humanistic perspective. If we want to continue humanistic traditions in the social sciences (and this is the only style of doing them that guarantees 'understanding' – which, essentially, people in the social sciences are generally interested in), we have to stop at the 'cultural a priori' and the differentiating role of individual experience. As can be seen, I do not feel persuaded by the arguments of those who seek the ideal of the social sciences in knowledge freed from values. A person is by their own nature a being that gives sense, formulates goals, decides upon values. There is no reason why knowledge that is the result of research efforts directed at themselves and their own behaviours should be ashamed of this, and try to free itself from features that are the most human in human life.

Both ethnographers and historians study society and cultures that are different from their own – distant in time or space, or in both time and space. They strive, in the process, not only to determine how certain events took place and take place, but also to answer the question of why something happens or does not, in this or another way. In other words, they try to render a foreign culture comprehensible for the participants of their own culture, and in this way to integrate a foreign capital of information into their native experience of culture. If sociologists can constantly cleave to the illusory conviction that they are conducting their studies as the presenters of humankind, freed from the limitations connected to belonging to a particular socio-cultural structure, this happens because: (a) they feel like members of a transcultural environment of scholars studying societies; and (b) they find themselves 'inside' of the culture that they study, and that is why they are not capable of perceiving their own cultural a priori, much like the flatlanders who are described in popular works on the theory of relativity cannot imagine what a three-dimensional world looks like. That is why sociologists, more frequently than historians and ethnographers, are inclined to classify the phenomena that they describe, not in reference to various socio-cultural phenomena and systems of value, but using terms such as 'advancement' and 'regression', 'enlightenment' and 'backwardness'.

## CULTURE AND KNOWLEDGE: POINTS OF INTERSECTION

Instead of summarizing what I said above, let us recount the 'points of intersection' between the cultural environment and processes of research – let us count these stages of research processes, in which the influence of culture is particularly essential.

1  Culture defines certain general positions in regard to reality and its exploration. It ascribes a high or low value to learning new facts and laws; places emphasis on understanding facts, or on the deeper understanding of eternal truths; appreciates new formulations and discoveries, or – the opposite – attachment to the legacies of the past.
2  Culture demarcates the place occupied in society by the 'presenters of knowledge'. Upon this depends whether these are, for instance, priests or liberal 'independent thinkers and artists', thinkers secluding themselves in cloisters or officials of bureaucratic institutions. It also depends on that culture whether they are seen as epiphanic apostles, prophets, or harmless maniacs, or as zealous social reformers, or also as impassive, occasionally unsafe, experts. And upon this depends what is expected from these presenters: the care for,

and interpretation of, an older, oral or written tradition; or the transformation of the perspective on the world and the explanation of secret ties linking the biographies of particular individuals with historical processes; or, in brief, providing the masses of average people with road signs, allowing them to find their way among the labyrinths and traps of life – or providing people in power with effective tools to govern.

3 Culture decides what is seen as the ultimate goal and ultimate form of the process of research: formulating systems of probability or laws of causality; reconstructing sequences of facts, or evolutionary schemes of human development. It is what decides on whether an adequate and satisfactory grasp is considered to be a typological and qualitative description, or one that finds expression in universal claims, which are relative and quantitative. From it also depends, what inhibitions the process of research will be subject to.

4 Culture defines the relative importance ascribed to various phenomena and aspects of mental experience, and in this way conditions forms of distinguishing 'wholes', 'facts', and 'figures' out of the amorphous material of intellectual impressions. It shapes the raw materials of the process of research, the way of seeing reality – initial, 'purely intellectual', 'pre-intellectual', ways of perceiving the world.

5 Culture influences ways of making sense of and intellectually organizing 'fundamental facts'. Every scholar wanting their ideas to be seen as accurate and met with acceptance must somehow adjust to inherited methodological traditions or to the collected resources of claims and perspectives, or to both canons at once. The scholar always begins there, and if these canons are considered 'verified', will often refer to them as unquestionable premises. This is the *sine qua non* condition for them to be considered as true members of the group of 'cultural brokers'. The postulates of continuity and accumulation of goods demand the more obedience, and are the more restrictive, the more advanced that the specialization of academic environments, and the subsequent isolation of their subdivisions (which subordinates certain scholars to one unquestioned influence, or a culturally unified environment, and gives them very little room for invention, for uncommon ideas, for truly creative innovation), is – and vice versa, these postulates contribute to specialization and its social consequences.

# IV

# Three Observations About Problems
# of Contemporary Education

The author of these three observations is not a pedagogue by training, and does not study the sociology of upbringing. These limitations leave their mark on the content of the text and the character of the observations that follow. These observations do not refer to any particular theory of education, nor are they based on a careful analysis of the course and effects of the procedures of education or upbringing used by any particular institution specializing in it. The author, studying the features of particular structures and cultures of industrial society – which, in an increasingly broader sense, and at an ever faster rate, are becoming the features of contemporary Polish society – came to several conclusions which, perhaps, explain the origins of certain particular difficulties that are repeatedly referred to in the contemporary practice of, and writing on, education. These are the conclusions that spurred him to formulate the following observations.

## THE LOST SOCIAL FUNCTION OF YOUTH

The complexity of the periodization of the life of an individual person in comparison to the similar periodization of animals is caused, as we know, by the layering of two criteria that are not necessarily synchronized: the biological (physiological maturing of the organism) and social (adapting to independent functioning in specific social situations by passing on, as part of cultural education – and thus as a process of learning – necessary tendencies, norms of behaviour and directives of value). As the accumulation of cultural resources and the heterogenization of society proceed, so the period of social adaptation preceding 'social maturity' has a tendency to get extended; because the development of culture is generally tied to the improvement of diet and the rationalization of paediatrics, this period of biological adaptation, preceding the achievement of 'physiological maturity', tends to have the opposite tendency. As a result, there emerges, and extends, a period dividing the moment of achieving sexual maturity from the moment when the human individual is acknowledged as 'adult', or mature in the social sense of the word. This period is generally considered the period of 'youth'. In modern industrial society, the phase of 'being young' has been significantly extended; this extension happened – alongside the slow pace of structural changes and cultural adaptations, typical for bygone times – incredibly quickly: so quickly that our civilization has not had time to create cultural institutions specialized in serving this new state of affairs. Sherwood Washburn pointed this out:

> Modern medicine and diet have accelerated puberty by about three years over what it was in the beginning of the nineteenth century. On the other hand, social development have tended to postpone the age at which people take responsible positions. For example, if puberty is at fifteen and a girl is married at seventeen there is a minimum delay between biology and society. However, if puberty is at twelve, and marriage at twenty, the situation is radically different (...) nothing in our system takes account of these facts.[1]

Non-European cultures that are technologically and culturally relatively stable, and have had many centuries of adaptation, have achieved in the past a maximum accordance between social and biological periodization. Rich material collected by anthropologists and ethnologists indicates one common feature of processes of upbringing in societies that are relatively stable: the process of social upbringing, or training young people for independent functioning in society, is completed at around the same time as when they achieve full physical and sexual maturity, making it possible for them to assume these innate functions. The lack of a period in which young people, as a result of partial 'social dyslexia', must be subjected to the minute control and intrusive authority of adults, although they are already biologically mature – in which raw social commands must constrain the natural desire to satisfy numerous needs – means that this relatively stable society does not know the phenomenon generally typical of our society, which is the 'stormy', turbulent period of youth, full of tensions and psychic crises. The anthropological data allow us to confirm, beyond all doubt, that a storminess and rebellious attitude are not innate features of young people, but the product of an internal contradiction of cultural systems along with mutual decomposition of cultural commands and the functional requirements of the social structure – or the phenomena that are plentiful in rapidly developing, liquid societies.

Extending the period of 'being young' gives rise not only to conflicts located in the sphere of social relations – biology. A second problem, no less essential – if not even more important – can be described as 'the disappearance of the social function of youth'.

Other factors intervene in the creation of the problem, beside the indicated cause of a general extension of the period of youth, to which we must ascribe the subsequent contraction of the content of this, after all, increasingly capacious period. The decrease in the percentage of time necessary for work that is indirectly productive in the general social balance of time characteristic of industrial societies leads to an increase in the pool of time that is, in this sense, 'free', which to a meaningful degree the youth take advantage of; the moment in which young people begin to assume a socially necessary role in the social division of productive functions is ever more delayed. Thus, the period in which young people participate in the redistribution of social products, without participating in producing them, is increased. Their participation in the redistribution of goods is tied to an emphasis on the element of law in the described social role, where their role in production is associated with an emphasis on the element of obligation. We can say that the immeasurable increase in personal life is subject to a period in which people enjoy the full extent of social rights because they are biologically mature; they have the ability to execute them, without carrying the associated responsibilities. This is a particular phase in which what is ignored – at a time acknowledged to be formative for the individual character – is a transcultural, general – as is shown by many studies – norm of reciprocity, or the equality of exchanged services.[2] This is all the more painful when there is no preparation for the violent transition into a situation of complete responsibility, which also does not follow logically from the period that preceded it; this practical revolution, tied to the leap into a qualitatively different 'adult' world, produces a crisis in the adaptation to the role of adult that is specific to industrial societies.

The phenomenon I have just described is again rather specific to our civilization. Primitive societies clearly formulated, in their cultural norms, the expectations for people belonging to each age category, and took into account those expectations in the general accounting of their economic production. Primitive agricultural societies, which achieved advances allowing them to delay the moment of integrating young people directly in productive work, sometimes formulated, from the ranks of youth, divisions of the army, located in special areas and under a strict discipline, subordinated to a clear set of responsibilities. So, in medieval European society, there were special functions demarcated for youth that corresponded to their social position: a young nobleman arrived in the Prince's court in the clearly defined capacity of squire or page, preparing for the process of becoming a soldier; a young burgher went as a student and apprentice to a master, following a clear path for attaining the master's position. Not so long ago, in traditional Polish rural society, there was still a custom of naming categories of young people in accordance with the function that, in the passing of time, fell to them in the social division of labour:

> When it comes to peasants, the following age groups are distinguished: 'chłopocek' [boy] – a child roughly 5-6 years old; 'pastuch' [shepherd] 6-10 years old, 'pastuch of cattle and horses' or 'pastuch of horses' from 10 to 16, 'podparobcok' or 'podparobek' [sub-farmhand] – a boy aged 16-20. A bachelor, from about the age of twenty until he got married was called a 'parobek' [farm-hand] or 'podparobcak'.[3]

All of these societies – aside from the contemporary industrial one – have devoted inordinate attention to the minute differentiation of function according to age, and have carefully initiated young people, step by step, into their new responsibilities. On the basis of this concern arose the collection of – most universal from a functional perspective, though still quite various in form – rituals that comprise what anthropologist Van Gennep called 'rites of passage'. In contemporary societies, we see only the a-functional relics of these rituals in certain spheres of life (for example, the ritual of conferring doctoral degrees), and – what is most important – we do not perceive their structural premises. Exiting the phase of childhood in a proper sense of the term is – to place it alongside similar moments in this or other types of civilization – in essence a 'passage into nowhere', similar to how entry into the adult world in many cases can be seen as 'arriving from nowhere'. One of the greatest researchers of American youth, August Hollingshead, conducted extensive studies and came to the conclusions that:

> an ill-defined no-man's land [...] lies between the protected dependency of childhood, where the parent is dominant, and the independent world of the adult, where the person is relatively free from parental controls. This no-man's land is a place where the maturing person works out the extremely important developmental tasks of freeing himself from his family, making heterosexual adjustments, selecting a vocation, gaining

an education, and [...] establishing a home of his own [...] The ado-
lescent's ambiguous position in the society may be a product of the
loss of function for this age group in our culture.[4]

How does our society strive to fill this empty space? When the
particular, exclusively 'youthful' social function disappears, filling the
interlude between the period of childhood and of 'maturity' can happen
only in two ways: by moving the borders of one of the two neighbouring periods. The information we have about all industrial countries
indicates that these two theoretically possible palliative measures are
realized in a tendency to move the social role that we traditionally associate with childhood towards ever higher upper limits. This
means that in, terms of the higher age groups, we do not expect the
precise responsibilities that we demand of adults; that, to ever higher
ages, we grant the social right to full dependency on parental care,
material rights and services; that, to an ever higher age limit moves
the moment from which we begin to bestow responsibility on young
people for their acts, and stop ascribing responsibility for them to
their parents. This means, in brief, that young people are 'children'
in a socio-cultural sense for longer amounts of time. As it seems,
there exists a clear tendency to take the boundaries of childhood up
to the lower boundaries of the phase of adulthood – in other words,
to completely encompass the phase of initiation and adaptation into
adulthood by the role of the child, or to completely eliminate the
institution of 'youth apprenticeship'.

In this tendency, I am inclined to discern one of the objective
problems dwelling at the root of difficulties experienced in contemporary upbringing. The frequently observed maladaptation of young
people to adult life, the crisis and helplessness of young families,
instability of career work of young people, etc., should in part be
attributed to the inadequacy of pedagogical content. In part, too, only
manipulating this content can level the effect of the decomposition
of cultural functions. Society's retreat from the regulation of the transitional period, narrowing the stage of transition from childhood to
adulthood to college entry exams, or entrusting its regulation to amorphous or anonymous collectives in academic dorms – these are expressions of an institutional inadequacy of contemporary pedagogy, and
not a crisis of models of upbringing.

## EXTRA-CULTURAL DETERMINANTS OF BEHAVIOUR

Other difficulties of contemporary upbringing lie beyond the reach
of its influences – in any case, the influences as narrowly under-

stood. The prerequisite condition of overcoming them is the significant expansion of the concept of pedagogy and taking into account pedagogic aspects of social activities, not often considered from this point of view.

Everyone will probably agree that the goal of an ambitious upbringing is to shape the future behaviours of people, and not only ideas about proper behaviour; an ambitious teacher will assess the effectiveness of their activities not by the fluidity with which students recite internalized normative lessons from rote memory, but in terms of their actual behaviour in situations that are not artificial, academic, but natural, part of life. The criteria for the assessment of pedagogical activity are contained beyond it – they are an instrumental factor in relation to social life.

If, now, the concerned pedagogue observes the discrepancy between the actual behaviour of teachers and their own pedagogical ideal, the causes of this discrepancy, considered theoretically, can be two: (a) young people are taught improper norms of behaviour, not in accordance with the ideal and (or, possibly, or) they are indoctrinated with the help of defective and ineffectual procedures; (b) on the actual behaviour of young people, there is an influence not only from norms schooled by teachers, but also from other determinants, which are not subject to the manipulative efforts of pedagogues.

I am not interested here in the intensity with which the first cause is manifested, though I am inclined to the opinion that most researchers of contemporary pedagogical institutions share: that the stormy changes of civilization have shocked pedagogues, caught them unawares – and that the result is a lack of behavioural models and didactic methods that are modernized in the same way as the conditions of life that they are to serve. It is enough to remember the widespread problems that even a talented and educated teacher encounters with the competing authority of academic information disseminated by the means of mass culture. These issues remain, however, in the realm of pedagogy as it is traditionally understood – and they should; what is most important – they can be considered by theoreticians and scholars of pedagogy, though in this case they cannot manage without reaching for the help of sociologists – at the very least to the phenomenal text crucial for teachers, Komorowska's study about the role of television in upbringing.[5]

It is worse with the second cause. In fighting its effects, the energies of professional pedagogues are decidedly insufficient. The greater its role, the more necessary are radical revisions to our imagination of what remains in the realm of the activities of educators, and what does not – or what pedagogy ought to occupy itself with.

The behaviour of a person in a given situation is determined, generally speaking, by two types of causes: (1) the wealth of information, norms of behaviour, and evaluative directives transmitted to people in the process of upbringing, whose content is the 'socialization' of an individual's personality – the 'interiorizing' of abilities to move through the social world in such a way as would be in accordance with the expectation and postulates of their peers. Factors of this type can be described as cultural determinants, because their concrete shape and direction of activities are defined by the culture of the environment of upbringing. (2) Factors that are not only genetic, but also actual – in the moment of action – external in regard to the acting person: the practical accessibilities of means essential to the realization of one of the alternative choices, the assemblage of punishments and rewards ascribed to particular alternatives, and the range of freedoms determined by the system of social influences. Factors of this type can be called, for a change, structural determinants, because it is precisely the social structure that defines their concrete shape and the direction in which they exert pressure on the acting individual.

Contemporary technological civilization – whose defining features are both the heterogeneity of society (society as a system of intersecting and autonomous centres of decision) and the multiple internal dependencies of people (tied to the growing autonomy of these productive activities of a person, which remain under their direct control) – is characterized by what is especially important for our reflections, the growth of the role of structural determinants in describing the behaviour of individual humans. The role of interiorized resources of models of behaviour gives way in the face of increased pressure from external necessity; in the case of conflicts between them, or internal necessity, the influence of interiorized models is annihilated, or a phenomenon takes place that Pavlov once called 'disintegration of dynamic stereotype', and which contemporary psychologists describe as frustrational neuroses, leading to increased aggression, or to apathy and escapist tendencies. Preventing such conflicts (not so much preventing them, as striving to prevent them; the dynamism and heterogeneity of society bids us assume that some residuum of conflicts, proportional to the variability of society, is unavoidable) can only happen in two ways: either by cutting the inculcated models into the actual shapes of external necessity, or the opposite – striving to manipulate those necessities so that the direction of pressures is in accordance with the direction of cultural determinants. Which of these two possibilities is selected as the premise of pedagogical strategy depends, of course, on the accepted pedagogical ideal, and not just on their pragmatically grasped effectiveness.

The planned direction of social processes is a constitutive feature of socialism – from this fact alone comes the necessity of selecting the second of the two theoretically possible solutions. Building social- ism – this is the major effort undertaken to shape a new type of person, whom we consider superior, more amenable to human fate, than the types of personality that were formed by previous systems. But socialist societies, like all other modern societies, are based on a technical civilization, and are also gifted with all of the attributes that characterize them. To them too, then refers the thesis about the growing role of structural determinants in shaping human behaviour.

One of the most troubling conclusions, to me, flowing from the study of models of success for Warsaw youth conducted a few years ago – a conclusion that is in accordance with the results of many other studies – is the significant discrepancy between the ideals of youth in school and the ideals expressed by youth that have already left school. Speaking in simplified terms, the ideals of schoolchildren were to a large degree activist, socially oriented, characterized by optimism, and the assumption of the great potential of human will and efforts. The ideals of children who had completed their education and started work, thus remaining under the influence of non-school environments, had a different structure: they were much more mini- malistic, egocentric, defensive; it seems that these young people yearned above all to carve out a small, private world of things and issues that were clear and controlled, from an uncertain and incomprehensible – and, what is most important, uncontrolled – 'larger world'. In light of these determinations, contemporary psychology can, with a great dose of probability, assume such attitudes to life are a reaction to the prior violence created by structural determinants, against the interior- ized models that we called cultural determinants.

It can almost be proved by deduction that pedagogical efforts have a more lasting effect on the views of people to whom they are directed, the more that the models inculcated are practically realized in typical situations that the individuals find themselves in in life. The dominant influence of the education system of Eton or Rugby on the students of these exclusive schools, on their way of thinking and behaviour throughout their lives, should be ascribed less to the creativity of their methods, as to its complete accordance with the conditions of life that stem from the social position and tasks of the English aristocracy. A graduate of Eton mingled socially outside of school with the gradu- ates of similar schools, and in the Indian or African colonial admin- istration or in the hallways of parliament they found themselves surrounded by ever new confirmations that the interiorized style of life was *comme il faut*. The authors of ancient texts emphasized the efficacy of pedagogy used on the Patrician youth, groomed for political leadership, for the requirements of oratory. As Tacitus writes:

> the youth, who was learning the form of oratory [...] was entrusted by his father or by a relative to a great orator of his age. He learned by accompanying him, being alongside him, he was present at public appearances and in gatherings of people, he listened to his arguments with opponents [...] he learned to fight through battle itself [...] Thus he did not lack a teacher [...] or opponents and competitors, fighting with actual weapons, and not wooden swords, or an auditorium, always full and ever new, composed of friends and foes both, so there was nowhere to hide, which was either fortunate or not.[6]

Anthropologists accordingly indicate the rigidity and resistance to change of these positions, inculcated into members of tribal society by a pedagogy that is, after all, even more primitive; the remarkable stability of pedagogical effects should be ascribed not to the perfection of methods of education, but again to the maximum accordance between the content of education and the requirements of actual situations encountered by a person in tribal life: cultural and structural determinants comprise two parallel vectors, which are also cumulative; education and life confirm each other, intensifying the acceptance of the models they impose. A similar rigidity and permanence of interiorized models could be observed recently in the traditional village, where – as a result of lack of choices – the lives of inhabitants were lived in the same society in which they were brought up.

And how is this matching up of cultural and structural determinants beginning to be realized among us, being a condition of the longevity of educational effects? Some light is thrown on this by the situation that Jan Szczepański describes in the following way:

> Wanting to present a social mechanism of hiring currently functioning in the job market, we could greatly simplify by comparing it to a machine producing various balls of specific sizes, which emerge from the machine (school) and fall into a system of holes of various sizes, and roll around on it until they find a hole of the appropriate size, that they fall into [...] As a result hiring happens spontaneously when the appropriate goals of the graduate encounter the appropriate goals of the workplace, in a word, when the ball encounters a hole that is the right size.[7]

This is, of course, only an intended model – the more symptomatic because the intended model is based on market principles and the regulating role of 'appropriateness' of education with the requirements of life entrusted to environment and chance; in our developing, planned country, human fates – even in their intention – remain under the control of the market. But an actual course of processes of mutual adaptation of individual attributes of a young person and of the requirements of life has more elements of the environment than the theoretical model.

This does not boil down to hiring school graduates. We were speaking of them rather as one ingredient of a broader problem of the confrontation of the cultural equipment offered by schools with the structural determinants awaiting them outside the school's gates. Educated by schools in the spirit of innovation and courage, the young graduate immediately encounters, in their first workplace, the bureaucratic brakes on innovation, about whose existence the school (out of a concern for the optimism of the young person) did not bother to inform him, and from these experiences they learn how much courage does not pay. Educated in school on traditional romantic heroes, the young person awakens suddenly into situations that are excessively prosaic, in which romanticism proves to be a not very useful model. Deciding to strenuously observe principles of equality and justice, the young person retreats helplessly before manifestations of indifference to human harm and the careful obedience of various laws and responsibilities. If school managed to inculcate a generous and open attitude towards people, the indifference and cynicism of his superiors swiftly cause him to see his previous convictions as illusory. As against the old adage about the experiences of youth forming the 'shell' of the adult, the first individual experiences of the adult readily reverse everything that teachers managed to instil in their student.

If accordance with cultural and structural determinants isn't immediately a given, on the strength of the homogeneity of society or the singular attribution of a type of education to the type of life situation ascribed to people's social position, it ought to be – in any case, in conditions of the building of socialism – achieved by the conscious shaping, in response to cultural premises, also in those situations that are the sources of structural pressures on a person when they emerge out of the direct curation of specialized educational institutions.

The concept of pedagogy, or the theory of conscious activity intended to educate a person, must be extended over a maximally broad sphere of situations, not belonging institutionally to the range of school pedagogy. And thus pedagogy must be acknowledged as a region of its own interests, studies, and responsibilities, in the location of the first employment of its pupils, the neighbourhood groups that they become members of after leaving the maternal home, even the uncounted organizations intervening in the process of satisfying the many needs of the young person. Taking them under its protection, pedagogy must take care that the necessities and opportunities for choice that it places before the young person confirm and stabilize, rather than negating, the claims about the rightness or practical utility of the models and behaviour and evaluative directives learned in school. In our planned-out country, it is not only the pedagogue who must plan – also, the person for whom plans are made must be a pedagogue.

## PROBLEM OF EMOTIONAL SAFETY

The roots of both of the difficulties discussed above lie outside of upbringing properly speaking, and defeating them does not lie within the bounds of possibility of specialized institutions of upbringing taken individually. The difficulty, to which I want to draw attention is, to a larger degree perhaps, 'internal' to upbringing – the influence of inadequacies of pedagogy itself as a lesson of contemporary upbringing.

The difficulty about which we are presently speaking is – similarly to what was discussed before – tightly connected to the fact of internal differentiation, the heterogeneity of modern society. With a tremendous social mobility and the ease of communicating in conditions of increasing specialization and professional isolation of environments, the member of modern society rubs up against in the course of his life, to a significant degree and at the same time, dozens of groups of people, who are different when considered from the viewpoint of social issues, collections of experiences, interests, likes, principles of action, environmental ideologies. They quickly come to the conclusion that there is no principle that would allow them to predict the behaviour of various individuals and the relationships they enter into in one or another situation; what is more, they become convinced that the behaviour of different people in similar situations can vary, which is doubtless a signal that they accept different models of behaviour and the equal status of these models, even if they are mutually exclusive. Surveying the opinions of different people, a person is doomed to construct an image of themselves from clashing elements and generally realizes the impossibility of containing them all in a unified, internally coherent system. This most frequently leads to the relativization of norms and models, which attests to their relativity, lack of absolutism, and not unconditional character.

According to contemporary psychology, even a superbly 'integrated' individual personality of a contemporary person is nothing other than an individual 'bundle of roles'; a person with a non-pathological personality is, for this reason, able to comfortably move through the contemporary world because they know which of the roles they have been taught they are to play in a given situation, and that the monologues gleaned from one script will not intrude unexpectedly into a scene played on an entirely different stage; in the workplace, they behave differently from in the family circle, and differently as well when interacting with friends, and again differently with the president of the Academy, etc. Because the rules for each of these roles are set by an automatic system of sanctions, the roles that each individual plays do not have to be in accordance with each other – and indeed, as a rule, they generally are not. Then one speaks of 'conflicting roles'; let us remember that this conflict is also interiorized – the personality of the contemporary person is internally contradictory. The situation is further complicated by the fact that there are few situations to which every person would assign the same role. Behaviour called for in a given situation by one group is often condemned by another one, and differs significantly from the demands of yet another codex. Thus, the contemporary person stands not only before a multitude of mutually independent and situations that are not contained within any one system, but also before a wealth of perspectives on what kind of behaviour is appropriate to each situation, taken individually. This is multiplied by the feeling of relativity – uncertainty about all directions and prohibitions.

This chronic state of personal, structural and cultural disintegration of modern society lies behind both the intensity of interest that philosophers today devote to the problem of 'the discrepancy between what should be and what is', and – which is frequently indicated in research and writing – the matter of the 'emotional instability' of the contemporary person, characteristic feelings of uncertainty, danger. In social psychology today, the view is also accepted (and up to now not overturned by the study of researchers outside of Europe) that emotional safety – the state of psychic balance, emerging from a sense of justice, rightness of one's own actions – is the condition of 'healthy' human individuality in every culture and every type of society. The lack of this feeling of rightness, a fear that is difficult to define rationally emerging from not knowing the principles of behaviour and the impossibility of predicting the actions of other people that is connected to it, from the lack of clarity in a situation – from the lack of possibilities for such a justification of one's actions that would be based on institutions that would produce, through their authority, a conviction about safety or freedom from responsibility – is generally experienced as painful by most people. This pain is probably one of the essential stimuli pushing people from various historical epochs to construct moral authorities, or to depend on already-constructed

authorities. In this emotional experience, and not in intellectual justifications, lurked, and still lurks, the secret of the attractiveness and
otherwise inexplicable endurance of religious beliefs, whose function
could only be replaced by a phenomenon of similar emotional
intensity.

The problems experienced by the modern person in a heterogeneous
society seeking new premises of emotional safety have a greater meaning
for upbringing than is generally acknowledged. Schools today strive
to ensure that their students have this essential feeling of emotional
safety with the assistance of means that seem to me traditional and
utterly unadapted to the actual demands of today's society. Their
traditional character is expressed in the insistent efforts to persuade
students of the existence of the objective – and therefore not vulner-
able to any methods of critique acknowledged in contemporary culture
– absolute and unshakeable rightness of a single model of behaviour;
it remains only to acquaint oneself with this model intellectually and
diligently adapt to it, in order to possess the feeling of untouched
strength supporting one's actions, in order to protect oneself from
the overwhelming feeling of personal responsibility for one's own
behaviours – in order to consider oneself not a subject, but an object,
a tool in the hands of a collective wisdom. In this way, the educator,
firstly, fuels in their students a desire to solve the problem of psychic
safety with the help of traditional, no longer effective, means; and,
secondly, sentences their students to discovering the relativity of all
models of behaviour on their own, and retreats at the most dramatic
and formative moment for shaping personality – at that moment when
the student experiences a profound psychic shock, evoked by the
discovery that the sky or history has 'gone up in flames'.

The effect of the first pedagogical error is the identification, by
people subjected to such procedures, of emotional safety with the
impersonality of their own actions, with evading responsibility for
their decisions – the deepening of the conviction that their own convictions and good faith do not offer sufficient justification for their
own views. The effect of the second error is developing their own
discovery of the relativity of models into a rebellion aimed primarily
at the principles inculcated by an 'absolutist' pedagogy; a person who
comes to the conclusion that they have been tricked sniffs out deceit
primarily in the place where they were most passionately convinced
of an absolute truth. Left to their own devices in a moment of most
painful experience, a person who has discovered 'on their own' the
relativity of principles of behaviour is, more so than others, inclined
to react to their own disillusionment with cynicism, nihilism towards
all norms and principles – a negation not only of absolute truths, but

also of the value of any criteria of differentiating better solutions from worse ones, more noble ones from less noble ones. Pedagogy, yearning to prophylactically cure relativism with absolutism, achieves, in my opinion, the opposite effect: it intensifies the unavoidable relativism, blowing it up, against its own design, into dimensions of cynicism and moral nihilism.

Meanwhile, as against good sense and the incontrovertible determinations of knowledge about the contemporary world, the thesis about the relativity of codexes of behaviour – ascribing them to particular environments and their interests – the responsibility of each individual person for their choices, and thus the location of the justification of human behaviour in those choices, is seen, among pedagogues, it seems, as something shameful. The thesis about the relativity of codexes, which is a descriptive claim, is equated with cynicism – which is a normative position – and ascribing to it all the sins and atrocities of the cynical position, this logically impoverished comparison expels it from the circle of truths acknowledged by pedagogy to be proper. From this wretched battle between an insufficiently dynamic form of upbringing and an excessively dynamic world, the greatest harm is suffered by the young person, the object of pedagogical procedures: doomed in the most dramatic moments of their lives to their own efforts, unequipped to solve the actual problems of the contradictions of real situations, unimagined in pedagogical utopia.

In every historical epoch, the most enlightened pedagogues have protested against raising children like hothouse flowers, against constructing pedagogical strategies that prepare young people for artificial, illusory conditions that are utterly unlike actual conditions. The intensity of propagating and using the slogan 'close to life' can be acknowledged as a criterion for progressive pedagogical thought. It is another thing altogether whether the sense of this 'life', to which people long to bring the model of education into proximity, is based on reliable knowledge about the conditions and requirements of social life, or whether it contains a utopia built on the bygone beliefs, no longer applicable to the actual arrangement of social relations.

In today's society, the grasp of 'life' must contain, among other things, an ingredient like confirming the multiplicity, variety, and relativity of codexes of behaviour. 'Closer to life' will be a behaviour that bravely and openly makes its pupils aware of this feature of the world, in which they will be moving. If it does not do so, this consciousness will arise anyhow, but it will happen in spite of their intentions and against their truths.

Replacing the vision of an absolute model of behaviour and all of its variations with a vision of many simultaneous competing models places before the work of upbringing new, more complicated tasks, but also opens it to new perspectives, and, most importantly, creates a completely new opportunity for the utility and permanence of educational influence. The new tasks consist of primarily a necessity to emphasize in upbringing not intellectual mastery, the memorization of a specific and finite instruction of norms of behaviour, but particular 'metanorms' – norms of selection between competing norms, criteria of selection among alternatives, directives to evaluate situations with ambiguous meaning. The main pressure, the strongest, must be placed on individual responsibility for their own choice. A young person must be prepared by an enlightened education, and not by the streets, for the fact that their life will be composed of a collection of individual decisions and choices, and that no one and nothing, neither divine plan nor historical necessity, will remove from them the burden of responsibility for their own actions. That is the new task. And the new opportunity, which comes from fulfilling these tasks? The new opportunity is a creative, innovative personality, a strength of consciousness that is self-reliant, and is far better equipped to confront disillusionment and cynicism, insured against a frustrated escape to a small private world. This opportunity is attractive enough to justify taking on these new tasks, although they will require great effort.

# V

## Masses, Classes, Elites: Semiotics and the Re-Imagination of the Sociological Function of Culture

### NOTE ONE: THE MATTER OF INFRASTRUCTURE

Probably the historical circumstances of the emergence of the term 'mass culture' decided on the particular research perspective in which the problematic connected to this term in American sociology – and not only American – is most typically located. First was the 'discovery' by sociologists of so-called means of mass communication and their demonic role in the revolutionary change of mechanisms of perceiving the world, and the degree of manipulability of those mechanisms; the term 'mass culture' arose from the term 'mass communication' – it was created to indicate everything that emerges from the massification of communication. In this way, on the strength of the genetic structure of thought, the concept of mass culture became tied with the concept of mass communication. Even more – they became connected into a cause-and-effect relationship. New technological means of mass communication – the cause. Mass culture – the effect. Sometimes this dependency is stated openly, but more frequently it is assumed as a premise, usually unreflexively. The term 'mass culture' frees in the mind associations with television, radio, mass journalism. And that is it. The circle of reasoning is fantastically closed: means of mass communication – that is what creates mass culture. Mass culture – is what is the child of these means. Even the primary theoretist of Marxist mass culture, Stefan Żółkiewski, although he made breakthroughs in the field, did not succeed entirely in freeing himself from it: in the excellent study On Polish People's Culture, the 'style' of mass culture is tied to features of the social structure, the mass-ness (type) of culture is ascribed to the mass of the range of transmission of cultural means of communication and its listeners.

The following note gives voice to doubts about the wisdom of research that closes this cycle and to the assumption that mass means of communication are not so much the causal factor of mass culture as a tool that shapes it – they play the role of channels through which cultural contents travel, filling chambers that were created earlier and independently of these means of 'mass' structure. The technical–social particularities of means of mass communication explain why they are able to fill this role. But it is only the particularities of the social structure that can explain why they fill this role effectively. For culture to become 'mass', it is not enough to establish a TV station. Something has to come before in the social structure. Mass culture is something like an elaboration on something that for the time being we will call 'mass social structure'.

Conflicts about the definition of mass culture have a long history and many participants. I do not want to be the 1,001st participant. I am not concerned at the moment with the definition, but only with what is generally meant when speaking of mass culture. What is meant is the following: in the framework of general social (national) culture, there were traditionally mutually differentiated variants: regional, ecological (village–town–city), class. The culture of a nation, with all of its universal features, was a collection of 'subcultures'. The 'massification' of culture is the disappearance of these cultures into a universal culture, identical for all members of society: speaking carefully, the weakening of 'subcultural' features and the accompanying growth of shared features.

I do not want to engage in arguments about the definition of culture. And in this case it is sufficient to note the delineation of problems generally located under the rubric of 'culture': norms, institutions, and models of individual behaviour, comprising 'culture' form, in sum, both a product and a premise of the active mutual adaptation of a person and their environment. Culture is the creation of the accumulated experiences of life processes of many generations, and simultaneously 'serves' those processes. On this service depends the social function of culture, and in this function lies the primary mechanism of selection of cultural elements, though not every socially functioning element of culture is 'functional' – the human collective that is in a state of normal ecological equilibrium manifests a tendency to absorb functional elements and a resistance to elements of other cultural systems.

If we agree with what has been said here on the subject of the contents of 'culture' in general, and 'mass culture' in particular, we can draw out the following conclusion: the various subcultures existing in the framework of 'national' culture – differentiated with regard to regional, ecological, or class difference – doubtless testify to the fact that this difference causes a strong differentiation in social situations, and that these situations must be served by different directives, institutions, and cultural models. Differentiated with regard to the difference of regional, ecological, or social-class factors, human collectives create something that, paraphrasing a term taken from genetics, we can call endocultural populations – this means populations having the property that cultural exchange with, and the accumulation of, internal cultural elements are much more intense than those involving external ones. From this perspective, even taking into account the 'equalizing' population exchanges that are constantly taking place, in every endocultural population, the mutation of cultural elements and the institutionalization of the products of these mutations, taking place relatively independently and in relative mutual isolation, produce relatively self-sufficient evolutionary tendencies of culture. From a general social perspective, this leads to the subsequent differentiation of subcultures. The essential nature of this differentiation is the greater, the more meaningful the differentiation of these features of the environment, which, taken abstractly, are, after all, shared, selected for their 'personal environment' by each member of the population. Because the social situation of the collective expresses itself in the first place in the means of producing, distributing, and acquiring goods satisfying its needs, this serves as the primary criterion of this selection – we can say that, in general, socio-cultural differentiation, the differences of subcultures are the greater, the more that the social situations of members of particular endocultural populations differ from each other. And the opposite – the general social culture is the more 'mass', in the previously worked-out sense, the greater the participation of general cultural elements within this culture; and the smaller the role of elements specific to the population of formerly endocultural groups, the less 'endocultural' these populations become, or the more convergent their socially understood environments become – that is, the more similar their ways of acquiring goods proper to each collective entering into the general fold become. In other words, for culture to become mass (or maybe it would be better to say 'universal'), it is necessary for the social situations of members of society to become uniform – and the criteria deciding on the functional utility of elements of culture.

The importance of this statement I seek not only in the ontological, but also in the methodological, sense. I am not interested right now in recreating the history of the massification of culture, but I am interested in the phenomenological arrangement of references in which the problematic of mass culture should be located, in order for it to be maximally comprehensible and for the mutual dependency of two variables, caused by the intervention of a third one typically remaining in the shadows, not to be mistaken for a relationship of cause and effect.

Television, radio, and mass journalism are the discoveries of most recent times; this does not mean, however, that earlier ages did not know means of mass communication. The defining features of means of mass communication are rightly considered to be: (1) transmitting the same information to a large number of people at once and not changing it according to the means of communication with various addressees; (2) transmitting this information in one, irreversible direction, practically excluding the possibility of an informed response, not to mention a discussion on varying grounds – the sharp polarization of a system of communication into informants and informees; (3) the particular suggestiveness of transmitted information, based on the high social authority of its sources, on the paramonopolistic situations of these sources and on the psychologically important premise that 'everyone' is listening, and listening respectfully, to the same thing. It is easy to discern that all of these characteristics are found, for instance, in the Catholic Church, that gigantic centre of transmission of medieval Europe, with the pulpits of parish churches in the role of television receivers. To the same Mass came the landlord, the peasant, and the craftsman; the same words of Mass were addressed to all of them, the same message sent to all. The movement of information was decidedly unidirectional, and no less irreversible than in the case of contemporary television. As to the authority and the widespread reach, the most creative telespecialists would find it hard to compete. But the Church did not produce mass culture. Not only the styles and modes of life, but also the ideals, and moral norms, and even beliefs, that were the least bit dependent on life situation, emerged differently among its audience. The words flowing from the pulpit were not identical to all of the faithful, but clearly the ears listening were coated in different kinds of glue, with a different level of stickiness – so to each ear, different contents adhered. It was first necessary to unify the chemical contents of the glue, in order for unified directives, that were unified in their transmission, also to be unified in their reception. Culture began to become mass not when the branches of the system began to spread on a mass scale, but when certain conditions of life and the social situation became mass – when those conditions and those situations ceased to be differentiated, and the selectivity of reception ceased to be differentiated.

If the means of mass communication today strengthen the contents of an ever-more mass (again, one would like to say 'universal') culture, then the premise of this fact should be sought in the universalization – transcending region, ecology, or class – of essential components of the social situation. More narrowly: the effectiveness of means of mass communication on the massification of culture is the greater, the more advanced the process of universalization of these components is. Let us consider then, what components enter into the picture here.

The first ingredient: dependence on the market. Even 120 years ago, the majority of people satisfied the majority of their needs outside the mediation of the market; with the help of labour power they were not selling – or the parts of it not sold – they created goods, which they used themselves. The process of satisfying the needs of this majority was therefore excluded from the macrosocial circulation of goods, and was relatively independent from the inter-regional, inter-environmental, or inter-class exchange. It formed its own particular infrastructure of the endocultural individual and their closest surroundings – the surroundings in whose realms was contained the circle of undeveloped exchange.

Today – in countries with developed industries, and also with a market – a relatively minuscule portion of the population satisfies a minuscule portion of their needs with goods that do not participate in the macrosocial exchange, made by themselves, embodying the identity of both producer and consumer. A decisive majority sells the most common of goods – labour power – in order to thereby acquire consumer goods. They enter the market in two ways: as a seller and as a buyer. Everyone, or almost everyone, sells. And – as sellers – in their successes and failures, hopes and disappointments, they depend on the market. On the labour market and the wage market, on the price of labour and the price of bread. The fascination with their own needs cannot in these conditions be expressed otherwise than in a fascination with the market. 'Market orientation' is, in these conditions, a social norm and a manifestation of psychic health. From psychophysical causes, a person in a macrosocial situation of the circulation of goods is susceptible to the culture-generating influences of the market. The material products of culture are necessary for the satisfaction of culturally modelled needs; these creations cannot be acquired otherwise than through the means of the market. Not by anyone: rich or poor, director or employee, burgher or farmer. This is the shared element of the social situation, one of the infrastructural universals of culture.

And the market – as the market does – makes uniform. Particularly the market based on mass and serial production. From the first moments of the industrial revolution, the development of industry was based – from the perpective of the market – on the serialization and universalization of the creation of goods that were previously, because of their rarity, accessible only to the privileged, and therefore endowed with particular prestige and accompanied by particular demand. The higher classes, in the role of consumers, serve the function of taste-makers; industry for the privileged becomes a reconnaissance, paving the way for mountains of mass-produced goods. (Let us notice, as an aside: from this, certainly, comes the astonishing jump in prices of 'rarity', connected to 'unrepeatability', observed in our times – possessing any of the industrial goods no longer produces a sweet feeling of safety and of the permanence of material symbols of high social status; today, the exclusive and 'only' – every creation of industry – if it only acquires the corresponding load of prestige because of its own exclusivity, will become a good in circulation, therefore invariably losing its prestige-making value. Thus the insane prices of original works of art, sculptures, ancient crafts, white crows: only there lies the guarantee that the rarity will not be transformed into commonality. Thus what is paid for is the unrepeatability – the price does not remain in any relationship to the aesthetic–use value. One buys symbols of social status: it is ever more difficult to acquire such a symbol on the market.) Thus it is not only that everyone satisfies their needs through the market. In proportion to the progress of serial production, they ever more frequently satisfy those needs with identical goods. This is the next infrastructural universal of culture.

The second ingredient: a dependence on organization. When society was composed of lords and their servants, or enterpreneurs and their hired hands, there was a need for two different cultures for serving diametrically different social situations: ruling and serving, powerful and powerless. When society is composed to a meaningful degree of functionaries of the organization, one culture is sufficient. The behaviour of the director has an influence on the behaviour of an ever greater number of people than the behaviour of the bureaucrats or workers under them – but the director, the bureaucrat, and the worker are all functionaries to an equal degree. The feudal lord was doomed to lordship, just like the serf to serfdom; the capitalist tycoon during times of turbulence and pressure, to making his own fate; the director, bureaucrat, and worker in the era of giant organizations are doomed to having their individual fates defined not so much by people, as by faceless powers, over whom they have no control or influence – bah, which they do not even understand the nature of. The tangled thicket of organizations, affiliations, and interdependencies (sorted out only in an abstract sociology far removed from reality), in connection to the far-advanced autonomization of decision-making by specialized formal organisms, means that there are no real social events that are neutral in regard to the fates of individuals, and there are a negligible number of neutral elements that an individual can influence – or could at least calculate. Sociologists keep rediscovering, with alarm, that the worker generally does not know what the factory, where he drills holes into steel cylinders, produces, and how. But those same sociologists rarely realize that in that same factory there is not a single person with a complete mental map of the entire process of production, including the details of each specific rule. It is said that the foreman knows more than the worker, the division head more than the foreman, the director more than the division head. But this is the view from the window of the director's office. The opposite saying is just as true: there are things that the worker knows, but not the foreman; the division head, but not the director. No one knows everything. In the situation of each of us, the number of unknowns exceeds our ability to calculate. That's how it is in the factory, that's how it is in the office, that's how it is in a multi-organization society – to a much greater degree than in the abstract, 'taken individually', factory. The organization is not so much impersonal, as inhuman. Absolutely and without exception. This is another universal of infrastructural culture.

In order to satisfy their needs, to acquire the goods necessary to do so, people must attain a position within an organization. Position in an organization becomes for everyone, regardless of the conduit, the primary instrumental value. Organizations differ amongst themselves, and the positions within them differ from each other, but the need for some kind of position in some kind of organization is common to all people. And the ways of acquiring those positions are, generally speaking, similar: appropriate to the level of education, behaviour appropriate to the organization's needs, crowned by a nomination decided by the appropriate members of the organization. In a way natural to each society, a fascination with need takes on the form of a fascination with organization and position within it – and it cannot take another form. Position within an organization is the fundamental determinant of all social situations and the legitimation of social identity. To the question, 'who is that?', the modern man without hesitation responds: 'This is director X in office Y', and not 'This is a very nice man', or 'This is a noble dreamer.' And this too is a universal of infrastructural culture.

But, in a pluralistic society, the power of every organization extends over only a portion of the socially necessary goods and only a portion of the human collective. No individual can contain the entire process of satisfying their own needs within a circle of goods and individuals within the domain of a single organization. Quite the opposite – in the course of this process, the individual will inevitably encounter the spheres of influences of many different and mutually autonomous organizations, and in only a very few will their individual influence be decisive. Every person is thus both the commander, and the petitioner; at one moment the subject, the next the object, of influence. Particular bilateral acts of cooperation polarize into subjects and objects – but society does not. The closer that a society approaches to an ideal model of pluralism, the closer the number of exceptions from this rule approaches to zero. Elements of objecthood and subjecthood are mingled in the situation of different individuals to different proportions, but they both appear in all of them. The differences are quantitative rather than qualitative. And thus the aspect of a situation, traditionally one of the most important sources of cultural differentiation, by degrees becomes also a premise of infrastructural universals.

The third ingredient: dependence on technology. The peasant weaving linen on a loom at home could rely solely on himself for satisfying his own needs. The farmer buying a shirt in the village store is relying on technology. A person shaving with a straight-razor is less reliant on technology than a person shaving with an electric razor. If a pebble falls into the turbines in the factory dozens of kilometres away, he will go unshaven. Technological equipment works well to make all of our activities easier, but also renders us helpless against the vagaries of fate. It is easier to tidy the house with a vacuum cleaner than a brush, but we don't know how to fix a broken vacuum cleaner. A macabre American joke says that American families go to sleep without dinner if the TV breaks: the lady of the house, not having listened to the newest commercials, won't know what to buy for dinner. Technology occupies the place of earlier natural disasters: when the tram goes off the tracks, we cannot return home after work. Within the family, fear of cars on the road has taken on the function of fears of wolves and snakes. But let us return to the business that is most important to us: more and more people, to an increasingly large degree, meet their needs with the help of technology: technology they don't produce themselves, whose mode of functioning they do not understand, and which they cannot make work without other people's help. Technology is a blessing, and technology is the materialization of constant anxiety. This ambivalence is notorious, much like the dualism of the feelings it engenders: wonder mixed with fear. The average person accepts the idea that a digital machine thinks in the same way that the Nootka Indian accepted the shaman's explanation that the fishing expedition was unsuccessful because the fish were angry that the proper dance was not performed before the line was lowered into the water: because the digital machine remains in some relationship to the satisfaction of his needs. A fascination with personal needs is expressed in a fascination with technology. This is also an infrastructural universal of culture.

But in the case of the Nootka Indian, the relationship between the sensitivity of the fish and his next dinner was direct and obvious. For our average contemporary, the relationship between the technology that he reads about in the newspaper and his dinner tonight, or even tomorrow, is far from this psychically pleasurable obviousness. The relationship between a new tool and the particular situation of the craftsman or farmer was once clear, the criteria of their evaluation simple: there is progress if my work is easier, or if I get more out of it, or both. Reading information about new bulldozers and trash compactors, a person is unsure whether there is a connection between them and their individual situation, and, if there is, what its character is. To connect these two variables, what is now necessary is abstract thought, theory, macrosocial synthesis. Not everyone can afford it – all the more so when verifiability lies outside the capabilities of the individual. New technological implements are certainly a multiplier of human power. But also of the individual's? We are far from the individualistic optimism of Adam Smith or the collectivist optimism of Charles Wilson of General Motors. The advancement of humanity and the advancement in the situation of an individual are not the same in practice and in individual consciousness today. Dependence on technology produces disorientation and fear, at least insofar as it always accompanies uncertainty and incomplete knowledge. Everyone feels threatened. No one can control the genie in this bottle. And this set of circumstances can be counted among infrastructural universals.

The importance of all three of these trans-regional, trans-ecological, trans-class – simply, universally common – ingredients of the social situation of people in industrial civilization emerges from the fact that these are the components of the most important life process: the process of satisfying human needs. Depending on the market, a human falls into an organization and technology becase they can't avoid them on the way to expending their creative energy in order to possess the goods necessary to regenerate it. In the increasing similarity of these paths, they perceive a significant message of a growing dominance of features that are common and universal in people's life situations over the ones that still remain different, and thus the growing dominance of those elements in a general social culture that have become macrosocial universals over those that remain subjugated to sub-cultural (regional, ecological, class) differentiation. Culture serves the life situations of people; mass culture (general) serves mass situations (universal ones).

This is, of course, a dependence on a model. On the one hand, the spread of culture must conquer the resistance of tradition, custom, and group homeostasis, and therefore is delayed in relation to the spread of infrastructural elements. On the other hand, the radiance of an actual cultural peak can introduce into the cultural system of this or that society elements adapted to the service of infrastructure which has not yet emerged; then the elements both precede and hasten (if considered in the collection of an individual national society, and not humanity as a whole) the corresponding changes in infrastructure.

In my deliberations up to this point, I could use the term 'needs' referring to the general meaning of the term and not troubling myself to define it. But in order to complete the list of infrastructural universals, it is necessary to make sense of the collection of elements included in this term. The most useful to this task seems to be the categorization offered by Abraham Maslow: 'needs of scarcity' and 'needs of existence'. To the first category belong, for instance, needs of satisfying hunger or guaranteeing safety; to the second, the need for the pleasure that is provided by aesthetic experiences or a feeling of one's own creative powers. The mutual relationship of both categories is characterized, generally speaking, by the following features: (1) when the needs of scarcity are not satisfied, they drown out or even eliminate the needs of existence; (2) when the needs of scarcity are satisfied, the needs of existence are the ones that are most troublesome and most insistently demand attention. Let us add that, in Maslow's view, the needs of necessity and existence differ, among other things, in that the first disappear at the moment they are satisfied, whereas with the others, it is the opposite – as they are satisfied, they grow; and the joy that the first can bring can be caused only by eliminating the tensions awoken by not satisfying them (this is 'negative joy'); the second, the opposite – they create tensions that are themselves a source of pleasure. Satisfying needs of scarcity, Maslow says, is only the condition of a lack of sickness; in order to be healthy, the needs of existence are necessary.

Using Maslow's terminology, then, we can say that another – not universal, but universalizing – ingredient of the life situation of the citizens of industrial civilization is the contraction of those parts of time and energy that are socially necessary for the satisfaction of needs of scarcity and – as a result – the universalization of the needs of existence. For the last few thousand years, in many parts of the globe, and certainly in the range of our oikoumene, the needs of existence, potentially serving every individual, emerged only among individuals who belonged to the idle and wealthy classes. The lives of all people around were fuelled by the effort to satisfy needs, but those needs were not only quantitatively, but also qualitatively different. A minority sought ways of satisfying problems of existence, but a majority coped with scarcity. The majority and the minority needed very different cultures. Along with the increase in the plenitude of goods satisfying the needs of scarcity, with the simultaneous decrease of people's direct participation, the effort of producing them, and the increase in the lower limit of participation in goods, a different situation appears: ever fewer people are fed by the life activities around satisfying needs of scarcity, and the needs of existence become ever more widepread. Thus, they gradually become psychological factors, which – similarly to infrastructual universals – become a premise of the universalization of culture, or the birth and triumph of mass culture.

Here we can conclude the first note. The idea that I wanted to express is relatively straightforward. On the level of a model, it can be presented in the following way: in order for the culture of society X to become mass – or for widespread acceptance and minimal differentiation according to regional, ecological, or class criteria – it is necessary in this society X for the social situations of individuals and the structure of their needs to be united to the degree that they must, and can, be served by one and the same cultural system. The model of this dependence is based among other things on the silently accepted – but never fulfilled in practice – premise of the cultural isolation of society X, and thus the non-existence of cultural diffusion from the outside. Because the above assumption is never met in practice, the relationship between culture on the one hand, and the infrastructure and structure of needs on the other, can be in this or that society more intricate than it would seem from the model. Thus, I am all the more inclined to insist on the value for research of the methodological directive stating that the system of reference for analysing the genesis and contents of mass culture should be processes taking place in social infrastructure and the structure of personality.

## NOTE TWO: IN THE MATTER OF 'HIGHER' AND 'LOWER' CULTURE

In this matter, opinions are divided. Some say that the view of some cultural values as 'higher' than others can be confirmed in an objective way; others – that it can't. But no one can really get by without both terms, or their variants.

I, too, would like to contemplate the meaning and reasonableness of the concept of 'higher' and 'lower' culture. To do this, however, we need to distinguish three spheres, in which these reflections on culture tend to be used.

1    Both concepts are used when we compare two or more cultural systems appearing in two or more different, temporally and geographically isolated, societies, and treated as distinct wholes. I discussed these uses of concepts of 'high' and 'low' in 'Bieguny analizy kulturowej' [Poles of cultural analysis].[1] These uses do not have the best reputation among contemporary anthropologists, even among those who, similarly to Steward or White, are devoted supporters of neo-evolutionist ideas. Both of these concepts elicit distaste among anthropologists because of the very feature that fans of concepts of 'higher' and 'lower' culture value: the sense – in the best case, subconscious – of evaluation. Higher is always in some sense 'better', 'more ideal', 'more worthy of appreciation'. In the case of comparisons between systems, this hidden meaning of the concept of 'higher' must in practice take sides with the cultural ethos from which all researchers are, in essence, recruited – in most general terms, industrial civilization; this means not only a predisposition towards this side, but acknowledging it as the 'best' – relatively speaking – stage that the other 'stages' lead to, i.e. all other cultures. If we accept, however, that culture A is 'higher' than culture B if and only if it disseminates, or leads to, a more meaningful output, or complicates cultural elements $Z_1, Z_2, \ldots Z_n$ more than culture B does, this can demonstrate that culture A is higher on the basis of the same definition only in such a way that elements $Z$ can be taken as typical only of it. Then the mind will be tormented by the suspicion that deliberations about high culture make no sense, other than being an effort to find a more dignified expression of the conviction of the merits of one's own culture. If this goes a step beyond the range of one's own cultural ethos, the issue immediately becomes more complex. The Eskimos, for instance, have fantastic technology and meagre sociology, but the Australian Arunta, quite the opposite. One could – though with difficulty – fit within the boundary of objective observations, while the evolutionary 'earliness' or 'lateness' of specific cultural systems are being decided; once you introduce to the reflection the terms 'higher' and 'lower', the objectivity of immanent theories immediately becomes questionable. If there is some kind of objectivity here, it has only a sociological nature; the claim that our cultural system – industrial civilization – is higher, means, and means only, that we are stronger economically and militarily, that we cut the roots of other cultural systems, or that we rework them in this or another way – or try to – into our own model. We could also formulate this as: the superiority of industrial cultures

– in the only objective sense of the term – does not indicate superiority in a necessary diachronic chain of evolutionary events, but in a synchronic, actual hierarchy of societies in a general human development. Let us observe how many people began to doubt the cultural superiority of the West when various 'primitives' sent to the UN representatives who were not so much exotic as stubborn.

2  We can use the concepts discussed here to compare two different cultural systems that can serve the same society. In practice, this is the use to which critics of their own civilization put concepts of 'higher' and 'lower', when they set cultural realities against a postulated ideal acknowledged to be 'higher', or rather described as 'higher' to strengthen its attractiveness and motivating social force. The classic example here is Edward Sapir's concept of 'genuine' and 'spurious' cultures, formulated in 1924 in the pages of the *American Journal of Sociology*. This was simply a critique of American civilization from the perspective of cultural values that were neglected by that civilization in its actual proceedings, though highly valued in ideology. It was given by the author, however, in the form of a general concept referring to all societies: no society is doomed to have one and only one culture, and there is no necessary correlation between a society and its culture – a society can select for itself a culture that is better or worse, genuine or spurious.

> A genuine culture is perfectly conceivable in any type or stage of civilization, in the mold of any national genius [...] It is merely inherently harmonious, balanced, self-satisfactory [...] a culture in which nothing is spiritually meaningless, in which no important part of the general functioning brings with it a sense of frustration, of misdirected or unsympathetic effort. [...] a genuine culture refuses to consider the individual as a mere cog, as an entity whose sole raison d'être lies in his subservience to a collective purpose that he is not conscious of or that has only a remote relevancy to his interests and strivings [...] The great cultural fallacy of industrialism, as developed up to the present time, is that in harnessing machines to our uses it has not known how to avoid the harnessing of the majority of mankind to its machines. The telephone girl who lends her capacities, during the greater part of the living day, to the manipulation of a technical routine that has an eventually high efficiency value but that answers to no spiritual needs of her own is an appalling sacrifice to civilization.[2]

Although Marx did not analyse capitalism in terms of culture, his critique of alienation stemming from capitalist industry, incomparably broader and more far-reaching than Sapir's critique, could be – if we take into account the contents, and not the specific wording – counted in the same category of reflection on 'higher' and 'lower' culture.

It is best to analyse this category in the terms proposed by Gramsci: the adequacy and historical rationality of the model, offered in the place of a system that actually exists. If we do not accept uncritically the values that existing culture is adapted to creating and spreading, when we perceive the essential flaws in the dissemination of values that a given culture adheres to in its ideology, we have the right to subject the dominant system of culture to critical analysis and offer a counter-proposition of another system. If the proposed system has better odds of serving already-existing needs, or evoking the needs that are stifled by the actually existing system, it is historically rational and adequate; the proposed idea then has the chance of concentrating social energies, sufficient to become a factor shaping social reality. In this process, the terms 'higher' and 'lower' function in the role of idea-mobilizing concepts of worldview.

3   The concepts analysed here are used in the comparison of fields of value (or also the type of needs served) in the framework of one society and one cultural system. In this sense we frequently speak of satisfying needs of the 'soul', or 'spiritual' needs; these are matters 'higher' than satisfying the needs of the 'gut', or material values – physiological sustenance. There was a period of several thousand years in human history when this division and its qualification had a narrow sociological meaning, they were 'sociologically objective': it was a period when societies divided internally into classes fascinated with spiritual nourishment and classes whose pursuit of physical nourishment did not leave time for the pleasures of the soul, and when the classes enjoying spiritual enjoyments were in their societies higher in this most objectively sociological meaning of the term, in that they dominated economically, politically, and ideologically. One field of culture being higher than another was thus objectively justified in the infrastructural higher-ness of the class that participated in it. The ground upon which trod the foot of a new Hawaiian ruler became holy; everything touched by the dominating class became 'higher'. These events explain the meaning of the concepts of 'higher' and 'lower' used in the way we are currently considering; they do not occur in conditions where all aspects of culture become to a greater or lesser degree accessible even to people from non-dominant classes – where, because of changes discussed in the first note, the satisfaction of both of the primary kinds of need becomes possible for an ever greater number of people – though in varying proportions. In these new conditions, using concepts of 'higher' or 'lower' to characterize various fields of culture can be explained in two ways: (a) as remembering old times, when aristocracy of class or money was also an aristocracy of the soul – this has already changed, but the associated

ideas remain, though people rarely reflect on their genesis; (b) the fact that – as has already been discussed – spiritual good and physiological-sustenance goods serve essentially qualitatively different human needs. Here, however, a complication appears: as Maslow, already cited, claims, the needs of existence are 'higher' than the needs of scarcity in no possible sense, except that, insofar as the needs of scarcity are not satisfied, the needs of existence are repressed and pushed into the subconscious. Every person, however, has need of both kinds – and Eupsychia, an ideal utopian culture propagated by Maslow, is characterized by this very feature: that all people in it would realize needs of both types – that is, they could satisfy their needs of existence, because their needs of scarcity would already have been met. But why use the evaluative term 'higher' to describe the relationship between the needs of existence and the needs of scarcity? Would it not be better, for example, to talk about first- and second-order needs? Or better to stop, as does Maslow, with two independent terms, not deciphering the mutual relationship between both types of needs through the act of choosing a name, but leaving it in empirical terms? Only such a solution can definitively liberate us from the nagging fear that residues of class infrastructure impose a schema of organizing affairs that the remnants of these infrastructures are specifically aiming to eliminate.

4  Finally, the last way of using the terms, which participants in discussions of mass culture usually have in mind, but which must first be separated from other cases where our terms also appear, in order to avoid extrapolating what will now be said about 'high' and 'low' culture.

The case that interests us now is based on using the concept of 'higher' or 'lower' to qualify various elements of culture located in the same cultural field and mutually exchangeable in satisfying the same need. And thus: everyone eats, but eating lobster is an act that is higher, culturally, than eating blood pudding. Everyone eats fish, but eating fish with two forks is an element of high culture rather than eating it with a knife and fork. Everyone gladly listens to music, but the pleasure experienced from the *Toccata* of Bach is of a higher order than that from Karin Stanek. Everyone reads books, but reading Camus is an activity of higher cultural value than reading Kraszewski.

I think that the reader who has made it to this point will readily understand what the author's views on such uses of the terms 'higher' and 'lower' are. Essentially, this view is the following: the elevation of eating with two forks over with a knife and a fork, or Camus over Kraszewski, is not an immanent one. If assertions about superiority have any objective meaning, that meaning should not be sought in the structures of classifying cultural good, and not even in culture, but in its infrastructure. Statements about superiority in the version that currently interest us can have only a sociological meaning: that those who listen to Bach and eat fish with two forks occupy a position in the social structure that is higher than those who listen to Karin Stanek and eat fish with a knife and fork. When I am asked 'Is cultural good X higher than cultural good Y?', I respond by asking 'Is class A, for whom X is a good, higher in the social structure than class B, for whom Y is a good?' If I receive a negative response, further deliberations about the superiority of X over Y seem meaningless to me.

Obviously, very few people will say: X is culturally superior to Y, because I, and 'we', value X more than Y, and we are members of group A, which is higher in the social hierarchy than group B, which values Y more than X. In general, the expression of a thought which – if it means anything – means precisely what I have said in the previous sentence is done in a form ostensibly more objective. We know many forms of such objectivization. Formerly, the genealogical determinant of sociological superiority reached for arguments of the type *Kinderstube*, 'innate elegance of the soul, achieved only through a multi-generational tradition', and, finally, 'This cannot be learned and it cannot be bought. One has it from birth.' Then there was a period in which the following formula was used: what is higher is that which 'is not typical, widespread' – or that which not everyone can afford. These forms of objectivization do not function any more in our conversations. The crowning place among 'objective criteria' (so, non-sociological ones?) is today occupied by the following postulate: 'What is culturally higher is that which is difficult and complicated, an appreciation for which must be learned.' I am passing over the empirical nonsensicalness and operational uselessness of such a criterion: in America, I encountered a general *horror* when I asked for a second fork for my fish (everyone there eats fish with a knife), and I was asking for a second fork because it suddenly turned out that eating fish with a knife and fork is much more difficult and complicated for me than eating it with two forks; an appreciation for Karin Stanek may require a much greater effort and study than enjoying listening to Bach. I am interested here in something else: this 'difficulty' and 'learning' that, in such a disarming way, betrays the social affiliations of the new form of objectivizing 'cultural superiority'. Of course, these are our intellectual affiliations as intelligentsia. The society of the era of great organizations places the highly educated expert at the top of the hierarchy, and transforms education into the catapult that launches one to social peaks, the way former societies used the catapult of genealogy or money. That is why it is not, 'You cannot learn it and you cannot buy it', or 'Not everyone can buy it', but 'Not everyone can learn it.' The human is the measure of all things; the social group organizes the social world with the help of its own hierarchy of values. The basis of our social position as intelligentsia is education – we like X, therefore X is higher, because appreciating it requires education. I know that such vivisection of the myth guaranteeing psychic safety is a painful process and generally infuriates the patient. But what are we to do? – although 'it is hard to listen' – as one of the author's heroes, belonging to lower culture, said – it is true. And the truth is necessary for us, because, after all, we intellectuals really create our society out of a new culture – we really are called to it by our place in social structure, and we will not answer this call if we do not look the truth in the eyes.

Thus, we must acknowledge certain truths in full, not stopping at the borders where our vested interest begins. Culture becomes the more mass (widespread, the same for everyone) the further advanced the infrastructural process of the transformation of society is, divided into neglected and privileged regions, ecological environments and classes – into societies of people in which social situations become increasingly similar in terms of their most essential aspects. The further such an infrastructural process progresses, the more the divisions into 'higher' and 'lower' cultures lose their ideological sense. Both processes correlated with each other – the cultural one and the infrastructural one – lead in the process of development to two changes that impact each other: to the disappearance of the division of people into higher and lower, and to the disappearance of dividing cultural values into higher and lower. This second division, similarly to the first, belongs, as Marx said, to the prehistory of the human species. Let us rid ourselves of it, the same way we wish to rid ourselves of the first one, if we want to begin to create the history of the human species. All the more so, as, in the two political forms known up to this point, in which we see industrial society with large organizations – the capitalist and the socialist – our own, socialist one is more effective at instituting the egalitarian process in infrastructure, and can therefore also further develop a culture where the terms 'higher' and 'lower' would become meaningless – in which there would cease to exist a Redfieldian division into the 'great' and 'little' cultural traditions.

But that is only half of the story. Shedding the baggage of the overly critical tendencies of the intelligentsia, let us try to determine whether deliberations about higher or lower culture did not conceal a problem that we cannot dismiss. This problem exists, it seems, and is not trivial. The thing is that the sociological conditions of 'higher' and 'lower' have served for the last few thousand years as the institutional frameworks, or the mechanism by whose assistance the development of culture progressed, introducing and disseminating new values in the cultural system. The sociological conditioning of higher and lower slowly retreat into the past – they persist most strongly only in human consciousness. Does this not perhaps mean the liquidation of the institutions that serve the development of culture? Does this not threaten us with stasis, cultural stagnation, halting the birth of new values?

It seems that in the traditional institutions serving the development of culture, we can distinguish the permanent elements, the ones that are the *sine qua non*, and elements that are conditional and fleeting. In capitalist industrialization, there was an element of private property, which essentially comprised its historical form, but which does not have to accompany industrialization, and was an element of complex cooperation, without which industrialization cannot proceed. An analogous accounting can be undertaken in the case of cultural development. Then the sociologically bolstered higher and lower properties of cultures can be counted among transitional, fleeting elements, in certain conditions functional, but not necessarily in every case of cultural development. However, the necessary element – and, as it seems, its necessity is not confined within the boundaries of one epoch, however long – is the existence of clusters or centers for free creation and propagation of new cultural values, not yet acknowledged and not widespread.

For the sake of logical argument, I have been emphasizing, especially in the first note, the 'homogeneous', uniform aspect of mass culture. Now I need to narrow these observations. And so: mass culture is 'widespread' or 'uniform' only in the sense of transcending region, ecology, class. In other words, the differentiation of people according to the cultural values that they prize and that they accept with particular eagerness is not generally marked, or is marked to a lesser degree, by regional, ecological, or class factors, or by extra-cultural infrastructural determinations of privilege or neglect. Yet another way of saying this: it is not exactly accurate to say that mass culture is a culture that does not have subcultures. A more rigorous formulation should be: mass culture is a culture in which the dissemination of particular subcultures is not defined by boundaries between regions that are developed or neglected, ecological environments, and classes (for this more narrow formulation, I am indebted to Krzysztof Zagórski). One would like for it to be a culture in which the internal differentiation of people would not be the result of stifling certain needs of certain people, but the opposite – allowing all needs of all people to be expressed; what is more, not only needs, but also a sociologically minor indicator such as individual taste. We can, of course, imagine (fortunately, only imagine) a culture on a given isolated territory, free from all internal differentiations, deprived of all subcultures. But in the framework of such a culture, instead of change, we would find only traditions; instead of progress, persistence. The history of culture, its development, began from its differentiation, first exo-socially, then endo-socially. For a few thousand years, this differentiation took place in the form of class privilege and oppression. We are slowly freeing it from this unfortunate, but luckily transitory, coating – but we are freeing it! Differentiation itself remains, and must remain, if we do not give up on the value of our culture, which is that culture's constant development and enrichment.

And so the victory over and casting off of regional, ecological, and class determinants of division into lower and higher does not mean that mass culture cannot be varied – leaving in its place many different, even controversial, values and their mutual competition. The consciousness of an objective, necessary, irreversible rightness is the necessary condition of an energetic propagation of its truth only for weak people. People who are strong, among other things in their consciousness, can easily make the effort in the name of values that they treasure, even when they are deprived of the blissful, comforting myth that these values are 'natural', 'in and of themselves' better than the ones they are fighting. What is more, only when freed from myth can people unleash all of the creative powers of their society, suspiciously looking at all declarations of cultural superiority and seeking in them the rebirth of sociological superiority.

Among various subcultures, which can appear and which should appear – for its own good – in the cradle of mass culture, only one subculture plays a particularly exalted role and will probably play it for a long time yet. This is the subculture of the creators of culture, or rather – in a developing (let us hope) democratization of cultural production – the subculture of environments, in which people are professionally striving to create cultural values. I am speaking of intellectuals. Before the human species mastered the globe and became the master of all creation, it first had to emerge as a group of mammals, ostensibly – because of its physiological 'indeterminacy' – fatally defenceless against fantastically physiologically well-adapted predators of the forest. Before a culture becomes widespread, it must first be born somewhere, and initially it will be an elite value (or, rather, from the perspective of later times, avant-garde), whose potential is far from clear. In order for the conflict over the adequacy and historical rationality of a given cultural value to be resolved, this value must

have the possibility of 'being selected', and those who are to decide
– namely the masses – must have an actual possibility of choice. With
the lack of such a possibility of choice 'on equal footing', the fact
that they choose value X, and not Y, is no proof of the thesis that
value X better serves their needs and tastes than does value Y. Butter
better satisfies my tastes and needs than margarine, but, when I eat
margarine, it only means that the nearby store was out of butter. I
know people who eat margarine all the time – some because, in their
youth, they had few opportunities to develop a taste for butter, and
others because of their budgetary constraints. From none of these
three facts can we conclude that margarine is better at satisfying
human needs than butter is. With this fatty analogy, I want to justify
the role of intellectual subculture in the culture of society. Elite or
avant-garde culture is not simply the culture of an isolated group; it
is the material of a future general social culture. This is only the case,
of course – let us add – if the group that comprises the base of avant-
garde culture does not prove to be an isolated group in an infrastructural sense. But that is the problem of the place of intellectuals in the
social structure of society.[3]

# Afterword

## Zygmunt Bauman, 2016

I admit that there was a 'Lévi-Straussian' period in my thinking, inquiries, and writing – and also that the indelible traces of his thought are still easily detected, even in my most recent publications.[1] Through a twist of fate, this period came at a time in my life (1965–70) that was uniquely inhospitable to systematic thinking and formulating extensive and far-reaching plans for research.

For ethnographers, anthropologists, and all other researchers of cultural personality, both those skilled in the discipline and those who are just starting out and are still unsure how to deal with the particularity, creativity, and sometimes the downright strangeness of cultural ideas and initiatives, the appearance of Claude Lévi-Strauss' works on the shelves of bookstores was a revelation. And of those beginners and adepts, there were many – of various kinds, in different parts of the academic world. For me, certainly, these works were a revelation – brilliant from my first encounters with them.

Fêted by hosts on the occasion of the World Sociological Congress in 1966 in Evian, with a tidy sum of francs intended for the purchase of books, the Polish delegates raced to the bookstore; as for me, I spent my portion of the funds, down to the last centime, on anything I could find with Lévi-Strauss' name on the cover. I was enchanted (bewitched?) by every sentence that I encountered on that first reading. And I will add that, during this time, we were debating amongst our group of friends from the Department of Sociology at the University of Warsaw, and with several regular visitors from neighbouring programmes, about a research programme devoted to the anthropology of Polish society, and this very ambitious plan called for the adoption of new, inventive ideas and propositions of structural sociology (or semiotics) whose pioneer was Claude Lévi-Strauss. From the point of view of the success of the prepared programme, the scientific revolution of the great anthropologist was truly a gift from above, and deriving conclusions from it was a task that could not be put off.

But what was it in Lévi-Strauss' works (returning in my mind to that moment) that could be the main cause of enchantment/bewitchment for me and my friends? Probably, it was that, in nearly every one of the sentences, at very least in every paragraph, were answers to questions that I had up to that point been unable to put into words – and which I realized that I, like many other 'culture-ologists', had long been fruitlessly struggling to formulate: some noticeably, but many more that were 'under the skin', as it were – just at, but not quite crossing, the threshold of consciousness. And, from nearly every side, there fluttered solutions devised by the method of structural anthropology to problems that I had up to that point only felt; but I did not know that they were problems, and thus issues that strenuously demanded deference, analysis, and solutions. In connecting one to the other, it emerged quite starkly that everything I had learned about culture up to that point, I urgently needed to revisit and rethink – and, to a large degree, to put away on a shelf, if not send to the dustbin. In brief – it was necessary to start all over, and from an entirely new point.

The biggest shock for me was how much I could rely on my memory, discovering culture as a *process*, rather than as a body of material that was constant, or set up for self-stabilization and permanence (to use the language of Talcott Parsons, who was an unquestioned authority and spiritual leader of sociology at the time, resolving conflicts and storms and restoring 'balance') – a weighty and inert body, surrounded by clear and carefully guarded boundaries and thus effectively separated from 'foreign' influences, self-sufficient and equipped with homeostatic and safety stopgaps tending to the monotonous recreation of norms and the elimination of all departures from them, and the expulsion of foreign bodies.

Culture appeared in this image as a servile, uniform, stable, unchanging order and resistance to pressures to change – the way of 'more of the same, and innovators begone!' The functional cohesion of the system rendered cultural change (it was not possible to ignore that it was taking place, or to deny its banality) a puzzle, demanding to be solved with the help of specific – rare, or even unique – circumstances: to put it one way, a remarkable accident. Stability, guaranteed by the monotony of self-recreation, was, however, the point (a goal, a 'telos'?) of social existence. Parsons' 'Structural functionalism' articulated (as

Ralf Dahrendorf first noticed[2]) a *utopia* controlling the intentions and strategies of 'solid modernity', in which stasis (limiting changes) was the goal of movement and also the defining term of a perfect state: an ideal, to which the only movement tolerated by the system aimed. Utopia – and thus a state of *things* (as opposed to a state of the *soul*) that was nowhere yet achieved, nowhere in actual society to be found, and probably never to be achieved. Lévi-Strauss turned Talcott Parsons' vision upside-down – in the same way that Karl Marx did with Hegel's dialectic.

And if I am once again to trust my memory, then I took the work of Lévi-Strauss as – in grasping culture and in studies of it – a path from utopia to practice: concretely and more specifically, from 'structure' to 'structurization'. The obsessive, compulsive rush to structurization (organizing, ordering, rendering intelligible) of human ways of being-in-the-world appeared to be, from then on, a way of being for cultural phenomena – and this quality did not render culture homeostatic, or a force for entrenching the 'system', but quite the opposite: a tool of constantly, insistently, obtrusively, and irrevocably dynamizing the human condition. Asking what culture does, when it is not structuring things, sounded to me from then on – and still does today – like an equally paradoxical question to 'What does the wind do when it is not blowing?' or 'What does the river do when it doesn't flow?'. I added to these two examples of ways of being, whose existence fits entirely into motion and setting into motion, also the question: 'What does modernity do, when it doesn't modernize?' It was not, after all, an accident that the concept of 'culture' entered into everyday language no sooner than in the third quarter of the eighteenth century.

As I learned from Lévi-Strauss' anthropological uses of Ferdinand de Saussure's linguistics (and then from others who followed his lead, particularly Mary Douglas and Edmund Leach), a particular kind of development used by culture is integration and separation, connection and disconnection, pairing and juxtaposing. From these manoeuvres, meaning emerges – by right of its provenance, shaky and unstable, changing and fluid. Umberto Eco, one of the most productive and multi-dimensional students of the structuralist school, described the profession he pursued (and which he, to a meaningful degree, created) by the name of 'semiologist', whose *métier* he described as 'the ability to identify messages where one might suppose that there were only gestures, to sense signs where it would be easier to see nothing more than objects'.[3] Signs are in constant motion: they take on meaning, spread it, and transmit it through the relationships they enter into with other signs. And I will add that – following Saussure – Lévi-Strauss divides the sign into two components that are mutually autonomous: *le signifiant* (that which signifies) and *le signifié* (that which is signified) – in relation to each other neither exclusively nor once-and-for-all associated, and able to move independently, not taking its partner along. This situation adds dynamism and a kaleidoscopic changeability to culture – and to a great degree. Culture is brimming with relics in the form of 'zombie' *signifiants* – namely, those where the old meanings have disappeared from view or fallen out of use – and it is also full of newly coined terms that are still seeking their referents and involved in forming relationships to objects that were already located in the semantic field. Languages (with the exception of artificial languages, produced for the use of disciplines actively interested in unequivocal meanings for their terms) are therefore (necessarily, as Leach emphasizes) organically freighted with an excess of terms – without which, however, in concern for fulfilling their communicative function, they cannot get by; the meaning of signs is carved out in a space, so to speak, that is 'inter-signs' – in spaces of proximate meaning and mutual opposition.

I have presented here a slim selection of examples of the inspiration that results from Lévi-Strauss' transfer, half a century ago, of the concept of culture from the sphere of *existence* to the category of *process*. Many of them have taken root in the practice of culture-ologists strongly enough for their relationship to the school of structuralists to have disappeared from memory; the emotions accompanying the intellectual revolution it produced have had time to cool, and, of the innovative and shocking effects that they were characterized by at the time of the creation of the book placed into the hands of readers today, only slim traces remain. Others did not succeed in joining the canon of cultural knowledge – which does not mean, however, that they have lost the power to inspire, or that their sentence of exile, carried out by the judgement of history, could not undergo revision. Because, as Georg Christoph Lichtenberg observed already in 1772 – namely two centuries before Thomas Kuhn shocked the academic world with his concept of a 'paradigm shift' – 'resolutions can be ratified only while they are still warm'.[4]

This book (as decreed by a fate that cannot be revised) is thus the result of the kind of strange anomaly that is relatively rare in the annals of publishing. Its first reading is to take place fifty years after it was written – a distance of time after which the emotions accompanying its composition have decisively cooled, and the events of its creation have been forgotten or completely evaded notice; after such a passage of time from the first publication, there is usually a second or third reading (or its no less significant lack), deepening or revising, confirming or refuting the previous claims. These particular circumstances mean that readers encountering the book for the first time half a century after its writing will find in its pages many pieces of information already known to them – but I wager that they will also find others, admittedly written long ago, but not to be found in current readings.

The fact that such a rare event came to pass – almost storybook-like in its uniqueness – is entirely thanks to the rare inquisitiveness and persistence of Dariusz Brzeziński, for which I will be forever grateful to him. The final proofs of *Sketches in the Theory of Culture* were finished in 1967, edited in 1968, and, not long after (during the March purge), scattered, and all available copies were ordered destroyed by those 'above', who – as I believed – also carefully ensured (I remind you that all of this took place in a world, unknown to today's youth, without computers, in the pre-disc era of typewriters and carbon copies) that the order was followed. Perhaps there is yet one other copy hiding somewhere, among many manuscripts confiscated from me, in the heaps of doctored works that the National Institute of Memory inherited from post-PRL censorship. My own copy was confiscated by officers from the Ministry of Public Security in customs uniforms as I left the country, and all subsequent efforts to recover it from later Polish authorities went unanswered. The author last accessed the text half a century ago.

Dr Brzeziński found it in 2016, and retrieved from nonexistence the only – as far as I know – copy to survive the conflagration, untouched by anyone except the author, uncorrected by editors and proofreaders; and Professor Raciborski, the head of Scholar Press, undertook to publish it. A story that is more like something from a mystery or Gothic novel than (fortunately) the typical academic process.

# Notes

## Part I  Sign and Culture

### 1  The Origins of the Semiotic Theory of Culture, or the Crisis of Cultural Anthropology

1 Translator's note: As the reference was missing, this is my translation of the quote.
2 Karl Marx, *Capital*, vol. I.
3 Translator's note: Citation missing, translation is my own.
4 Translator's note: This quote is actually located in Book II of the *Histories*.
5 Werner Jaeger, *Paideia*, vol. I, Oxford University Press, p. 152.
6 Margaret Mead, *Anthropology: a Human Science: Selected Papers, 1939-1960*, Princeton, Toronto, London, New York: D. Van Nostrand Company, Inc., 1970, p. 170.
7 M. Montaigne, *Próby* [Essays], trans. T. Boya-Żeleński, vol. I, Warsaw: Państwowy Instytut Wydaniczy, 1957, pp. 306–8 [my translation – KB].
8 C. Lévi-Strauss, *Tristes Tropiques*, trans. from the French by John and Doreen Weightman, New York: Penguin, 1974, pp. 383–4.
9 See K. E. Bock, 'Theories of progress and evolution', in *Sociology and History*, ed. Werner J. Cahnman and Alvin Boskoff, New York: Free Press of Glencoe, 1964, pp. 24–5.
10 Paul Bohannan, *Justice and Judgment Among the Tiv*, London, New York: Published for the International African Institute by Oxford University Press, 1957, pp. 69 and 212.
11 Walter Goldschmidt, *Comparative Functionalism: An Essay in Anthropological Theory [by] Walter Goldschmidt*, Berkeley: University of California Press, 1966, p. 6.

12 Ibid., p. 7.
13 Lévi-Strauss, *Tristes Tropiques*, pp. 332–3.
14 Ibid., pp. 387 and 391.
15 B. Baczko, *Rousseau – samotność i wspólnota* [Rousseau – solitude and community], Warsaw: Państwowego Wydawnictwa Naukowego, 1964, pp. 166 and 167.
16 See G. Charbonnier, 'Horloges et machines à vapeur', in *Entretiens avec Claude Lévi-Strauss*, Paris, 1961.

## 2   Towards a Semiotic Theory of Culture

 1 F. Znaniecki, *Cultural Sciences, Their Origin and Development*, Urbana: University of Illinois Press, 1963, p. 132.
 2 Ibid., p. 120.
 3 C. Lévi-Strauss, *The Raw and the Cooked*, University of Chicago Press, p. 12.
 4 Ibid., p. 341.
 5 C. Lévi-Strauss, *Anthropologie structurale*, Paris: Plon, 1958, p. 44.
 6 Tadeusz Milewski, *Językoznawstwo* [Linguistics], Warsaw: Państwowe Wydawnictwo Naukowe, 1965, p. 9.
 7 A. A. Zinoviev, 'Ob osnowach abstraktnoj teorii znakow [On the foundations of an abstract theory of signs]', *Problemy Struktury Lingwistyki* [Problems of structural linguistics] (1963).
 8 M. W. Popowicz, *O fiłosofskom analizie jazyka nauki* [On the philosophical analysis of linguistics], Kiev: Naukowa dumka, 1966, p. 48.
 9 Ibid., pp. 50–1.
10 L. A. Abramian, *Gnoseologiczeskije problemy tieorii znaków znaków* [Gnoseological problems of the theory of signs], Yerevan, 1965, pp. 56–7.
11 L. D. Reznikow, *Gnoseologiczeskije woprosy semiotiki* [Gnoseological questions of semiotics], Leningrad: Izdatielstwo Leningradskogo uniwiersitieta, 1964, p. 19.
12 D. P. Gorski, 'Formalnaja logika i jazyk [Formal logic and language]', in *Fiłosofsfeije problemy sowremionnoi formalnoj logiki* [Philosophical problems of formal logic], Moscow: Izdatielstwo Akadiemii nauk SSSR, 1962, p. 55.
13 Charles E. Osgood, 'On the nature of meaning' [1952], in *Current Perspectives in Social Psychology*, ed. E. P. Hollander and H. G. Hunt, New York: Oxford University Press, 1963.
14 Lev Vygotsky, 'Razwitie wyszszych psichiceskich funkcji' [The development of higher psychological functions], in *Iz nieopublikowanych trudow* [Unpublished works], Moscow: Izdatielstwo Akadiemii piadegogiczeskich nauk, 1960, p. 225.
15 I believe that the term 'isomorphism' was introduced into linguistics by Jerzy Kuryłowicz (*Recherches structurales*, Copenhagen: Nordsk Sprog- og Kulturforlag, 1949, pp. 48–60).

16  See F. de Saussure, *Kurs językoznawstwa ogólnego* [Course in general linguistics], trans. K. Kasprzyk, Warsaw: Państwowe Wydawnictwo Naukowe, 1961, p. 79. It is worth noting that Roman Jakobson ('À la recherche de l'essence du langage', *Diogène* 51 (1965)) protested strongly against the idea accepted among linguists, that it was Saussure who discovered the difference between the 'signifier' and the 'signified'. Jacobson argues that, already within Stoic philosophy, there is the assertion that the sign (*semeion*) constitutes a relation between the '*semainon*' and the '*semainomenon*' – the first of these is sensory (*aistheton*); the second, mental (*noeton*). There is a similar idea in St Augustine's distinction between two elements within the *signum* – the *signans* and the *signatum*. It turns out that this topic has a long history. However, the distinction entered into modern linguistics via Saussure.

17  R. Jakobson, 'Dwa aspekty języka i dwa typy zakłóceń afazyjnych [Two aspects of language and two types of aphasic disturbance]', in R. Jakobson and M. Halle, *Podstawy języka* [Fundamentals of language], Wrocław: Zakład Narodowy im. Ossolińskich, 1964, p. 112. See also A. Martinet, *Éléments de linguistique générale*, Paris: Colin, 1960, pp. 205–7.

18  J. D. Apresjan, 'O poniatach i mietodach strukturnoj leksikołogii [On understandings and methods of structural lexicology]', *Problemy Struktur Lingwistyki* [Problems of linguistic structure] (1962).

19  Roman Suszko, *Wykłady z logiki formalnej* [Lectures in formal logic], Warsaw: Państwowe Wydawnictwo Naukowe, 1965, ch. 1, p. 41.

20  A. Martinet, *La linguistique synchronique*, Paris: Presses Universitaires de France, 1965, p. 4.

21  Henri Lefebvre, *Le langage et la société*, Paris: Gallimard, 1966, pp. 322–3.

22  B. Malinowski, *Szkice z teorii kultury* [Sketches in the theory of culture], trans. H. Buczyńska, Warsaw: Ksiażka I Wiedza, 1958, pp. 31 and 38 [my translation – KB].

23  Cited in A. Pierce, 'Durkheim and functionalism', in *Emile Durkheim*, ed. K. H. Wolff, Columbus: Ohio State University Press, 1960.

24  A. R. Radcliffe-Brown, 'The concept of function in social science', *American Anthropologist* (1935).

25  See B. Salzberg, 'What is information theory?' in *Information Storage and Neutral Control*, ed. W. S. Fields and W. Abbott, Springfield, IL: C. C. Thomas, 1963.

26  Jacobson, 'À la recherche'.

27  These terms were introduced by Kenneth Lee Pike in *Language* (Glendale: Summer Institute of Linguistics, 1954), and elaborated on by A. Capella, *Studies in Sociolinguistics*, The Hague: Mouton, 1966.

28  Raymond Firth, *Elements of Social Organization*, London, 1951, p. 153. The author expresses similar ideas in *Primitive Polynesian Economy*, New York, 1950, ch. 10, and in the article 'Orientations in economic life' (in *The Institutions of Primitive Society*, ed. E. E. Evans-Pritchard et al., Glencoe: The Free Press, 1954).

29 Melville J. Herskovits, *Economic Anthropology*, New York: Knopf, 1952, p. 488.

30 Marshall D. Sahlins, 'Political power and the economy in primitive society', in *Essays in the Science of Culture*, ed. G. E. Dole and R. L. Carneiro, New York: Crowell, 1960, p. 391.

31 H. I. Hogbin, *Transformation Scene: The Changing Culture of a New Guinea Village*, London: Routledge & Paul, 1951, p. 122.

32 B. Malinowski, *Argonauts of the Western Pacific*, London: Routledge & Sons, 1950, pp. 97 and 175.

33 E. Leach, *Political Systems of Highland Burma*, London: London School of Economics and Political Science, 1954, p. 163.

34 Saussure, *Kurs*, p. 80.

35 E. Benveniste, 'Nature du signe linguistigue', *Acta Linguistica*, 1 (939).

36 C. Bally, 'Sur la motivation du signe linguistique', *Bulletin de la Société de Linguistique de Paris* (1940).

37 Wacław Sierpiński, *Teoria mnogości* [Set theory], Warsaw: Państwowe Zakłady Wydawnictw Szkolnych, 1964, p. 47.

38 See L. Apostel, B. Mandelbrot, and J. Piaget, *Logique et équilibre*, Paris: Presses Universitaires de France, 1957, p. 122.

39 See F. Harary and others in *Structural Models: An Introduction to the Theory of Directed Graphs*, New York: Wiley, 1963; also O. W. Biełych and E. W. Bielajew, 'Wozmożnosti promienienija tieorii grafow w socjologii', in *Czełowiek i Obszczestwo*, vol. I, Leningrad, 1966.

40 Saussure, *Kurs*, pp. 121–2.

41 Jakobson, 'À la recherche'.

42 See Z. Bauman, 'Trzy uwagi o problemach współczesnych wychowania' [Three observations about problems of contemporary education], *Kwartalnik Pedagogiczny*, 4 (1965).

43 A. J. Greimas, *Semantique structurale*, Paris: Larousse, 1966, p. 19.

44 Lévi-Strauss, *The Raw*, p. 347.

45 Max Gluckman, *Les rites de passage*; citation from the author's manuscript.

46 *Principles of Self-organization*, Oxford, 1962; Russian translation, ed. A. J. Lernera, Moscow: Izd. Mir., 1966.

47 See 'Niekotoryje osobiennosti piererabotki informacji czelowiekom [Certain features of information processing in humans]', in *Kibernetika, myszlenie, żizń* [Cybernetics, thought, life], ed. A. N. Berga et al., Moscow: Izd. 'Mysl', 1964, pp. 234–5.

48 E. I. Bojko, 'Modelirowanie funkcji mozga i wysszaja nejrodin'amiita [Modelling functions of the brain and higher processes]', in Berga et al., eds., *Kibernetika*, p. 302.

49 Lévi-Strauss, *Anthropologie structurale*, p. 30.

50 Karl Marx, Friedrich Engels, and C. J. Arthur, *The German Ideology*, London: Lawrence & Wishart, 1974 [1947], pp. 121, 47.

51 T. Parsons, *Essays in Sociological Theory*, New York: Free Press, 1964, pp. 21–2.

52 See, for instance, Paul Radin, *The World of Primitive Man*, New York: H. Schuman, 1953, p. 249.
53 S. Goodenough, 'Cultural anthropology and linguistics', in *Language in Culture and Society*, ed. D. Hymes, New York: Harper & Row, 1964, p. 38.
54 Claude Lévi-Strauss, 'Le triangle culinaire', *L'Arc*, 26 (1965), pp. 19–29.
55 Z. Bauman, *Kultura a społeczeństwo* [Culture and society], Warsaw: Państwowe Wydawnictwo Naukowe, 1966, ch. 1.
56 L. W. Szczerba, 'Opyt obszczej tieurii leksykografii [Experiences in the general theory of lexicography]', in *Izbannyje raboty po jazykoznaniju i fonetike* [Work on linguistics and phonetics], vol. I, Leningrad: Izdatielstwo Leningradskogo uniwiersitieta, 1958.
57 A. A. Leontiev, *Słowo w rieczewoj diejatielnosti* [The word in practical activity], Moscow: Izd. AN SSSR, 1965.
58 Stefan Żółkiewski, *Zagadnienia stylu* [Questions of style], Warsaw: Państwowy Instytut Wydawniczy, p. 248.

## 3   Man and Sign

1 René Descartes, *Discourse on the Method*, Part V.
2 René Descartes, *The Passions of the Soule in Three Books*, 1650, Articles 12 and 16.
3 J. O. de La Mettrie, *Człowiek – maszyna* [Man – machine], trans. S. Rudniański, Warsaw: Państwowe Wydawnictwo Naukowe, 1953, pp. 68–9 [my translation – KB].
4 G. W. Zopf, 'Relation and context', in *Principles of Self-Organization*, ed. Heinz von Foerster and George W. Zopf Jr, Oxford, 1962; *Cyt. wg rosyjskiego przekładu pod red. A. J. Lernera*, Moscow: Izd. Mir., 1966, p. 411.
5 See M. Mazur, *Cybernetyczna teoria układów samodzielnych* [Cybernetic theory of autonomous systems], Warsaw: Państwowe Wydawnictwo Naukowe, 1966, pp. 50–7.
6 Walter B. Cannon, *The Wisdom of the Body*, New York: W. W. Norton & Co., 1932. Citations from the 1939 edition.
7 Ibid., p. 238. [Translator's note: although I located both the 1932 and the 1939 editions of the text, this quote was not to be found in either one. Thus, the translation is my own.]
8 J. M. Fletcher, 'Homeostasis as the explanatory principle in psychology', *Psychological Review*, 49 (1) (1942), pp. 81–7.
9 See, for example, Jean Piaget, *The Origins of Intelligence in Children*, trans. Margaret Cook, Madison, CT: International Universities Press, 1952.
10 J. Piaget, 'Genèse et structure en psychologie', in *Entretiens sur les notions de genèse et de structure*, ed. Maurice de Gandillac et al., Paris: Mouton, 1965, p. 43.

11 J. Piaget, *Narodziny inteligencji dziecka* [Origins of intelligence in children], trans. Maria Przetacznikowa, Warsaw, 1966, p. 14.

12 W. S. Tiuchtin, 'Suszcznost' otrażenija i tieoria informacji [The essence of reflection and information theory]', in *Kibernietika, myszlenie, żiżń* [Cybernetics, thought, life], ed. A. W. Berga et al., Moscow: Izd. 'Misl', 1964, p. 311.

13 R. Chauvin, *Życie i obyczaje owadów* [The life and habits of insects], trans. A. Straszewicz, Warsaw: Państwowe Wydawnictwo Naukowe, 1966, p. 100.

14 W. McDougall, *Psychology: The Study of Behaviour*, New York: Holt, 1912; *An Outline of Psychology*, New York: Macmillan, 1923.

15 E. Rabaud, *L'instinct et le comportement animal*, Paris: Colin, 1949.

16 See, for example, K. Z. Lorenz, *King Solomon's Ring: New Light on Animal Ways*, New York: Thomas Y. Crowell Company, 1952.

17 See, for example, N. Tinbergen, *The Study of Instinct*, Oxford, 1951; *Social Behaviour in Animals*, London: Wiley, 1953.

18 Chauvin, *Życie* [Life], p. 92.

19 V. C. Detier and E. Stellar, *Animal Behavior, Its Evolutionary and Neurological Basis*, Englewood Cliffs: Prentice-Hall, 1964, p. 71. [Translator's note: I was unable to find this book, or indeed, any evidence of its existence. Thus, the translation is my own.]

20 G. Viaud, *Instynkty* [Instincts], trans. H. Waniczek, Warsaw: Państwowe Wydawnictwo Naukowe, 1965, p. 44.

21 W. Ross Ashby, in von Foerster and Zopf Jr (eds.), *Principles*, p. 316.

22 H. Frings and M. Frings, *Animal Communication*, New York: Blaisdell Pub., 1964, p. 51.

23 Cited in A. N. Montiew and E. P. Kripczyk, 'Niekotoryje ossobiennosti procesja piererabotki informacji człowiekom [Some features of individual processes of information processing in humans]', in Berga et al., eds., *Kibernetika* [Cybernetics], pp. 238–9.

24 Detier and Stellar, *Animal Behavior*, p. 97.

25 Syunzo Kawamura, 'The process of sub-culture propagation among Japanese monkeys', in *Primate Social Behaviour*, ed. C. H. Southwick, Princeton: Van Nostrand, 1963, p. 84.

26 A. Remane, *Życie społeczne zwierząt* [The social life of animals], trans. W. Serafiński, Warsaw: Państwowe Wydawnictwo Naukowe, 1965, p. 182.

27 G. A. Pask, 'The model of evolution', in von Foerster and Zopf Jr, eds., *Principles*, p. 290 [my translation – KB].

28 M. Lindauer, *Communication among Social Bees*, Cambridge, MA: Harvard University Press, 1961.

29 C. R. Carpenter, 'Societies of monkeys and apes', in Southwick, ed., *Primate Social Behaviour*, p. 27.

30 Kinji Imanishi, 'Social behaviour in Japanese monkeys', in Southwick, ed., *Primate Social Behaviour*, p. 76.

31 See S. L. Washburn and I. De Vore, 'The social life of baboons', in Southwick, ed., *Primate Social Behaviour*, p. 107.

32 Cited in E. Brehant, *An Encyclopedist of the Dark Ages,* New York: Columbia University Press, 1912, pp. 207ff.

33 M. T. Hogden, *Early Anthropology in the Sixteenth and Seventeenth Centuries,* Philadelphia: University of Pennsylvania Press, 1946, p. 30.

34 S. F. Washburn, 'Tools and human evolution', in *Man Before History,* ed. C. Cabel, Englewood Cliffs: Prentice-Hall, 1964, p. 14.

35 C. Geertz, 'The transition to humanity', in *Horizons of Anthropology,* ed. Sol Tax, London: Allen & Unwin, 1964, p. 46.

36 P. Teilhard de Chardin, *The Phenomenon of Man,* trans. B. T. Walla, London, 1959, p. 165.

37 Carpenter, 'Societies', p. 49.

38 Cited in A. Spirkin, *Pochodzenie świadomości* [Origins of consciousness], trans. R. Hekker, Warsaw, 1966, pp. 66–8.

39 E. Cassirer, *An Essay on Man,* New Haven: Yale Univeristy Press, 1944, pp. 27ff.

40 For a similar – though not identical – account, see M. W. Popowicz, *O fiłosofskom analizie jazyka nauki* [On the philosophical analysis of linguistics], Kiev: Naukows dumka, 1966, p. 83.

41 See A. Martinet, *La linguistique synchronique: Études et recherches,* Paris: Presses Universitaires de France, 1965, p. 2.

42 Piaget, *Narodziny* [Origins], p. 19.

43 Ibid., p. 205.

44 See E. R. Wolf, 'The study of evolution', in Tax, ed., *Horizons,* p. 112.

45 G. Charbonnier, *Entretiens avec Claude Lévi-Strauss,* Paris: Julliard, 1961, p. 43.

46 A. M. Turing, 'Computing machinery and intelligence', *Mind,* 59 (236) (1950), pp. 433–60.

47 A. Newell, J. C. Shaw, and H. Simon, 'Elements of a theory of human problem solving', *Psychological Review,* 63 (3) (1958), pp. 151–66.

48 Michel Scriven, 'The mechanical concept of mind', *Mind,* 64 (246) (1953), pp. 230–40 [I was not able to locate this text; my translation – KB].

49 Keith Gunderson, 'The imitation game', *Mind,* 73 (290) (1964), pp. 234–5 [I was not able to locate this text; my translation – KB].

50 Anatol Rapaport, 'An essay on mind', in *Theories of the Mind,* ed. J. M. Scher, New York: Free Press of Glencoe, 1962.

51 I. B. Nowik, 'K woprosu o jedinstwie priedmieta i metoda kibiernietiki' [Towards a response to the unity of the object and method of cybernetics], in Berga et al., eds., *Kibernetika* [Cybernetics], p. 130.

## 4   The Problem of Universals and the Semiotic Theory of Culture

1 J. Piaget, *Narodziny inteligencji dziecka* [Origins of intelligence in children], trans. Maria Przetacznikowa, Warsaw: Państwowe Wydawnictwo Naukowe, 1966, p. 12.

2 E. Leach, *The New Directions in the Study of Language,* ed. Eric H. Lenneberg, Cambridge, MA: MIT Press, 1964.

3 See B. Z. Seligman, 'The problem of incest and exogamy, a restatement', *American Anthropologist*, 52 (3) (1950), pp. 305–16.

4 J. M. Scher, 'Mind as participation', in *Theories of Mind*, ed. Scher, New York: Free Press of Glencoe, 1962, p. 360.

5 M. Mead, 'Our educational emphasis in primitive perspective', *American Journal of Sociology*, 48 (6) (1943), pp. 633–9 [my translation – KB].

6 See Marshall, 'Sharing, taking and giving: relief of social tensions among Kung Bushmen', *Africa*, 31 (3) (1961), pp. 231–49.

7 H. I. Hogbin, *Transformation Scene: The Changing Culture of a New Guinea Village*, London: Routledge & Paul, 1951, p. 86.

8 S. M. Shirokogoroff, *Social Organization of the Northern Tungus*, Shanghai: Commercial Press, 1929.

9 M. Reay, *The Kuma*, Melbourne University Press, 1959, p. 107.

10 M. Mead, ed., *Cooperation and Competition among Primitive Peoples*, New York: McGraw-Hill Book Co., 1937, p. 31.

11 C. Lévi-Strauss, *La pensée sauvage*, Paris: Plon, 1962, p. 24.

12 M. W. Popowicz, *O filosofskom analizie języka nauki* [On the philosophical analysis of linguistics], Kiev: Naukowa dumka, 1966, p. 84.

13 Piaget, *Narodziny* [Origins], p. 205.

14 E. Leach, 'Anthropological aspects of language: animal categories and verbal abuse', pp. 35, 37–8 [my translation – KB].

15 See S. M. Lambert, *A Yankee Doctor in Paradise*, Boston: Little, Brown and Co., 1941, p. 304.

16 L. Berkovitz, 'The judgmental process in personality functioning', *Psychological Review*, 67 (2) (1957), pp. 130–42.

17 H. Hogbin, *Social Change*, London: Watts, 1959, p. 189.

18 E. V. Stonequist, *The Marginal Man: A Study in Personality and Culture Conflict*, New York: Charles Scribner's Sons, 1927. Citations from the 1961 edition.

19 E. Neyman, 'Typy marginesowości i ich rola w zamianie społecznej [Types of marginality and their role in social change]', *Studia Socjologiczne*, 4 (23) (1966), pp. 35–62.

20 G.M. Williams, *Understanding India*, Coward-McCann, New York 1928, s. 168.

21 Stonequist, *The Marginal Man*, pp. 221, 154–5.

## 5 Some Research Problems in the Semiotic Theory of Culture

1 See, for instance, S. K. Szaumian, 'Preobrazowanie informacji w procesie poznania i dwuchsatupienczataja teoria strukturnoj lingwistiki [Transformation of information in cognitive process and the theory of structural linguistics]', *Problemy Strukturnoj Ligwistiki* (1962).

2 A. Chapanis, 'Man, machines, and models', *American Psychologist*, 16 (3) (1961), pp. 113–31.

3 We find a similar diagram, though in a different context, in C. Friesa, 'Meaning and linguistic analysis', *Language*, 30 (1) (1954), pp. 57–68.

4 M. H. Marx, 'The central nature of theory construction', in *Theories in Contemporary Psychology*, ed. M. H. Marx, New York: Macmillan, 1963 [my translation – KB].

5 W. Spence, 'Types of constructs in psychology', *Psychological Review*, 51 (1) (1944), pp. 47–68 [my translation – KB].

6 F. de Saussure, *Kurs językoznawstwa ogólnego*, trans. Krystyna Kasprzyk, Warsaw: Państwowe Wydawnictwo Naukowe, 1961, p. 25 [*Course in General Linguistics*, ed. and annotated Roy Harris, London, New Delhi, New York, and Sydney, p. 77].

7 See S. Żółkiewski, 'O regułach analizy strukturalnej [On the principles of structural analysis]', *Kultura i społeczeństwo*, 10 (4) (1966), pp. 73–106.

8 W. B. Pillsbury, 'Meaning and image', *Psychological Review*, 15 (3) (1908), p. 156 [my translation – KB].

9 Kenneth L. Pike, 'Towards a theory of the structure of human behaviour', in *Language in Culture and Society*, ed. Dell Hymes, New York: Harper & Row, 1964, p. 57.

10 E. Benveniste, '"Structure" en linguistique', in *Sens et usages du terme structure dans les sciences humaines et sociales*, ed. E. Bastide, Gravenhage: Mouton, 1962, pp. 38–9.

11 Kenneth Lee Pike, *Language in Relation to a Unified Theory of the Structure of Human Behavior*, Glendale: Summer Institute of Linguistics, 1954, p. 54.

12 S. F. Nadel, *The Theory of Social Structure*, London: Cohen and West, 1957.

13 Ibid., pp. 8, 10.

14 Ibid., pp. 44, 57.

15 I have presented my own interpretation here, and not a minute summary of Nadel's theory; I tried to 'reformulate' it in such a way as to make it maximally correspond to the tasks that I set myself in the following sketch. I must refer readers wanting to acquaint themselves with this very interesting theory in its natural form to the author's own work.

16 See R. Jakobson, 'Typological studies and their contribution to historical comparative linguistics', in *Proceedings of the Eighth International Congress of Linguistics*, Oslo University Press, 1958.

17 T. Milewski, 'Zasady językoznawstwa typologicznego [Principles of linguistic typology]', *Biuletyn Polskiego Towarzystwa Językoznawczego* (1962).

18 See W. W. Martinov, *Kibernetika, Semiotika, Lingwistyka* [Cybernetics, semiotics, linguistics], Mińsk: Nauka i technika, 1966, Semiotika 3: Aksjomy Porożdzienija.

19 Ibid., pp. 87–8.

20 See L. Hjelmslev, *Prolegomena to a Theory of Language*, Baltimore: Waverly Press, 1953.

21 See A. J. Greimas, *Sémantique structurale*, Paris: Larousse, 1966.

22 N. Chomsky, 'Explanatory models in linguistics', in *Logic, Methodology and Philosophy of Science*, ed. E. Nagel et al., Stanford University Press, 1962, pp. 535, 536.

23 P. Smoczyński, *Przyswojenie przez dziecko podstaw system językowego*, [A child's acquisition of the basics of the language system], Łódź: Ossolineum, 1965.
24 A. A. Leontiev, *Słowo w rieczewoj diejatielnosti* [The word in practical activity], Moscow: Izdatielstwo AN SSSR, 1965.
25 J. Piaget, *Narodziny inteligencji dziecka*, [Origins of intelligence in children], trans. Maria Przetacznikowa, Warsaw: Państwowe Wydawnictwo Naukowe, 1966, p. 12
26 Ibid., pp. 426–8.
27 Translator's note: I was unable to locate this source; thus, the translation is my own.

## PART II   Culture and Social Structure

## 1   Cultural and Extra-Cultural Organization of Society

1 Cited in *Filozofia egzystencjalna* [Existential philosophy], produced by Leszek Kołakowski and Krzysztof Pomian, Warsaw: Państwowe Wydawnictwo Naukowe, 1965, p. 348.
2 Ibid., p. 451.
3 Karl Marx, Friedrich Engels, and C. J. Arthur, *The German Ideology*, London: Lawrence & Wishart, 1974 [1947]).
4 *Humanistic Viewpoints in Psychology*, ed. Frank T. Severin, New York: McGraw-Hill, 1965, p. 35.
5 Ibid., p. 51.

## 2   Economics, Culture, and Typologies of Societies

1 See part I, chapter 2, 'Towards a Semiotic Theory of Culture'.
2 R. Redfield, *Peasant Society and Culture*, University of Chicago Press, 1956, pp. 67–9.
3 R. Linton, *The Cultural Background of Personality*, New York: Appleton-Century-Crofts, 1945, p. 5
4 R. Benedict, *Patterns of Culture*, New York: Houghton Mifflin Co., 1934, p. 253.
5 L. A. White, *The Evolution of Culture*, New York: McGraw-Hill, 1959, p. 242.
6 W. Kula, *Problemy i metody historii gospodarczej* [Problems and methods of economic history], Warsaw: Państwowe Wydawnictwo Naukowe, 1963, pp. 251, 252–7.
7 W. Kula, *Teoria ekonomiczna ustroju feudalnego*, Warsaw: Państwowe Wydawnictwo Naukowe, 1962, pp. 45–6.
8 J. Rutkowski, *Studia z dziejów wsi polskiej XVI–XVIII wieku* [Studies in the history of Polish villages from the 16th to the 18th centuries], Warsaw: Państwowe Wydawnictwo Naukowe, 1956, pp. 301, 333.

9 *Materiały do dziejów uwłaszczenia chłopów w Królestwie Polskim* [Materials for a history of peasant enfranchisement], Wrocław: Zaklad Narodowy im. Ossolińskich, 1961, p. 9.
10 Cited in J. Chmurą, *Problem siły roboczej w rolnictwie Królestwa Polskiego* [The problem of labour power in the agriculture of the Kingdom of Poland], Warsaw: Państwowe Wydawnictwo Naukowe, 1959, p. 243.
11 Koszutski gives the number for 1845 as 46,397 workers, and for 1857–6 as 364 (*Rozwój przemysłu wielkiego w Królestwie Polskim* [The development of major industry in the Kingdom of Poland], Warsaw: Redakcya Gazety Handlowej, 1901, p. 167); Kempner gives 50,000 in 1850 (*Dzieje gospodarcze Polski porozbiorowej w zarysie*, vol. I, Warsaw: Druk. K. Kowalski, 1920, p. 47).
12 W. Kula, *Historia gospodarcza Polski 1864–1918*, Warsaw: Spoldzielnia Wydawnicza 'Wiedza', 1947, p. 40.
13 M. Mieszczankowski, *Struktura agrarna Polski międzywojennej*, Warsaw: Państwowe Wydawnictwo Naukowe, 1960, p. 312.
14 *Młodzież sięga po pracę*, Warsaw: Instytut Spraw Spolecznych, 1938, p. 108.
15 J. Michałowski, *Wieś nie ma pracy* [The village has no work], Warsaw: Fundusz Pracy, 1935, pp. 1–2, 67, 70.
16 Ibid., pp. 24, 48.
17 K. Marx, *Kapitał*, ed. P. Hoffman, vol. I, Warsaw: Ksiażka i Wiedza, 1956, p. 581 [K. Marx, *Capital*, trans. Samuel Moore and Edward Aveling, ed. Frederick Engels, vol. 1, pt 6, ch. 19, p. 381].
18 S. Śreniowski, *Uwłaszczenie chłopów w Polsce* [Enfranchisement of Polish peasants], Warsaw: Państwowe Wydawnictwo Naukowe, 1956, pp. 55–6.
19 Kula, *Problemy*, p. 564.
20 B. Gałęski, *Chłopi a zawód rolnika* [Peasants and the profession of farmer], Warsaw: Państwowe Wydawnictwo Naukowe, 1963, pp. 127–8.
21 Ibid., p. 54.
22 *Materiały*, pp. 24, 28.
23 Kula, *Problemy*, pp. 250–1.

### 3　Cultural Determinants of the Research Process

1 A. Montagu, *Anthropology and Human Nature*, New York: McGraw-Hill, 1963, pp. 16 and 105 [my translations – KB].
2 See A. Korzybski, *Manhood of Humanity*, New York: E. P. Dutton, 1921.
3 C. Lévi-Strauss, *Structural Anthropology*, New York: Basic Books, 1963, p. 84.
4 D. Lee, *Freedom and Culture*, Englewood Cliffs, NJ, 1959, p. 1.
5 E. Cassirer, *An Essay on Man*, New Haven, CT: Yale University Press, 1964, p. 25.

6  A. F. Wallace, *The Psychic Unity of Human Groups*, w: *Studying Personality Cross-Culturally*, ed. Bert Kaplan, Evanston, IL: Row, Peterson, 1961, pp. 131–2.
7  G. F. Kneller, *Educational Anthropology: An Introduction*, New York: Wiley, 1965, p. 81.

## 4  Three Observations About Problems of Contemporary Education

1  Cited in B. Berelson and G. A. Steiner, *Human Behavior: An Inventory of Scientific Findings*, New York: Harcourt, Brace and World, 1964, p. 83.
2  See. A. W. Gouldner, 'The norm of reciprocity', *American Sociological Review* (April 1960), pp. 161–78; H. Becker, *Man in Reciprocity*, New York: F. A. Praeger, 1956; L. T. Hobhouse, *Morals in Evolution*, London: Chapman and Hall, 1906.
3  D. Markowska, *Rodzina w środowisku wiejskim*, Wrocław: Zakład Narodowy im. Ossolińskich, 1964, pp. 50–1.
4  A. B. Hollingshead, *Elmtown's Youth*, New York: J. Wiley, 1945, p. 149.
5  J. Komorowska, *Telewizja w życiu dzieci i młodzieży* [Television in the life of the youth], Łódź and Warsaw: Państwowe Wydawnictwo Naukowe, 1963.
6  Cited in G. E. Żurakowskij, *Oczerki po istorii anticznoj pedagogiki* [Essays in the pedagogy of antiquity], Moscow: Akademia Piedagogiczeskich Nauk RSFR, 1963, p. 353.
7  J. Szczepański, *Socjologiczne zagadnienia wyższego wykształcenia* [Sociological questions of higher education], Warsaw: Państwowe Wydawnictwo Naukowe, 1963, p. 340.

## 5  Masses, Classes, Elites: Semiotics and the Re-Imagination of the Sociological Function of Culture

1  Z. Bauman, 'Bieguny analizy kulturowej', *Studia Socjologiczne*, 3 (1964).
2  Edward Sapir, 'Culture, genuine and spurious', *American Journal of Sociology*, 29 (4) (Jan. 1924), pp. 401–29, 409, 410, 411.
3  Jak wynika z datowanego na 20 maja 1967 r. listu Zygmunta Baumana do Wydawnictwa Ossolineum – znajdującego się obecnie w Archiwum Zakładu Narodowego im. Ossolińskich we Wrocławiu – niniejszy tekst, a zatem i cała książka, miał się kończyć paragrafem pt. *Dialektyka demokratyzacji*. Ustęp ten nie zachował się jednak w ocalonym, niepełnym egzemplarzu korektowym, i nie ma go też w teczce redakcyjnej *Szkiców z teorii kultury*. Rozdział ten – zrekonstruowany na podstawie artykułu opublikowanego w "Kulturze i Społeczeństwie" nr 1 z 1965 r. – uznać należy więc za niedokończony (przyp. red. nauk.).

## Afterword

1 Editor's note. In this commentary to *Sketches in the Theory of Culture*, completed by Zygmunt Bauman in September 2016, the author draws connections between his biography and the development of the book, and presents a contemporary assessment of his earlier theory of culture.
2 Ralf Dahrendorf, 'Out of Utopia: toward a reorientation of sociological analysis', *American Journal of Sociology*, 64 (2) (Sept. 1958).
3 See his 'Signs of the times', in Umberto Eco, Stephen Jay Gould, Jean-Claude Carriere, and Jean Delumeau, *Conversations about the End of Time* (London: Penguin, 1999), p. 171.
4 *Afforisms*, in the English translation by R. J. Hollingdale (London: Penguin, 1990), p. 42.

# Index

Abramian, L. A. 37, 257n10
accommodation–assimilation
	process 28, 65, 78, 90, 91,
	98, 106, 145, 150, 158
adaptation 67, 70, 83, 86, 112,
	158, 220
  behavioural 204
  biological 66, 87, 90, 217
  capacity common to all living
	organisms 29
  concepts to reality 144
  crisis in 218
  cultural 217, 244
  decisive meaning for 56
  ego 133
  entirely plastic 97
  evolutionary 77
  good 54
  human needs of 207
  ideas advantageous for 98
  information valuable for 210
  mutual 225, 232
  organic 79
  passive 143
  poor 54
  social 216, 217

Africa see South Africa; Western
	Africa
alienation xv, 32, 158, 243
Allport, Gordon W. 168
Altamira Cave Paintings 85
*American Journal of Sociology*
	243, 263n5, 267n2 (ch. 5),
	268n2
American psycholinguistics
	38
amorphousness viii, 54, 56-8,
	149, 210, 215, 220
Anglo-Indians 115
animals 57, 63, 67-9, 89, 161,
	170, 185, 194
  domestic 14
  features inherited by humans
	from 204
  game 100, 104
  periodization of 216
  signs and 70-9, 88, 90
  teaching and learning
	205
  traits of particular species in
	totemic systems 26
  wild 100, 101

anthropology xxiin14, 9, 20, 34,
100, 161, 251
contemporary 19, 182
crisis of 17, 19, 21
economic 177
social 18
*see also* cultural anthropology;
structural anthropology
anthropomorphism 62, 64,
171
*see also* praxeomorphism
anti-evolutionarism 20
antinomy 18, 22
Apostel, L. 259n38
Archimedes 64
aristocracy 12, 244-5
English 223
Aristotelianism 84, 171
Armenians 174
Ashby, W. Ross 54-6, 67, 73, 92,
261n21
Aspresjan, J. D. 39
assimilation 2, 62, 67, 95, 96, 99,
111, 181
active 144
biological 144
cultural 112
*see also* accommodation–
assimilation process;
individual-assimilating
process
Australian Arunta 242
autonomization
decision-making 237
functionally distinguished
structures 165
fundamental 161
human needs 164
information circulating in
society 206
meanings 205
autonomy of culture 177
relative 203-6

Baczko, Bronisław xxin5
Bally, C. 48, 259n36
Bantu people 105
Bateson, Gregory xxiiin17
Baudouin de Courtenay, Jan 33,
137
Bauman, Janina xi–xii
Będziń county (Poland) 186
bees 26, 70
behaviour *see* human
behaviour(s); symbolic
behaviour; territorial
behaviours
Benedict, Ruth 16, 163, 182,
265n4 (ch. 2)
Benveniste, E. 48, 126, 259n35,
264n10
Berlyne, D. E. 150
Boas, Franz 16, 19, 20
Bohannan, P. J. 18, 256n10
Boulez, Pierre 27
Brazil 21, 22
Brus, Włodzimierz xxin5
Brzeziński, Dariusz xi, xx, xxin1,
255
Bücher, K. W. 174
Burma 47

Cannon, Walter B. 65-6, 260n6
capitalism 45, 103, 134, 179,
183, 185, 190, 236, 247
contemporary societies 51
early individualism 195
market laws 198
Marx's critique of alienation
stemming from 243
private property in 248
range of implementation of
values xii
transition to socialism 197
Carpenter, C. R. 82, 261n29,
262n37
Cartesian visions 64-5

Carthailhac, E. 85
Cassirer, Ernst 88, 208, 262n39, 267n5 (ch. 3)
Central Union of Polish Industry 189
ceremonies 23, 40, 53, 125, 159
Chauvin, Remy 70-1, 261nn13/18
China 85
Chlewisk 194
Chmura, Julian 186, 266n10
Chomsky, Noam 125, 142, 143, 265n22
class privilege 51, 249
classes 41, 50, 146, 158, 163, 193, 232, 235, 241, 245-8
  hegemonic 160
  higher 51, 81, 236, 244
  idle and wealthy 240
  superior 47
  working 51
classification 11, 68, 88, 89, 107, 110, 115, 134, 174
  alternative to 95
  always distanced from reality 117
  amplitude and minuteness of 94
  folk 18
  language a principle of 123
  modes of 114
Columbus, Christopher 84
congruence 49, 60
Corneille, Pierre 24
cultural anthropology viii, xiii, 30
  see also Benedict; Boas; Douglas; Lévi-Strauss; Malinowski; Mead
cultural brokers xv, 164
  category of people playing the role of 211-12
  true members of the group of 215

cultural changes xiv, xviii, 199, 201, 252
  infrastructure of 178-83, 189, 200
  marketization and 189-97
cultural determinants xv, xxin6, 2, 203-15, 222-5
  presentism emerging from 172
cultural differences xxiin13, 189
  erasing 201
  glaring 178
  Romantic attitude towards 12
  sensitivity to 9
cultural differentiation xvii, 20, 99, 131, 139, 159, 233, 249
  cultural determination and 209-14
  important sources of 238
  observed 177
  see also socio-cultural events
cultural diffusion 180, 181
  non-existence of 241
cultural diversity 9, 10
cultural evolution viii, xii, xvi–xix, xxiin15, 86
  general principles of 197
  infrastructure in total process of 182
  new level of 117
  relatively self-sufficient tendencies of 233
cultural fields 109, 140, 152, 245
  border between 83
  patterns corresponding to xiv
  phylogenetic questions about 139
  research problems in ontogenesis of 141-5
  synchronic analysis of 131-6
  threatened unequivocality of meaning of 111
cultural hybrids 114

cultural meaning 59, 102, 127, 141, 208, 241-2
  agreed upon 125
  ambivalence in 115
  assigned 45
  excess of 109
  marginal sphere subordinated to 113
  multiplicity of 115, 116
  phenomenon for 173
cultural norms xviii, 181, 218
cultural signs 146
  accessible 149
  ideal 145
  position-creating or position-derivative character of 152
  role of 25
    advance of information to 150
  social structure and 145
cultural superiority 11, 12, 243, 249
  objectivizing 246
cultural taboos 85, 114, 151, 173
  visible incarnation of 84
cultural universals 97, 107, 116-17
  blank spots cannot be 109
  fervent searches for 20
  problem of 95
  searching for 98
  site of 96
  sought-after 99
Cushing, Frank 18, 22
customs 8, 24, 44, 100, 175, 181, 240, 255
  beliefs and 22
  better and worse 12
  innateness of 10
  manners and 10
  naming 219
  primordial 13

  superiority of one's own 101
  urban 200
Cwojdziński, S. 64
cybernetic machines 66, 91
  famous mouse 92
  path of development for 93
cybernetics xvii, 34, 37, 119, 156, 171
  new perspectives opened up by 54
  potential of viii
  technical successes of 7
  transformations examined by 155
  unity of object and method of 262n51
Czarnowski, Stefan 8

Dahrendorf, Ralf 253
Dart, Raymond 85
Darwin, Charles 84, 92
Descartes, René 68, 260nn1-2
  *see also* Cartesian visions
determinants 169-70, 182
  class 249
  ecological 249
  extra-cultural 220-6
  fundamental 237
  genealogical 246
  independent 29
  psychological external/personal 31
  regional 249
  semiotic function as 52-6
  structural 222, 223, 224, 225
  *see also* cultural determinants
Deutsch, J. A. 92
development of culture 85-6, 217, 248
  research problems in 145-52
dichotomism 147, 155, 168, 174, 206, 207
  cybernetic 171

gnoseological 156
information–energetic 167
Diderot, Denis 167
differences 12-17
  class 233, 239
  similarities and 197-202
  *see also* cultural differences
differentiation 28, 38, 43, 46, 51,
      82, 91, 109, 147, 149,
      167, 176, 182, 229, 232,
      234
  behaviour 83, 87, 90, 145
  class 50, 81, 233, 239, 241,
      248
  function according to age
      219
  generation 50
  internal 226, 248, 249
  language 126
  pattern 132
  role 80, 129
  sex 50, 79, 80, 100
  signifying opposition 75, 110,
      140, 177
  social position 148
  socio-cultural 233
  sphere 102, 106
  *see also* cultural differentiation
Dilthey, Wilhelm 31, 124
division of labour 41, 91, 183,
      186
  social 193, 195, 219
DNA (deoxyribonucleic acid) 68
Dollard, J. 151
Douglas, Mary 253
Durkheim, Émile 41

Eco, Umberto 253
education 29, 142, 194, 199,
      201, 237, 246
  basis of social position as
      intelligentsia 247
  creation of a ladder of 192-3

cultural 11, 216
  problems of xv, xxin6, 216-30
  spreading information through
      unification of 211
egalitarianism 17, 20, 247
  mass 50
egocentrism 10, 144, 223
Egyptians 10
Eisler, Jerzy xxin4
electricity 64, 76, 165-6
empathy 24, 103, 213
  reheating old dreams of 18
  unreflexive 11
English language 75
entropy 23, 57, 91
  *see also* negentropy
Eskimos 242
ethnography 1, 8, 96, 100, 103-6,
      122, 173, 213-14, 251
  diversity of ritual forms as
      described in 53
  European 12, 14, 15, 16
  pioneers of 13
  *see also* Bohannan; Cushing;
      Lévi-Strauss; Malinowski;
      Mead; Murdock
Euclidean space 97
Eupsychia 245
Eurasians 115
Eurocentric civilization 17
Evans-Pritchard, E. E. 105,
      258n28
evolution 16, 17, 40, 68, 84, 194,
      242, 243
  balance considered to be the
      purpose of 66
  collection of unconditional
      stimuli becomes smaller
      with progress of 78
  linear 20
  Polish grammar x
  *see also* cultural evolution;
      human evolution

evolutionary development 77, 81
  communication in animal
    world 75
evolutionary schemas 175
external reality 88, 206, 207,
    213
  human mind and 208-9
  sign and 48
  unchanging characteristics of
    77

Fabre, Jean-Henri 71
feedback 99, 119-20, 137, 176
  energy 155, 162
  information 155
feudalism 51, 146, 179, 181-6,
    188-90, 194, 236
Fichte, J. G. 9
Firth, Raymond 45, 46, 103, 105,
    176, 177, 258n28
Fletcher, J. M. 66, 260n8
folk systems 18
folwark 189-90
foreign cultures 12, 44, 214
Fortes, Meyer 101
Francastela, Pierre 97, 98
functionalism
  individual 16
  pure 17-18
  structural 252-3

Gałęski, Bogusław 192, 193, 200,
    266n20
General Motors 239
generalizations 37, 82, 94, 95,
    97, 139
  empirical 1, 2, 108-9, 121-2,
    123
  statistical 1
  theoretical 2
  true 19
generative grammar 125, 142
Glanzer, M. 150

Gluckman, Max 53, 259n45
gnoseological mechanisms 109,
    156, 168, 257n10
Goldschmidt, Walter 19, 256n11
Golovin, N. E. 7
Górski, D. P. 38, 257n12 (ch. 2)
grammar
  intellectual 25
  laws of 25
  Polish x
  syntactic 142
  syntagmatic 143
  *see also* generative grammar
Gramsci, Antonio xi, 244
Great Society term 164
Greco-Roman culture 12
Greeks 9, 11, 156, 174
Greimas, A. J. 51, 140, 259n43,
    264n21

Harvey, O. J. 114
Hegel, G. W. F. 110, 253
Helvetius, C. A. 167
Henry, Jules 105
Herodotus 10
Herskovits, Melville J. 45, 46,
    176, 259n29
Hesiod 11
higher–lower culture 241-50
Hildebrandt, B. 17499
Hindus 115
Hippocrates 66
Hirszowicz-Bielińska, Maria
    xxin5
Hjelmslev, L. 126, 140, 264n20
Hochfeld, Julian xxiin10
Haeckel, Ernst 71
Hogbin, H. I. 46-7, 259n31,
    263nn7/17
Hogden, Margaret T. 9, 262n33
Holbach, Paul-Henry Thiry,
    baron 167
*Homo oeconomicus* 189

*Homo sapiens* 84, 86, 90
  essential species characteristics
    of 81
  specifics of semiotic system
    proper to xiv
  unified 20
homogeneous cultures 178, 197
  beliefs of people from 10
Hovland, C. I. 114
Hull, C. L. 70
human action(s) 57, 60, 96,
    169-70, 207
  analysis of 42
  antimony of 171
  comprehensible 213
  conscious, objects of 166
  content of 48
  determinants of 29, 31
  existence of 8
  forms of 1, 48
  general and widespread modes
    of 54
  informational function of 43
  interpreted 52, 185
  meaning of 61
  psychological foundation for
    20
  shared characteristics 1
  situation of 177
  stimuli most frequently
    determined by 29
  understanding of 1, 31, 176
  untangling from semiotic roles
    44
human behaviour(s) 48, 52, 53,
    122, 159
  called for / condemned 227
  extra-cultural determinants of
    220-6
  growing role of structural
    determinants in shaping
    223
  heterogeneous systems and 167

  information function contained
    in 130
  irreducibility of 169
  justification of 229
  meaning of 39-47
  meaningful 128
  mutual dependency between
    economy and patterns of
    173
  observable 33
  premise integrated into 207
  semiotic function of 51
  significantly less stereotypical
    205
  structuring of xiv, 156
  study of 120, 128
  wave-like nature of 127
human evolution 170
  biosocial 204
  cultural instruments of 181
  gap between closest relative
    and 83
  modern views on 204
human individuals xvii, 31, 40,
    146, 167-71, 173
  collective, social existence of
    161
  developing mind of 145
  objectivization of 90
  study of the cooperation of
    120
human praxis 1, 96
  internally distinguished
    102
  organized system of reference
    for 2
  redemption of soul the primary
    goal of 98
  two signs of 91
humanistic coefficient 31
humanists xvii, 32, 165-8
  understanding of socio-cultural
    processes 213

humanities 31, 36, 39, 124, 165
  contemporary xix, 26, 33, 167
  former enthusiasms for
    physicalistic imitations
    126
  goals of research in 32
  Marxist 33
  methodological distinction
    between naturalism and 32
  positivistic 168, 169
  two principles of defining 166
Husserl, Edmund 36

Imanishi, Kinji 82, 261n30
incest 101
indeterminacy xviii, 67, 113, 117,
    134, 158
  eliminating 108, 132, 141
  foundational 111
  limits of 28
  liquidation of 58, 106, 108,
    130
  minimalization of 107
  physiological 249
  reducing 43, 51, 59, 96, 108,
    110, 131, 177
  removing 44, 57
  repeated 111
Indians 21, 22, 180, 223
  Nootka 238-9
individual-assimilating process
    157, 158
individualization viii, xix, 79, 135
  development of xviii
  no room for 134
  rush to 150
information theory 7
infrastructure 201, 202, 231-41,
    244, 246, 248, 250
  class 245
  cultural changes 178-83, 189,
    200
innate ideas 97, 98

input and output 119-20, 123,
    175
intelligent machines 92
interiorization xxiin15, 29, 157-9,
    161, 207, 208, 222-4, 227
intra-species communication 73,
    79-87
Isidore of Seville 84
isomorphic structures 27, 42, 78,
    86, 88, 90
  acquired 67
  connecting with intellectually
    accessible signs 25
  existence of 39
  external world and human
    mind 99, 144
  individual behaviours and
    human collective 29
  interiorized patterns 159
  mutually congruent 60
  natural selection and 55
  world of the human and
    human thoughts 96
isomorphism xvi, 40, 43, 100,
    157, 158
  culture 96
  lack of 149
  law of 77
  opposition 24, 39, 173
  sought-after 120
IV (intervening variable) term 121

Jabłoński, Henryk xxin5
Jacobsen, Michael Hviid xxiin9
Jaeger, Werner 11, 256n5
Jakobson, Roman 50, 125, 137,
    258nn16-17, 259n41,
    264n16
Jews 134, 174

Kadiueo people 22, 24
Kawamura, Syunzo 78, 261n25
Keynes, J. M. 185

kinship 20, 23, 114, 176
  collective broader than
    common ties of 179
  oppositions in 24
  structures of xiv, 95
    elementary 124
Klemm, Gustav 8, 9
Kłosowska, Antonina 180
knowledge 65, 95, 128, 137, 167,
    169, 213
  academic 94
  cultivating 166
  cultural determination of
    209
  culture and 17, 23, 107, 111,
    214-15, 254
  defined 207
  descriptive 87
  development of 83
  direct 159
  efforts to acquire 111
  elements of
    a priori 209
    new 208
  empirical 94
  ethnography as a field of 12
  falsifying 209
  foundational 27
  functions of 208
  gnoseological mechanisms of
    109
  hunger for 158
  incomplete 239
  incontrovertible determinations
    of 229
  insider and outsider 115
  making sense of 171
  new 94
  normative 87
  patterns and 162
  reliable 229
  scholastic 165
  social resources of 28

structure of 157
trained into the memory 143
Kołakowski, Leszek xxin5
Koreber, K. 85
Krajewski, Janusz ix, x
Kraśko, Nina x
Kripczyk, E. P. 55, 261n23
Kubicki, Roman xxiiin18
Kuhn, Thomas 254
Kuma people 105
Kung tribe 105
Kuroń, Jacek xii

La Mettrie, J. O. 68, 260n3
Lange, Oskar 179
language 22-4, 39, 49, 83, 87-8,
    89, 208, 211
  acoustic 125
  acquisition of 142, 143
  artificial 254
  aspects of 258n17
    anthropological 100
  behavioural 47
  characterized by incredible
    richness of semantic axes
    90
  common 165, 166
  concepts given names in 108
  cuisine of a given society as 60
  ear untrained in differentiating
    between sounds 110
  everyday 162, 253
  foreign 11, 19
  full analysis of a system 26
  function of 34
    communicative 40
  history of 138
  individual interactions as 122
  laws of grammar in 25
  learning 142-3
  long and short vowels in
    meaningful opposition
    in 75

language (cont.)
  period when child does not yet
    use 145
  plural and singular in 50
  relationship to its empirical
    symptoms 123
  semantically important
    phonemes in 59
  simultaneous use of taboo and
    108
  society forced to master 16
  sociological 162
  structure of 48, 123, 128
  study of 40, 126
  understanding the properties of
    126
  wave-particle nature of 127
  words in 41
  *see also* linguistics; theory of
    language
Leach, Edmund 47, 100-9, 113,
    253, 254, 259n33, 263n2
    (ch. 4), 263n14
Leakey, L. S. B. 85
Leakey, Mary 85
Lefebvre, Henri 40, 258n21
Lenin, V. I. 163
Leontiev, A. A. 60, 260n57,
    265n24
Leontiev, A. N. 55
Lévi-Strauss, Claude xvii, 15, 19,
    22, 27, 33-4, 51-2, 60,
    100, 107, 124, 157, 161,
    207, 251-4, 260n54
  *Anthropologie structurale* xiii,
    23-6, 33, 159, 257n5,
    259n49, 266n3
  *Du miel aux cendres* 24
  *La pensée sauvage* 23-4, 159,
    263n11
  *Le cru et le cuit* 24, 33, 257n3,
    259n44
  *Mythologiques* 25, 26

*Totémisme aujourd'hui* 24
*Tristes Tropiques* 21, 23, 24,
    26, 256n8, 257n13 (ch. 1)
Lichtenberg, Georg Christoph
    254
Lindauer, M. 80, 261n28
linguistics 48, 89, 91, 122, 123,
    208, 253
  analogies in 126, 127-8, 129
  historical 137
  humanities scholars turning to
    39
  propositions worked out
    in 140
  theoretical methods developed
    in 125
  *see also* American
    psycholinguistics;
    grammar; meaning(s);
    phonetics; phonology;
    semantics; structural
    linguistics
Linnaeus, Carl 84
Linton, Ralph 182, 265n3
    (ch. 2)
liquidity viii, xix, xx
List, Friedrich 174
Loeb, J. 71
Lombards 174
London 167
Lorenz, K. 70, 71, 72, 261n16

Macdonald, K. B. 180
Malinowski, Bronisław 16, 17,
    19, 20, 25, 41, 47, 100,
    105, 258n22, 259n32
Mandelbrot, B. 259n38
Maori people 105
marketization
  cultural changes and 189-97
  process of satisfying needs
    183-9, 197
  village labour power 199

marriage 159, 217, 219
  neighbours as potential
    candidates for 101
Martinet, A. 40, 258nn17/20,
  262n41
Martinov, W. W. 138, 139,
  264n18
Marx, Karl 9, 27, 34, 57, 62, 66,
  91, 136, 160, 163, 167,
  171, 173, 174, 181-2, 189,
  243, 247, 253
Marx, Melvin H. 121
Marxism 2, 33, 123, 168
  activist 27, 37
  Bauman and xi, x
  dialectic of praxis 66
  interpretation of social
    structure 1
  materialist 27
  Marxism premises of xiii
  primary theorist of mass
    culture 231
Marxist–Leninist thinking xii
Maslow, Abraham 240, 245
mass communication 181, 197
  means of xvi, 231, 232, 234,
    235
mass culture vii, xviii, 165, 221,
  234, 239, 245
  birth and triumph of 241
  conflicts about the definition of
    232
  cradle of 249
  development of 2
  emergence of 180, 231
  homogenic 200
  margins xxin6
  Marxist, primary theorist of
    231
  new 200, 201
  norms of 149
  tool that shapes 232
  uniformity of 248

Mauss, Marcel 21
McDougall, W. 71, 261n14
Mead, Margaret 11, 101, 106,
  163, 256n6, 263nn5/10
meaning(s) xxiin15, 35, 48, 51-2,
  55, 69, 71, 77, 126, 145,
  158, 160, 181, 183, 201-2,
  228
  accessible 120, 208
  acquired 12, 27
  adaptive 163, 203
  ambiguous 230
  analysis of 152
  assigned 130
  autonomization of 205
  blurring together of 110
  categories of 2
  chaos of experience transforms
    into consistentsystem of 58
  cognitive–creative 99
  comprehensible 122
  contradictory 111
    mutually 110
  crises of 141
  decisive 56
  decoding 36
  delineated 72
  dialectic 66
  discrepancies of 116
  dual 111
  dynamic 66
  emergence of 253
  emphasized xiv, xv
  encoded 122
  essence and xii
  essential xix, xx
  eternal struggle to give 60
  excess of 157
  expressed 17, 125
  fixed xvi
  free 207
  function of 116
  fundamental elements of 140

meaning(s) (cont.)
gaps between 110
general 240
grasped 38, 178
hidden 242
human behaviour 39-47, 61, 83, 122
important 102
informational 204
instrumental 46
intellectual 107
lack of 88, 109
learned 207-10
lexical 39
long-discussed problem of 34
marginal regions of xviii, 117
mutually significative 34
necessary clarity and singleness of 79
necessary condition of 51
new 66, 88
non-economic 193-4
not all things observed by the senses has 76
not necessarily coherent models and xviii
object has 37
objective 246
opposition of 140
owed to statistical associations 175
proximate 254
relationship of 110
objectified 88
religious 191
semiotic 37, 177
separation of 206
shared xvi
signifying 72-3, 75
signs are determined by 36
singular 110, 111, 114, 117
social 191

sociological 246
narrow 244
solidified 81
spatial-temporal 138
status-related 191
structures of 26, 27, 34
well-known 45
temporary deprivation of 149
things without 161
thinking 128
tightly restricted 74
uncovering 70
unequivocal 81, 111, 132, 254
unified 89
web of 57
*see also* cultural meaning; multiplicity of meanings
Merleau-Ponty, Maurice 163
methodological ahistoricism 16
methodological premises 174-8
Michałowski, Jerzy 188-9, 266n15
Milewski, Tadeusz 35, 36, 88, 138, 140, 257n6, 264n17
Mill, John Stuart 71, 122
Miller, E. 151
modernity
imperatives created by xx
liquid xix, xx
transformation of viii
Modzelewski, Karol xii
monsters 84, 85
Montagu, Ashley 204, 266n1
Montaigne, Michel de 13, 15, 16, 256n7
Montgomery, K. C. 150
Morawski, Stefan xxin5
Morris, Charles 38
multiplicity of meanings 111, 118
chronic 115
immanent 112
semiotic 117
Murdock, G. P. 20, 95

Nadel, S. F. 129-31, 264nn12/15
National Science Centre ix, xxin1
nativism 98
needs 13, 31, 69, 87, 96, 106,
 144, 207, 245, 249
 aesthetic 40
 animal 71, 86
 biological 57
 collective 24, 41, 80
 individual 24, 41
 satisfying 28, 29-30, 33, 40,
  41, 44, 57, 99, 104, 131,
  134, 164, 173, 177,
  179-89, 197, 239-41, 250
 serving 18, 33, 244, 250
 specialization and
  autonomization of 164
 spiritual 243
 stifling 248
 structure of 90, 95, 241
 vital 181
negation 170
 negation of 21-6, 37
negentropy 57, 59
nervous systems 64
 bilaterally symmetrical 78
 well-developed 85
New Guinea 46-7, 105
 Arapesh people 106
Neyman, Elżbieta 114-15,
 263n19
Nowik, I. B. 93, 262n51
Nuer people 105

Oceania (Siuai people) 105
Office of Polish People's
 Anthropology xii
Ogden, C. K. 38
ontogenetic processes 14, 68, 73,
 76-80, 130, 141-2, 144
organization of space 97, 99, 122
 sacral 98
 urban type of 202

Osgood, Charles 38, 257n13
Ossolineum ix, x, xxin2,
 xxiin12
Ossowski, Stanisław 8, 20, 213
otherness 10, 21
 cultural 17
 ever more savage 22
output 242
 input and 119-20, 123, 175

paradigm shift 254
Parsis 174
Parsons, Talcott 58, 157, 252-3,
 259n51
Pascal, Blaise 78
Pask, G. A. 80, 261n27
Pavlov, Ivan 70, 78, 170, 222
*Pedagogical Quarterly* xxin6
Peirce, C. S. 36, 44, 48, 49
People's Poland xi
Peter Martyr 84
Petrycy of Pilzno, Sebastian 147
Phoenicians 174
phonetics 44
 syntagmatic 143
phonology 44, 125, 127
phylogenetic processes 64, 68, 69,
 71-3, 76, 130, 159
Piaget, Jean 66, 89, 90, 97, 107,
 143-5, 259n38, 260n9
 *Narodziny inteligencji dziecka*
  261n11, 262nn42/1,
  263n13, 265n25
Pike, Kenneth L. 125, 127-9, 131,
 258n27, 264nn9/11
Pilaga people 105
pilgrims 9
Pillsbury, W. B. 125, 264n8
Plato 47, 155
plebeians 12
Pliny the Elder 84
pluralism xix, 237, 238
Plutarch 11

Poland vii, xi
  development of major industry
    266n11
  problem of labour power in
    agriculture 266n10
  socialist revolution 197
  socio-cultural events (1968) viii
  villages and cities xv, 179-90,
    199-201
Polish Academy of Sciences ix,
  xxinn1/4
Polish Philosophical Society ix
Polish United Workers' Party x
Pomerania 189
Popovich, M. W. 37, 107
Poznań 189
Prague Linguistic Circle 33,
  125-6
praxeomorphism 7, 64-70
praxis
  directed 60
  Marxist dialectic of 66
  *see also* human praxis
presentism 103, 172, 175
proto-societies 80, 81, 82, 86
psychological tools 38, 41, 42
psychology 12, 20, 21, 30, 69,
    108, 120-3, 150-2, 169,
    171, 177, 188, 234, 241
  animal 71
  contemporary 222, 223, 226-7
  developmental 142
  positivistic 168
  rise of 38
  social 168, 227
  *see also* Berlyne; Chomsky;
    Glanzer; Golovin;
    Kripczyk; Leontiev;
    Montgomery; Pavlov;
    Piaget; Skinner; Vygotsky

Rabaud, E. 71, 261n15
racial hybrids 114

Radcliffe-Brown, A. R. 18, 41,
  100, 258n24
Rapaport, Anatol 92, 262n50
rationalizations 217
  semiotic and technical 52
reality 17, 27, 35, 57, 58, 59,
    135, 203, 204, 215
  abstract sociology far removed
    from 236
  active character that structures
    82
  active creation of 48
  adaptation of concepts to
    144
  analysis of xiv
  convictions treated as attributes
    of 212
  cultural 210
  culture defines general positions
    in regard to 214
  delineation of general positions
    of the individual towards
    xv
  divorce from 179
  experienced 208
  false image of 161
  formation of 11
  full arc of classification always
    distanced from 117
  fundamental reality in relation
    to 60
  linguistic 126
  marking 29
  opportunities hidden in 91
  organizing 76, 81
  perceived in liminal categories
    xviii
  resistance to confrontation with
    155
  signs with meaning on a
    different level of 39
  *see also* external reality; social
    reality

reciprocity 25, 28, 34, 63, 162, 218
  equivalent 104
  generalized 46, 103, 105, 135
  mutual 103-4
Redfield, R. 179, 180, 247, 265n2 (ch. 2)
reflex arcs 71, 89
reflexivity 170
  *see also* unreflexivity
religious mythology 10-11
research
  goals of 32
  problems in 141-52
  structure of the act of 206-9
Reznikow, L. D. 38, 257n11
Richards, I. A. 38
RNA (ribonucleic acid) 68
Rococo salons 64, 167
Rousseau, Jean-Jacques 23
Rysakova, S. A. 76
Rzeszów region (Poland) 188

safety 99, 194, 236, 252
  emotional 226-30
  guaranteeing 240
Sahlins, Marshall D. 103, 259n30
Sartre, Jean-Paul 163
Saussure, Ferdinand de 21, 33, 47-8, 49, 60, 123, 126, 253, 258n16, 259nn34/40, 264n6
Sautuola, Marcelino 85
savages 13, 14, 22, 23
Scher, Jordan M. 101, 263n4
schismogenic mechanisms xxiiin17
Scriven, Michael 92, 262n48
self-stimulation 38
Seligman, Brenda Z. 100-1, 263n3
semantic ambivalence 83
  fear of 92

semantic axes 90, 141
  higher–lower 80
  possible assemblages of 140
  relatively rich 82
semantic complexity 77
semantic divisions 85
semantic fields 113, 254
  irreducible 140
semantic intuition 179
semantic oppositions,
  fundamental 58
  role of 110
semantic unequivocality 74, 83
semantics 26, 39, 45, 50, 129, 146, 173
  important phonemes 59
  methods of structural analysis in 140
  specialized traits 70
  structural 127
  untangling mutual elements 122
semiotic function xiv, 43, 51, 52-61, 70, 146-7, 148, 173, 178
  realizing 108, 111, 115, 116
  satisfying needs 29-30, 44, 177
  understanding human behaviours in 40
semiotic sentences 138
  constant creation of 139
semiotic theory of culture 7-152
semiotics xiii, xvi, xix, 1, 2, 34, 53, 252
  sociological 48
  Soviet 37
  *see also* signs
sensory apparatus 24, 79, 90-1
  organs in animals and humans 76, 97
sensory experience 90, 95, 98, 107, 119, 122, 123
sensory-motor aspects 97, 144

sexual relationships 217, 219
  organization of 20
  partners
    common and appealing 100
    potential 74, 101
  pre-marital initiation 100
Shannon, C. E. 43, 68
Sherif, M. 114
Siek, Janusz ix, x
Sierpiński, Wacław 49, 259n37
Siewierz 186
signifieds 36, 48, 51, 61, 110,
    156, 207, 254
  signifier and 49, 60, 258n16
  system of 39, 40, 159
signs 7, 28, 44, 46, 69, 120, 158
  absorbed 149
  acoustic 88
  acquired 75
  animals and 70-9, 88, 90
  articulated 126
  artificial 37
  behavioural 52
  collection of 51, 145-6
  communicative 79, 88
  complex 49
  contemporary concept of
    35-8
  creation and dissemination of
    156-7
  deciphering 17
  determined by meaning 36
  differentiating 38, 75, 99, 110,
    148, 149
  divided into mutually
    autonomous components
    253-4
  exchange of 147
  feature that differentiates 38
  function of 17
  human 8, 88, 90, 91
  identifying 135
  intellectually accessible 25

  isomorphic oppositions in the
    world of 173
  linear relationships with 39
  linguistic 48, 91
  meaning of 42, 254
  meaningful 25, 35, 39
  natural 36, 37, 70
  new 138-9, 148, 159
  observable phenomena as 35-6
  opposition of 80
    artificial 29
  phenomena fulfilling the
    function of 36
  phylogenetic mechanism of
    producing 76
  position-creating xiv, 150
  position-derivative xiv, 146,
    147-8, 150
  positional 159
  problem of 39
  road 25
  selecting 78
  specialized 39, 70, 150
  unfettered access to 149
  univocality of 85
  *see also* cultural signs;
    signifieds; system of signs;
    theory of signs
Silesia 189
Simon, Herbert A. 120
Skinner, B. F. 70
Smith, Adam 239
Smoczyński, P. 143, 265n23
social functions 166, 191, 232
  culture and 30
  endogamously increasing
    complexity of 140
  lost 216-20
  painful conflict between 195
  specialization of 195, 198, 201
  viable 173
social reality 29, 48, 126
  creating xvii

factor shaping 244
semiotic function that
    structures 53
structuring xvii, 128
vision of multiple aspects of
    182
social space 147
  Leach's theory of realms of
    100-7
social structure 18, 29, 45, 46,
    51, 82, 131, 147-8, 159
  actions interpreted as adequate
    portion of 50
  change in 163
  class and 246
  contradictions of 24
  cultural signs/factors and 145,
    177
  culture and xii, xiii, 2, 33, 96,
    161, 206, 222, 231
  dysfunction of 160
  economics and 173
  functional requirements of 218
  homogeneity in the field of
    xxiin13
  human behaviours and 33, 52
  Marxist interpretation of 1
  mass 232
  oppositions in 178
  place of intellectuals in 247,
    250
  portion crucial for construction
    of given situation 44
  position in 162
  problem of 152
  simplest way of coding for use
    of individual 80
  theory of 129
socialism 178, 179, 198, 199,
    200, 247
  British xi
  building 223, 225
  constitutive feature of 223

range of implementation of
    values xii
  transition from capitalism to
    197
socialization 82, 143, 157, 158,
    207, 222
  decisive stage of 145
  possibility of 23
socio-cultural events viii, xvii,
    101, 220
  changes in xviii, xix–xx
  character of analytical facts/
    context 32, 151
  differentiation 233
  transformation xv
socio-cultural factors 177
  conditions for subordinating
    economics to 176
socio-cultural processes 203
  development of xix
  humanistic understanding of
    213
socio-cultural structure
  key to decomposing xviii
  limitations connected to
    belonging to 214
socio-cultural systems 160-7
  rush to individualization
    known to 150
sociology 33, 53, 146, 169, 172
  abstract 236
  American 157, 231
  analytical 32
  behavioural 168
  meagre 242
  neopositivist conception of 32
  one-sided cultural version of
    159
  Polish xii
  positivistic 168
  structural 252
  superficial economization of
    177

sociology of politics xi
sociology of upbringing 216
Solinus, Gaius Julius 84
Sommerhoff, G. 54
South Africa 26
  Sterkfontein, Swartkrans, and
    Koomdrai 85
Soviet Union 37, 55, 76, 88, 143,
  180
space *see* organization of space;
  social space
specialization 82, 91, 96, 140,
  237
  academic environment 215
  behaviours in the semiotic
    function 53
  code 149
  communicative 125, 226
  cultural institution 217
  educational 216, 225
  eliminating regions of
    indeterminacy 108
  human needs 164
  informational 161, 164, 203,
    204
  personality 183
  professional 199
  semantics trait 70
  sign 39, 70, 150
  social function 195, 198, 201
  technological sphere 24
Spence, Kenneth W. 121
Spencer, Herbert 66
spheres
  amorphous 57
  anonymous 173
  appropriate 23
  border 102, 112-13
  boundaries between 107
  broader 176, 212, 225
  concentric 98, 102, 104, 106
  congruence of 49
  cultural 9, 212

  distinction between 135
  economic 181
  expansion of 101
  external 99, 102, 104, 106
  functionally distinguished 96
  global 106
  intermediate 102, 103, 106
  internal 102, 104
  intersection of 112, 116
  liminal 102
  marginal 102, 113
  non-linguistic 125-6
  notorious discrepancy between
    164
  phenomenal 24
  psychic 197
  psychological 31
  signifying 48-9
  specialized 24
  technological 24
  terrifying 92
  unregulated contact with 104
Spinoza, B. 66
Steward, J. 242
stimulation 33, 38, 112
stimuli 1, 72, 76, 122, 135, 146
  accidental collection of 71
  association of specific
    behaviour with 29
  atypicality of 151
  catalysing 73
  characterized 205
  constant 149
  departure from habitual,
    expected structure 150
  environmental 67
  essential 227
  external 67, 71, 73, 88, 166
  function of the novelty of 151
  known and easily distinguished
    108
  most frequently determined by
    human action 29

organized into a system 206
perceived or remembered 210
purely informational 205
reaction to xvii, 67, 71, 86, 120-1, 166, 169
response to 204, 205
seemingly meaningless 203
semantically unequivocal 74
semiotic 148
strongest of cultural production 159
sudden 150
unconditional 78
Stonequist, Everett V. 114, 115, 263nn18/21
Strachey, William 14
structural analysis 27, 140
modern methods of 24
structural anthropology 33, 252
*see also* Lévi-Strauss (*Anthropologie*)
structural linguistics 25-6, 27, 34
contemporary 142
developments in 110
infamous methods of 125
resources offered by 137
thinking proper to 126
structuralism xiii, xix, 27, 128, 253, 254
application to Diltheyesque problems 124
basic principle of 126
French xiv
fundamental principle of 126
humanities advocated to assimilate 33
Marxist 2
potential of viii
problem central to 125-6
*Studies in Philosophy* xxin6
subjective–objective symbols 102
Suszko, Roman 40, 258n19

Swidler, Ann xxiin14
symbolic behaviour 124-31
Syrians 174
system of signs 82-3, 90
crucial function of 40
culture as 87, 152
efforts to interpret culture as 2
inherited 70
relationship between system of signifieds and 40
selection criteria for construction of 78
Szczepański, Jan 224, 267n7 (ch. 4)
Szczerba, L. W. 60, 187, 260n56

taboos 18, 92, 109, 152, 174
ambivalence connected to 108, 112
highly socially significant area of 113
justifying the use of 111
merciless 84
utilization of the institution of 116
*see also* cultural taboos
Tacitus 224
Tanganyika (Olduvai Gorge) 85
Tarkowska, Elżbieta vii, xii
Taylor, James 8, 128
technology xviii, 86-7, 181, 217, 222
academic reflection on 11
achievements of xvi
cradle of 7
dependence on 238, 239
fantastic 242
fascination with 239
meaning of xiv
new 231, 239
socially accessible 28
specialized spheres of 24

Teilhard de Chardin, Pierre 87, 262n36
Tel Aviv x
territorial behaviours 74-5
Tester, Keith viii, xi, xxiin9
Thales of Miletus 7
theory of language 125
  structuralist 128
  synchronic 137
theory of signs 34
  abstract 257n7
  gnoseological problems of 257n10
Thomas Aquinas, St 18, 175
Thucydides 15
Tich, N. A. 88
Tikopia 105
Tinbergen, N. 70, 72, 74, 261n17
Tiuchtin, W. S. 67, 261n12
Tolman, E. C. 70
transformations xii, xiii, xix, xx, 16, 26, 37, 116, 138, 139, 179, 180, 197, 198, 215
  constant xvii, 66
  endless 148
  examined by cybernetics 155
  goods/articles into commodities 183, 185
  human 171
  incredibly quick, impossible-to-predict viii
  infrastructural process of 247
  intensification of 160
  meaningful xi, 185
  meanings can be subject to 206
  reciprocal 25
  revolutionary 64
  social xvi
  socio-cultural xv
  visible 25
Trobriand Islands 16, 18, 47, 105

Tungusic peoples 105
Turing, A. M. 92

UNESCO (UN Educational, Scientific and Cultural Organization) xxiin10
uniqueness 87-91, 255
universals
  disciplinary 20
  infrastructural 235, 238, 239, 240, 241
  macrosocial 239
  pre-cultural 20
  problem of xiv, xviii, 2, 94-118
  *see also* cultural universals
University of Leeds ix, x
University of Warsaw ix, xii, xxiin10, 2, 251
unreflexivity 8, 10, 11, 15, 191, 231
urbanization xv, 2, 8
urbanization of villages xxin6, 178-81, 183, 185, 189, 191-4, 200-2

Vygotsky, L. S. 38, 40, 41, 120, 257n14

wage labour 187, 189, 190
  creation of large market of 193
  growth of need for 183
Wallas, Graham 164
Walter, W. G. 92
Washburn, Sherwood 217, 261n31, 262n34
Weber, Max 31
Wesley, John 14, 15
Western Africa (Tellensi people) 101
White, Leslie A. 182, 242, 265n5 (ch. 2)

Wiatr, Jerzy xi, xii
Williams, G. M. 115
Wilson, Charles 239
Wissler, Clark 8

youth 216-20

Zagórski, Krzysztof 248
Zeidler-Janiszewska, Anna
  xxiiin18

Zinoviev, Alexander 36, 40,
  257n7
Znaniecki, F. 8, 18, 31-2, 34,
  257n1
Żólkiewski, Stefan xii–xiii, xxin4,
  xxiin12, xxv, 3, 60, 124,
  231, 260n58, 264n7
Zopf, G. W. 54, 56, 65, 260n4,
  261nn21/27
Zuni Bow Priesthood 18